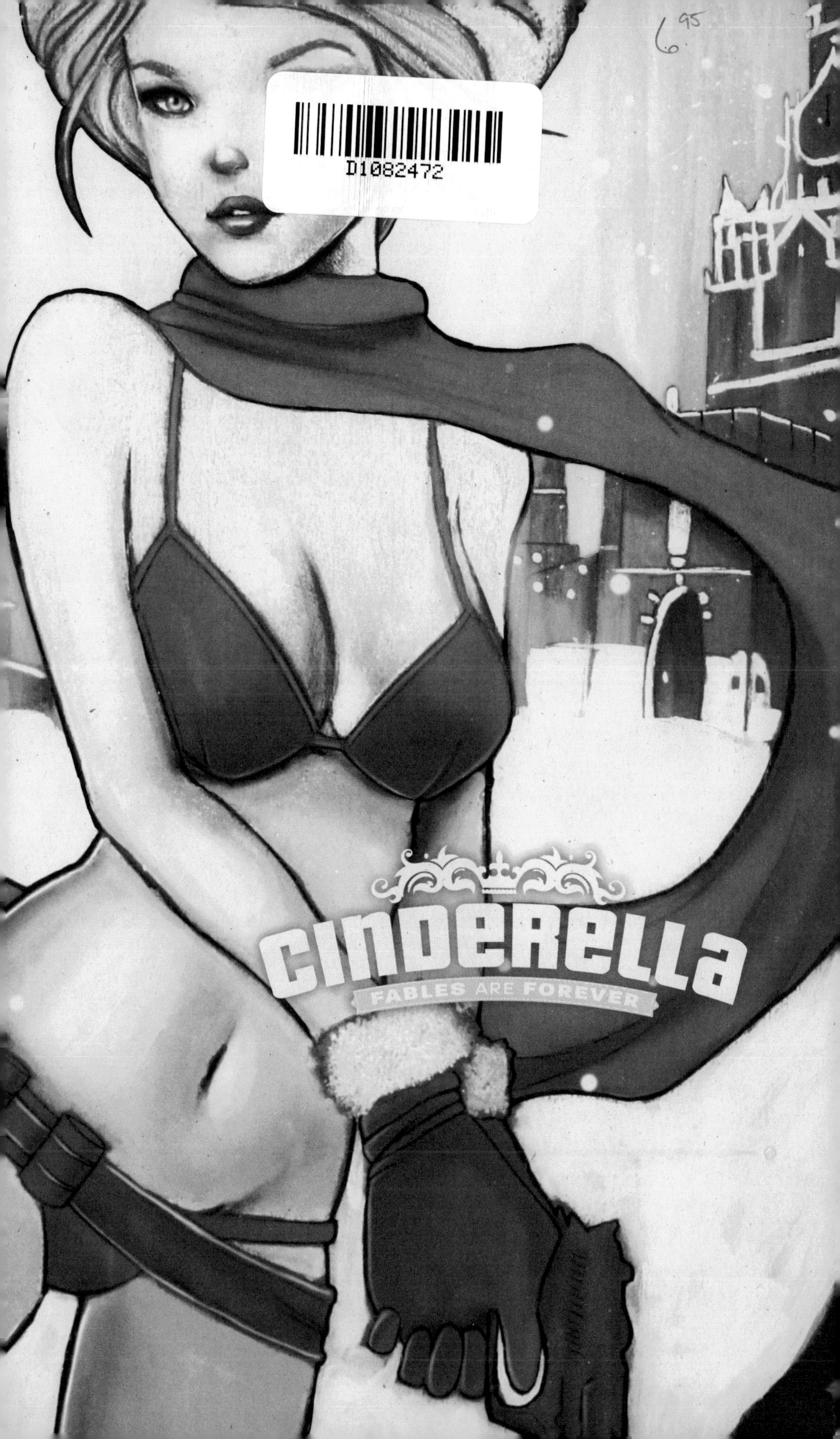
CINDERELLA
FABLES ARE FOREVER

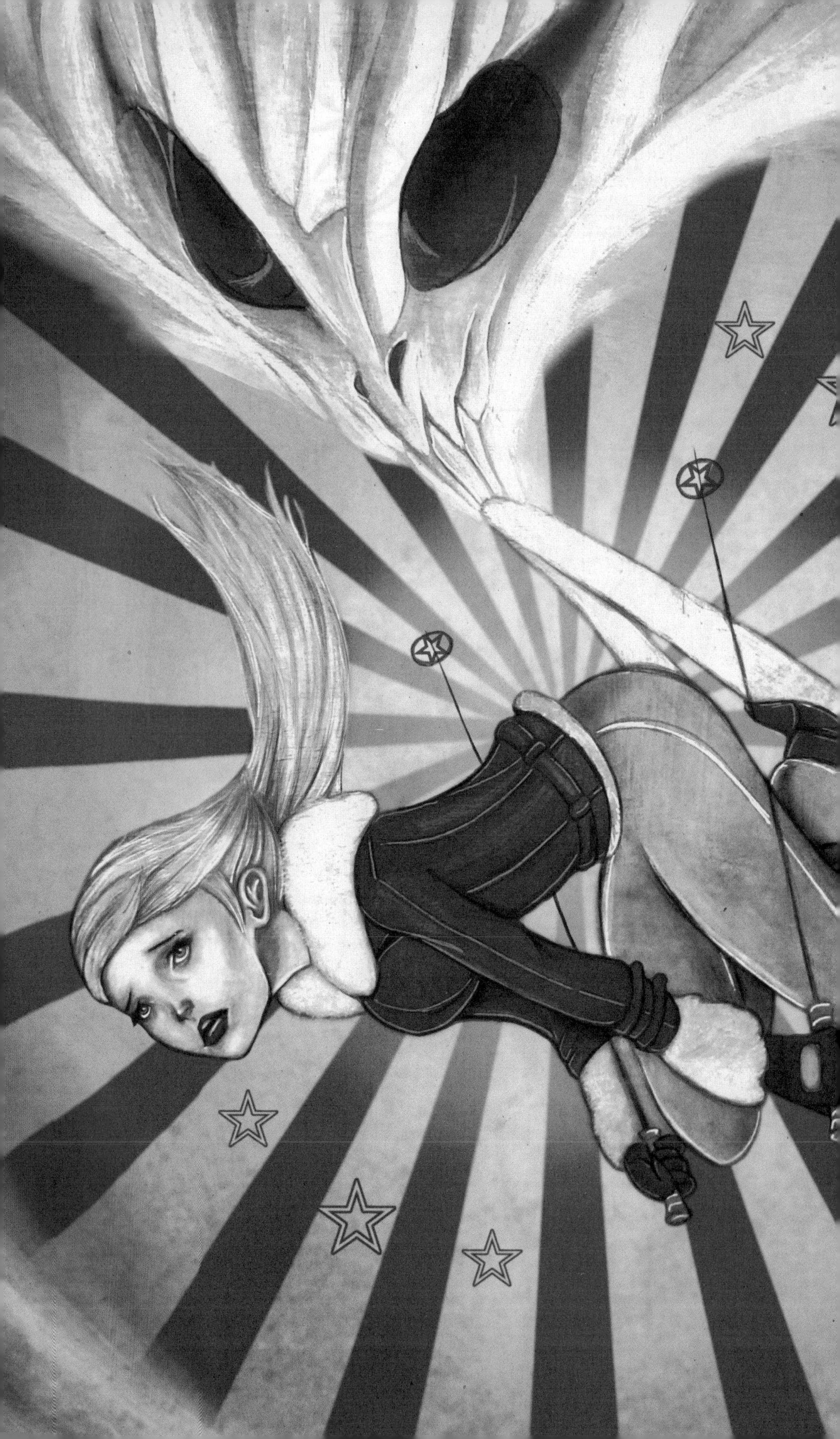

## CINDERELLA
### FABLES ARE FOREVER

Chris Roberson Writer
Shawn McManus Artist
Bill Willingham Consultant
Chrissie Zullo Cover Artist
Lee Loughridge Colorist
Todd Klein Letterer

FABLES created by Bill Willingham

Shelly Bond, Editor – Original Series
Gregory Lockard, Assistant Editor – Original Series
Robin Wildman, Editor
Robbin Brosterman, Design Director – Books

Karen Berger, Senior VP – Executive Editor, Vertigo
Bob Harras, VP – Editor - in - Chief

Diane Nelson, President
Dan DiDio and Jim Lee, Co-Publishers
Geoff Johns, Chief Creative Officer
John Rood, Executive VP – Sales, Marketing and Business Development
Amy Genkins, Senior VP – Business and Legal Affairs
Nairi Gardiner, Senior VP – Finance
Jeff Boison, VP – Publishing Operations
Mark Chiarello, VP – Art Direction and Design
John Cunningham, VP – Marketing
Terri Cunningham, VP – Talent Relations and Services
Alison Gill, Senior VP – Manufacturing and Operations
David Hyde, VP – Publicity
Hank Kanalz, Senior VP – Digital
Jay Kogan, VP – Business and Legal Affairs, Publishing
Jack Mahan, VP – Business Affairs, Talent
Nick Napolitano, VP – Manufacturing Administration
Sue Pohja, VP – Book Sales
Courtney Simmons, Senior VP – Publicity
Bob Wayne, Senior VP – Sales

CINDERELLA: FABLES ARE FOREVER

DC Comics, 1700 Broadway, New York, NY 10019
A Warner Bros. Entertainment Company.
Printed in the USA. 3/16/12. First Printing.
ISBN: 978-1-4012-3385-3

SUSTAINABLE FORESTRY INITIATIVE    Certified Sourcing
www.sfiprogram.org
SFI-01042
APPLIES TO TEXT STOCK ONLY

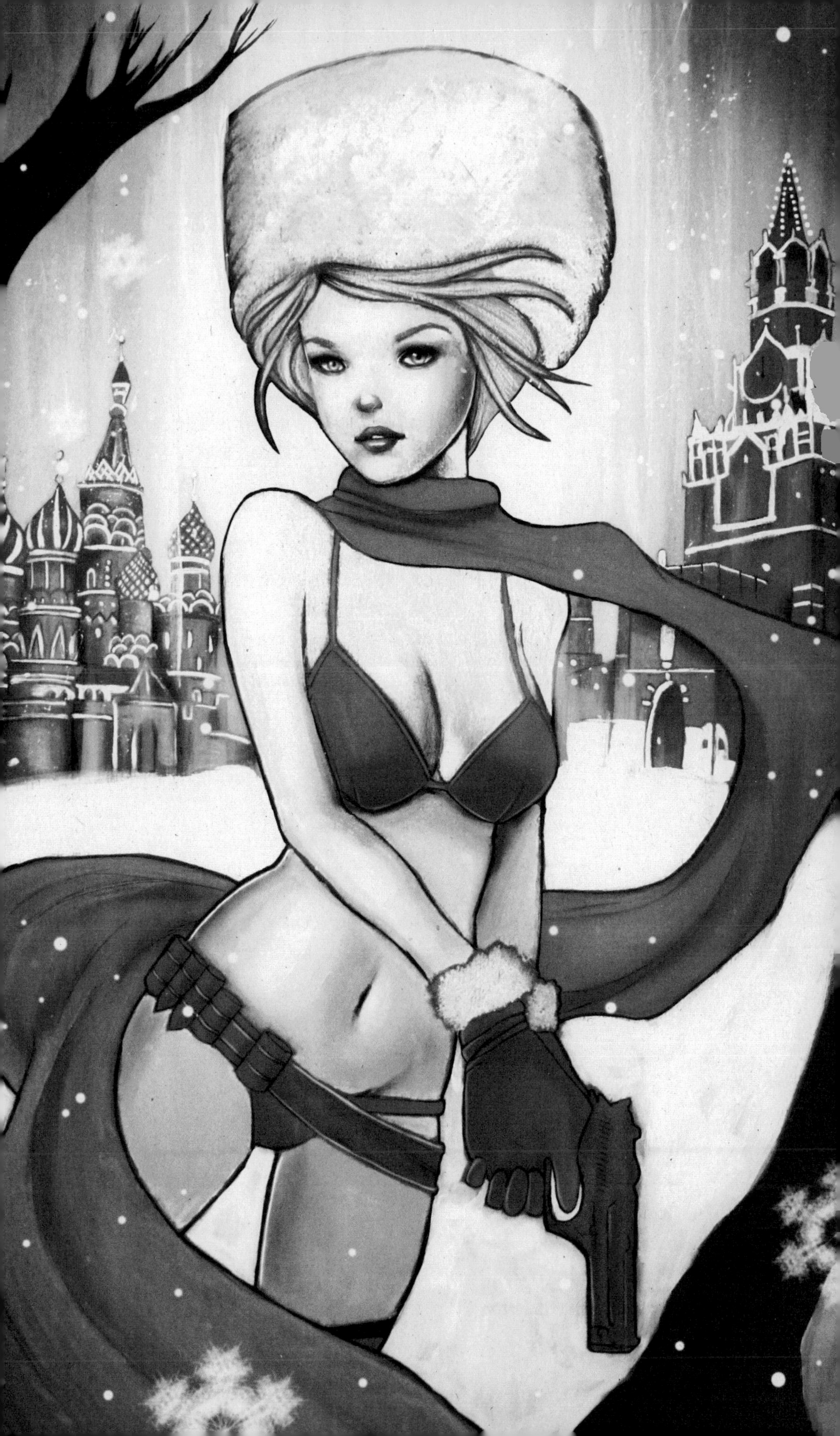

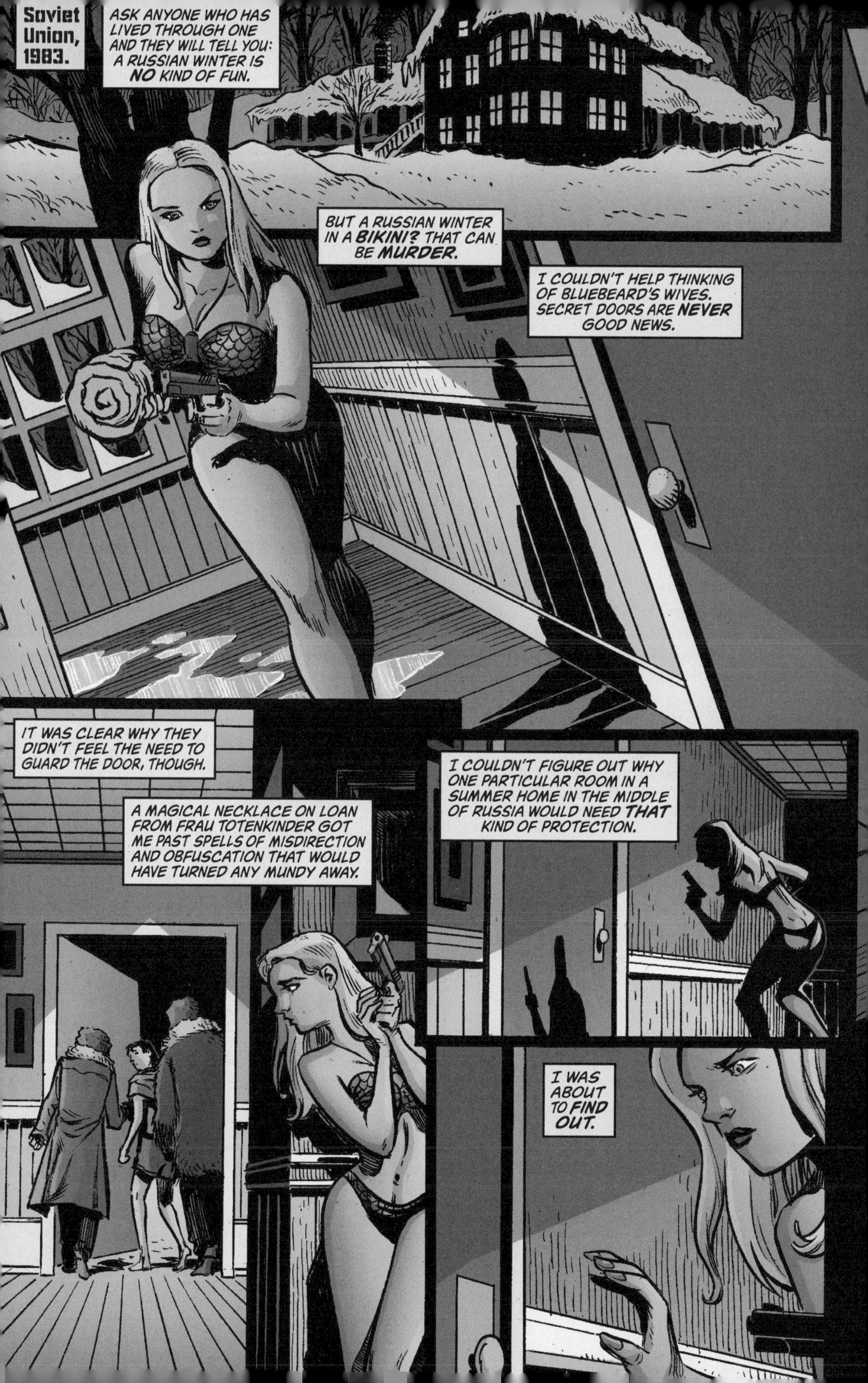
Soviet Union, 1983.
ASK ANYONE WHO HAS LIVED THROUGH ONE AND THEY WILL TELL YOU: A RUSSIAN WINTER IS NO KIND OF FUN.
BUT A RUSSIAN WINTER IN A BIKINI? THAT CAN BE MURDER.
I COULDN'T HELP THINKING OF BLUEBEARD'S WIVES. SECRET DOORS ARE NEVER GOOD NEWS.
IT WAS CLEAR WHY THEY DIDN'T FEEL THE NEED TO GUARD THE DOOR, THOUGH.
A MAGICAL NECKLACE ON LOAN FROM FRAU TOTENKINDER GOT ME PAST SPELLS OF MISDIRECTION AND OBFUSCATION THAT WOULD HAVE TURNED ANY MUNDY AWAY.
I COULDN'T FIGURE OUT WHY ONE PARTICULAR ROOM IN A SUMMER HOME IN THE MIDDLE OF RUSSIA WOULD NEED THAT KIND OF PROTECTION.
I WAS ABOUT TO FIND OUT.

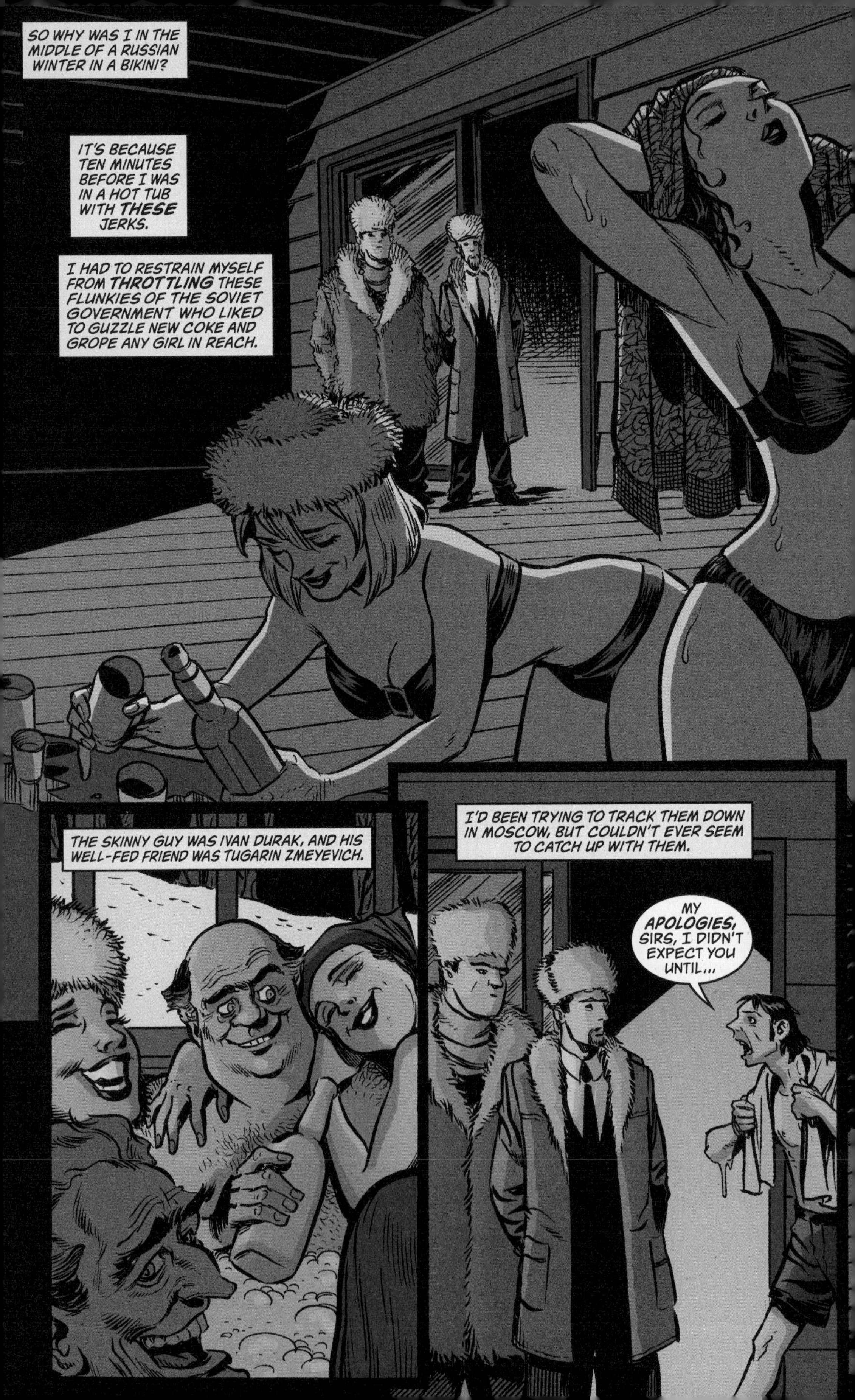
SO WHY WAS I IN THE MIDDLE OF A RUSSIAN WINTER IN A BIKINI?
IT'S BECAUSE TEN MINUTES BEFORE I WAS IN A HOT TUB WITH **THESE** JERKS.
I HAD TO RESTRAIN MYSELF FROM **THROTTLING** THESE FLUNKIES OF THE SOVIET GOVERNMENT WHO LIKED TO GUZZLE NEW COKE AND GROPE ANY GIRL IN REACH.
THE SKINNY GUY WAS IVAN DURAK, AND HIS WELL-FED FRIEND WAS TUGARIN ZMEYEVICH.
I'D BEEN TRYING TO TRACK THEM DOWN IN MOSCOW, BUT COULDN'T EVER SEEM TO CATCH UP WITH THEM.
MY **APOLOGIES**, SIRS, I DIDN'T EXPECT YOU UNTIL...

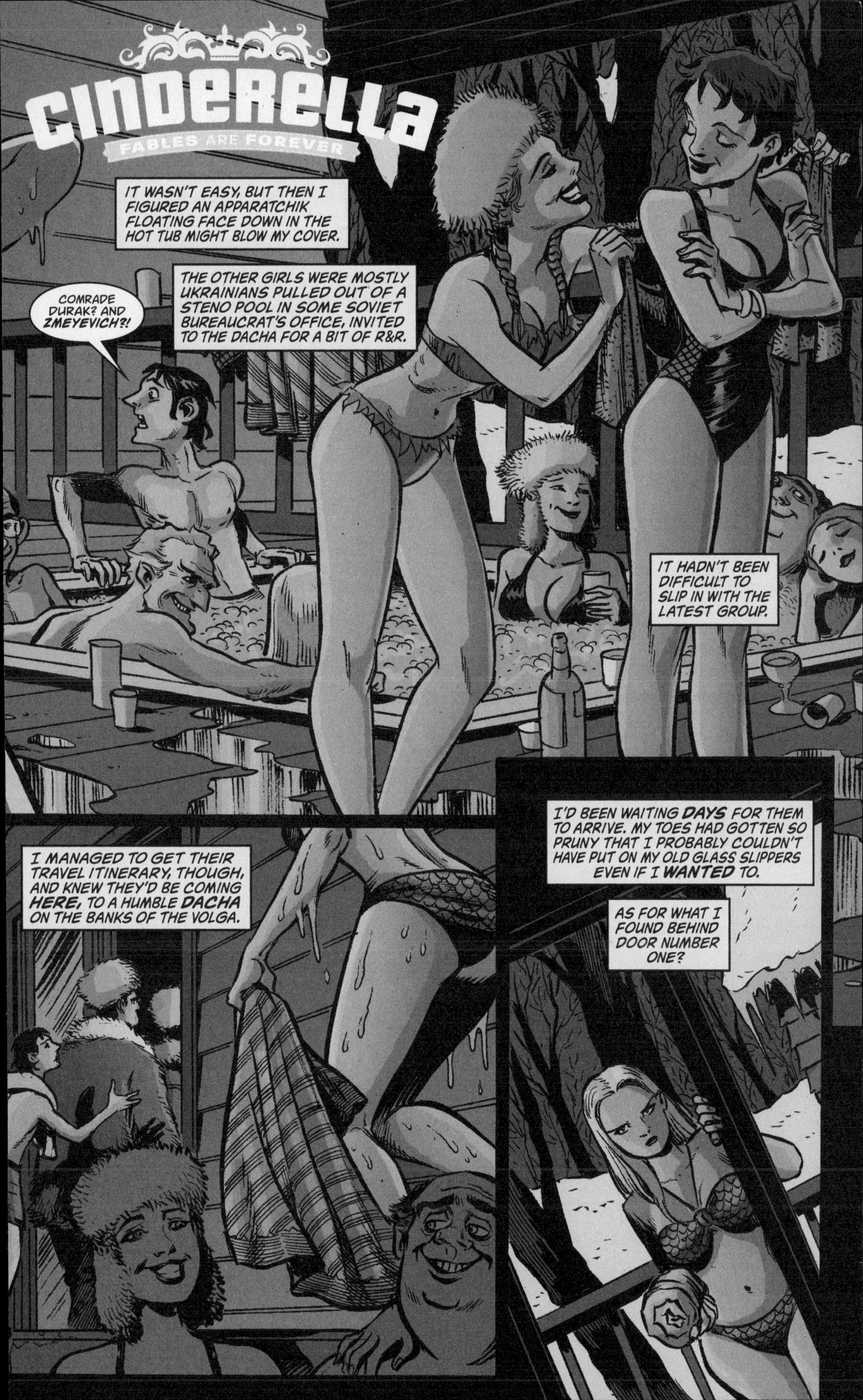
CINDERELLA
FABLES ARE FOREVER
IT WASN'T EASY, BUT THEN I FIGURED AN APPARATCHIK FLOATING FACE DOWN IN THE HOT TUB MIGHT BLOW MY COVER.
THE OTHER GIRLS WERE MOSTLY UKRAINIANS PULLED OUT OF A STENO POOL IN SOME SOVIET BUREAUCRAT'S OFFICE, INVITED TO THE DACHA FOR A BIT OF R&R.
COMRADE DURAK? AND ZMEYEVICH?!
IT HADN'T BEEN DIFFICULT TO SLIP IN WITH THE LATEST GROUP.
I MANAGED TO GET THEIR TRAVEL ITINERARY, THOUGH, AND KNEW THEY'D BE COMING HERE, TO A HUMBLE DACHA ON THE BANKS OF THE VOLGA.
I'D BEEN WAITING DAYS FOR THEM TO ARRIVE. MY TOES HAD GOTTEN SO PRUNY THAT I PROBABLY COULDN'T HAVE PUT ON MY OLD GLASS SLIPPERS EVEN IF I WANTED TO.
AS FOR WHAT I FOUND BEHIND DOOR NUMBER ONE?

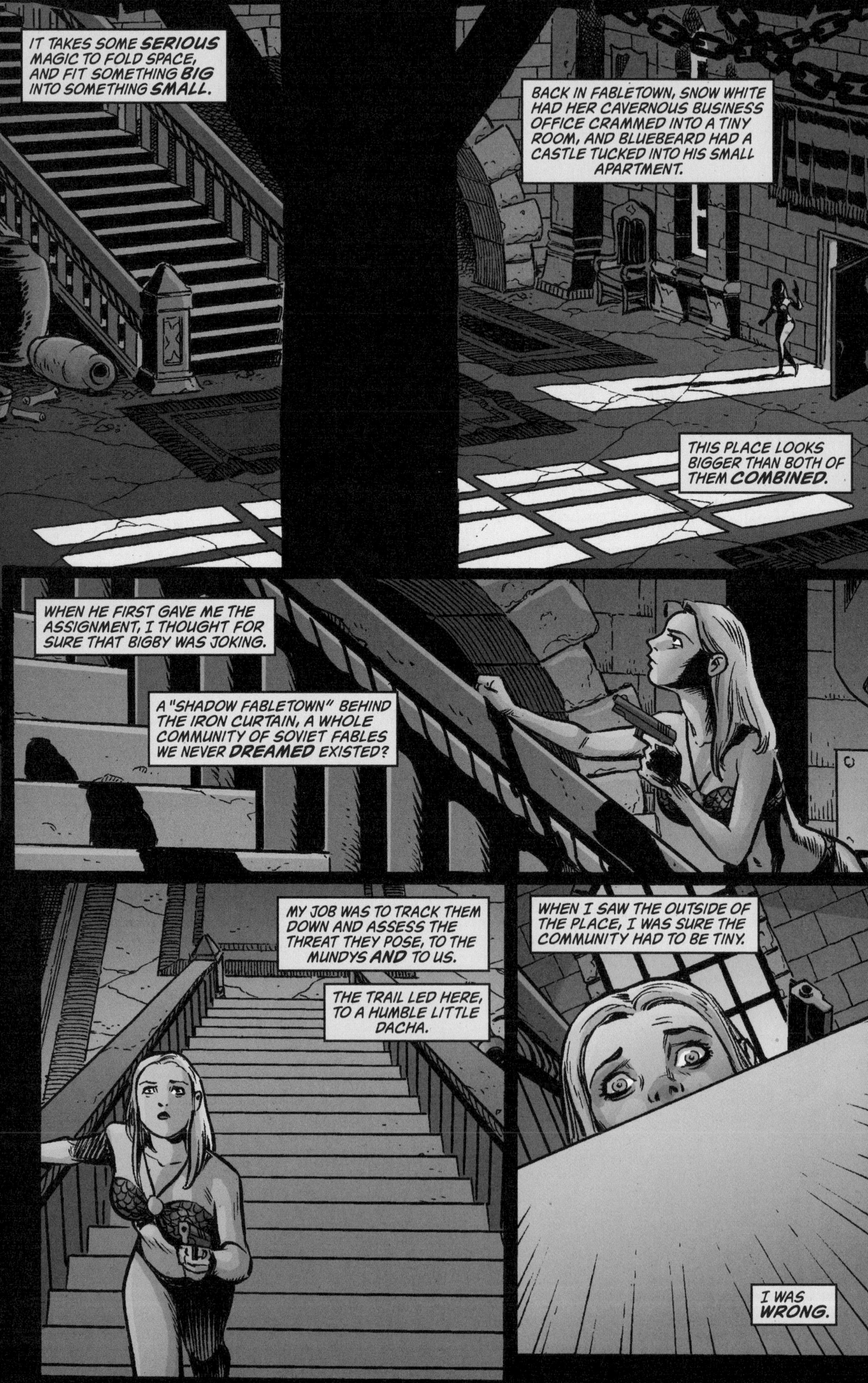
IT TAKES SOME SERIOUS MAGIC TO FOLD SPACE, AND FIT SOMETHING BIG INTO SOMETHING SMALL.
BACK IN FABLETOWN, SNOW WHITE HAD HER CAVERNOUS BUSINESS OFFICE CRAMMED INTO A TINY ROOM, AND BLUEBEARD HAD A CASTLE TUCKED INTO HIS SMALL APARTMENT.
THIS PLACE LOOKS BIGGER THAN BOTH OF THEM COMBINED.
WHEN HE FIRST GAVE ME THE ASSIGNMENT, I THOUGHT FOR SURE THAT BIGBY WAS JOKING.
A "SHADOW FABLETOWN" BEHIND THE IRON CURTAIN, A WHOLE COMMUNITY OF SOVIET FABLES WE NEVER DREAMED EXISTED?
MY JOB WAS TO TRACK THEM DOWN AND ASSESS THE THREAT THEY POSE, TO THE MUNDYS AND TO US.
THE TRAIL LED HERE, TO A HUMBLE LITTLE DACHA.
WHEN I SAW THE OUTSIDE OF THE PLACE, I WAS SURE THE COMMUNITY HAD TO BE TINY.
I WAS WRONG.

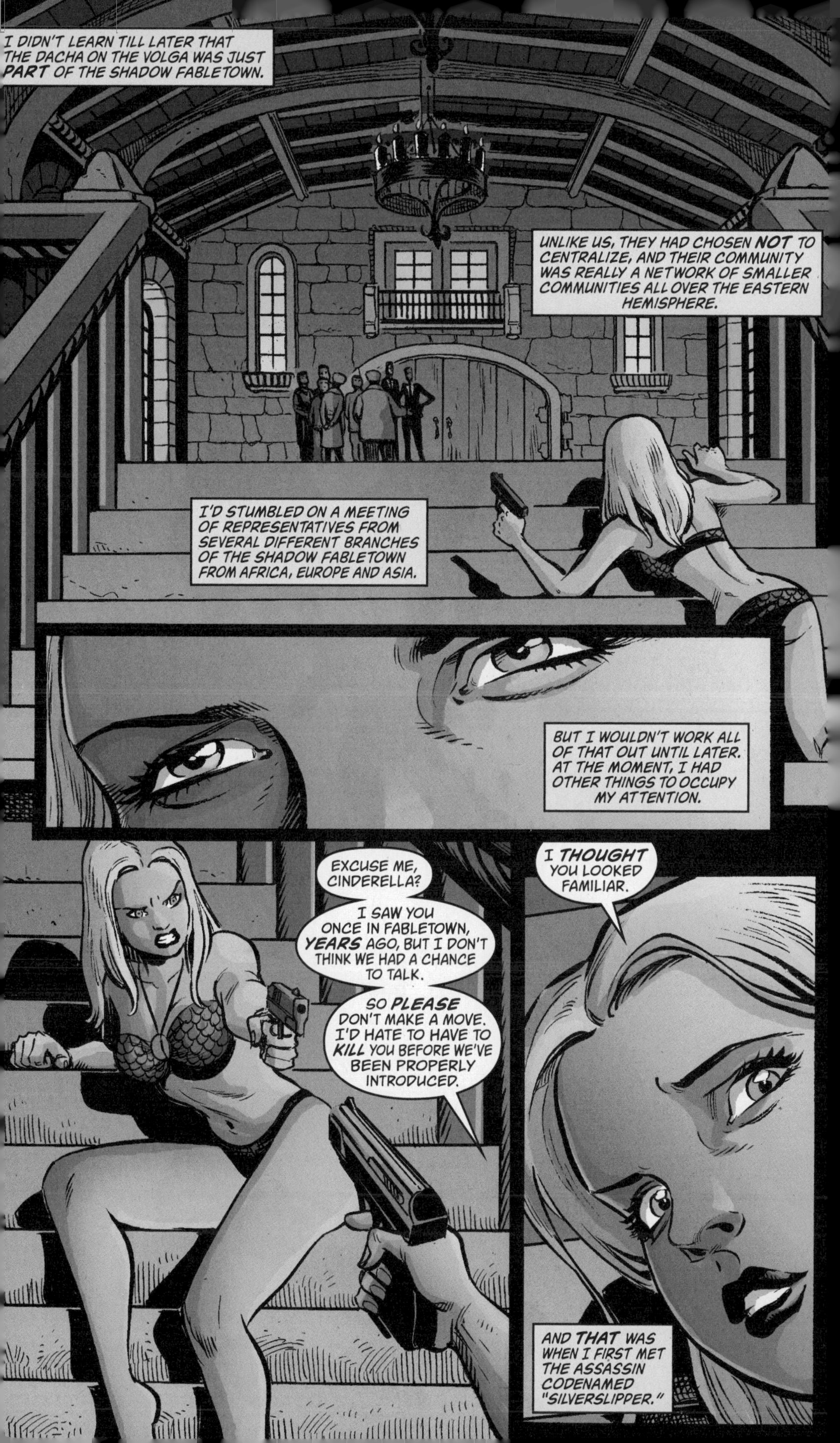
I DIDN'T LEARN TILL LATER THAT THE DACHA ON THE VOLGA WAS JUST PART OF THE SHADOW FABLETOWN.
UNLIKE US, THEY HAD CHOSEN NOT TO CENTRALIZE, AND THEIR COMMUNITY WAS REALLY A NETWORK OF SMALLER COMMUNITIES ALL OVER THE EASTERN HEMISPHERE.
I'D STUMBLED ON A MEETING OF REPRESENTATIVES FROM SEVERAL DIFFERENT BRANCHES OF THE SHADOW FABLETOWN FROM AFRICA, EUROPE AND ASIA.
BUT I WOULDN'T WORK ALL OF THAT OUT UNTIL LATER. AT THE MOMENT, I HAD OTHER THINGS TO OCCUPY MY ATTENTION.
EXCUSE ME, CINDERELLA?
I SAW YOU ONCE IN FABLETOWN, YEARS AGO, BUT I DON'T THINK WE HAD A CHANCE TO TALK.
SO PLEASE DON'T MAKE A MOVE. I'D HATE TO HAVE TO KILL YOU BEFORE WE'VE BEEN PROPERLY INTRODUCED.
I THOUGHT YOU LOOKED FAMILIAR.
AND THAT WAS WHEN I FIRST MET THE ASSASSIN CODENAMED "SILVERSLIPPER."

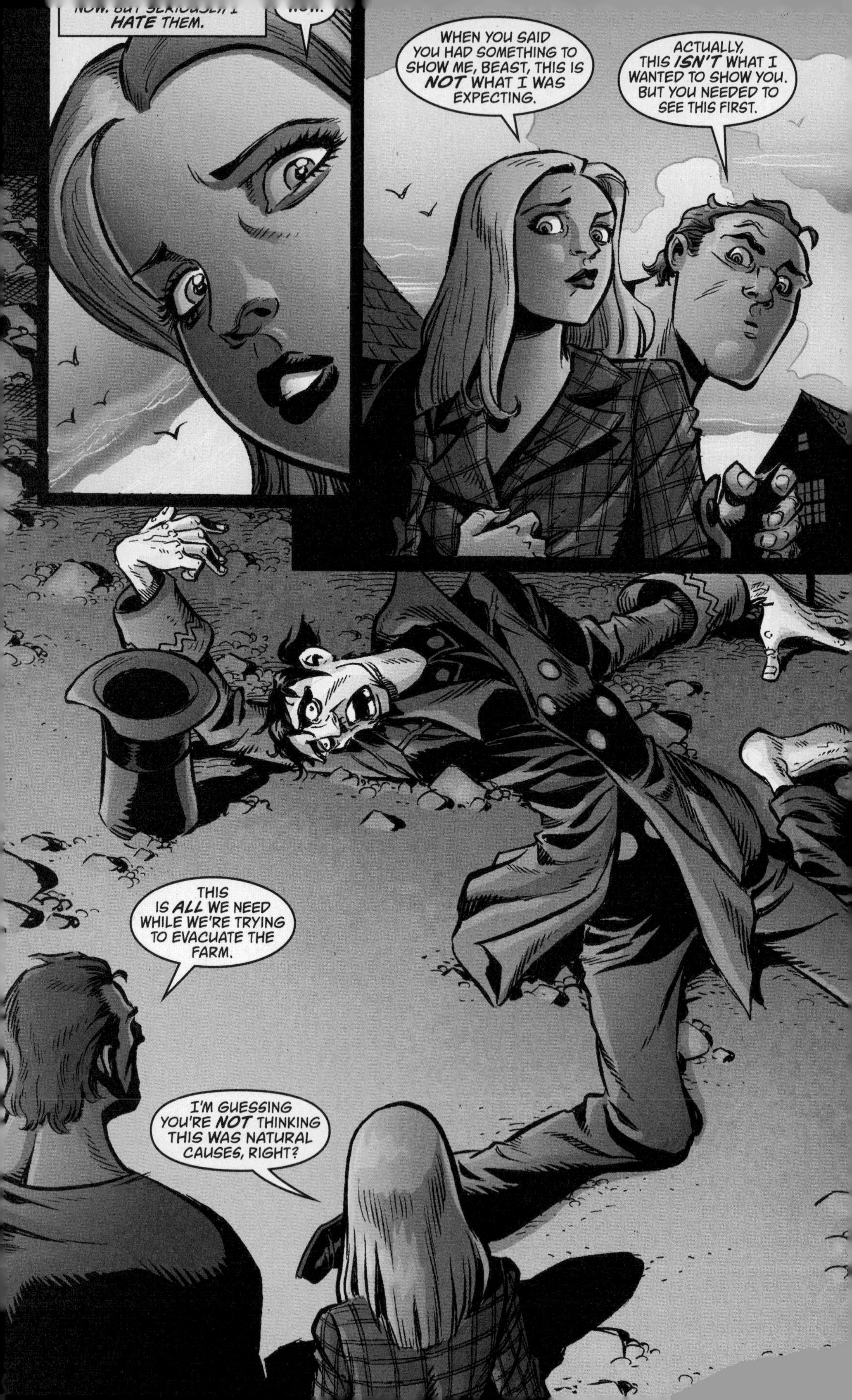
HATE THEM.
WHEN YOU SAID YOU HAD SOMETHING TO SHOW ME, BEAST, THIS IS NOT WHAT I WAS EXPECTING.
ACTUALLY, THIS ISN'T WHAT I WANTED TO SHOW YOU. BUT YOU NEEDED TO SEE THIS FIRST.
THIS IS ALL WE NEED WHILE WE'RE TRYING TO EVACUATE THE FARM.
I'M GUESSING YOU'RE NOT THINKING THIS WAS NATURAL CAUSES, RIGHT?

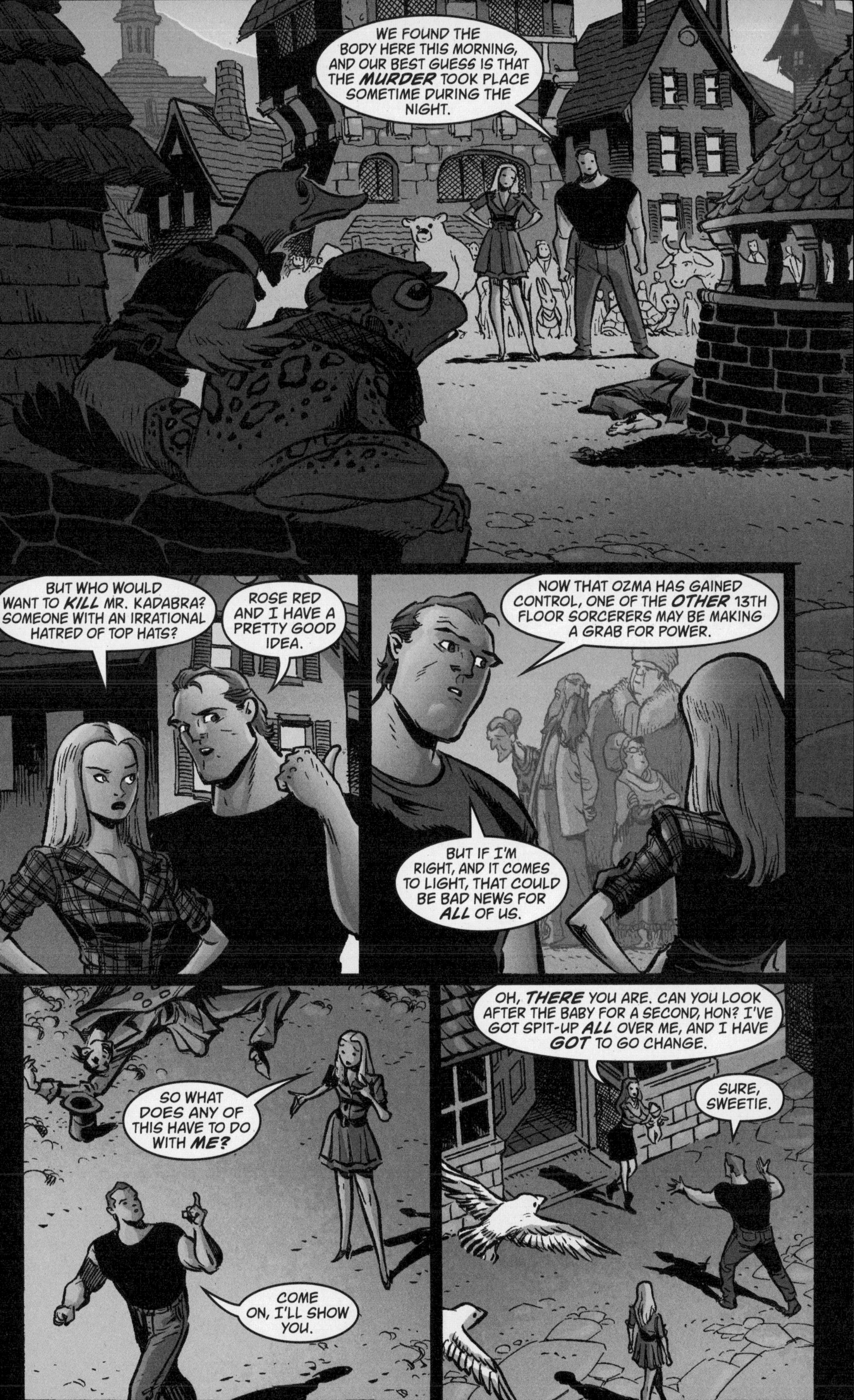
WE FOUND THE BODY HERE THIS MORNING, AND OUR BEST GUESS IS THAT THE MURDER TOOK PLACE SOMETIME DURING THE NIGHT.
BUT WHO WOULD WANT TO KILL MR. KADABRA? SOMEONE WITH AN IRRATIONAL HATRED OF TOP HATS?
ROSE RED AND I HAVE A PRETTY GOOD IDEA.
NOW THAT OZMA HAS GAINED CONTROL, ONE OF THE OTHER 13TH FLOOR SORCERERS MAY BE MAKING A GRAB FOR POWER.
BUT IF I'M RIGHT, AND IT COMES TO LIGHT, THAT COULD BE BAD NEWS FOR ALL OF US.
SO WHAT DOES ANY OF THIS HAVE TO DO WITH ME?
COME ON, I'LL SHOW YOU.
OH, THERE YOU ARE. CAN YOU LOOK AFTER THE BABY FOR A SECOND, HON? I'VE GOT SPIT-UP ALL OVER ME, AND I HAVE GOT TO GO CHANGE.
SURE, SWEETIE.

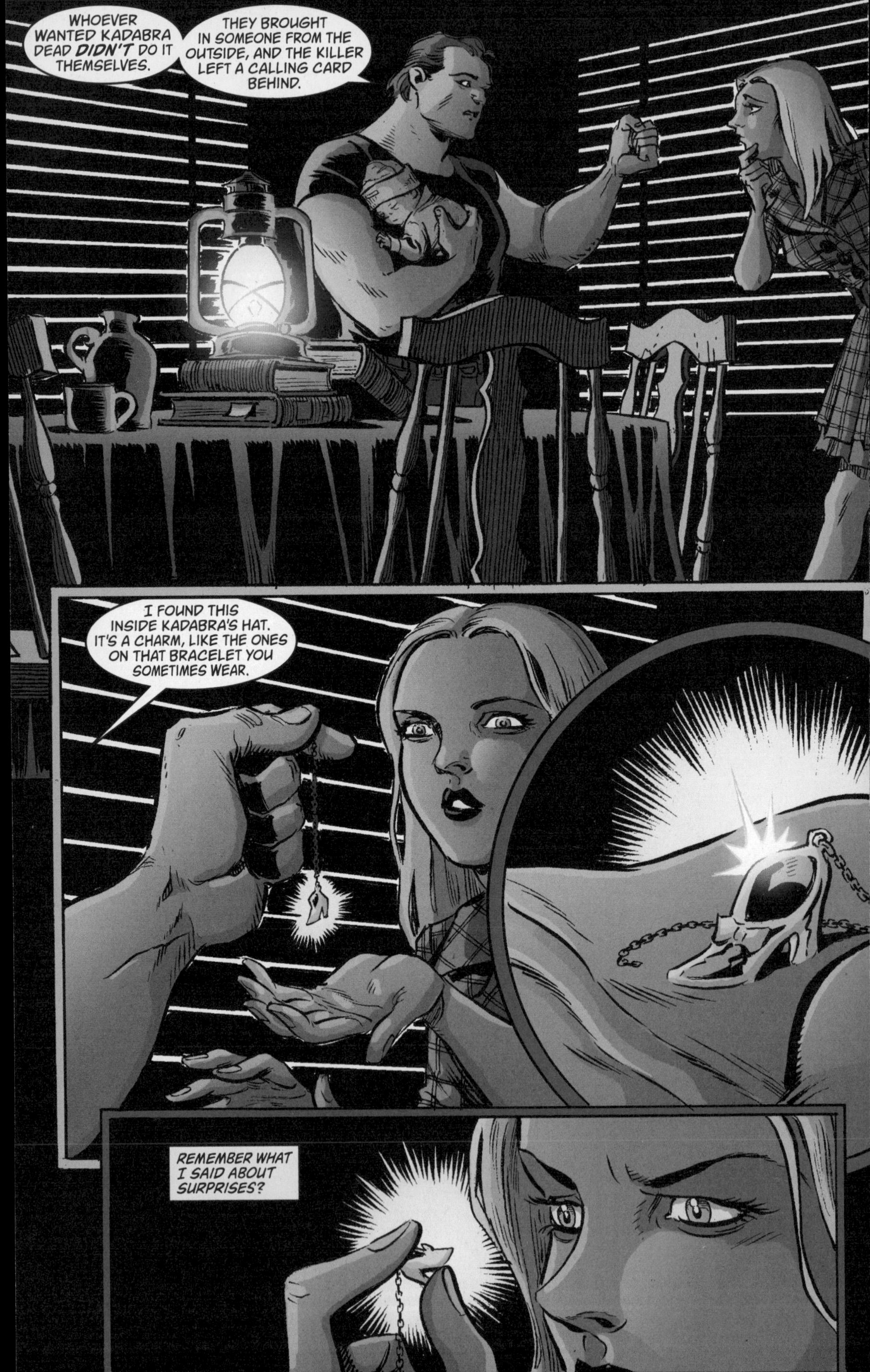
WHOEVER WANTED KADABRA DEAD **DIDN'T** DO IT THEMSELVES.
THEY BROUGHT IN SOMEONE FROM THE OUTSIDE, AND THE KILLER LEFT A CALLING CARD BEHIND.
I FOUND THIS INSIDE KADABRA'S HAT. IT'S A CHARM, LIKE THE ONES ON THAT BRACELET YOU SOMETIMES WEAR.
REMEMBER WHAT I SAID ABOUT SURPRISES?

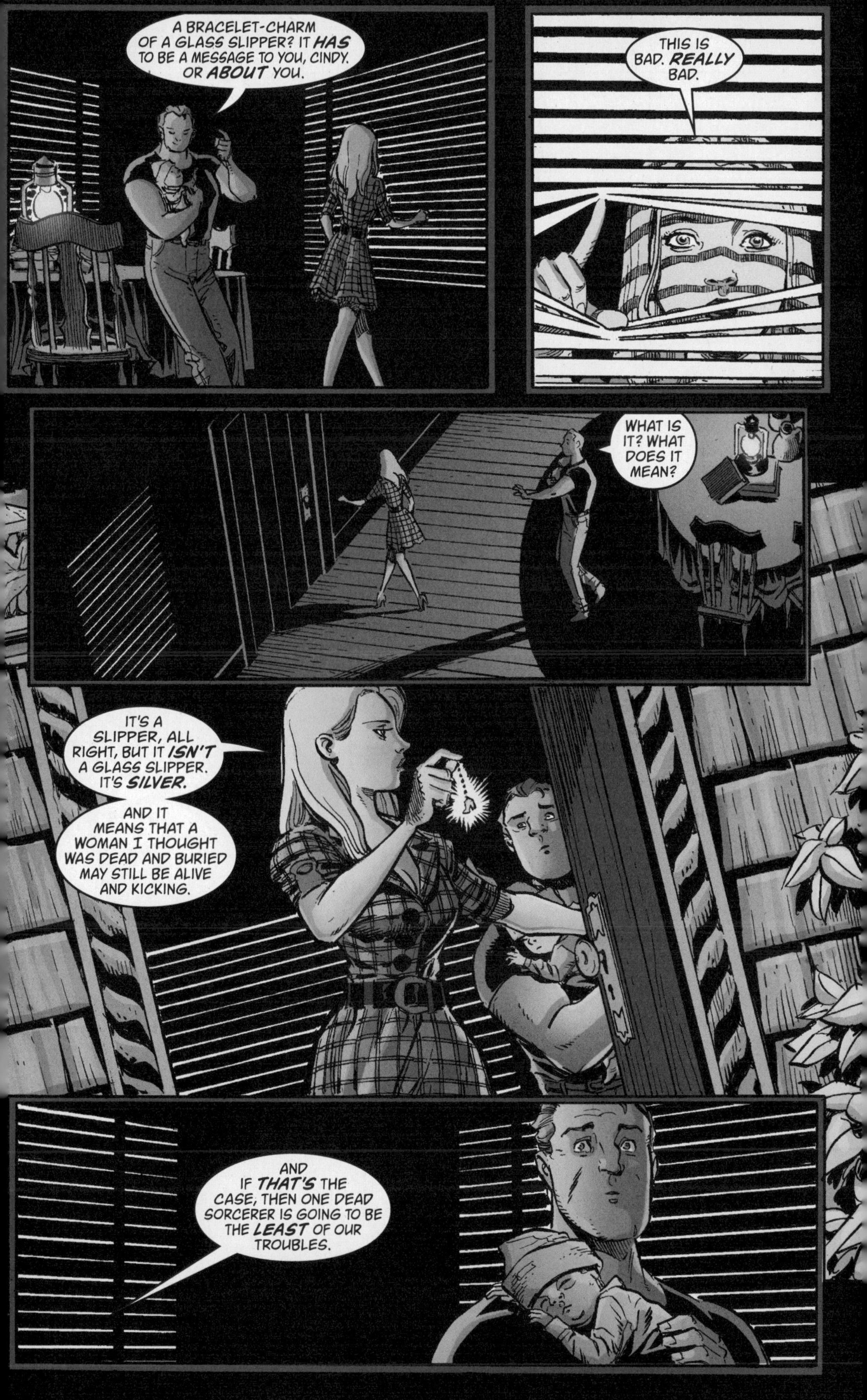
A BRACELET-CHARM OF A GLASS SLIPPER? IT HAS TO BE A MESSAGE TO YOU, CINDY. OR ABOUT YOU.
THIS IS BAD. REALLY BAD.
WHAT IS IT? WHAT DOES IT MEAN?
IT'S A SLIPPER, ALL RIGHT, BUT IT ISN'T A GLASS SLIPPER. IT'S SILVER.
AND IT MEANS THAT A WOMAN I THOUGHT WAS DEAD AND BURIED MAY STILL BE ALIVE AND KICKING.
AND IF THAT'S THE CASE, THEN ONE DEAD SORCERER IS GOING TO BE THE LEAST OF OUR TROUBLES.

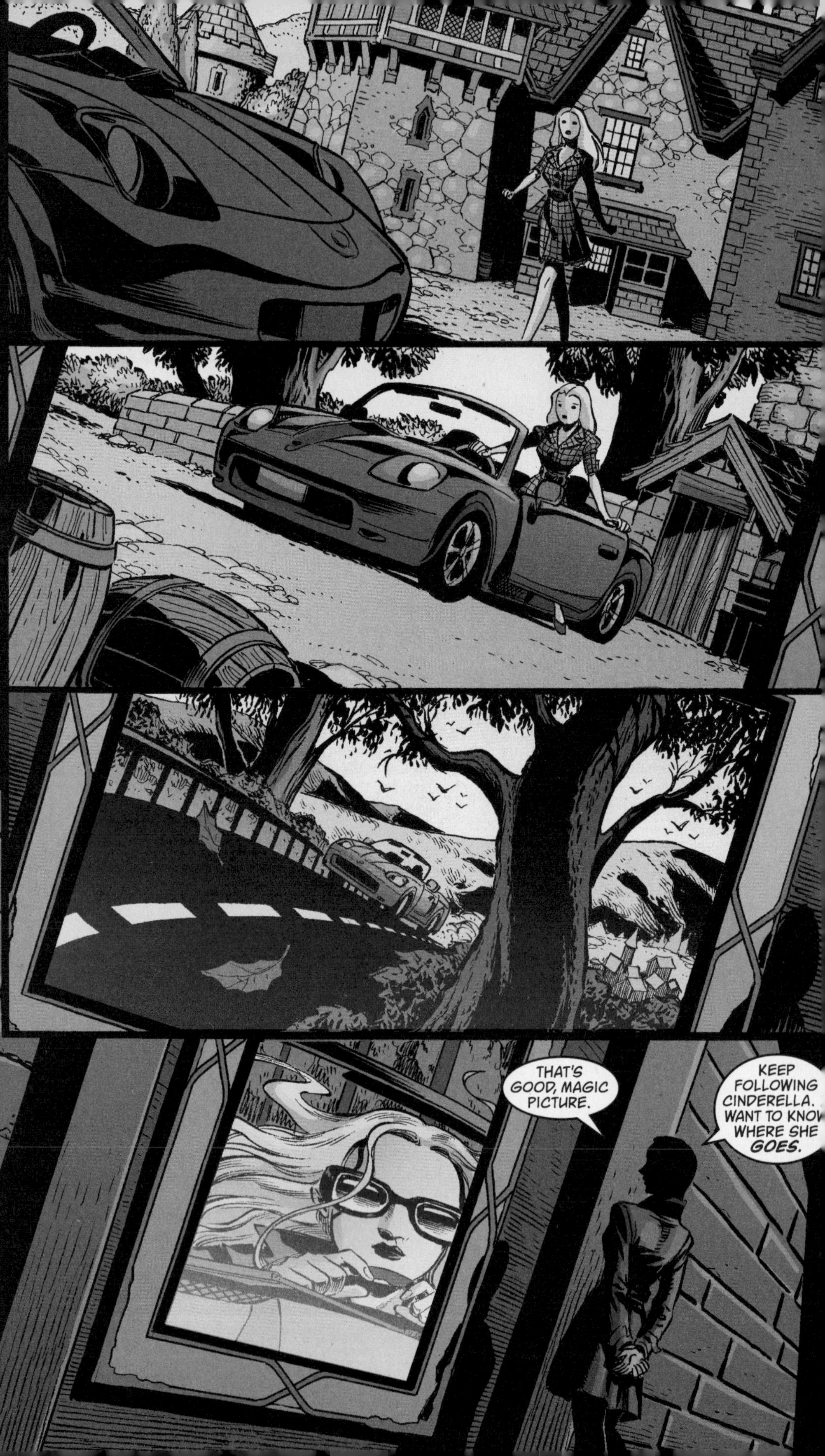
THAT'S GOOD, MAGIC PICTURE.
KEEP FOLLOWING CINDERELLA. WANT TO KNOW WHERE SHE GOES.

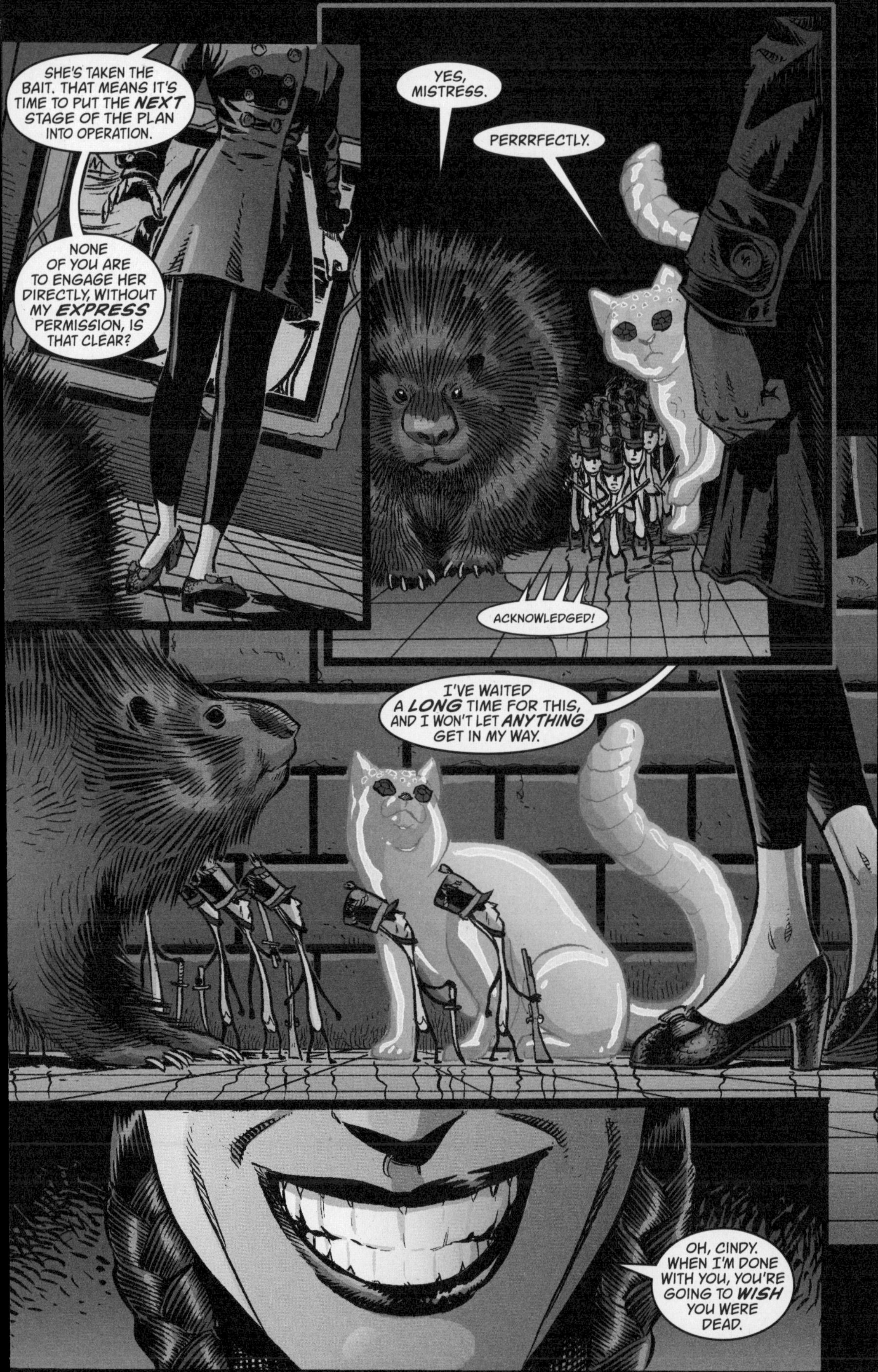
SHE'S TAKEN THE BAIT. THAT MEANS IT'S TIME TO PUT THE NEXT STAGE OF THE PLAN INTO OPERATION.
NONE OF YOU ARE TO ENGAGE HER DIRECTLY, WITHOUT MY EXPRESS PERMISSION, IS THAT CLEAR?
YES, MISTRESS.
PERRRFECTLY.
ACKNOWLEDGED!
I'VE WAITED A LONG TIME FOR THIS, AND I WON'T LET ANYTHING GET IN MY WAY.
OH, CINDY. WHEN I'M DONE WITH YOU, YOU'RE GOING TO WISH YOU WERE DEAD.

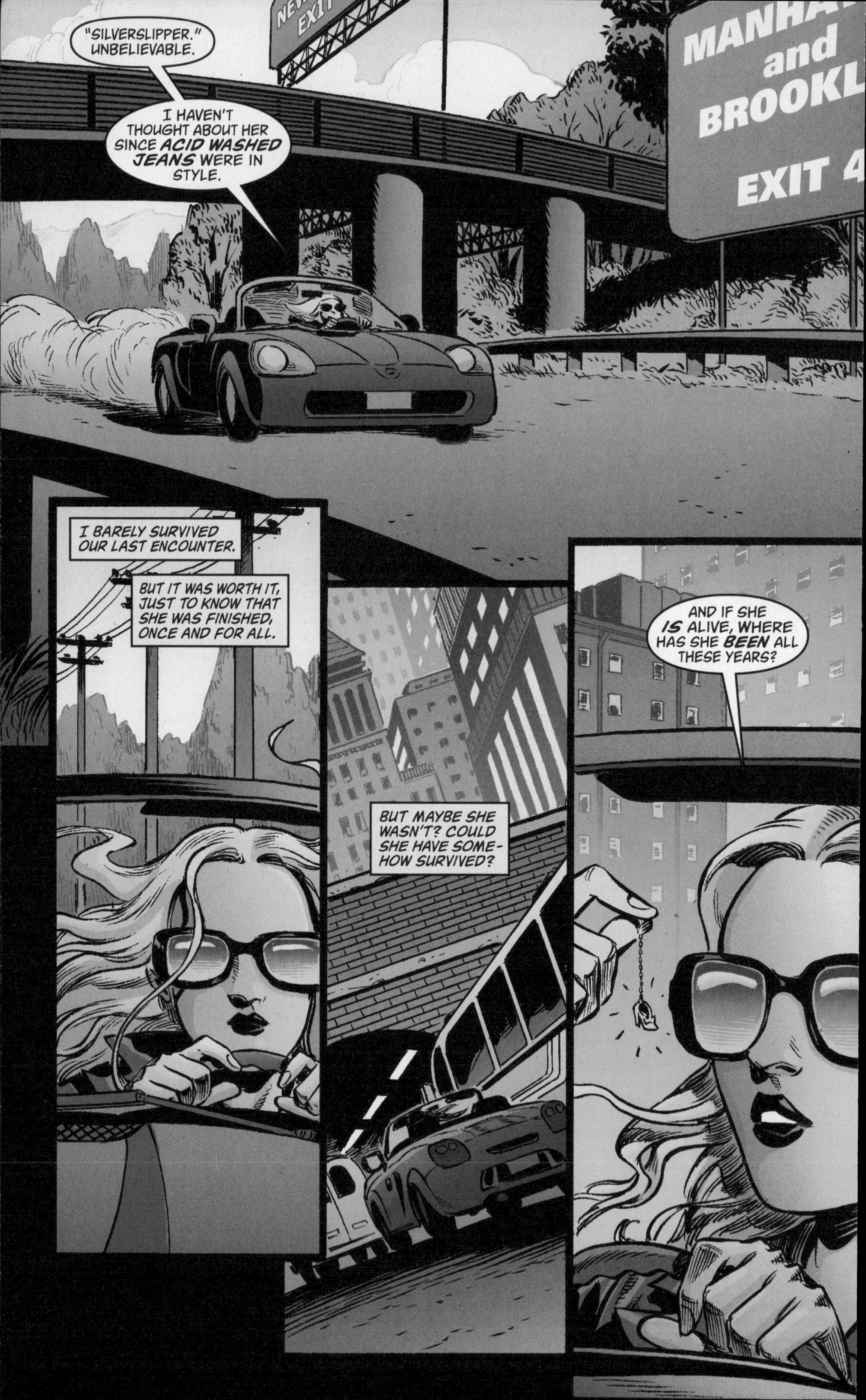
NEW
EXIT
MANHA
and
BROOKL
EXIT 4
"SILVERSLIPPER." UNBELIEVABLE.
I HAVEN'T THOUGHT ABOUT HER SINCE ACID WASHED JEANS WERE IN STYLE.
I BARELY SURVIVED OUR LAST ENCOUNTER.
BUT IT WAS WORTH IT, JUST TO KNOW THAT SHE WAS FINISHED, ONCE AND FOR ALL.
BUT MAYBE SHE WASN'T? COULD SHE HAVE SOME-HOW SURVIVED?
AND IF SHE IS ALIVE, WHERE HAS SHE BEEN ALL THESE YEARS?

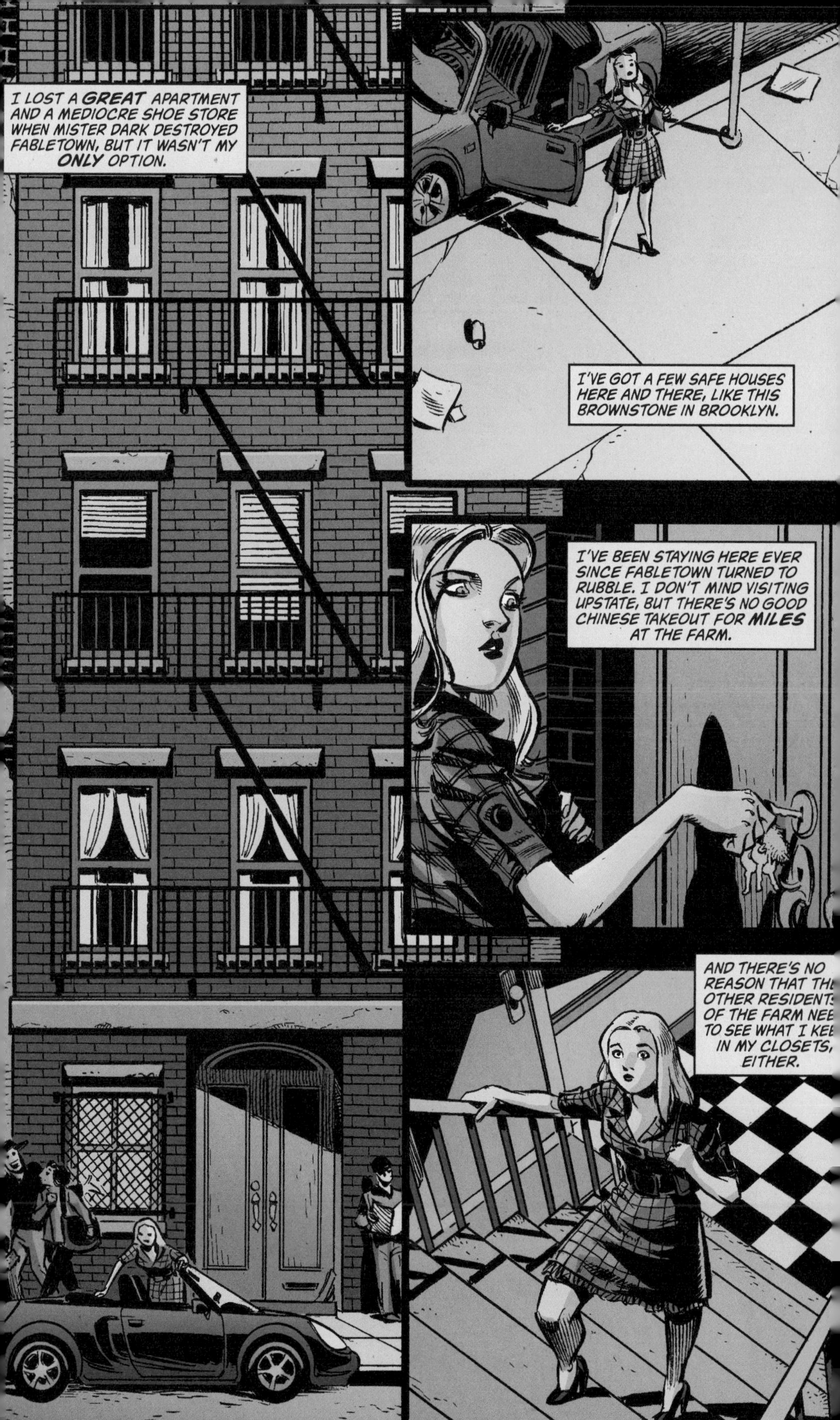
I LOST A GREAT APARTMENT AND A MEDIOCRE SHOE STORE WHEN MISTER DARK DESTROYED FABLETOWN, BUT IT WASN'T MY ONLY OPTION.
I'VE GOT A FEW SAFE HOUSES HERE AND THERE, LIKE THIS BROWNSTONE IN BROOKLYN.
I'VE BEEN STAYING HERE EVER SINCE FABLETOWN TURNED TO RUBBLE. I DON'T MIND VISITING UPSTATE, BUT THERE'S NO GOOD CHINESE TAKEOUT FOR MILES AT THE FARM.
AND THERE'S NO REASON THAT THE OTHER RESIDENTS OF THE FARM NEE TO SEE WHAT I KEE IN MY CLOSETS, EITHER.

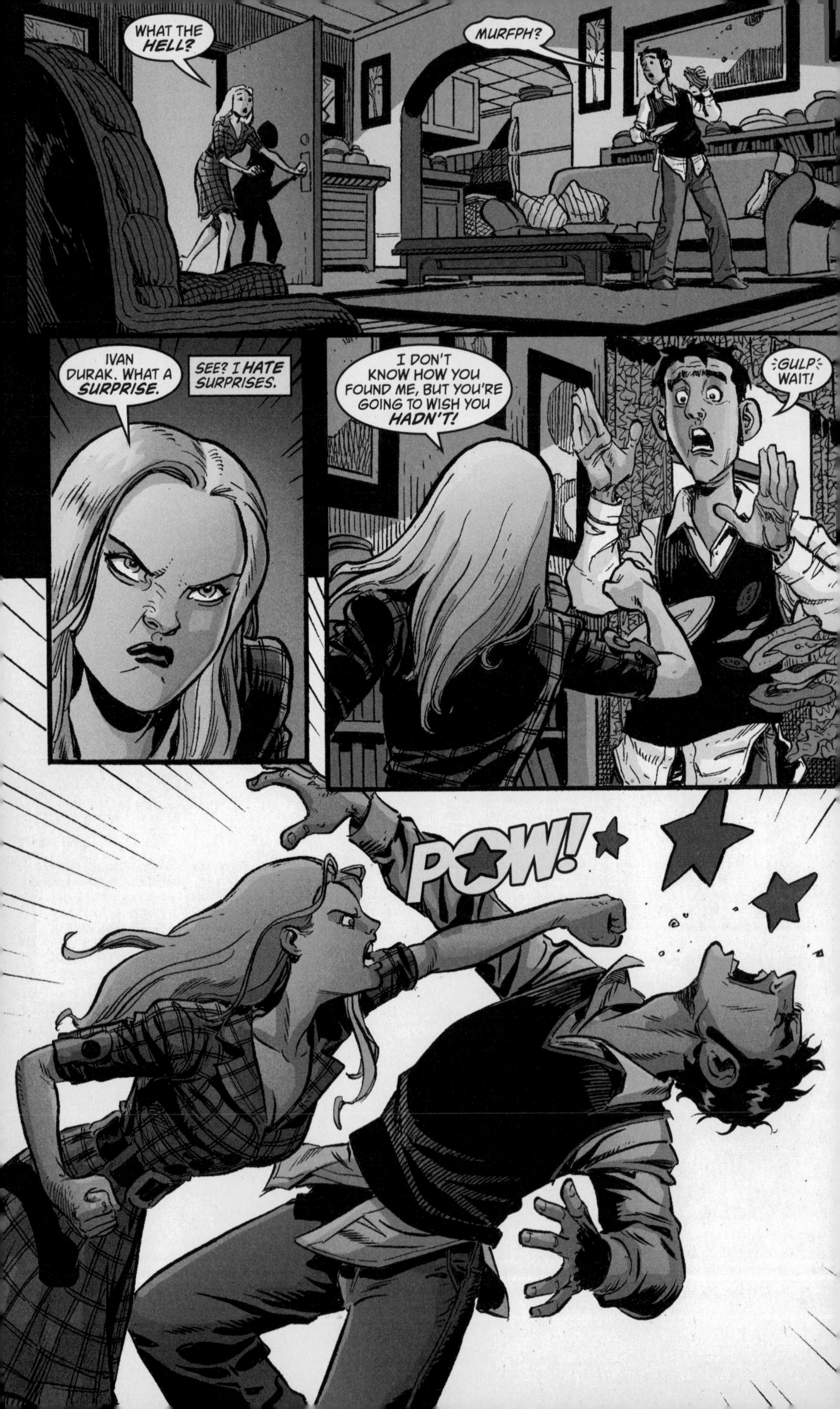
WHAT THE HELL?
MURFPH?
IVAN DURAK. WHAT A SURPRISE.
SEE? I HATE SURPRISES.
I DON'T KNOW HOW YOU FOUND ME, BUT YOU'RE GOING TO WISH YOU HADN'T!
GULP WAIT!
POW!

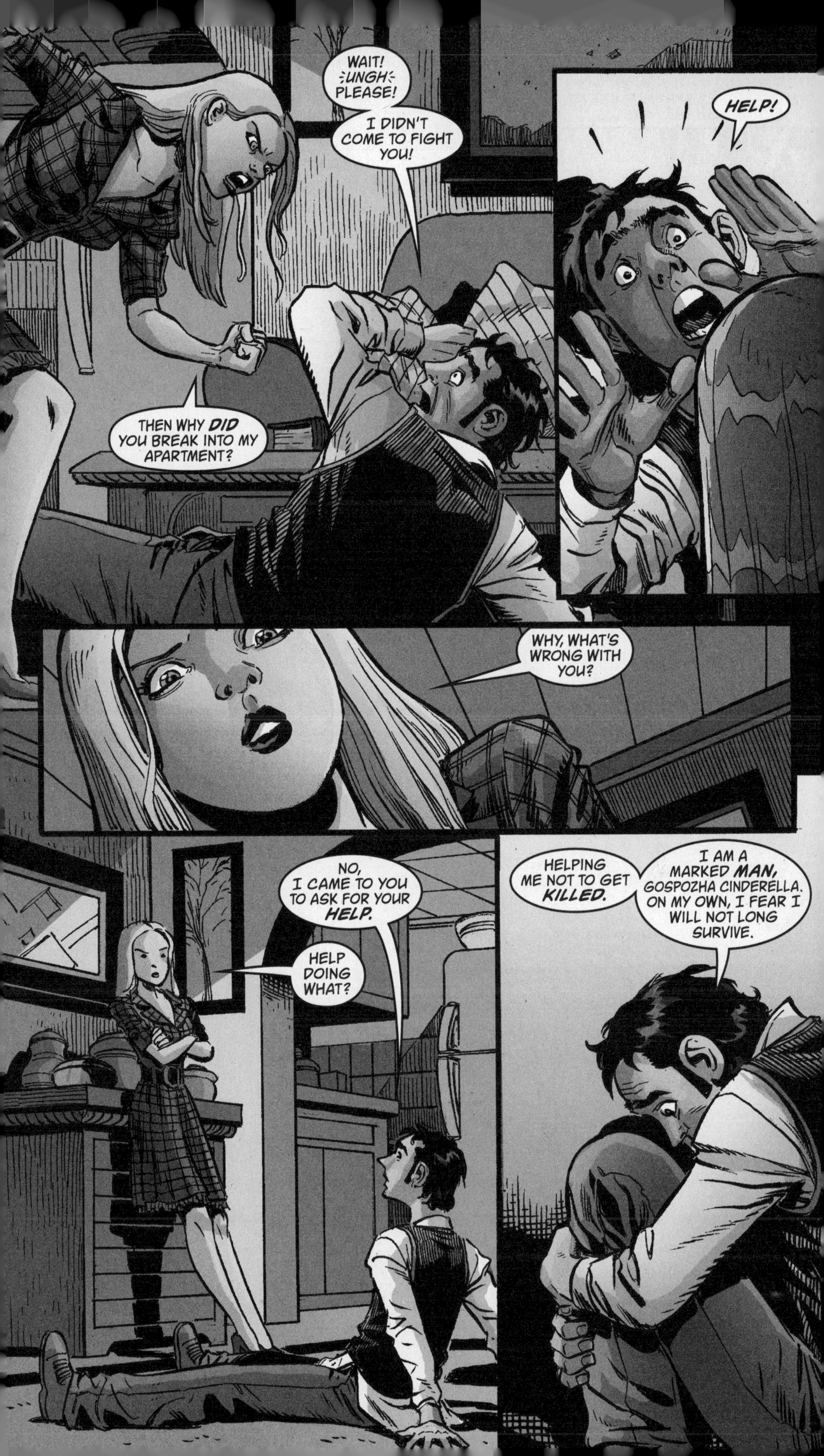
WAIT! UNGH PLEASE!
I DIDN'T COME TO FIGHT YOU!
THEN WHY DID YOU BREAK INTO MY APARTMENT?
HELP!
WHY, WHAT'S WRONG WITH YOU?
NO, I CAME TO YOU TO ASK FOR YOUR HELP.
HELP DOING WHAT?
HELPING ME NOT TO GET KILLED.
I AM A MARKED MAN, GOSPOZHA CINDERELLA. ON MY OWN, I FEAR I WILL NOT LONG SURVIVE.

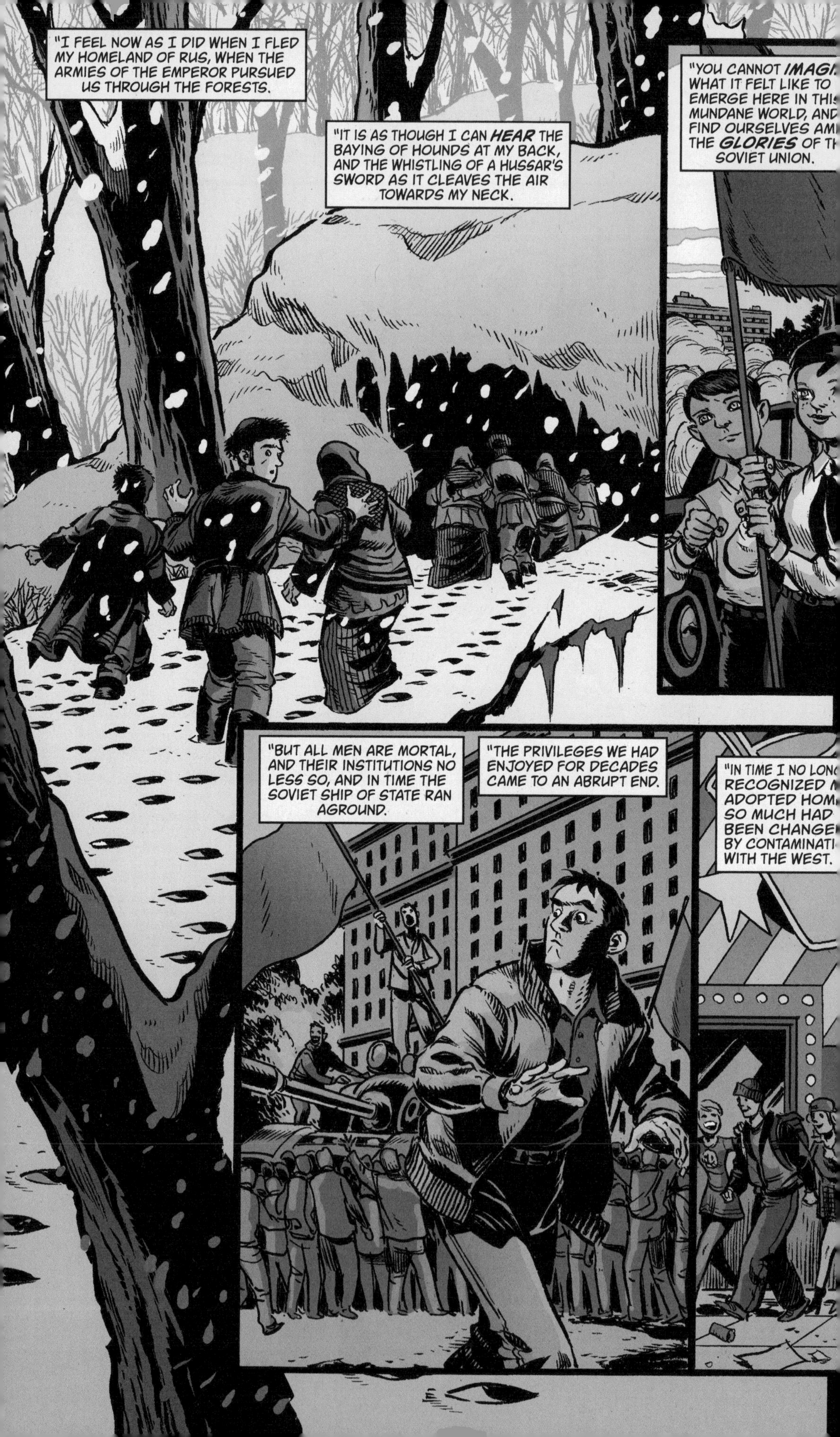
"I FEEL NOW AS I DID WHEN I FLED MY HOMELAND OF RUS, WHEN THE ARMIES OF THE EMPEROR PURSUED US THROUGH THE FORESTS.
"IT IS AS THOUGH I CAN HEAR THE BAYING OF HOUNDS AT MY BACK, AND THE WHISTLING OF A HUSSAR'S SWORD AS IT CLEAVES THE AIR TOWARDS MY NECK.
"YOU CANNOT IMAGI WHAT IT FELT LIKE TO EMERGE HERE IN THI MUNDANE WORLD, AND FIND OURSELVES AM THE GLORIES OF T SOVIET UNION.
"BUT ALL MEN ARE MORTAL, AND THEIR INSTITUTIONS NO LESS SO, AND IN TIME THE SOVIET SHIP OF STATE RAN AGROUND.
"THE PRIVILEGES WE HAD ENJOYED FOR DECADES CAME TO AN ABRUPT END.
"IN TIME I NO LON RECOGNIZED ADOPTED HOM SO MUCH HAD BEEN CHANGE BY CONTAMINATI WITH THE WEST.

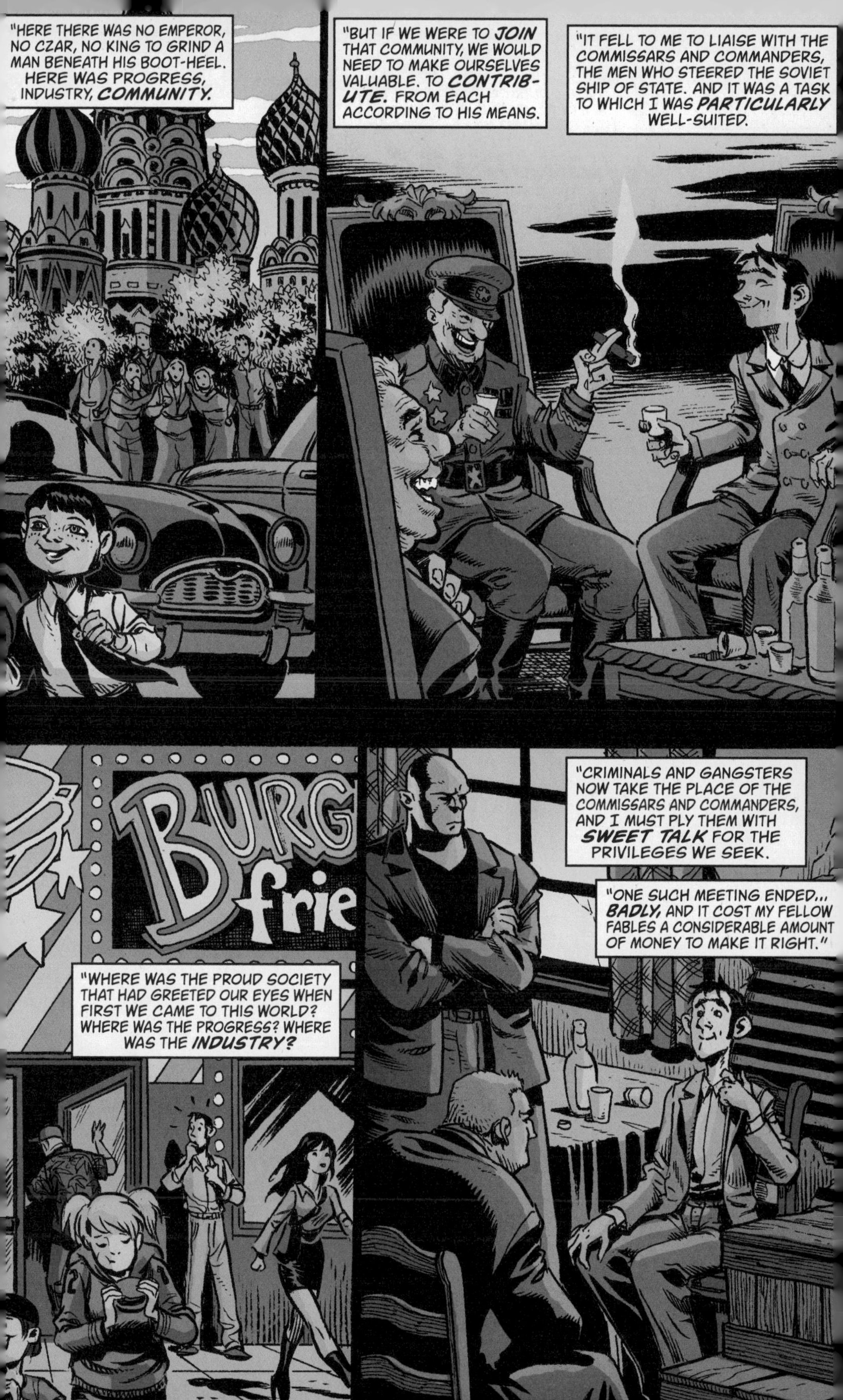
"HERE THERE WAS NO EMPEROR, NO CZAR, NO KING TO GRIND A MAN BENEATH HIS BOOT-HEEL. HERE WAS PROGRESS, INDUSTRY, COMMUNITY.
"BUT IF WE WERE TO JOIN THAT COMMUNITY, WE WOULD NEED TO MAKE OURSELVES VALUABLE. TO CONTRIB-UTE. FROM EACH ACCORDING TO HIS MEANS.
"IT FELL TO ME TO LIAISE WITH THE COMMISSARS AND COMMANDERS, THE MEN WHO STEERED THE SOVIET SHIP OF STATE. AND IT WAS A TASK TO WHICH I WAS PARTICULARLY WELL-SUITED.
BURG
frie
"WHERE WAS THE PROUD SOCIETY THAT HAD GREETED OUR EYES WHEN FIRST WE CAME TO THIS WORLD? WHERE WAS THE PROGRESS? WHERE WAS THE INDUSTRY?
"CRIMINALS AND GANGSTERS NOW TAKE THE PLACE OF THE COMMISSARS AND COMMANDERS, AND I MUST PLY THEM WITH SWEET TALK FOR THE PRIVILEGES WE SEEK.
"ONE SUCH MEETING ENDED... BADLY, AND IT COST MY FELLOW FABLES A CONSIDERABLE AMOUNT OF MONEY TO MAKE IT RIGHT."

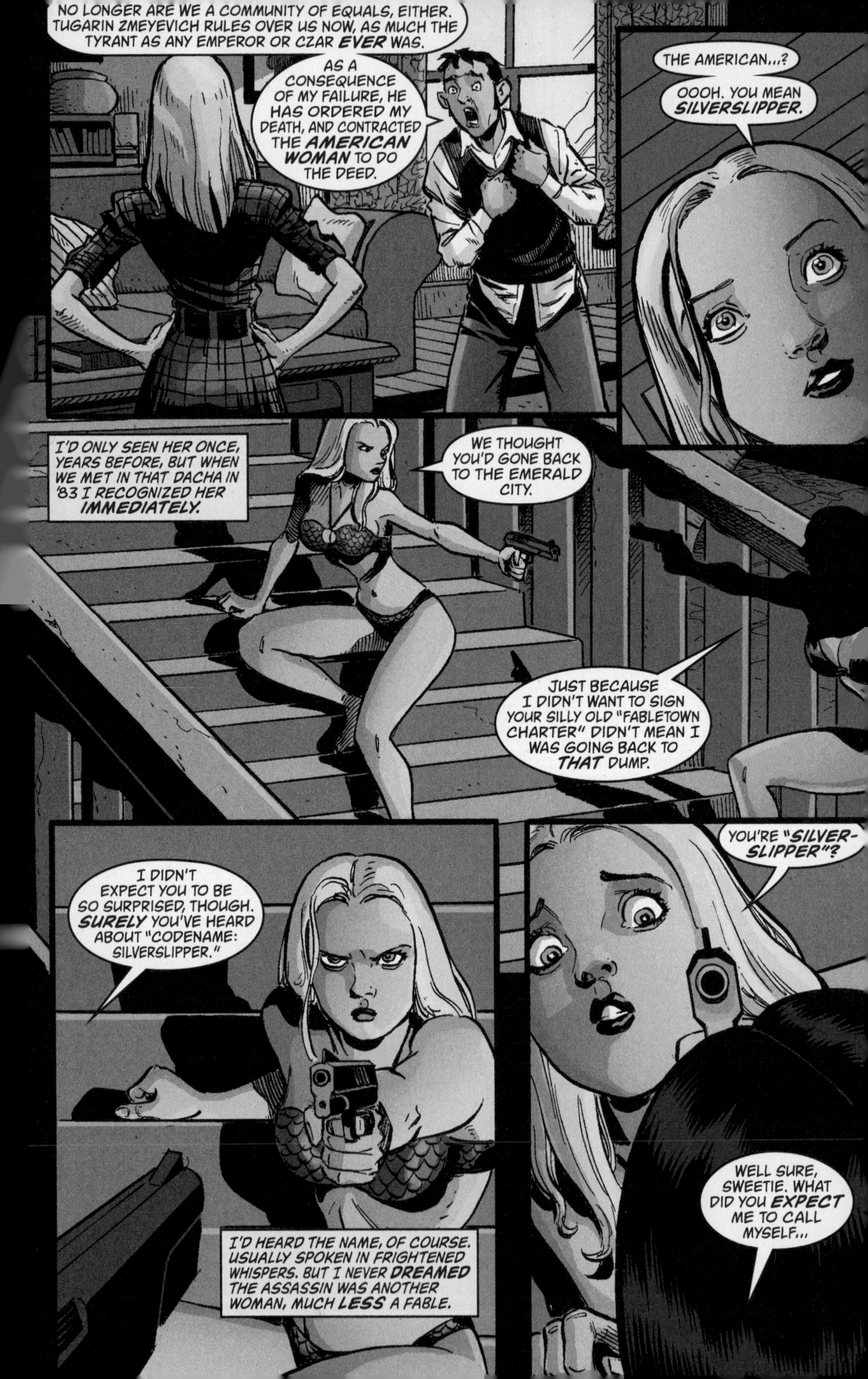
NO LONGER ARE WE A COMMUNITY OF EQUALS, EITHER. TUGARIN ZMEYEVICH RULES OVER US NOW, AS MUCH THE TYRANT AS ANY EMPEROR OR CZAR EVER WAS.
AS A CONSEQUENCE OF MY FAILURE, HE HAS ORDERED MY DEATH, AND CONTRACTED THE AMERICAN WOMAN TO DO THE DEED.
THE AMERICAN...?
OOOH. YOU MEAN SILVERSLIPPER.
I'D ONLY SEEN HER ONCE, YEARS BEFORE, BUT WHEN WE MET IN THAT DACHA IN '83 I RECOGNIZED HER IMMEDIATELY.
WE THOUGHT YOU'D GONE BACK TO THE EMERALD CITY.
JUST BECAUSE I DIDN'T WANT TO SIGN YOUR SILLY OLD "FABLETOWN CHARTER" DIDN'T MEAN I WAS GOING BACK TO THAT DUMP.
I DIDN'T EXPECT YOU TO BE SO SURPRISED, THOUGH. SURELY YOU'VE HEARD ABOUT "CODENAME: SILVERSLIPPER."
I'D HEARD THE NAME, OF COURSE. USUALLY SPOKEN IN FRIGHTENED WHISPERS. BUT I NEVER DREAMED THE ASSASSIN WAS ANOTHER WOMAN, MUCH LESS A FABLE.
YOU'RE "SILVER-SLIPPER"?
WELL SURE, SWEETIE. WHAT DID YOU EXPECT ME TO CALL MYSELF...

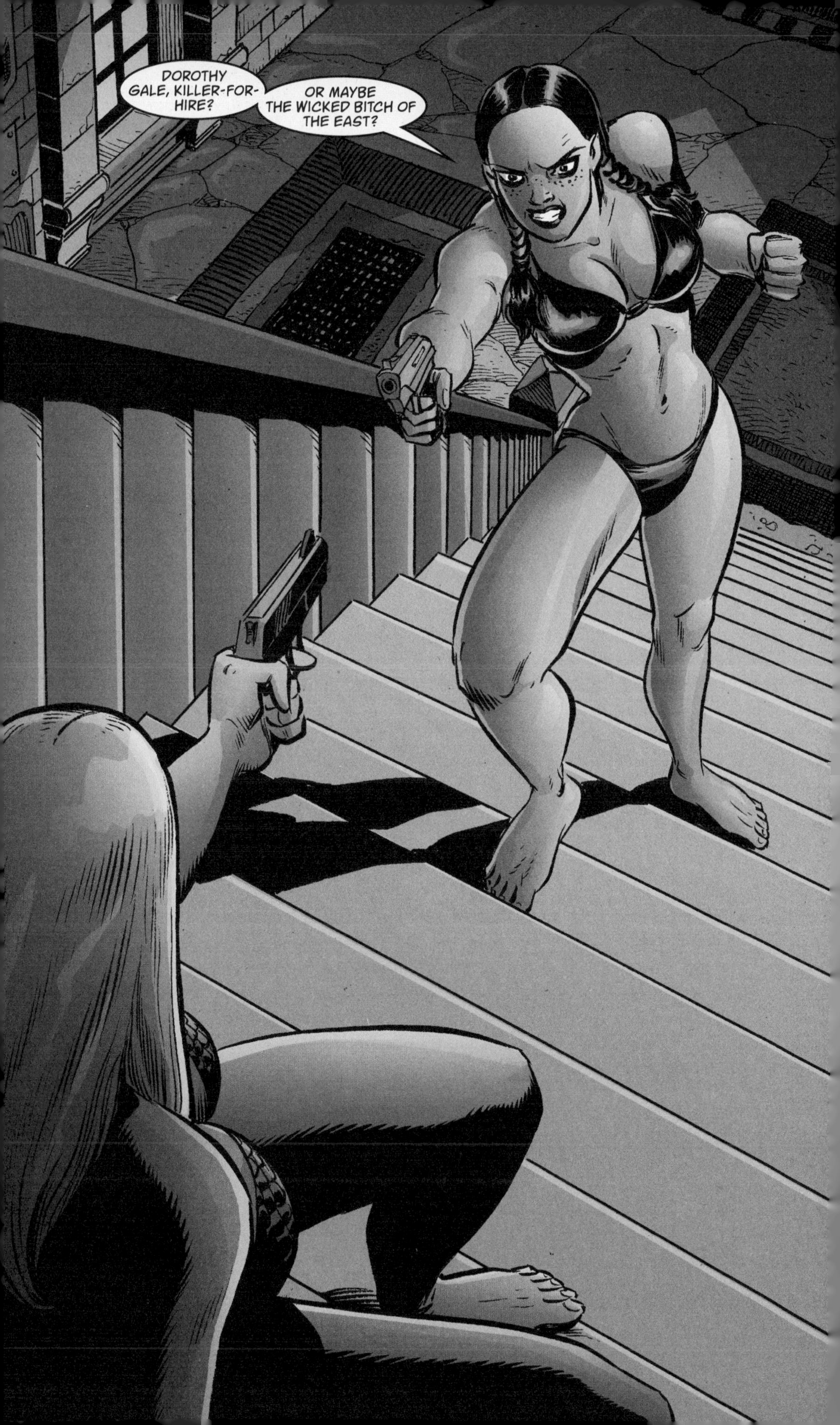
DOROTHY GALE, KILLER-FOR-HIRE?
OR MAYBE THE WICKED BITCH OF THE EAST?

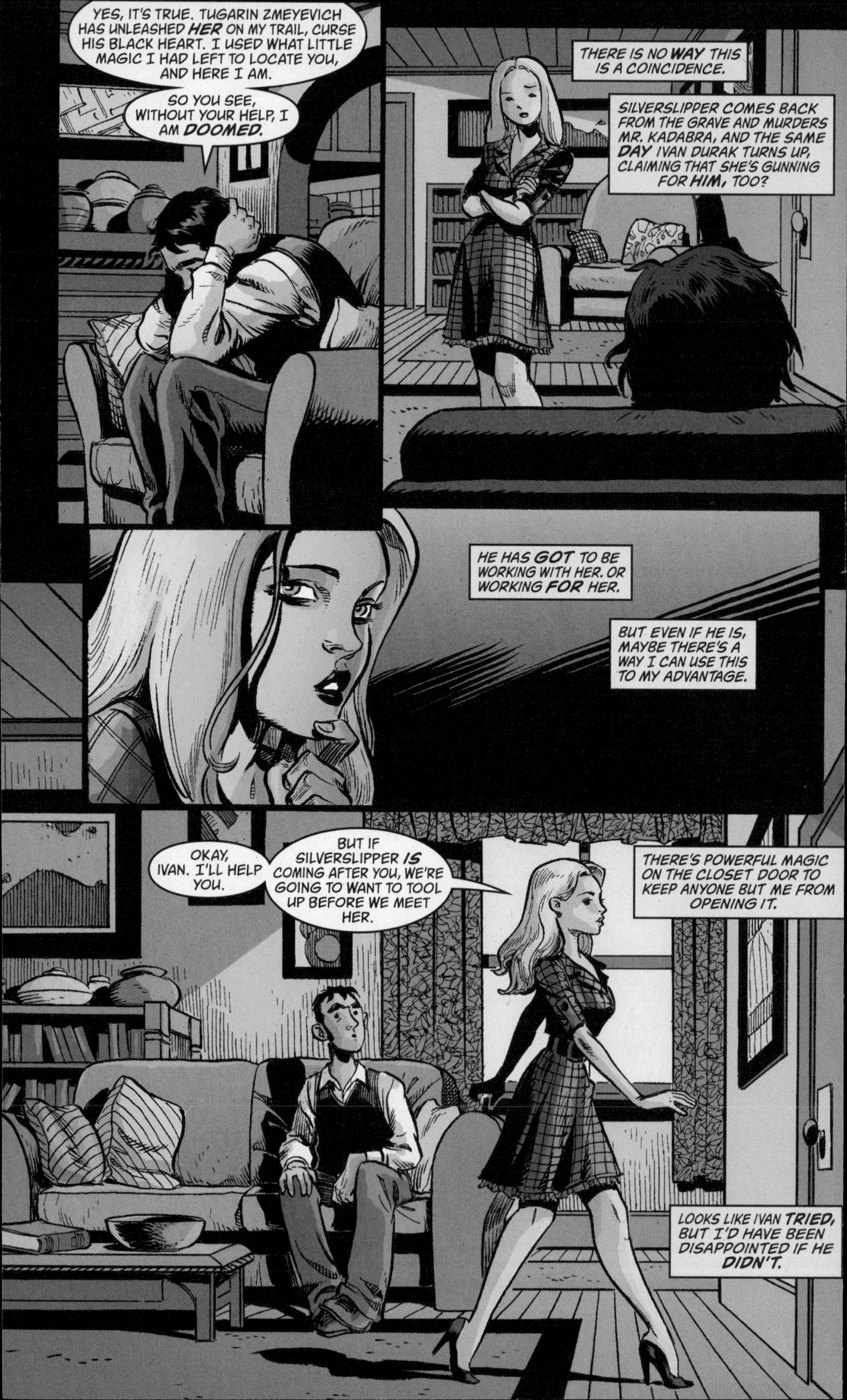
YES, IT'S TRUE. TUGARIN ZMEYEVICH HAS UNLEASHED HER ON MY TRAIL, CURSE HIS BLACK HEART. I USED WHAT LITTLE MAGIC I HAD LEFT TO LOCATE YOU, AND HERE I AM.
SO YOU SEE, WITHOUT YOUR HELP, I AM DOOMED.
THERE IS NO WAY THIS IS A COINCIDENCE.
SILVERSLIPPER COMES BACK FROM THE GRAVE AND MURDERS MR. KADABRA, AND THE SAME DAY IVAN DURAK TURNS UP, CLAIMING THAT SHE'S GUNNING FOR HIM, TOO?
HE HAS GOT TO BE WORKING WITH HER. OR WORKING FOR HER.
BUT EVEN IF HE IS, MAYBE THERE'S A WAY I CAN USE THIS TO MY ADVANTAGE.
OKAY, IVAN. I'LL HELP YOU.
BUT IF SILVERSLIPPER IS COMING AFTER YOU, WE'RE GOING TO WANT TO TOOL UP BEFORE WE MEET HER.
THERE'S POWERFUL MAGIC ON THE CLOSET DOOR TO KEEP ANYONE BUT ME FROM OPENING IT.
LOOKS LIKE IVAN TRIED, BUT I'D HAVE BEEN DISAPPOINTED IF HE DIDN'T.

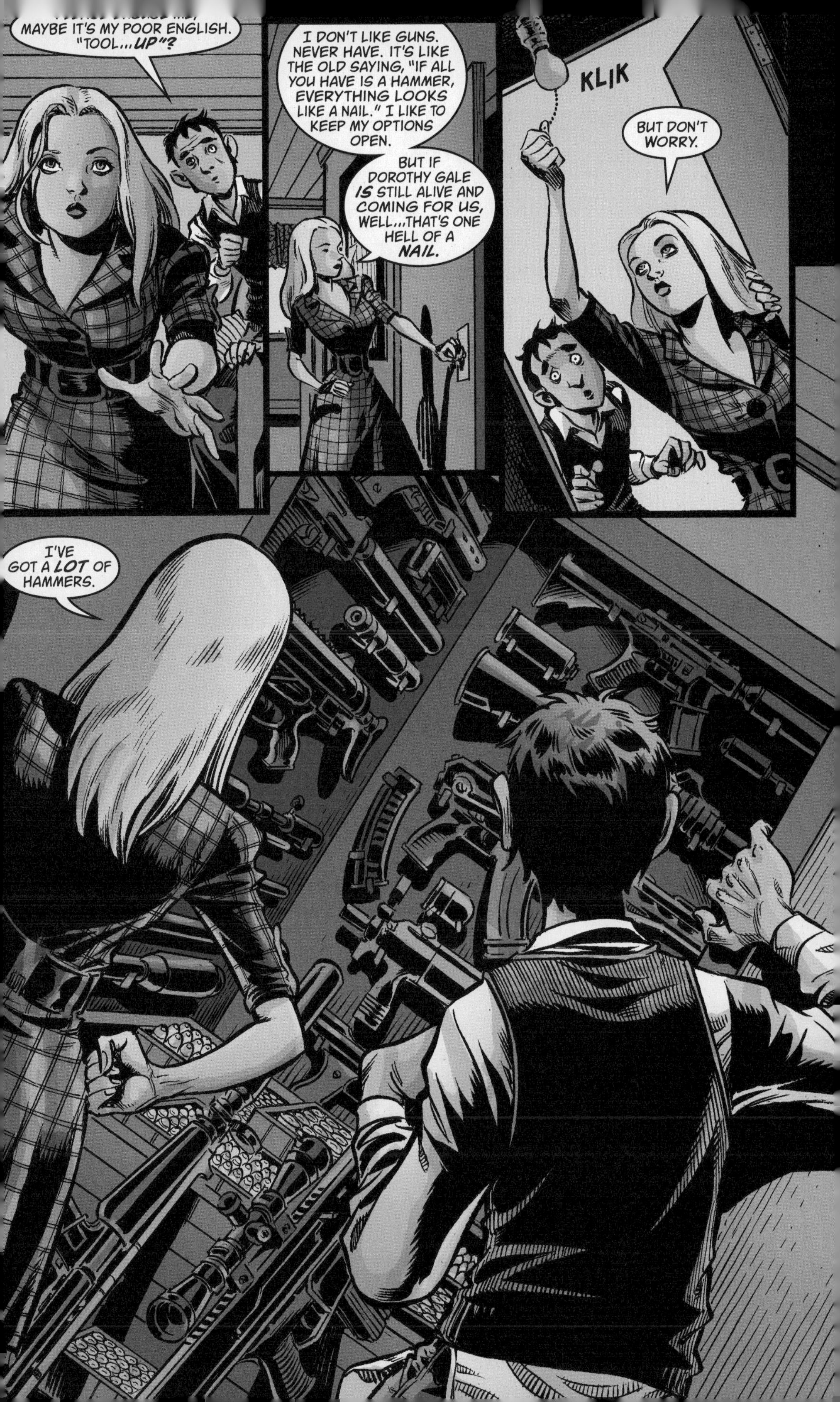
MAYBE IT'S MY POOR ENGLISH. "TOOL...UP"?
I DON'T LIKE GUNS. NEVER HAVE. IT'S LIKE THE OLD SAYING, "IF ALL YOU HAVE IS A HAMMER, EVERYTHING LOOKS LIKE A NAIL." I LIKE TO KEEP MY OPTIONS OPEN.
BUT IF DOROTHY GALE IS STILL ALIVE AND COMING FOR US, WELL...THAT'S ONE HELL OF A NAIL.
KLIK
BUT DON'T WORRY.
I'VE GOT A LOT OF HAMMERS.

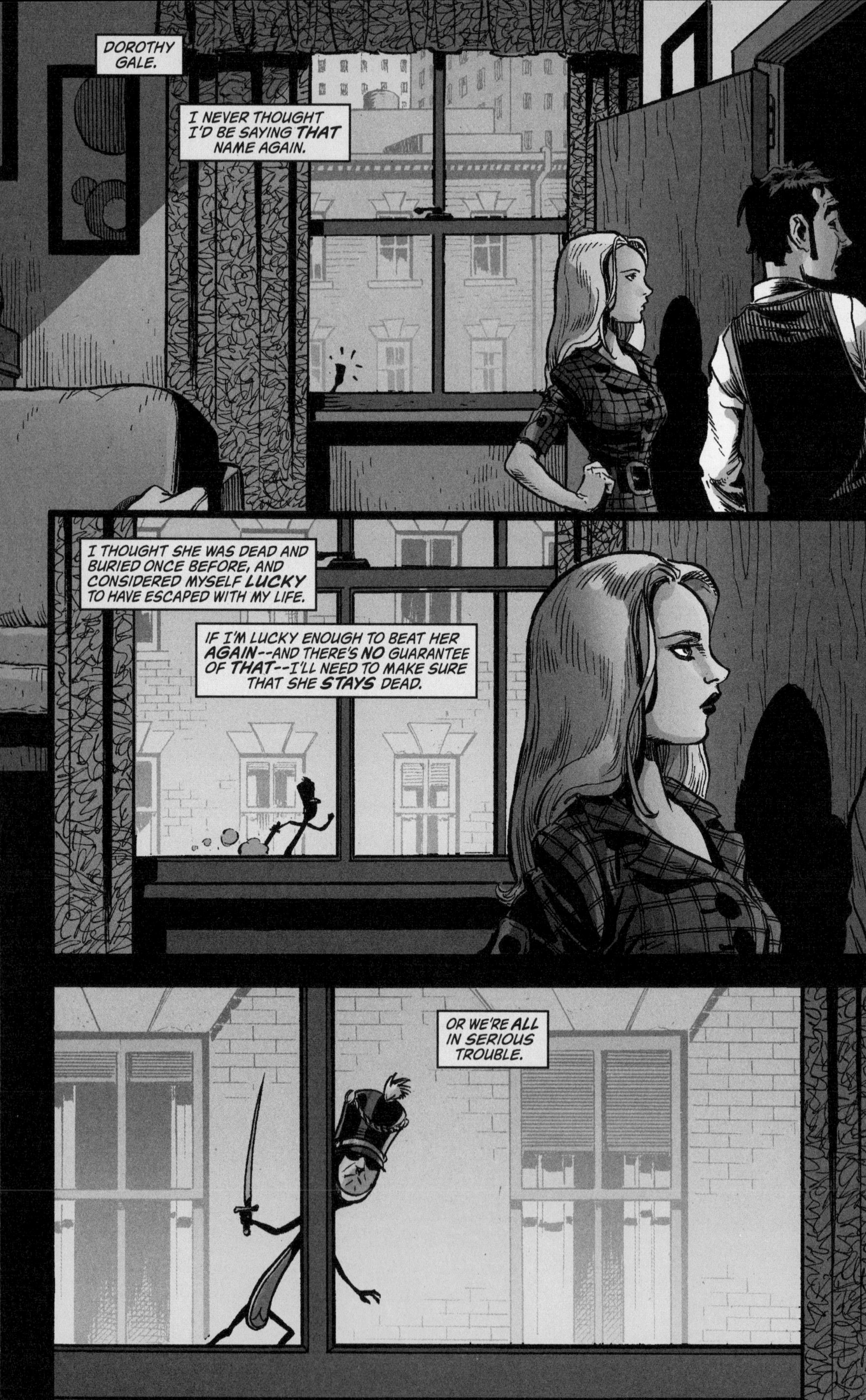
DOROTHY GALE.
I NEVER THOUGHT I'D BE SAYING THAT NAME AGAIN.
I THOUGHT SHE WAS DEAD AND BURIED ONCE BEFORE, AND CONSIDERED MYSELF LUCKY TO HAVE ESCAPED WITH MY LIFE.
IF I'M LUCKY ENOUGH TO BEAT HER AGAIN--AND THERE'S NO GUARANTEE OF THAT--I'LL NEED TO MAKE SURE THAT SHE STAYS DEAD.
OR WE'RE ALL IN SERIOUS TROUBLE.

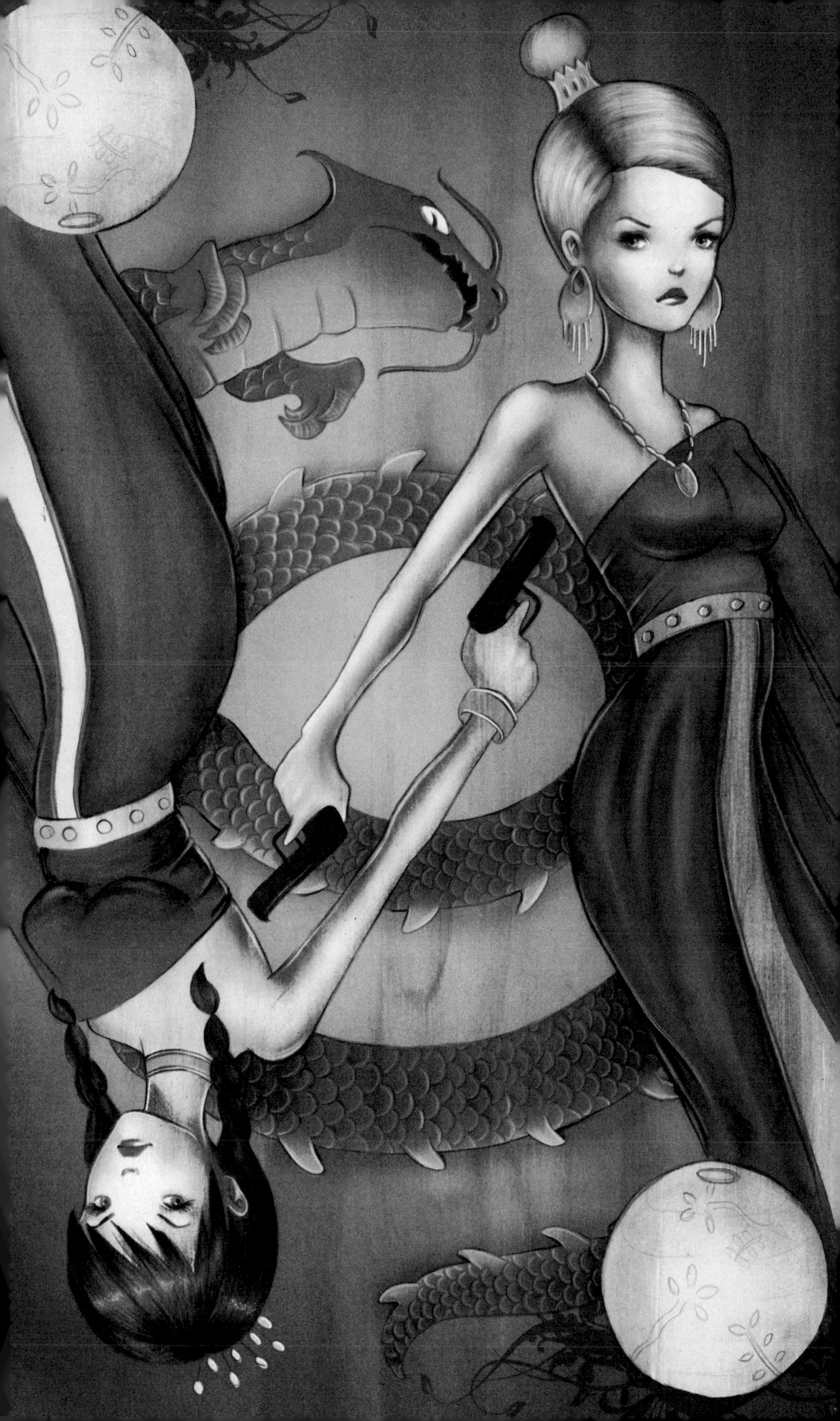

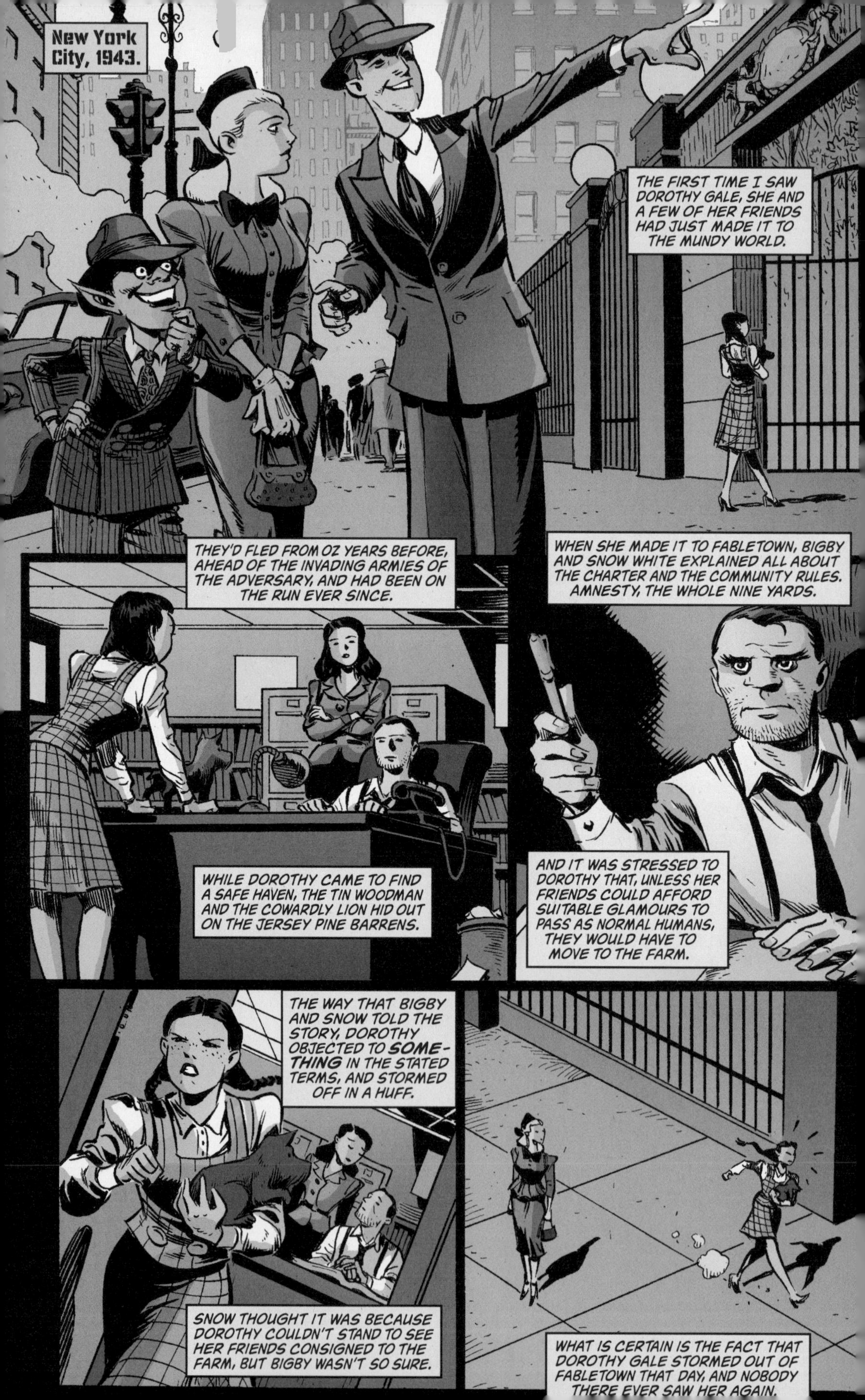
New York City, 1943.
THE FIRST TIME I SAW DOROTHY GALE, SHE AND A FEW OF HER FRIENDS HAD JUST MADE IT TO THE MUNDY WORLD.
THEY'D FLED FROM OZ YEARS BEFORE, AHEAD OF THE INVADING ARMIES OF THE ADVERSARY, AND HAD BEEN ON THE RUN EVER SINCE.
WHILE DOROTHY CAME TO FIND A SAFE HAVEN, THE TIN WOODMAN AND THE COWARDLY LION HID OUT ON THE JERSEY PINE BARRENS.
WHEN SHE MADE IT TO FABLETOWN, BIGBY AND SNOW WHITE EXPLAINED ALL ABOUT THE CHARTER AND THE COMMUNITY RULES. AMNESTY, THE WHOLE NINE YARDS.
AND IT WAS STRESSED TO DOROTHY THAT, UNLESS HER FRIENDS COULD AFFORD SUITABLE GLAMOURS TO PASS AS NORMAL HUMANS, THEY WOULD HAVE TO MOVE TO THE FARM.
THE WAY THAT BIGBY AND SNOW TOLD THE STORY, DOROTHY OBJECTED TO SOMETHING IN THE STATED TERMS, AND STORMED OFF IN A HUFF.
SNOW THOUGHT IT WAS BECAUSE DOROTHY COULDN'T STAND TO SEE HER FRIENDS CONSIGNED TO THE FARM, BUT BIGBY WASN'T SO SURE.
WHAT IS CERTAIN IS THE FACT THAT DOROTHY GALE STORMED OUT OF FABLETOWN THAT DAY, AND NOBODY THERE EVER SAW HER AGAIN.

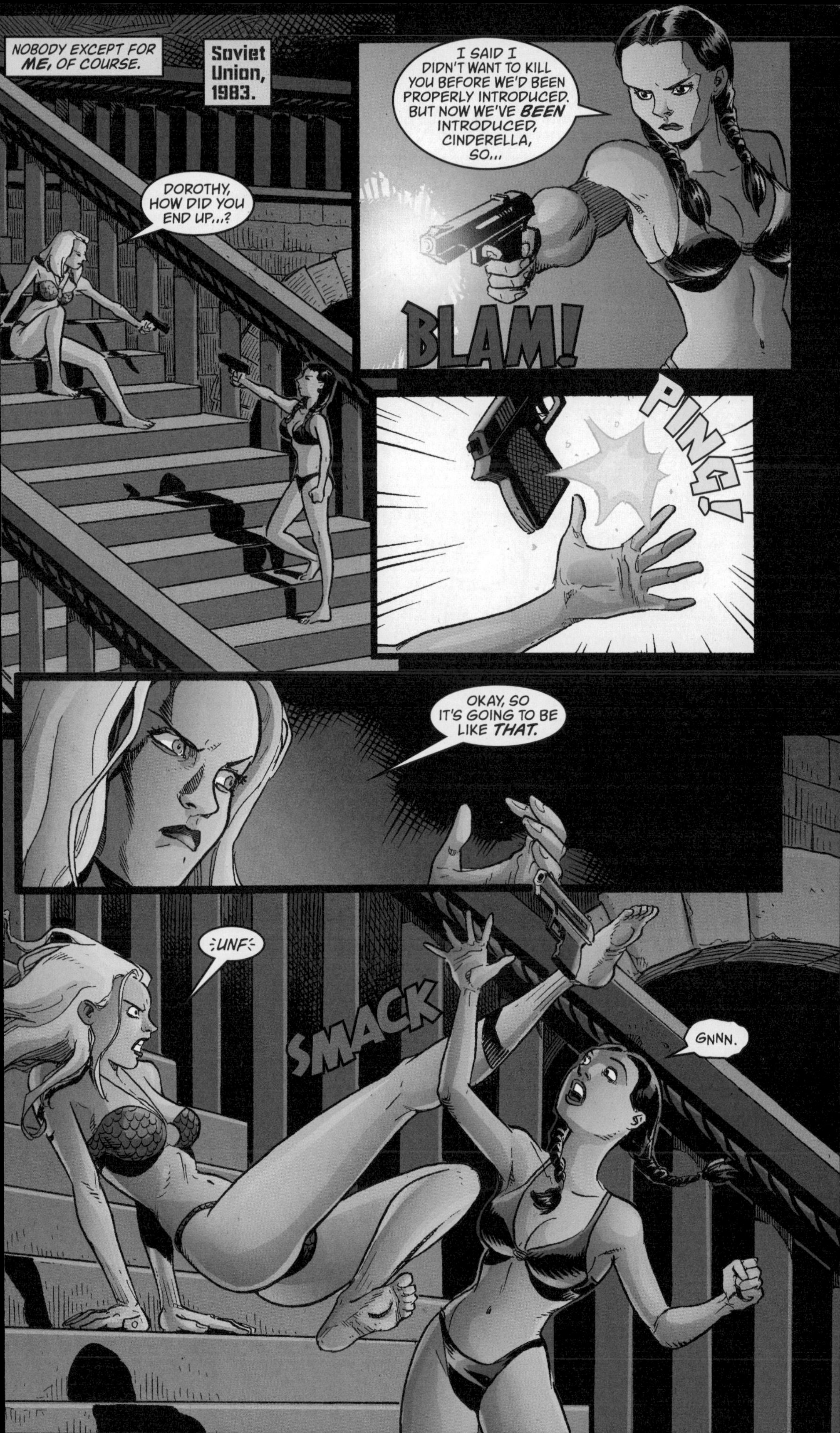
NOBODY EXCEPT FOR ME, OF COURSE.
Soviet Union, 1983.
DOROTHY, HOW DID YOU END UP...?
I SAID I DIDN'T WANT TO KILL YOU BEFORE WE'D BEEN PROPERLY INTRODUCED. BUT NOW WE'VE BEEN INTRODUCED, CINDERELLA, SO...
BLAM!
PING!
OKAY, SO IT'S GOING TO BE LIKE THAT.
UNF
SMACK
GNNN.

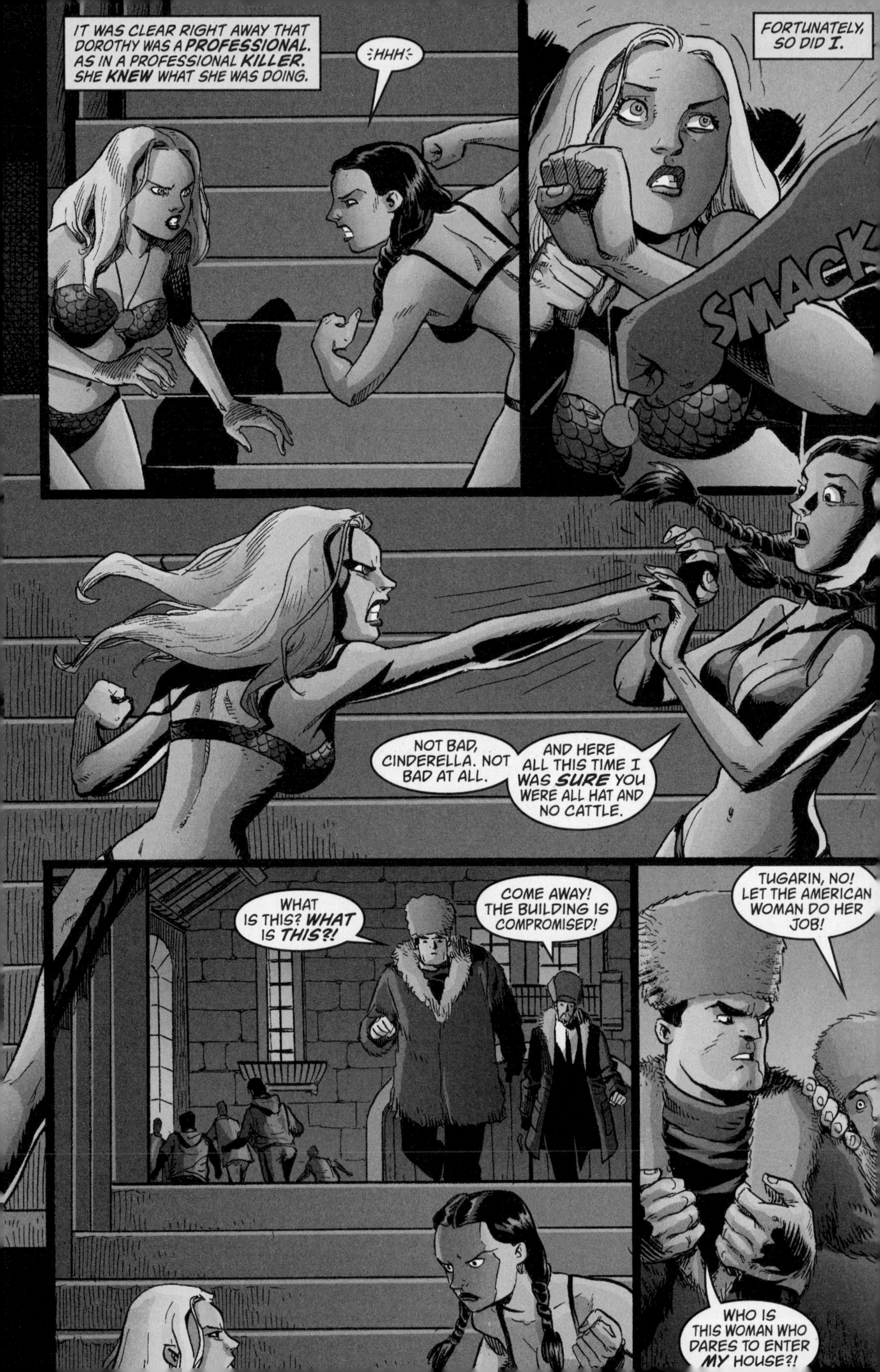
IT WAS CLEAR RIGHT AWAY THAT DOROTHY WAS A PROFESSIONAL. AS IN A PROFESSIONAL KILLER. SHE KNEW WHAT SHE WAS DOING.
HHH
FORTUNATELY, SO DID I.
SMACK
NOT BAD, CINDERELLA. NOT BAD AT ALL.
AND HERE ALL THIS TIME I WAS SURE YOU WERE ALL HAT AND NO CATTLE.
WHAT IS THIS? WHAT IS THIS?!
COME AWAY! THE BUILDING IS COMPROMISED!
TUGARIN, NO! LET THE AMERICAN WOMAN DO HER JOB!
WHO IS THIS WOMAN WHO DARES TO ENTER MY HOUSE?!

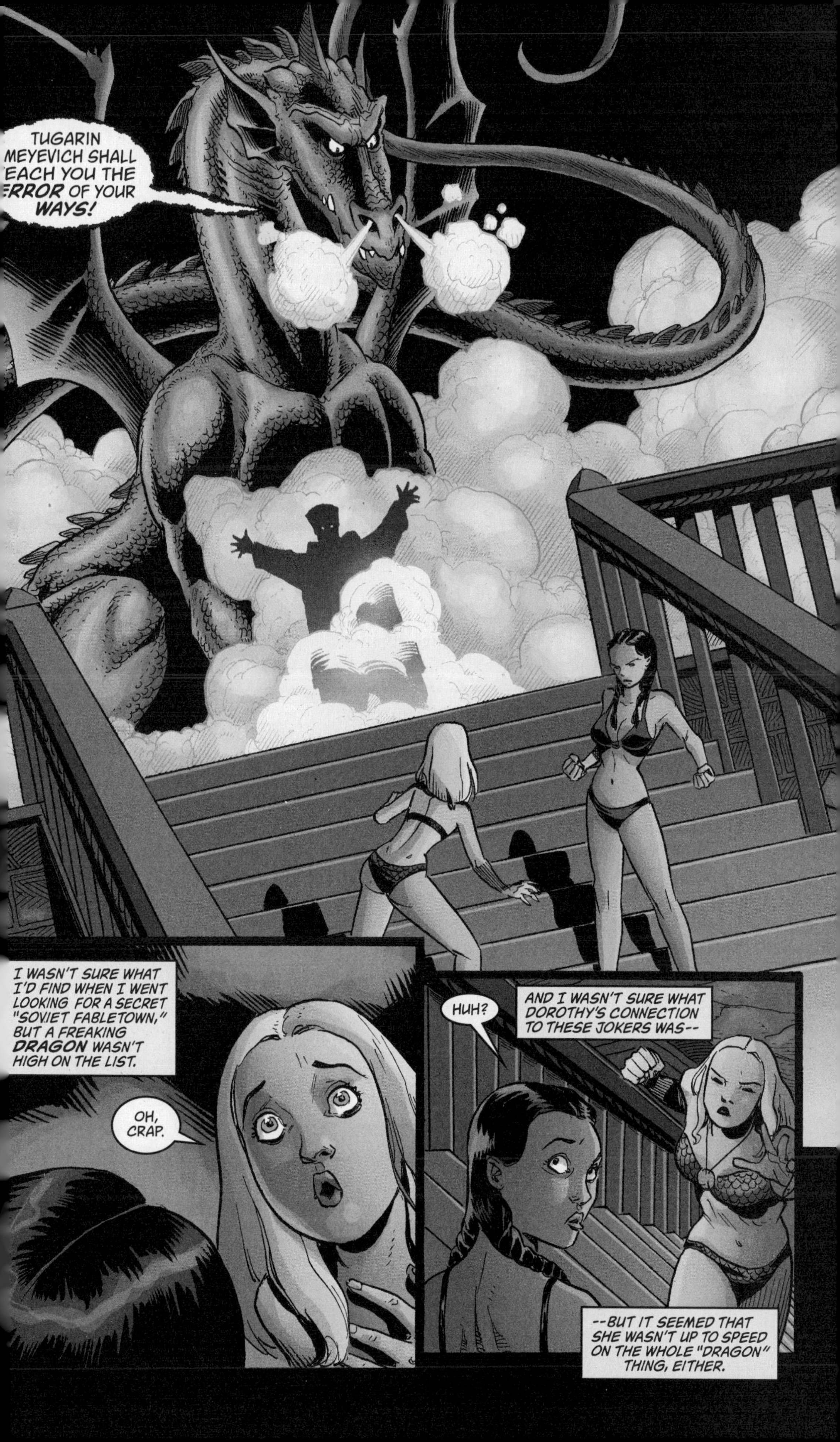
TUGARIN
MEYEVICH SHALL
TEACH YOU THE
ERROR OF YOUR
WAYS!
I WASN'T SURE WHAT I'D FIND WHEN I WENT LOOKING FOR A SECRET "SOVIET FABLETOWN," BUT A FREAKING DRAGON WASN'T HIGH ON THE LIST.
OH, CRAP.
AND I WASN'T SURE WHAT DOROTHY'S CONNECTION TO THESE JOKERS WAS--
HUH?
--BUT IT SEEMED THAT SHE WASN'T UP TO SPEED ON THE WHOLE "DRAGON" THING, EITHER.

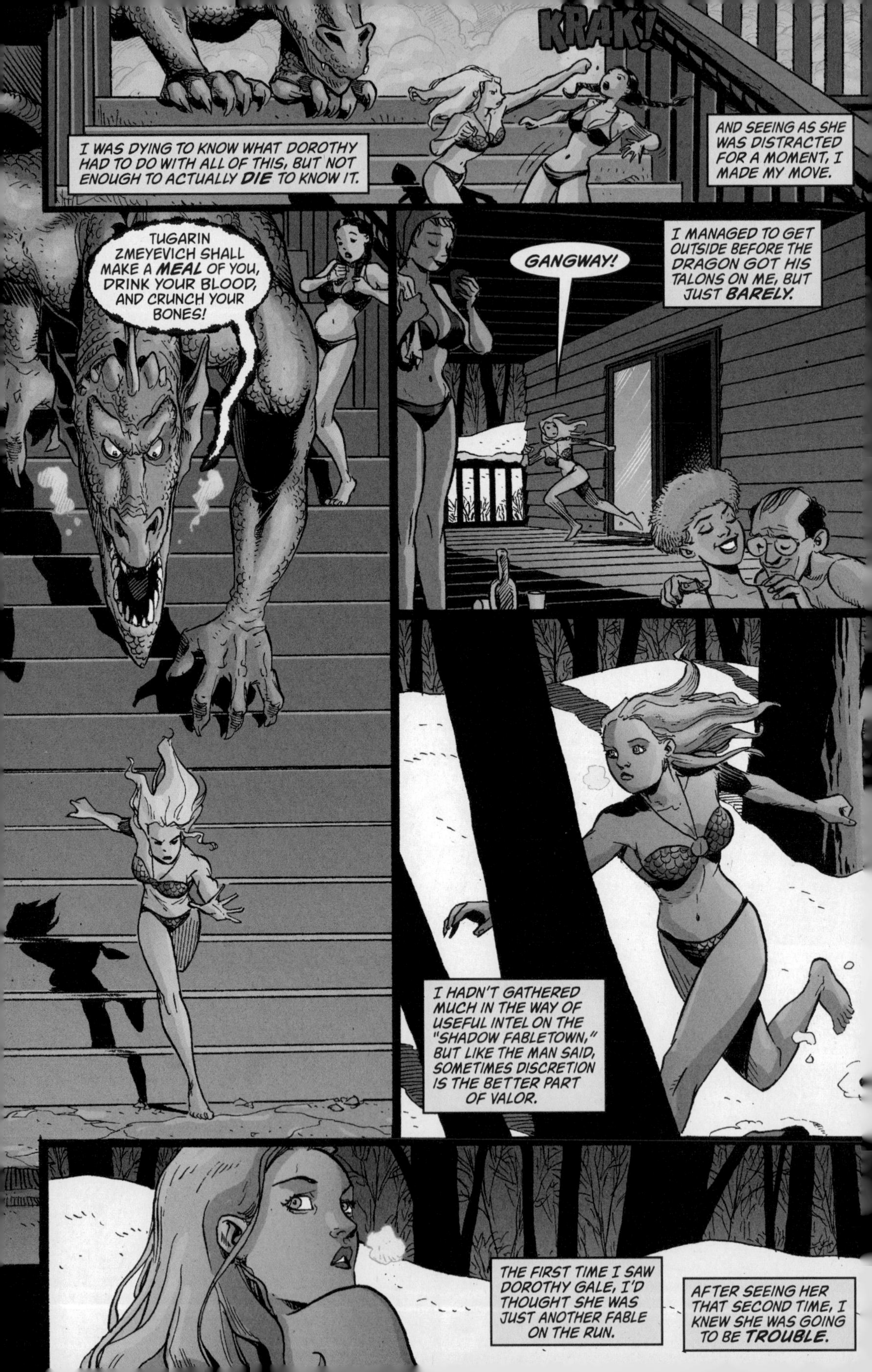
KRAK!
I WAS DYING TO KNOW WHAT DOROTHY HAD TO DO WITH ALL OF THIS, BUT NOT ENOUGH TO ACTUALLY DIE TO KNOW IT.
AND SEEING AS SHE WAS DISTRACTED FOR A MOMENT, I MADE MY MOVE.
TUGARIN ZMEYEVICH SHALL MAKE A MEAL OF YOU, DRINK YOUR BLOOD, AND CRUNCH YOUR BONES!
GANGWAY!
I MANAGED TO GET OUTSIDE BEFORE THE DRAGON GOT HIS TALONS ON ME, BUT JUST BARELY.
I HADN'T GATHERED MUCH IN THE WAY OF USEFUL INTEL ON THE "SHADOW FABLETOWN," BUT LIKE THE MAN SAID, SOMETIMES DISCRETION IS THE BETTER PART OF VALOR.
THE FIRST TIME I SAW DOROTHY GALE, I'D THOUGHT SHE WAS JUST ANOTHER FABLE ON THE RUN.
AFTER SEEING HER THAT SECOND TIME, I KNEW SHE WAS GOING TO BE TROUBLE.

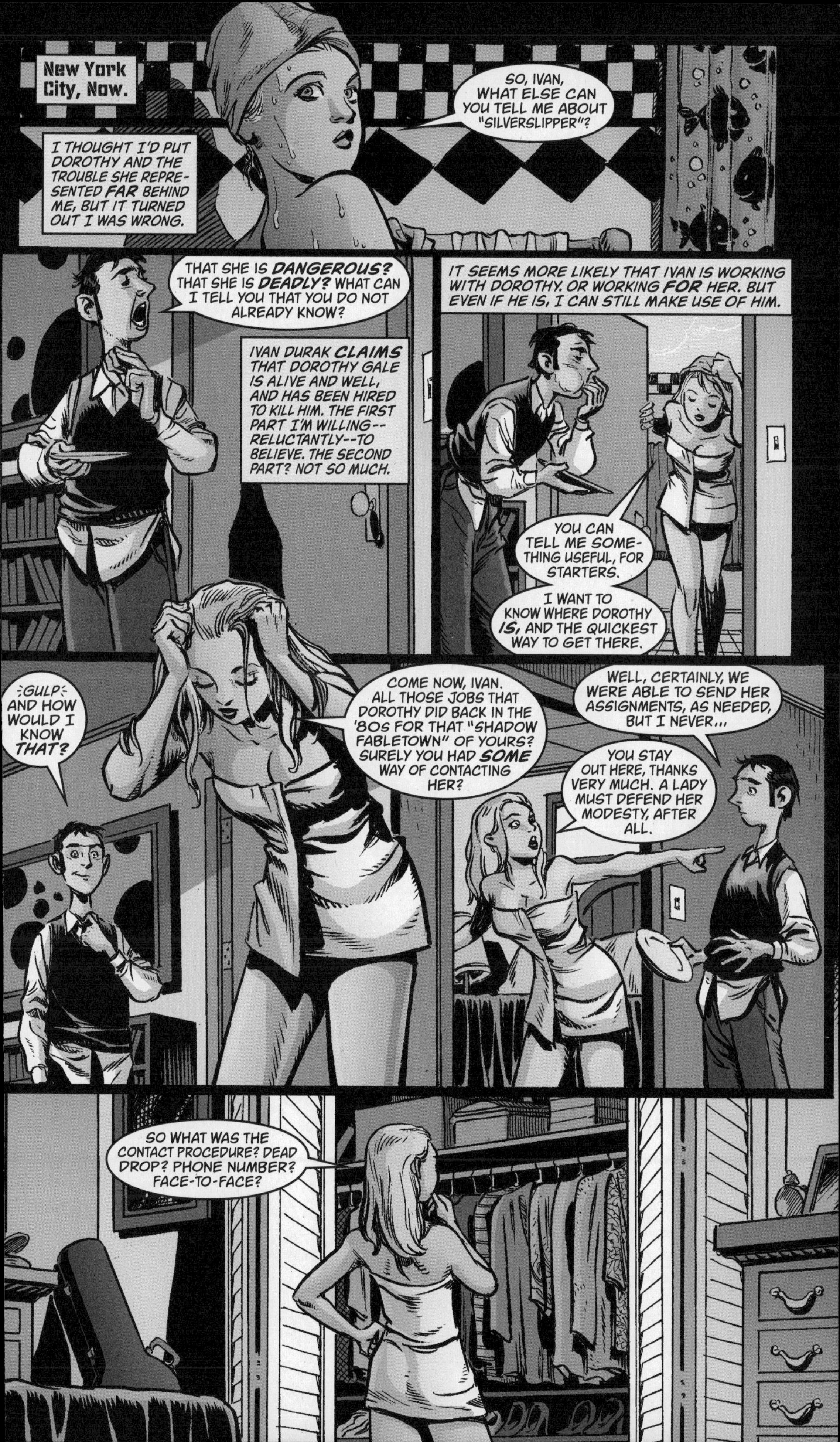
New York City, Now.
I THOUGHT I'D PUT DOROTHY AND THE TROUBLE SHE REPRESENTED FAR BEHIND ME, BUT IT TURNED OUT I WAS WRONG.
SO, IVAN, WHAT ELSE CAN YOU TELL ME ABOUT "SILVERSLIPPER"?
THAT SHE IS DANGEROUS? THAT SHE IS DEADLY? WHAT CAN I TELL YOU THAT YOU DO NOT ALREADY KNOW?
IVAN DURAK CLAIMS THAT DOROTHY GALE IS ALIVE AND WELL, AND HAS BEEN HIRED TO KILL HIM. THE FIRST PART I'M WILLING--RELUCTANTLY--TO BELIEVE. THE SECOND PART? NOT SO MUCH.
IT SEEMS MORE LIKELY THAT IVAN IS WORKING WITH DOROTHY. OR WORKING FOR HER. BUT EVEN IF HE IS, I CAN STILL MAKE USE OF HIM.
YOU CAN TELL ME SOMETHING USEFUL, FOR STARTERS.
I WANT TO KNOW WHERE DOROTHY IS, AND THE QUICKEST WAY TO GET THERE.
GULP AND HOW WOULD I KNOW THAT?
COME NOW, IVAN. ALL THOSE JOBS THAT DOROTHY DID BACK IN THE '80S FOR THAT "SHADOW FABLETOWN" OF YOURS? SURELY YOU HAD SOME WAY OF CONTACTING HER?
WELL, CERTAINLY, WE WERE ABLE TO SEND HER ASSIGNMENTS, AS NEEDED, BUT I NEVER...
YOU STAY OUT HERE, THANKS VERY MUCH. A LADY MUST DEFEND HER MODESTY, AFTER ALL.
SO WHAT WAS THE CONTACT PROCEDURE? DEAD DROP? PHONE NUMBER? FACE-TO-FACE?

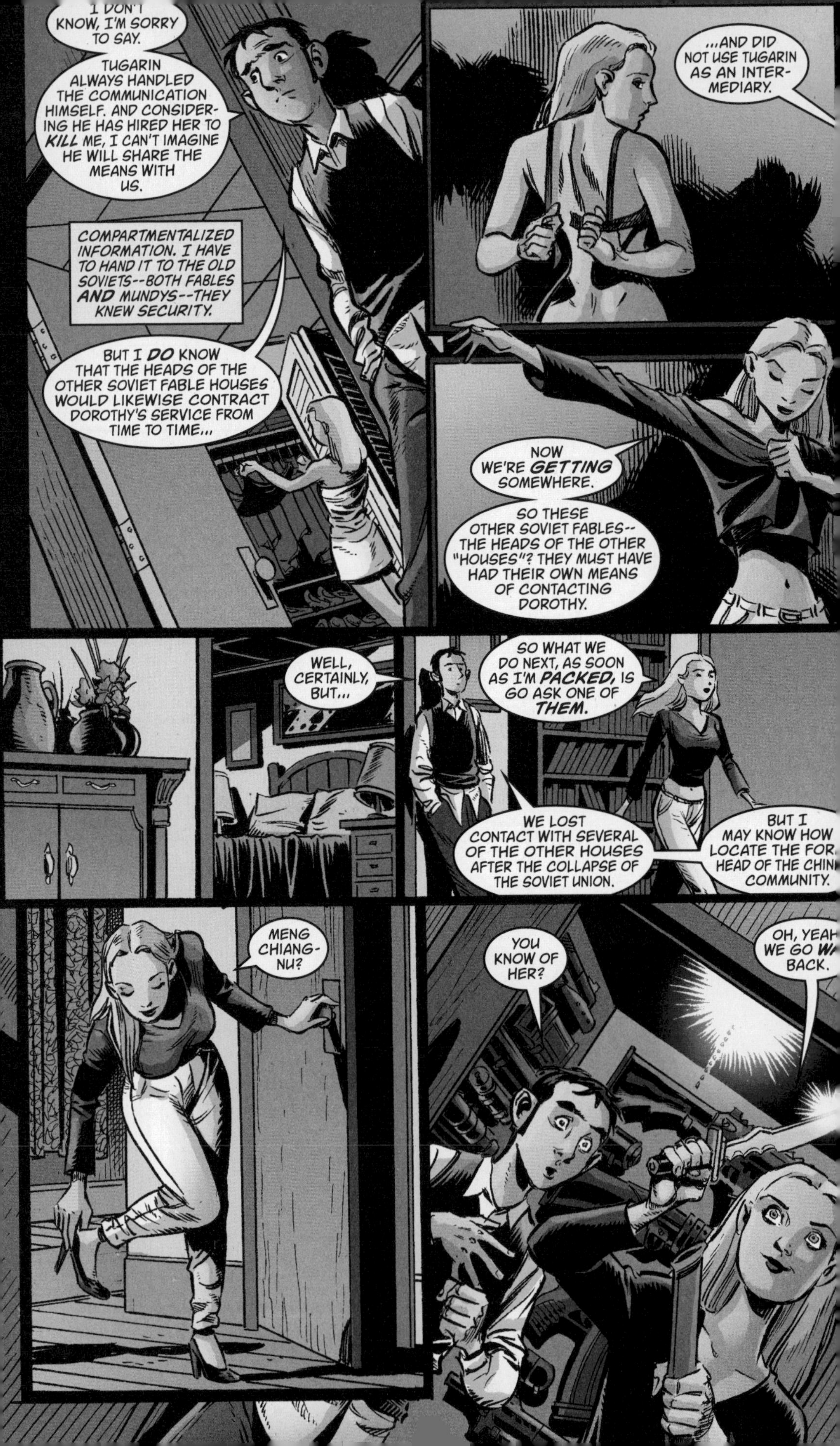
I DON'T KNOW, I'M SORRY TO SAY.
TUGARIN ALWAYS HANDLED THE COMMUNICATION HIMSELF. AND CONSIDERING HE HAS HIRED HER TO KILL ME, I CAN'T IMAGINE HE WILL SHARE THE MEANS WITH US.
COMPARTMENTALIZED INFORMATION. I HAVE TO HAND IT TO THE OLD SOVIETS--BOTH FABLES AND MUNDYS--THEY KNEW SECURITY.
BUT I DO KNOW THAT THE HEADS OF THE OTHER SOVIET FABLE HOUSES WOULD LIKEWISE CONTRACT DOROTHY'S SERVICE FROM TIME TO TIME...
...AND DID NOT USE TUGARIN AS AN INTERMEDIARY.
NOW WE'RE GETTING SOMEWHERE.
SO THESE OTHER SOVIET FABLES--THE HEADS OF THE OTHER "HOUSES"? THEY MUST HAVE HAD THEIR OWN MEANS OF CONTACTING DOROTHY.
WELL, CERTAINLY, BUT...
SO WHAT WE DO NEXT, AS SOON AS I'M PACKED, IS GO ASK ONE OF THEM.
WE LOST CONTACT WITH SEVERAL OF THE OTHER HOUSES AFTER THE COLLAPSE OF THE SOVIET UNION.
BUT I MAY KNOW HOW LOCATE THE FOR HEAD OF THE CHIN COMMUNITY.
MENG CHIANG-NU?
YOU KNOW OF HER?
OH, YEAH WE GO WA BACK.

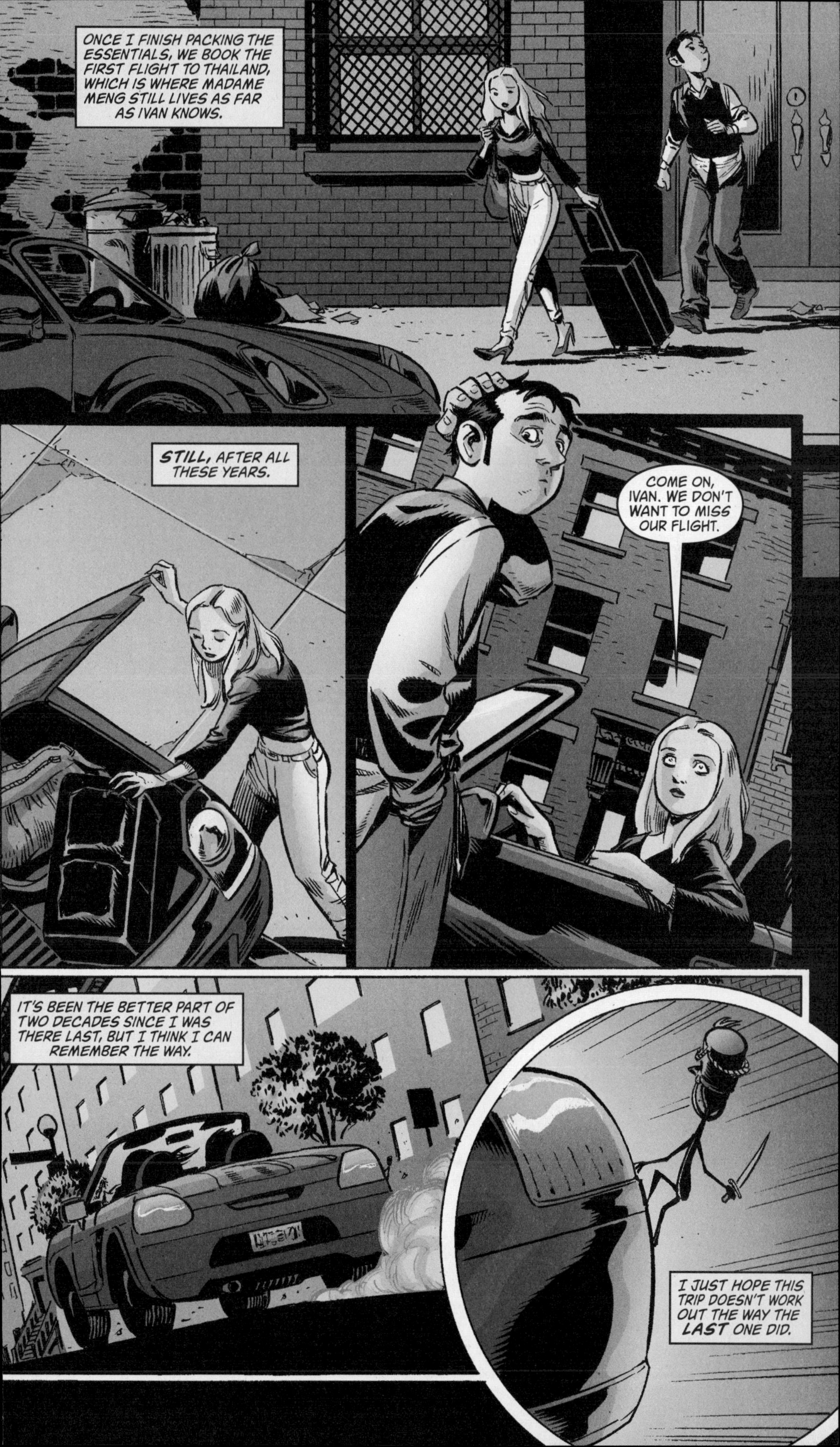
ONCE I FINISH PACKING THE ESSENTIALS, WE BOOK THE FIRST FLIGHT TO THAILAND, WHICH IS WHERE MADAME MENG STILL LIVES AS FAR AS IVAN KNOWS.
STILL, AFTER ALL THESE YEARS.
COME ON, IVAN. WE DON'T WANT TO MISS OUR FLIGHT.
IT'S BEEN THE BETTER PART OF TWO DECADES SINCE I WAS THERE LAST, BUT I THINK I CAN REMEMBER THE WAY.
I JUST HOPE THIS TRIP DOESN'T WORK OUT THE WAY THE LAST ONE DID.

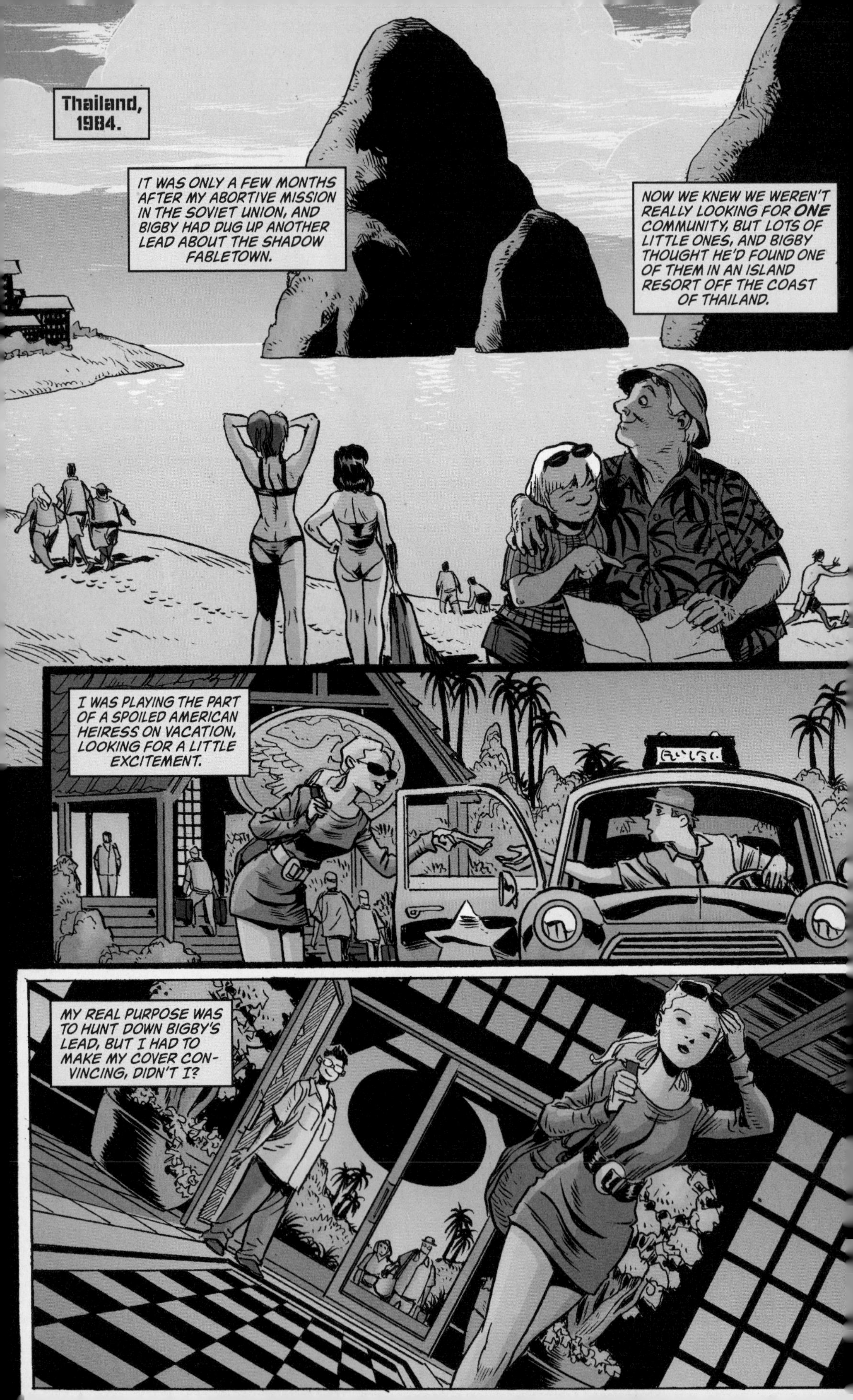
Thailand, 1984.
IT WAS ONLY A FEW MONTHS AFTER MY ABORTIVE MISSION IN THE SOVIET UNION, AND BIGBY HAD DUG UP ANOTHER LEAD ABOUT THE SHADOW FABLETOWN.
NOW WE KNEW WE WEREN'T REALLY LOOKING FOR ONE COMMUNITY, BUT LOTS OF LITTLE ONES, AND BIGBY THOUGHT HE'D FOUND ONE OF THEM IN AN ISLAND RESORT OFF THE COAST OF THAILAND.
I WAS PLAYING THE PART OF A SPOILED AMERICAN HEIRESS ON VACATION, LOOKING FOR A LITTLE EXCITEMENT.
MY REAL PURPOSE WAS TO HUNT DOWN BIGBY'S LEAD, BUT I HAD TO MAKE MY COVER CON-VINCING, DIDN'T I?

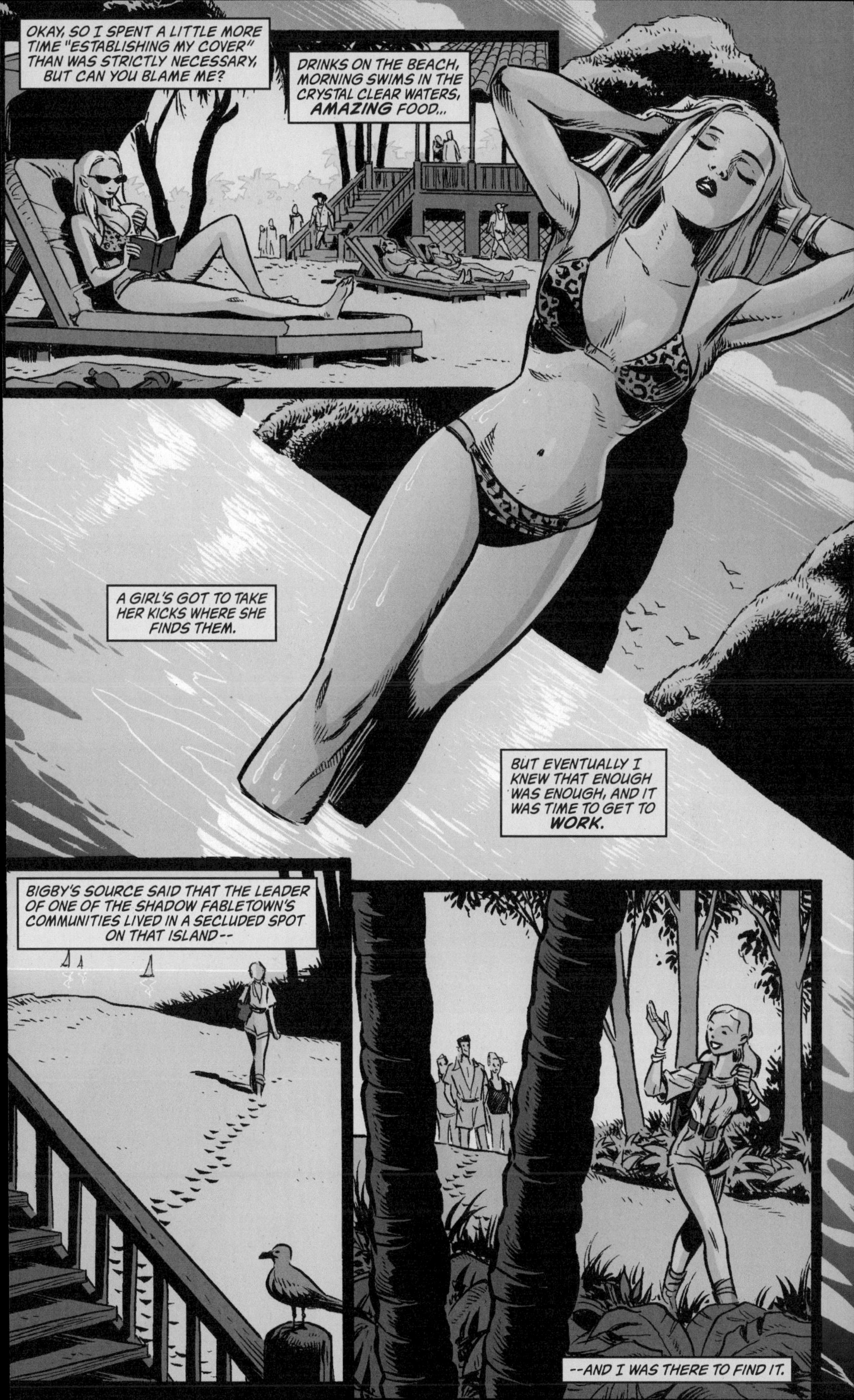
OKAY, SO I SPENT A LITTLE MORE TIME "ESTABLISHING MY COVER" THAN WAS STRICTLY NECESSARY, BUT CAN YOU BLAME ME?
DRINKS ON THE BEACH, MORNING SWIMS IN THE CRYSTAL CLEAR WATERS, AMAZING FOOD...
A GIRL'S GOT TO TAKE HER KICKS WHERE SHE FINDS THEM.
BUT EVENTUALLY I KNEW THAT ENOUGH WAS ENOUGH, AND IT WAS TIME TO GET TO WORK.
BIGBY'S SOURCE SAID THAT THE LEADER OF ONE OF THE SHADOW FABLETOWN'S COMMUNITIES LIVED IN A SECLUDED SPOT ON THAT ISLAND--
--AND I WAS THERE TO FIND IT.

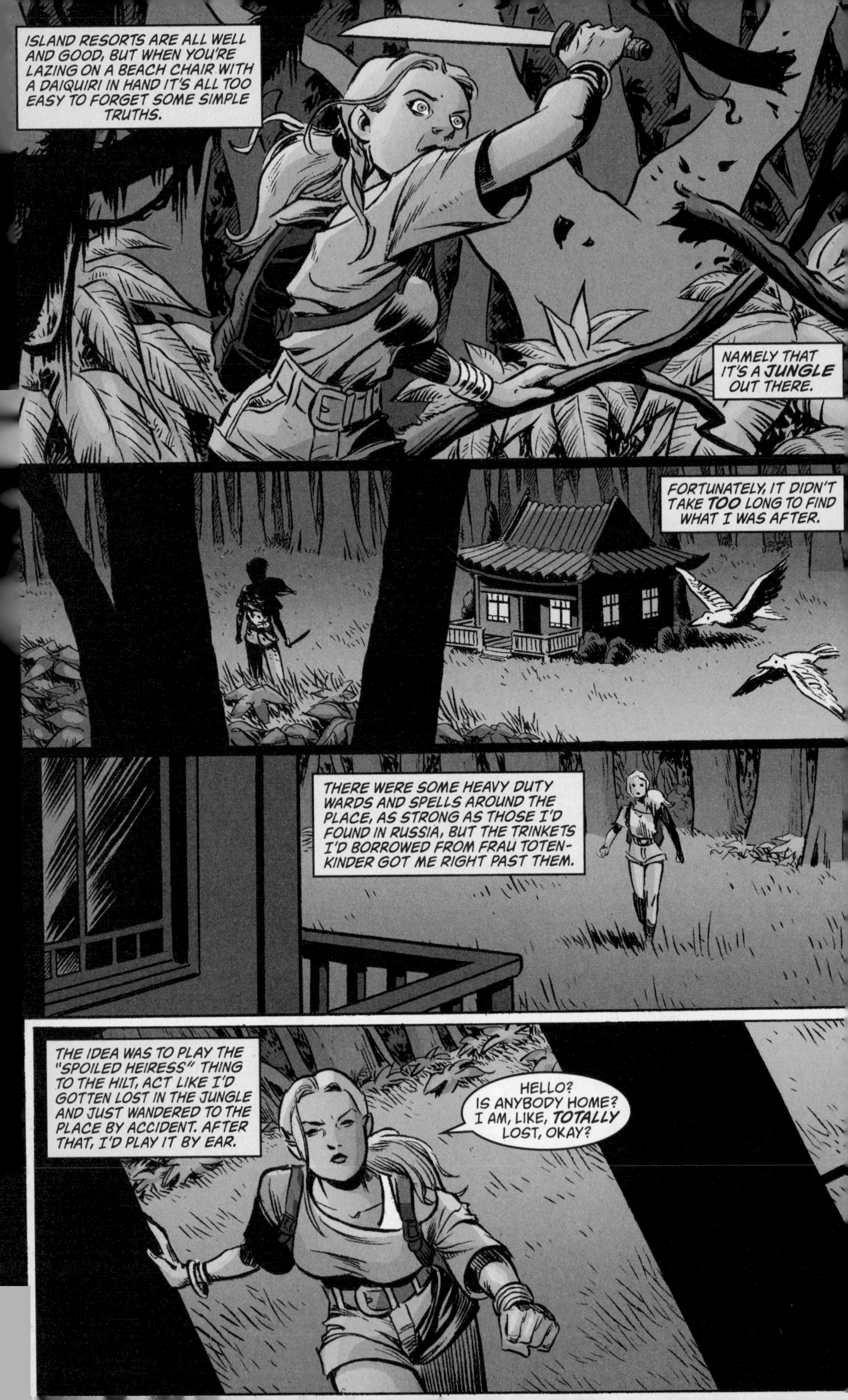
ISLAND RESORTS ARE ALL WELL AND GOOD, BUT WHEN YOU'RE LAZING ON A BEACH CHAIR WITH A DAIQUIRI IN HAND IT'S ALL TOO EASY TO FORGET SOME SIMPLE TRUTHS.
NAMELY THAT IT'S A **JUNGLE** OUT THERE.
FORTUNATELY, IT DIDN'T TAKE **TOO** LONG TO FIND WHAT I WAS AFTER.
THERE WERE SOME HEAVY DUTY WARDS AND SPELLS AROUND THE PLACE, AS STRONG AS THOSE I'D FOUND IN RUSSIA, BUT THE TRINKETS I'D BORROWED FROM FRAU TOTEN-KINDER GOT ME RIGHT PAST THEM.
THE IDEA WAS TO PLAY THE "SPOILED HEIRESS" THING TO THE HILT, ACT LIKE I'D GOTTEN LOST IN THE JUNGLE AND JUST WANDERED TO THE PLACE BY ACCIDENT. AFTER THAT, I'D PLAY IT BY EAR.
HELLO? IS ANYBODY HOME? I AM, LIKE, **TOTALLY** LOST, OKAY?

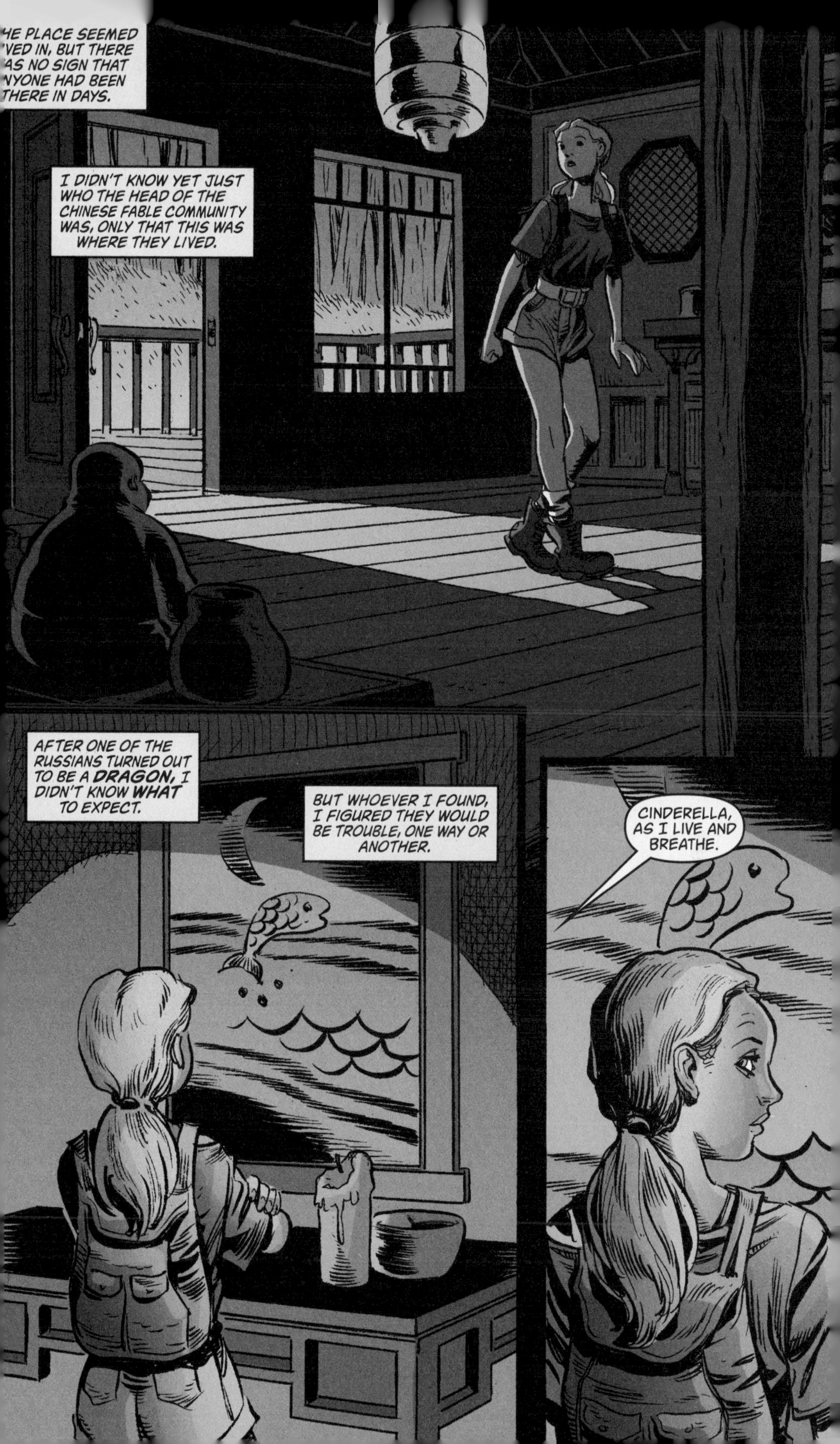
HE PLACE SEEMED
VED IN, BUT THERE
AS NO SIGN THAT
NYONE HAD BEEN
THERE IN DAYS.
I DIDN'T KNOW YET JUST WHO THE HEAD OF THE CHINESE FABLE COMMUNITY WAS, ONLY THAT THIS WAS WHERE THEY LIVED.
AFTER ONE OF THE RUSSIANS TURNED OUT TO BE A DRAGON, I DIDN'T KNOW WHAT TO EXPECT.
BUT WHOEVER I FOUND, I FIGURED THEY WOULD BE TROUBLE, ONE WAY OR ANOTHER.
CINDERELLA, AS I LIVE AND BREATHE.

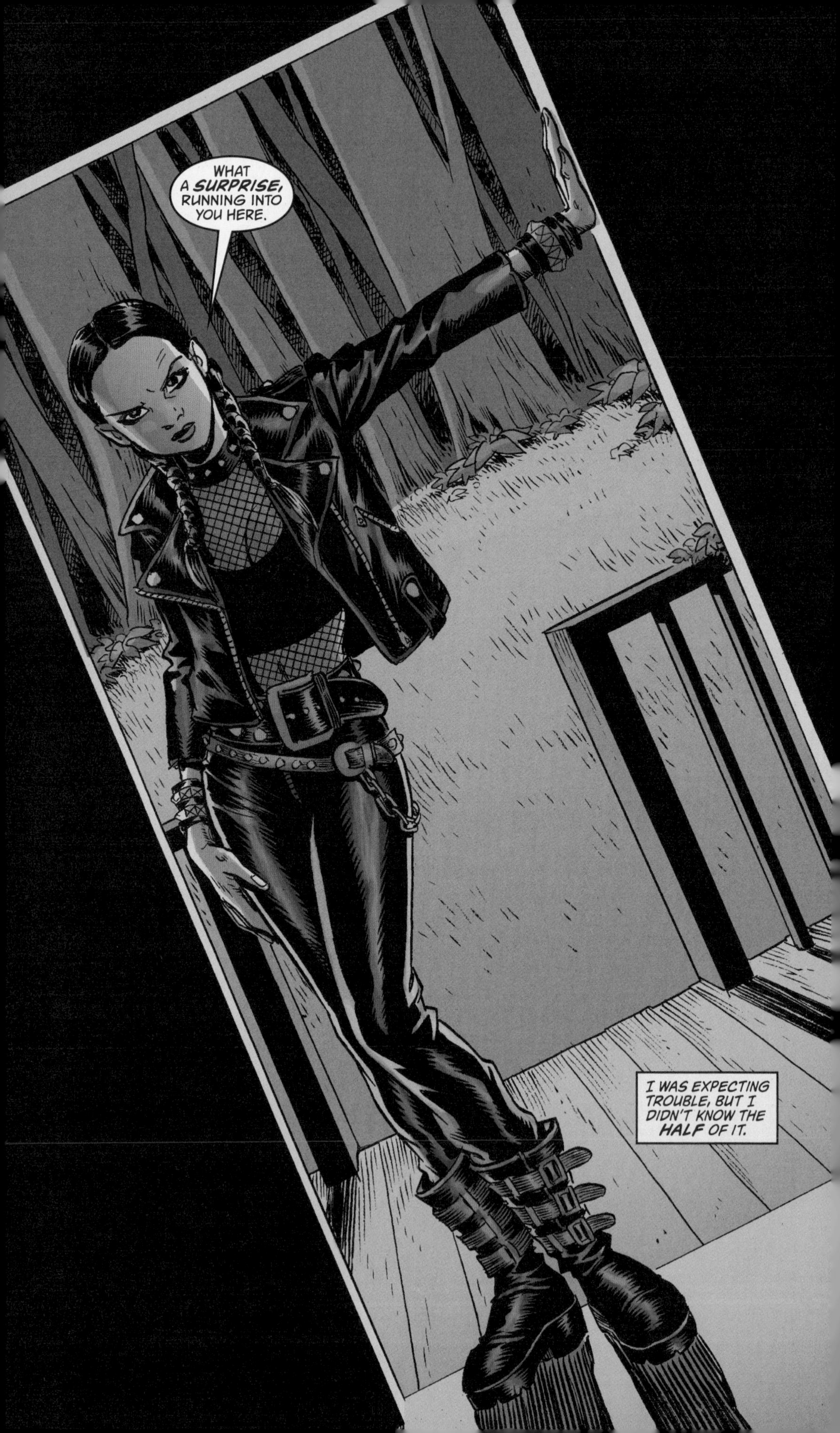
WHAT A **SURPRISE,** RUNNING INTO YOU HERE.
I WAS EXPECTING TROUBLE, BUT I DIDN'T KNOW THE **HALF** OF IT.

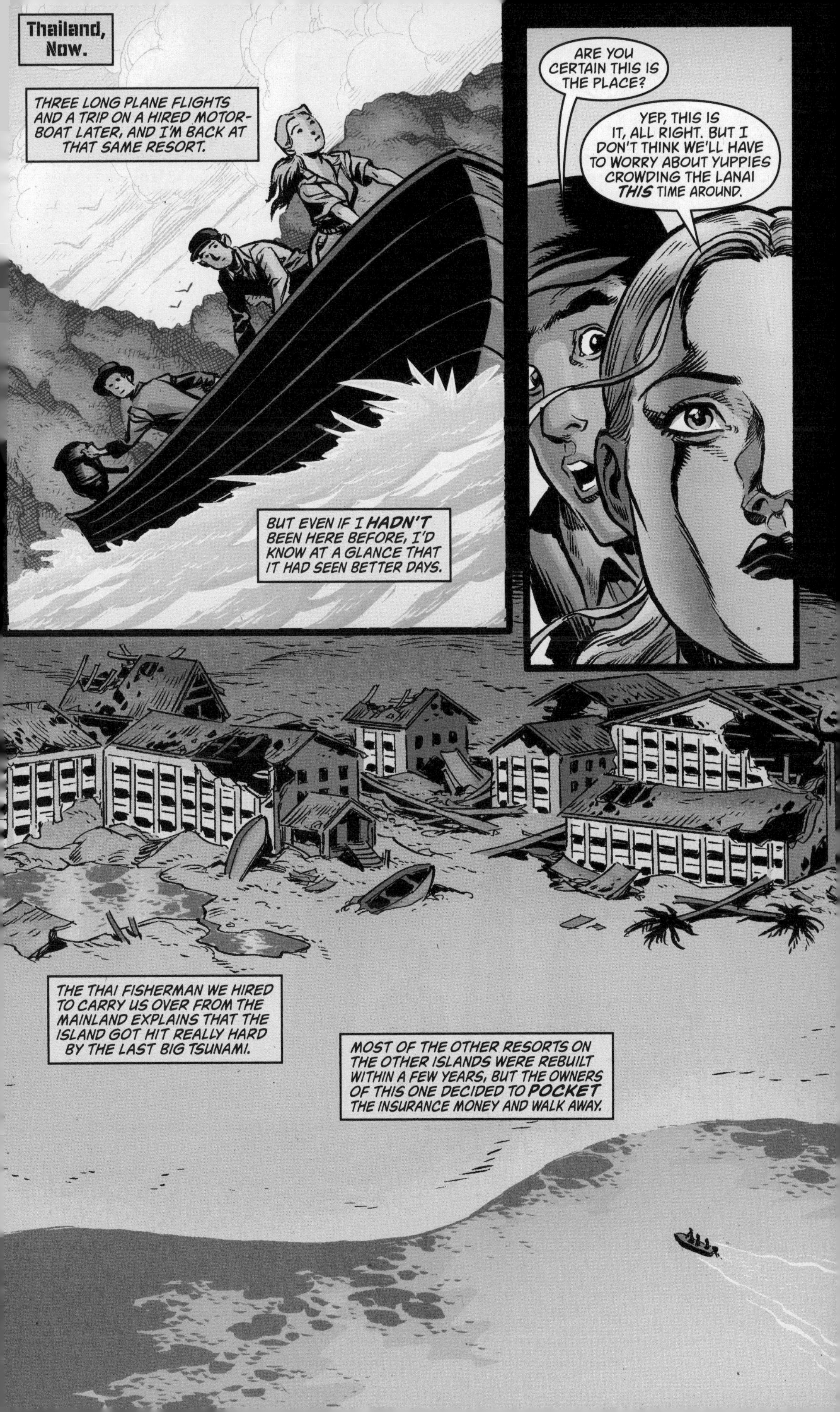

Thailand, Now.
THREE LONG PLANE FLIGHTS AND A TRIP ON A HIRED MOTOR-BOAT LATER, AND I'M BACK AT THAT SAME RESORT.
BUT EVEN IF I HADN'T BEEN HERE BEFORE, I'D KNOW AT A GLANCE THAT IT HAD SEEN BETTER DAYS.
ARE YOU CERTAIN THIS IS THE PLACE?
YEP, THIS IS IT, ALL RIGHT. BUT I DON'T THINK WE'LL HAVE TO WORRY ABOUT YUPPIES CROWDING THE LANAI THIS TIME AROUND.
THE THAI FISHERMAN WE HIRED TO CARRY US OVER FROM THE MAINLAND EXPLAINS THAT THE ISLAND GOT HIT REALLY HARD BY THE LAST BIG TSUNAMI.
MOST OF THE OTHER RESORTS ON THE OTHER ISLANDS WERE REBUILT WITHIN A FEW YEARS, BUT THE OWNERS OF THIS ONE DECIDED TO POCKET THE INSURANCE MONEY AND WALK AWAY.

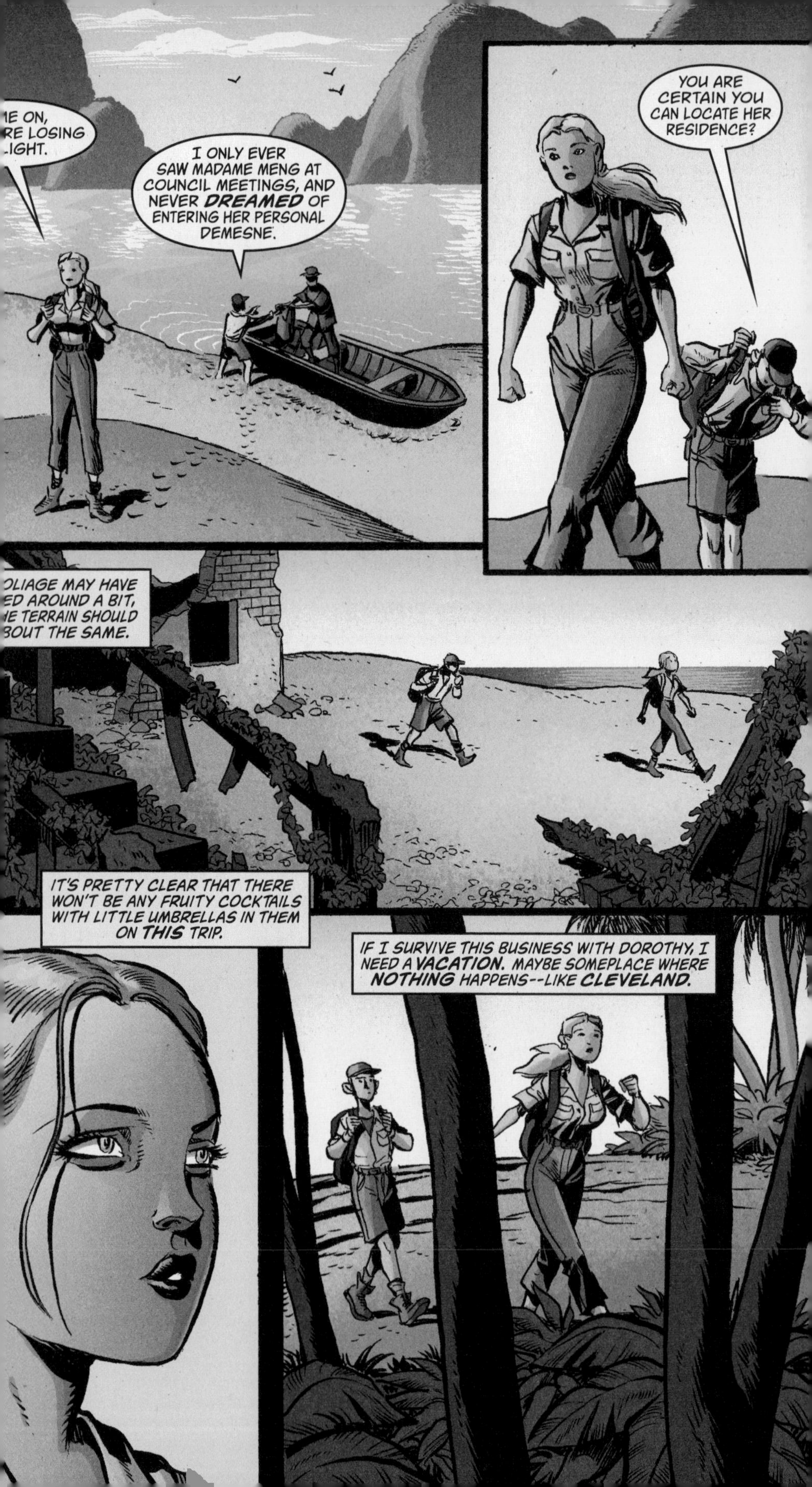

IE ON,
RE LOSING
LIGHT.
I ONLY EVER SAW MADAME MENG AT COUNCIL MEETINGS, AND NEVER DREAMED OF ENTERING HER PERSONAL DEMESNE.
YOU ARE CERTAIN YOU CAN LOCATE HER RESIDENCE?
OLIAGE MAY HAVE ED AROUND A BIT, IE TERRAIN SHOULD BOUT THE SAME.
IT'S PRETTY CLEAR THAT THERE WON'T BE ANY FRUITY COCKTAILS WITH LITTLE UMBRELLAS IN THEM ON THIS TRIP.
IF I SURVIVE THIS BUSINESS WITH DOROTHY, I NEED A VACATION. MAYBE SOMEPLACE WHERE NOTHING HAPPENS--LIKE CLEVELAND.

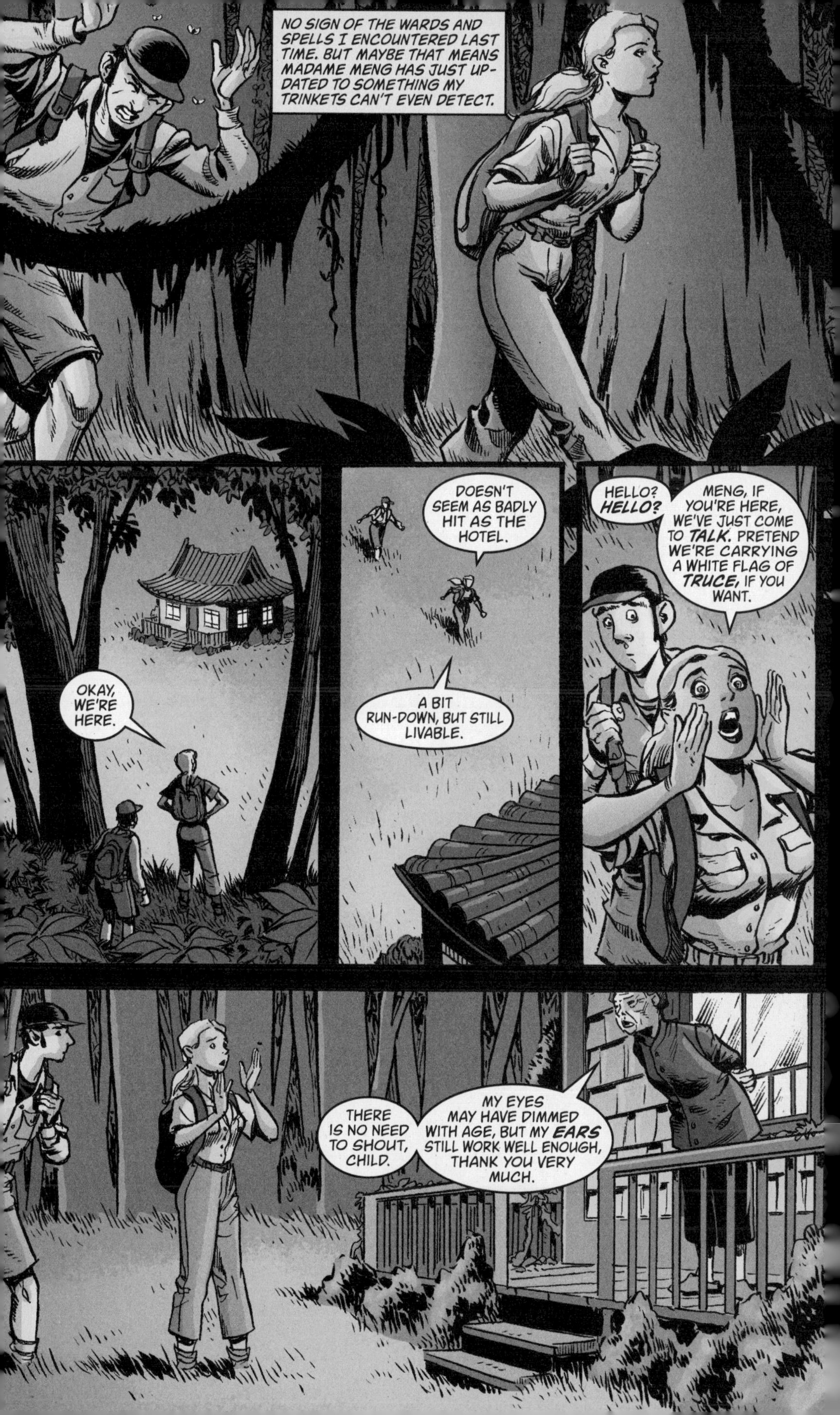

NO SIGN OF THE WARDS AND SPELLS I ENCOUNTERED LAST TIME. BUT MAYBE THAT MEANS MADAME MENG HAS JUST UP-DATED TO SOMETHING MY TRINKETS CAN'T EVEN DETECT.
OKAY, WE'RE HERE.
DOESN'T SEEM AS BADLY HIT AS THE HOTEL.
A BIT RUN-DOWN, BUT STILL LIVABLE.
HELLO? HELLO?
MENG, IF YOU'RE HERE, WE'VE JUST COME TO TALK. PRETEND WE'RE CARRYING A WHITE FLAG OF TRUCE, IF YOU WANT.
THERE IS NO NEED TO SHOUT, CHILD.
MY EYES MAY HAVE DIMMED WITH AGE, BUT MY EARS STILL WORK WELL ENOUGH, THANK YOU VERY MUCH.

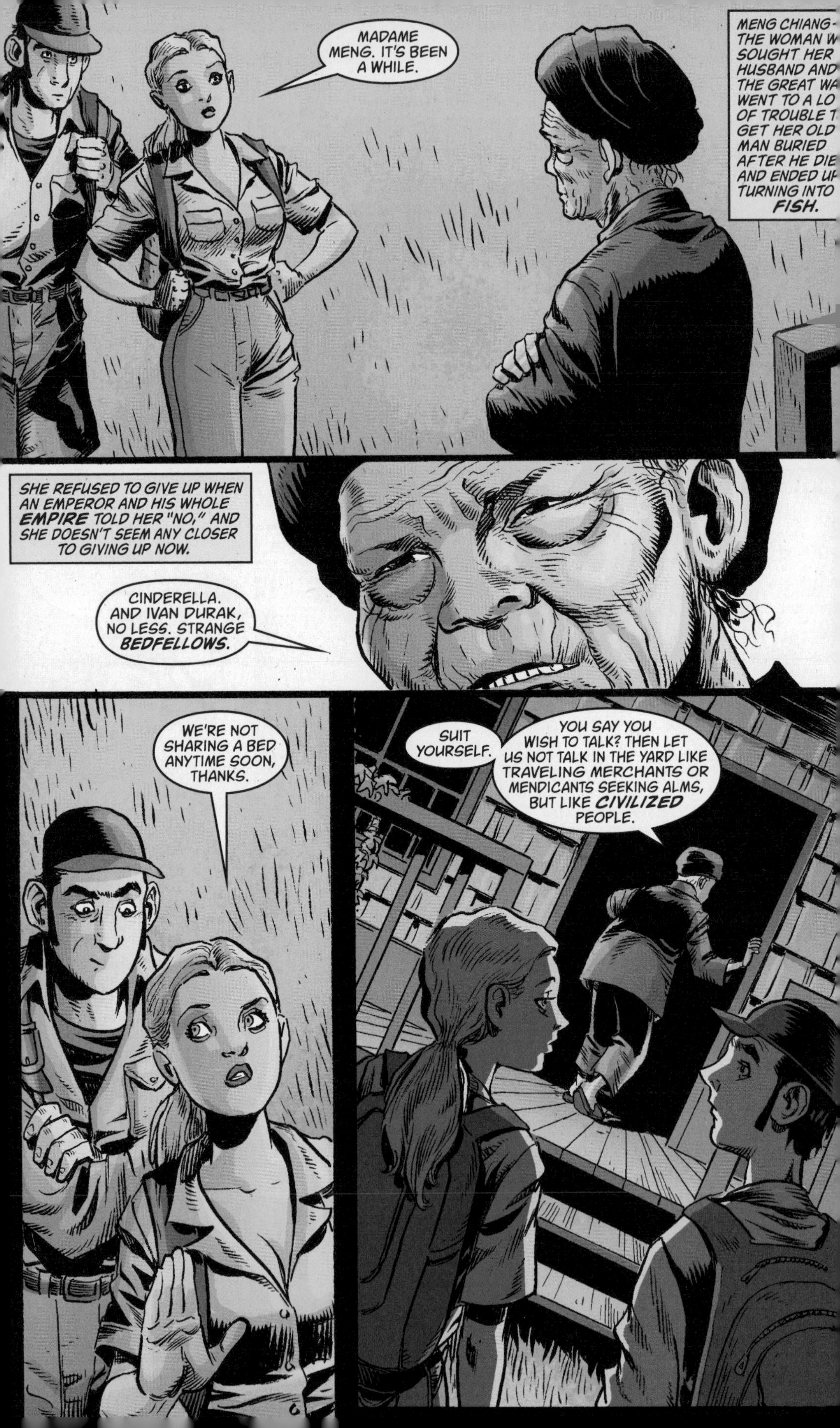
MADAME MENG. IT'S BEEN A WHILE.
MENG CHIANG-- THE WOMAN W SOUGHT HER HUSBAND AND THE GREAT WA WENT TO A LO OF TROUBLE T GET HER OLD MAN BURIED AFTER HE DIE AND ENDED UP TURNING INTO FISH.
SHE REFUSED TO GIVE UP WHEN AN EMPEROR AND HIS WHOLE EMPIRE TOLD HER "NO," AND SHE DOESN'T SEEM ANY CLOSER TO GIVING UP NOW.
CINDERELLA. AND IVAN DURAK, NO LESS. STRANGE BEDFELLOWS.
WE'RE NOT SHARING A BED ANYTIME SOON, THANKS.
SUIT YOURSELF.
YOU SAY YOU WISH TO TALK? THEN LET US NOT TALK IN THE YARD LIKE TRAVELING MERCHANTS OR MENDICANTS SEEKING ALMS, BUT LIKE CIVILIZED PEOPLE.

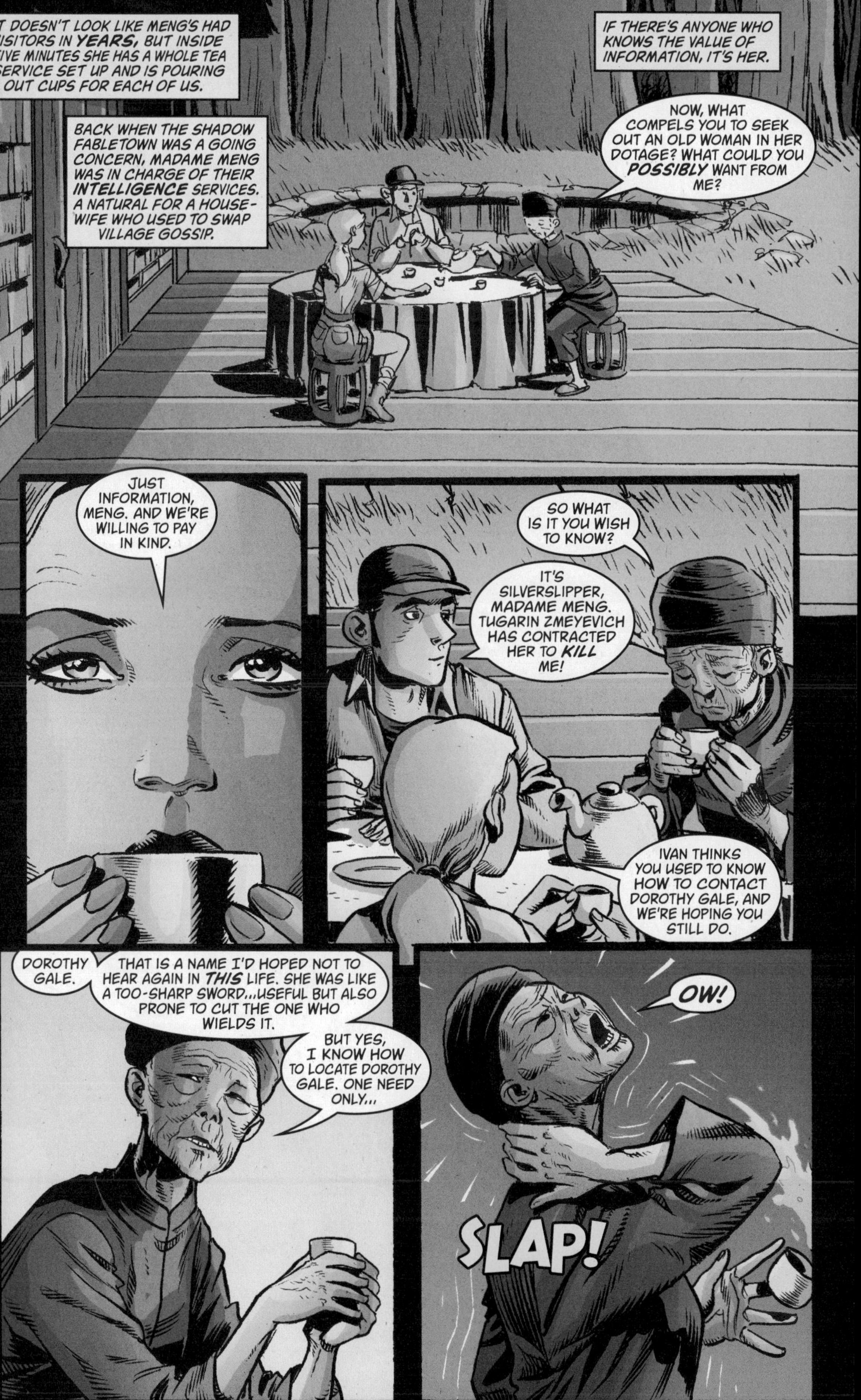
IT DOESN'T LOOK LIKE MENG'S HAD VISITORS IN YEARS, BUT INSIDE FIVE MINUTES SHE HAS A WHOLE TEA SERVICE SET UP AND IS POURING OUT CUPS FOR EACH OF US.
IF THERE'S ANYONE WHO KNOWS THE VALUE OF INFORMATION, IT'S HER.
BACK WHEN THE SHADOW FABLETOWN WAS A GOING CONCERN, MADAME MENG WAS IN CHARGE OF THEIR INTELLIGENCE SERVICES. A NATURAL FOR A HOUSE-WIFE WHO USED TO SWAP VILLAGE GOSSIP.
NOW, WHAT COMPELS YOU TO SEEK OUT AN OLD WOMAN IN HER DOTAGE? WHAT COULD YOU POSSIBLY WANT FROM ME?
JUST INFORMATION, MENG. AND WE'RE WILLING TO PAY IN KIND.
SO WHAT IS IT YOU WISH TO KNOW?
IT'S SILVERSLIPPER, MADAME MENG. TUGARIN ZMEYEVICH HAS CONTRACTED HER TO KILL ME!
IVAN THINKS YOU USED TO KNOW HOW TO CONTACT DOROTHY GALE, AND WE'RE HOPING YOU STILL DO.
DOROTHY GALE.
THAT IS A NAME I'D HOPED NOT TO HEAR AGAIN IN THIS LIFE. SHE WAS LIKE A TOO-SHARP SWORD...USEFUL BUT ALSO PRONE TO CUT THE ONE WHO WIELDS IT.
BUT YES, I KNOW HOW TO LOCATE DOROTHY GALE. ONE NEED ONLY...
OW!
SLAP!

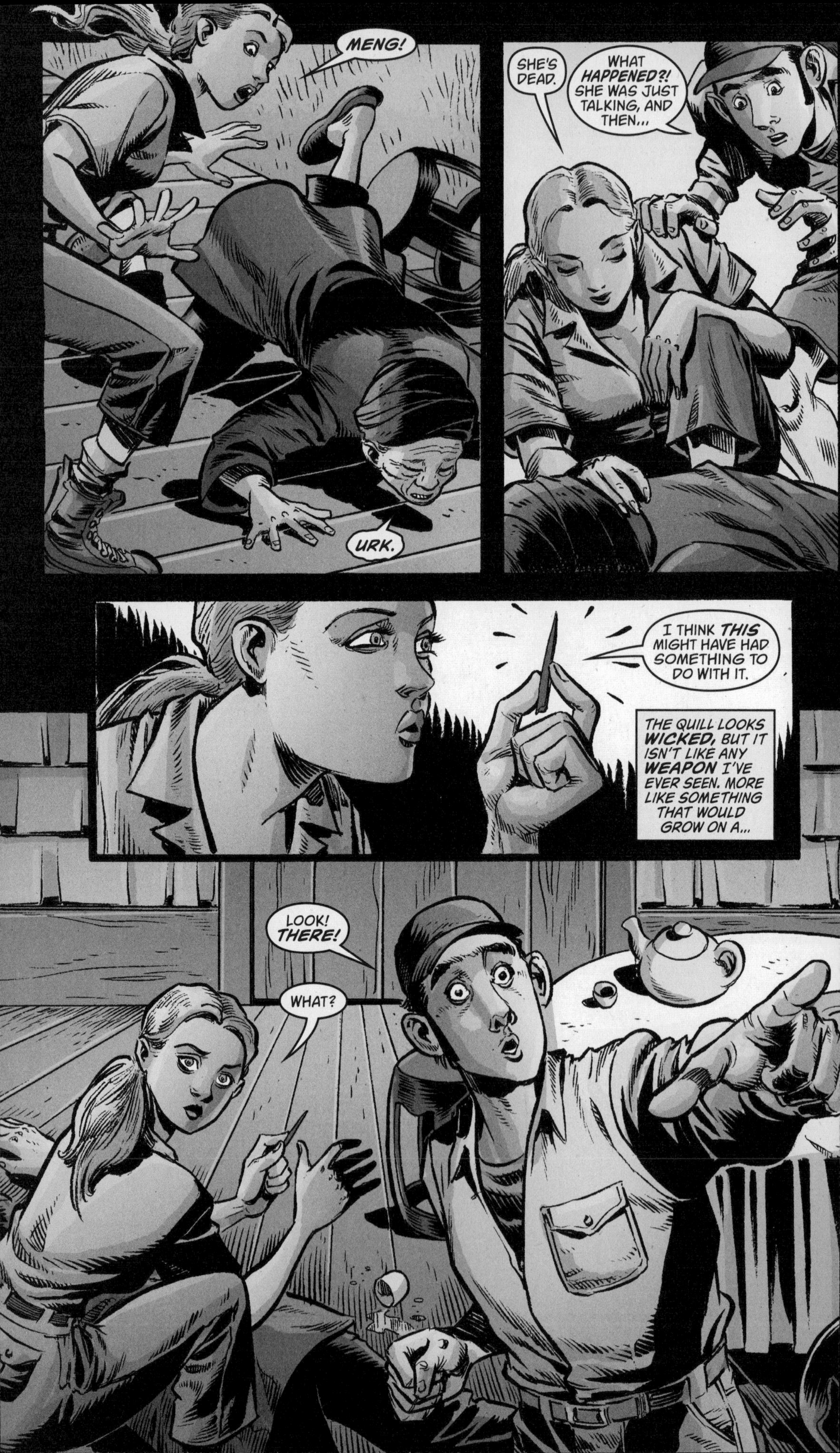
MENG!
URK.
SHE'S DEAD.
WHAT HAPPENED?! SHE WAS JUST TALKING, AND THEN...
I THINK THIS MIGHT HAVE HAD SOMETHING TO DO WITH IT.
THE QUILL LOOKS WICKED, BUT IT ISN'T LIKE ANY WEAPON I'VE EVER SEEN. MORE LIKE SOMETHING THAT WOULD GROW ON A...
LOOK! THERE!
WHAT?

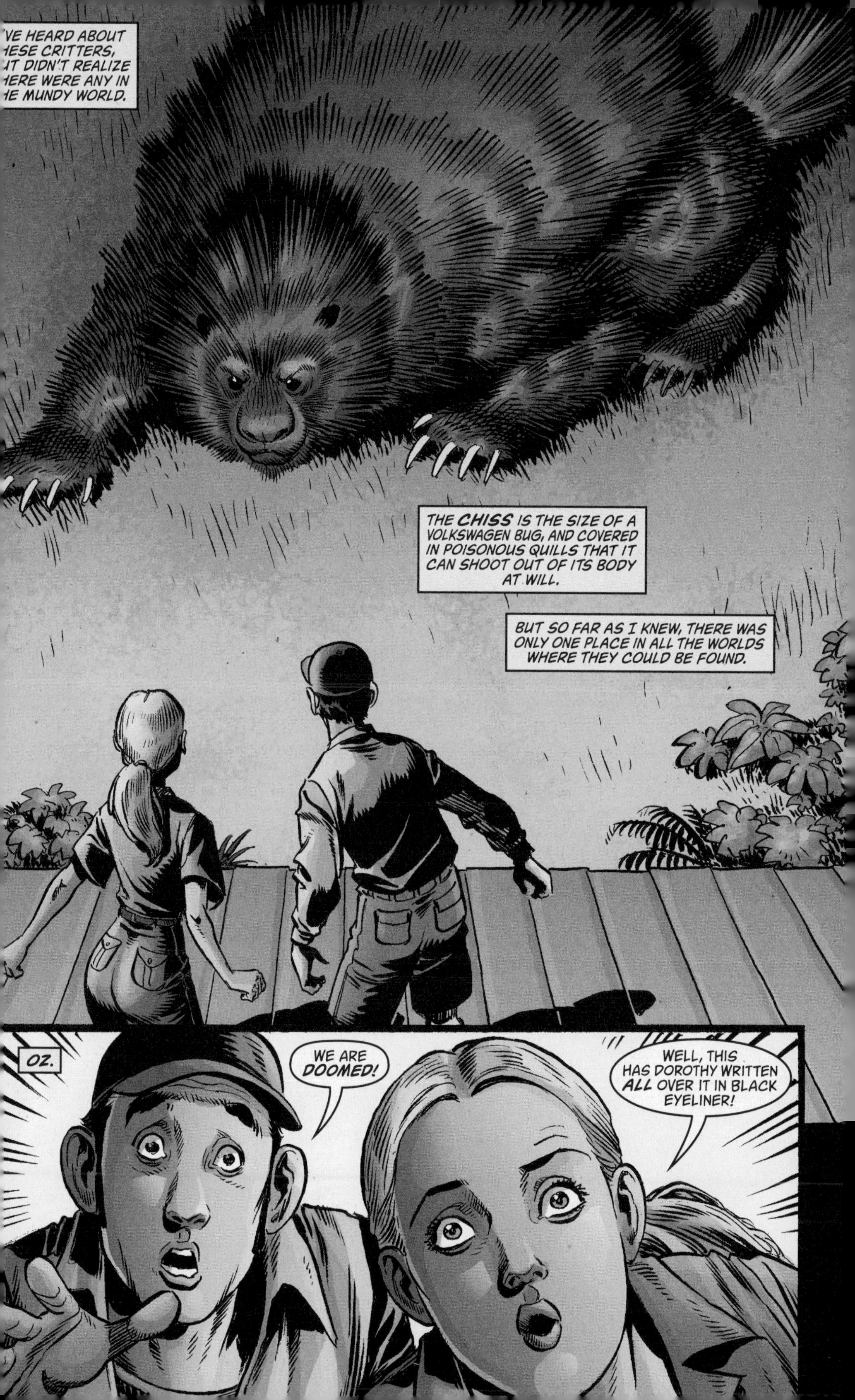

'VE HEARD ABOUT HESE CRITTERS, UT DIDN'T REALIZE HERE WERE ANY IN HE MUNDY WORLD.
THE CHISS IS THE SIZE OF A VOLKSWAGEN BUG, AND COVERED IN POISONOUS QUILLS THAT IT CAN SHOOT OUT OF ITS BODY AT WILL.
BUT SO FAR AS I KNEW, THERE WAS ONLY ONE PLACE IN ALL THE WORLDS WHERE THEY COULD BE FOUND.
OZ.
WE ARE DOOMED!
WELL, THIS HAS DOROTHY WRITTEN ALL OVER IT IN BLACK EYELINER!

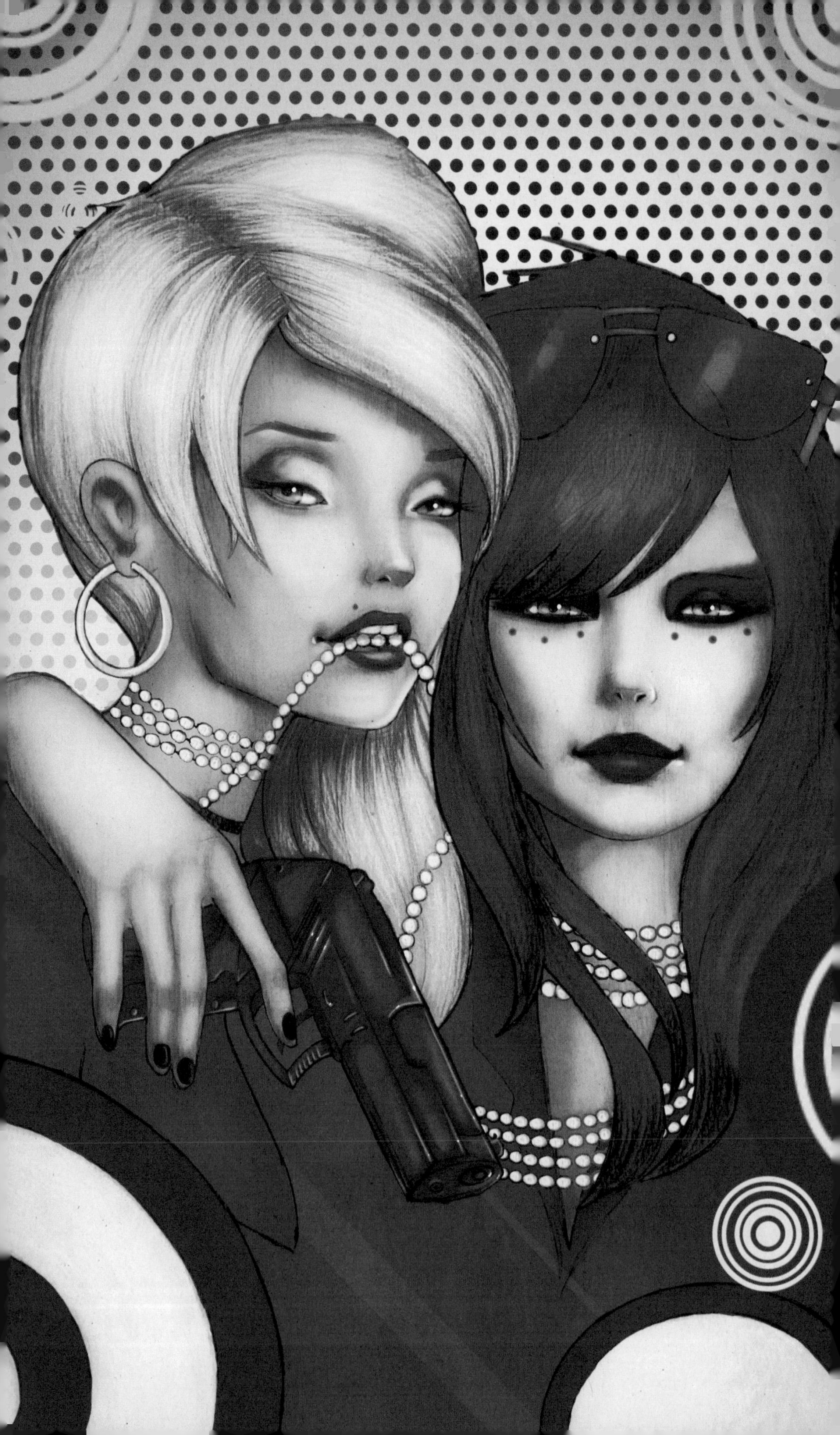

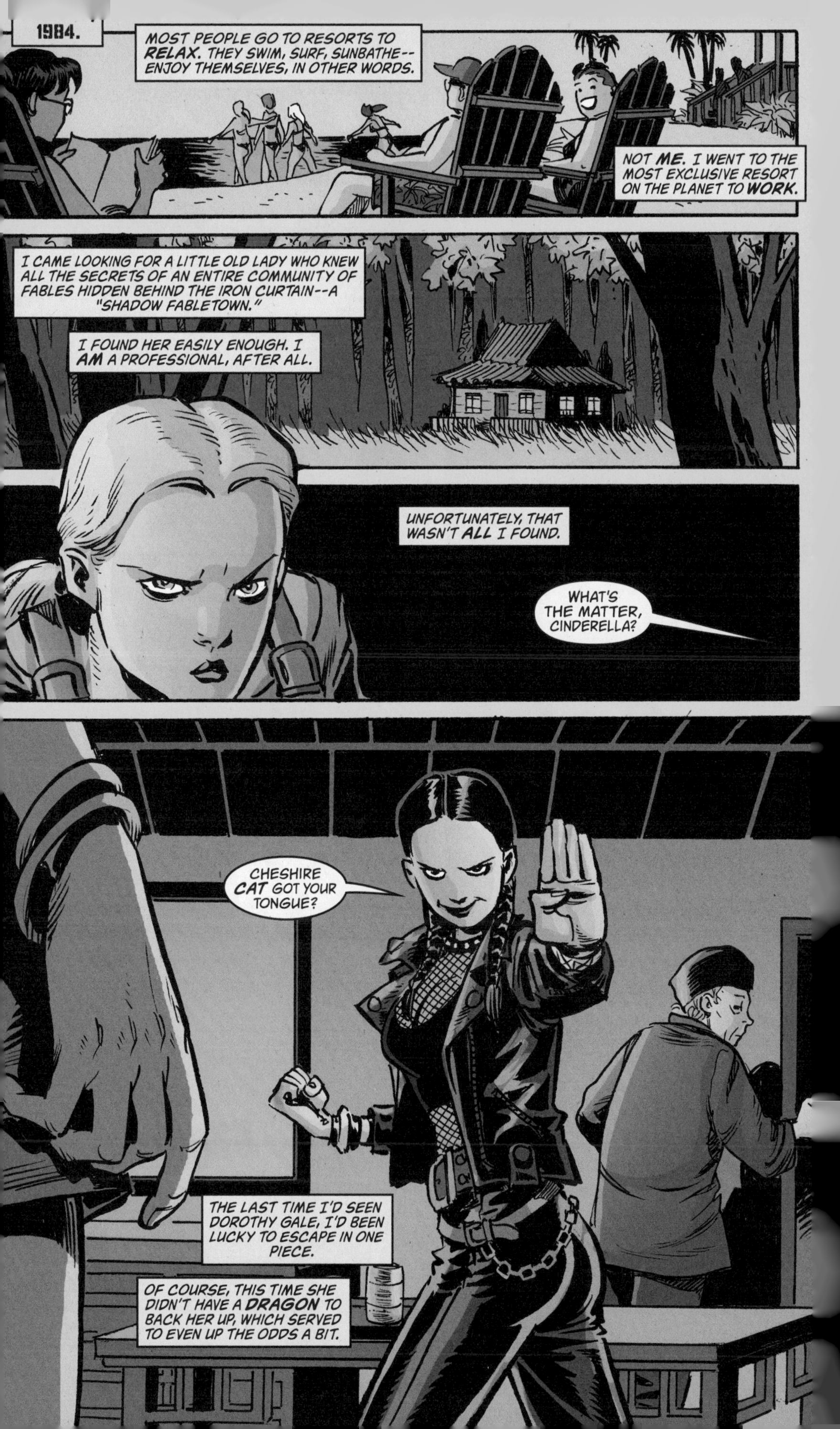

1984.
MOST PEOPLE GO TO RESORTS TO RELAX. THEY SWIM, SURF, SUNBATHE-- ENJOY THEMSELVES, IN OTHER WORDS.
NOT ME. I WENT TO THE MOST EXCLUSIVE RESORT ON THE PLANET TO WORK.
I CAME LOOKING FOR A LITTLE OLD LADY WHO KNEW ALL THE SECRETS OF AN ENTIRE COMMUNITY OF FABLES HIDDEN BEHIND THE IRON CURTAIN--A "SHADOW FABLETOWN."
I FOUND HER EASILY ENOUGH. I AM A PROFESSIONAL, AFTER ALL.
UNFORTUNATELY, THAT WASN'T ALL I FOUND.
WHAT'S THE MATTER, CINDERELLA?
CHESHIRE CAT GOT YOUR TONGUE?
THE LAST TIME I'D SEEN DOROTHY GALE, I'D BEEN LUCKY TO ESCAPE IN ONE PIECE.
OF COURSE, THIS TIME SHE DIDN'T HAVE A DRAGON TO BACK HER UP, WHICH SERVED TO EVEN UP THE ODDS A BIT.

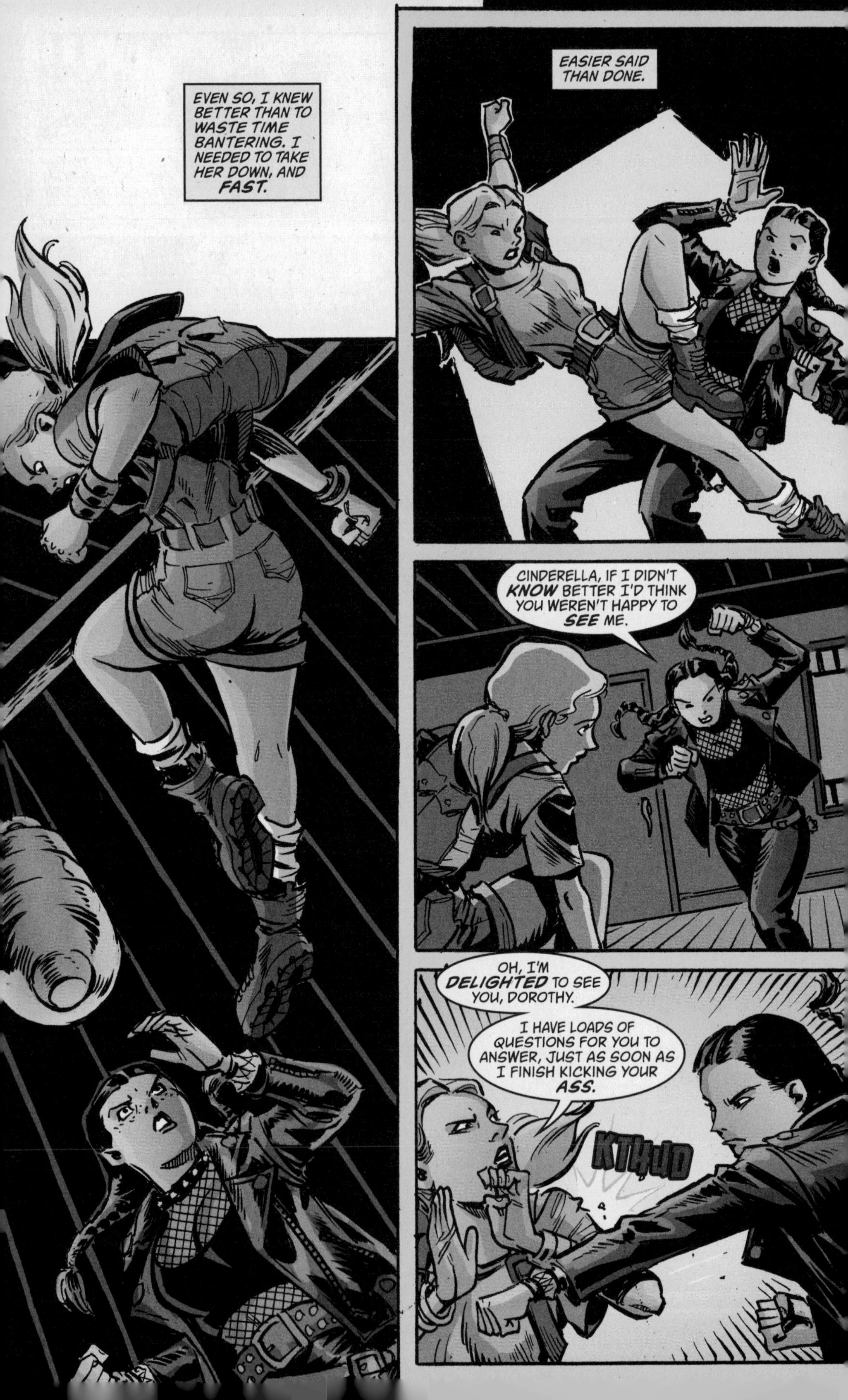
EVEN SO, I KNEW BETTER THAN TO WASTE TIME BANTERING. I NEEDED TO TAKE HER DOWN, AND FAST.
EASIER SAID THAN DONE.
CINDERELLA, IF I DIDN'T KNOW BETTER I'D THINK YOU WEREN'T HAPPY TO SEE ME.
OH, I'M DELIGHTED TO SEE YOU, DOROTHY.
I HAVE LOADS OF QUESTIONS FOR YOU TO ANSWER, JUST AS SOON AS I FINISH KICKING YOUR ASS.
KTHUD

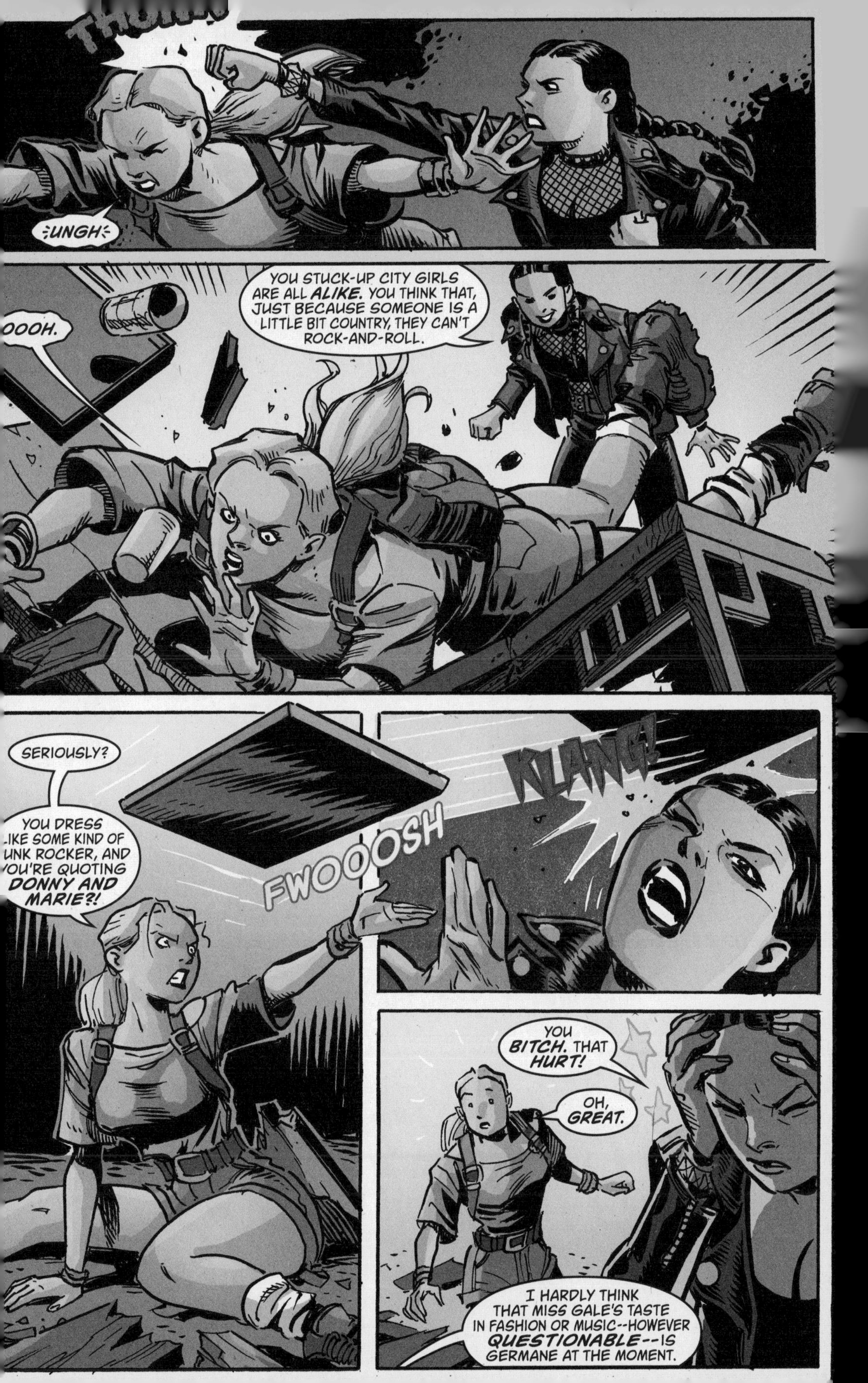
THUNK
UNGH
OOOH.
YOU STUCK-UP CITY GIRLS ARE ALL ALIKE. YOU THINK THAT, JUST BECAUSE SOMEONE IS A LITTLE BIT COUNTRY, THEY CAN'T ROCK-AND-ROLL.
SERIOUSLY?
YOU DRESS LIKE SOME KIND OF UNK ROCKER, AND YOU'RE QUOTING DONNY AND MARIE?!
FWOOOOSH
KLANG!
YOU BITCH. THAT HURT!
OH, GREAT.
I HARDLY THINK THAT MISS GALE'S TASTE IN FASHION OR MUSIC--HOWEVER QUESTIONABLE--IS GERMANE AT THE MOMENT.

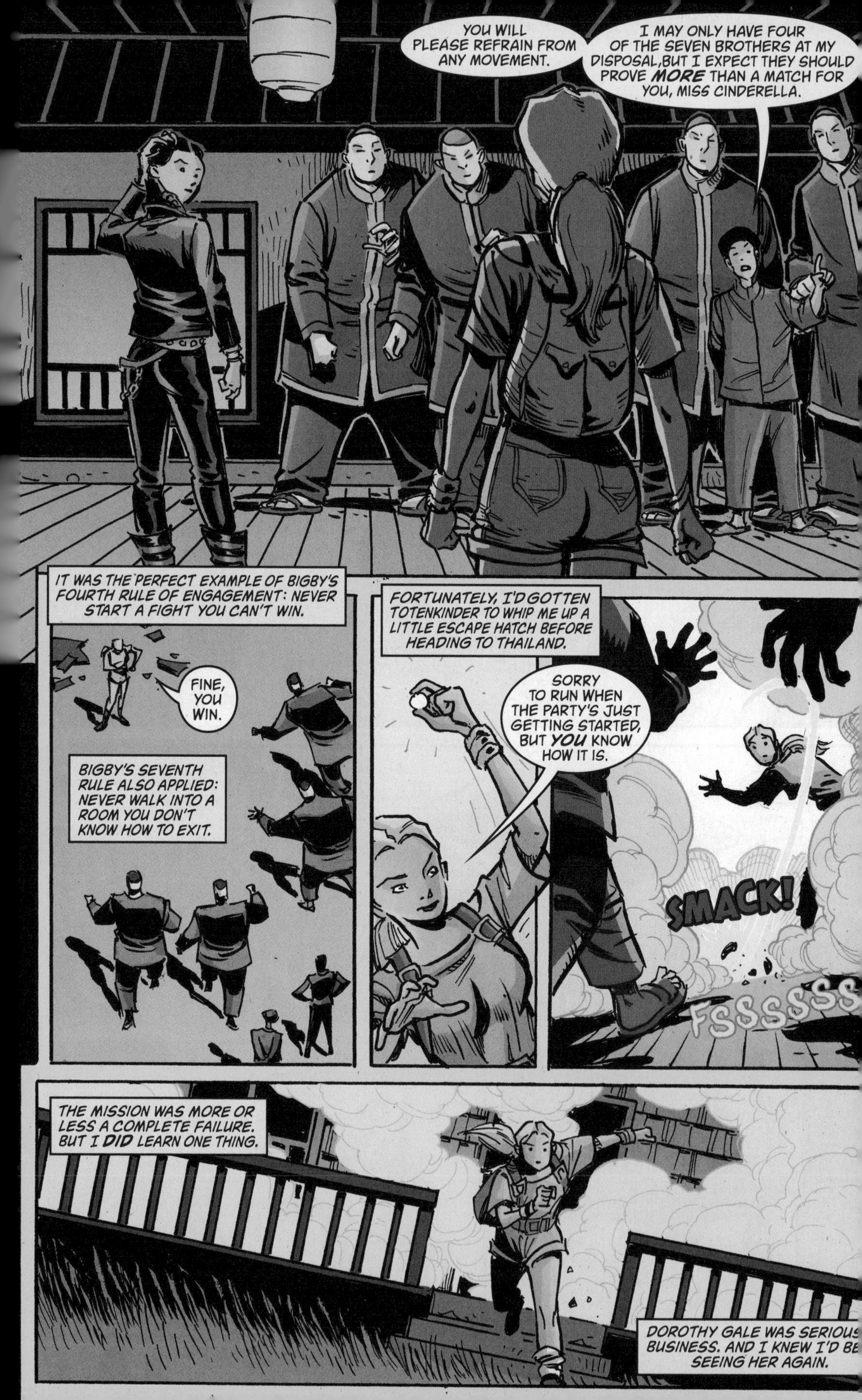
YOU WILL PLEASE REFRAIN FROM ANY MOVEMENT.
I MAY ONLY HAVE FOUR OF THE SEVEN BROTHERS AT MY DISPOSAL, BUT I EXPECT THEY SHOULD PROVE MORE THAN A MATCH FOR YOU, MISS CINDERELLA.
IT WAS THE PERFECT EXAMPLE OF BIGBY'S FOURTH RULE OF ENGAGEMENT: NEVER START A FIGHT YOU CAN'T WIN.
FINE, YOU WIN.
BIGBY'S SEVENTH RULE ALSO APPLIED: NEVER WALK INTO A ROOM YOU DON'T KNOW HOW TO EXIT.
FORTUNATELY, I'D GOTTEN TOTENKINDER TO WHIP ME UP A LITTLE ESCAPE HATCH BEFORE HEADING TO THAILAND.
SORRY TO RUN WHEN THE PARTY'S JUST GETTING STARTED, BUT YOU KNOW HOW IT IS.
SMACK!
FSSSSSSS
THE MISSION WAS MORE OR LESS A COMPLETE FAILURE. BUT I DID LEARN ONE THING.
DOROTHY GALE WAS SERIOUS BUSINESS. AND I KNEW I'D BE SEEING HER AGAIN.

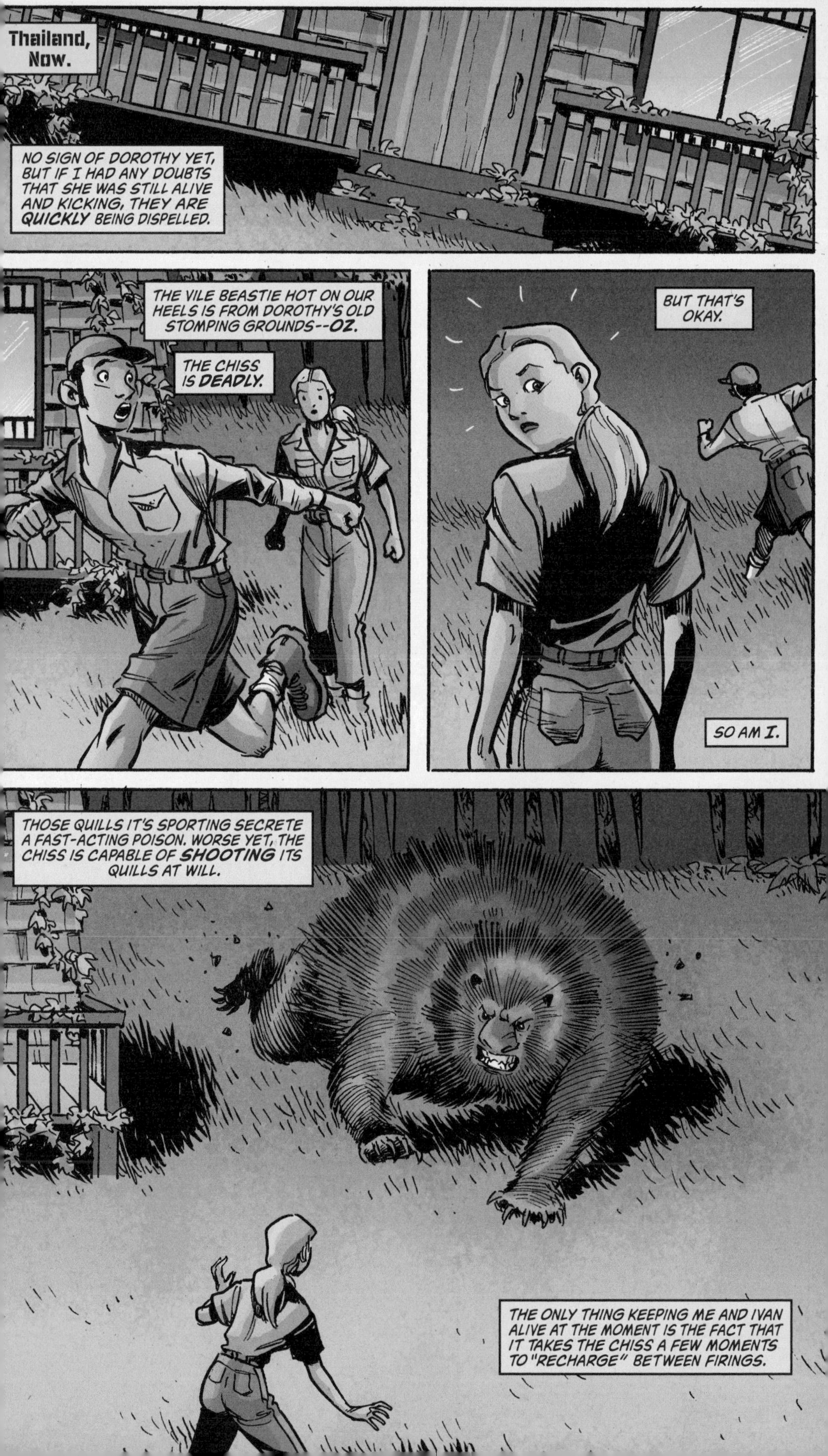
Thailand, Now.
NO SIGN OF DOROTHY YET, BUT IF I HAD ANY DOUBTS THAT SHE WAS STILL ALIVE AND KICKING, THEY ARE QUICKLY BEING DISPELLED.
THE VILE BEASTIE HOT ON OUR HEELS IS FROM DOROTHY'S OLD STOMPING GROUNDS--OZ.
THE CHISS IS DEADLY.
BUT THAT'S OKAY.
SO AM I.
THOSE QUILLS IT'S SPORTING SECRETE A FAST-ACTING POISON. WORSE YET, THE CHISS IS CAPABLE OF SHOOTING ITS QUILLS AT WILL.
THE ONLY THING KEEPING ME AND IVAN ALIVE AT THE MOMENT IS THE FACT THAT IT TAKES THE CHISS A FEW MOMENTS TO "RECHARGE" BETWEEN FIRINGS.

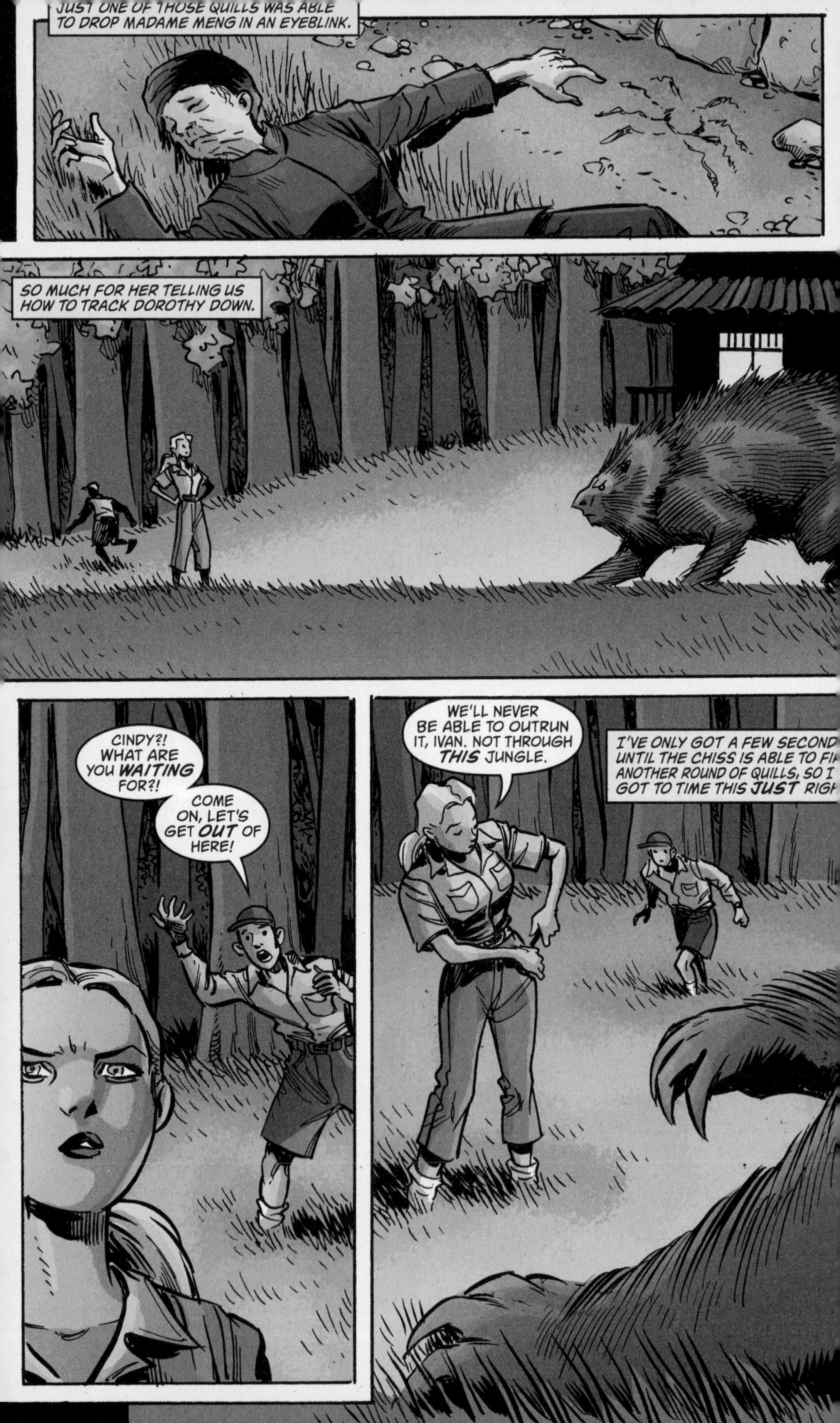
JUST ONE OF THOSE QUILLS WAS ABLE TO DROP MADAME MENG IN AN EYEBLINK.
SO MUCH FOR HER TELLING US HOW TO TRACK DOROTHY DOWN.
CINDY?! WHAT ARE YOU WAITING FOR?!
COME ON, LET'S GET OUT OF HERE!
WE'LL NEVER BE ABLE TO OUTRUN IT, IVAN. NOT THROUGH THIS JUNGLE.
I'VE ONLY GOT A FEW SECOND UNTIL THE CHISS IS ABLE TO FI ANOTHER ROUND OF QUILLS, SO I GOT TO TIME THIS JUST RIGH

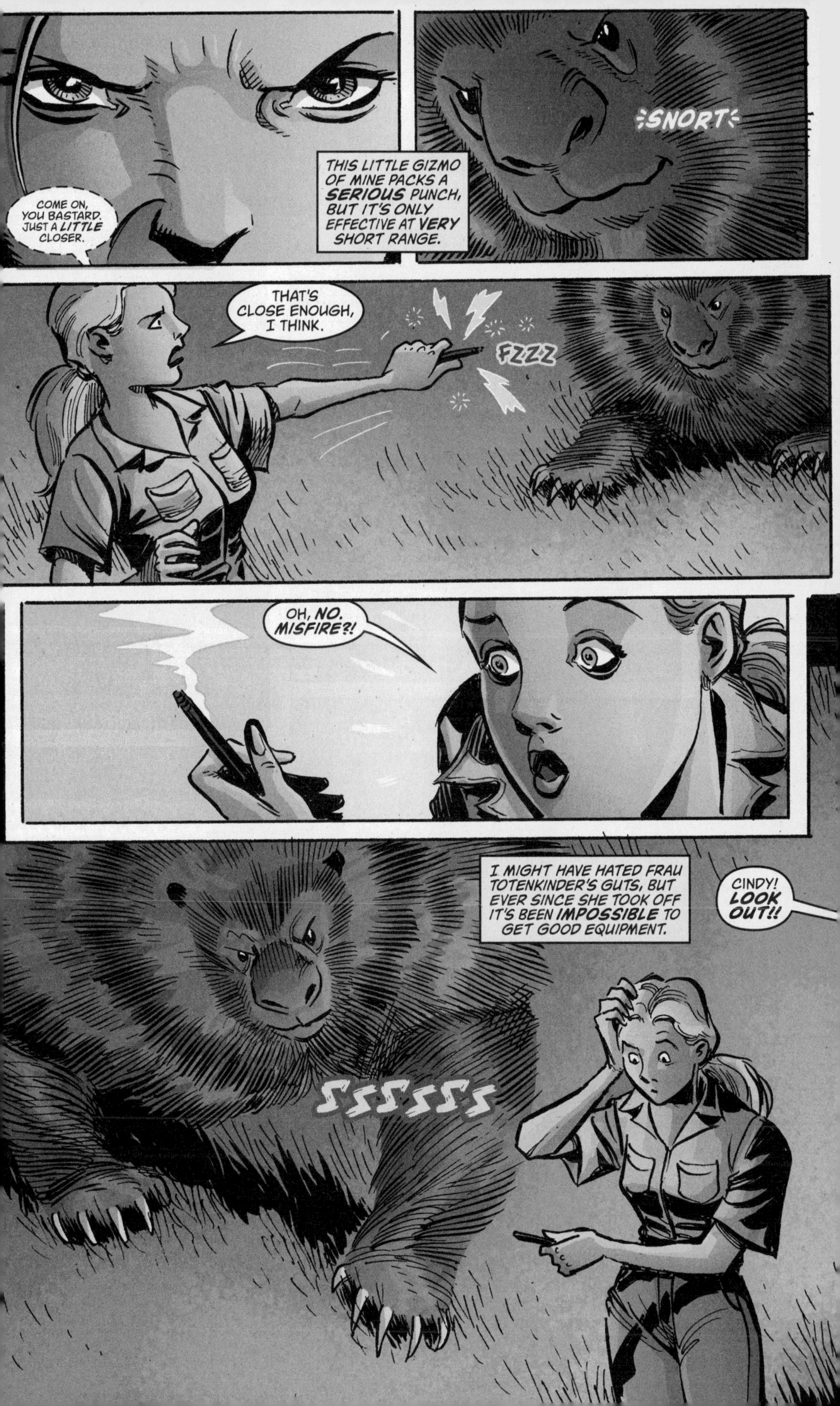
COME ON, YOU BASTARD. JUST A LITTLE CLOSER.
THIS LITTLE GIZMO OF MINE PACKS A SERIOUS PUNCH, BUT IT'S ONLY EFFECTIVE AT VERY SHORT RANGE.
SNORT
THAT'S CLOSE ENOUGH, I THINK.
FZZZ
OH, NO. MISFIRE?!
I MIGHT HAVE HATED FRAU TOTENKINDER'S GUTS, BUT EVER SINCE SHE TOOK OFF IT'S BEEN IMPOSSIBLE TO GET GOOD EQUIPMENT.
CINDY! LOOK OUT!!
SSSSSS

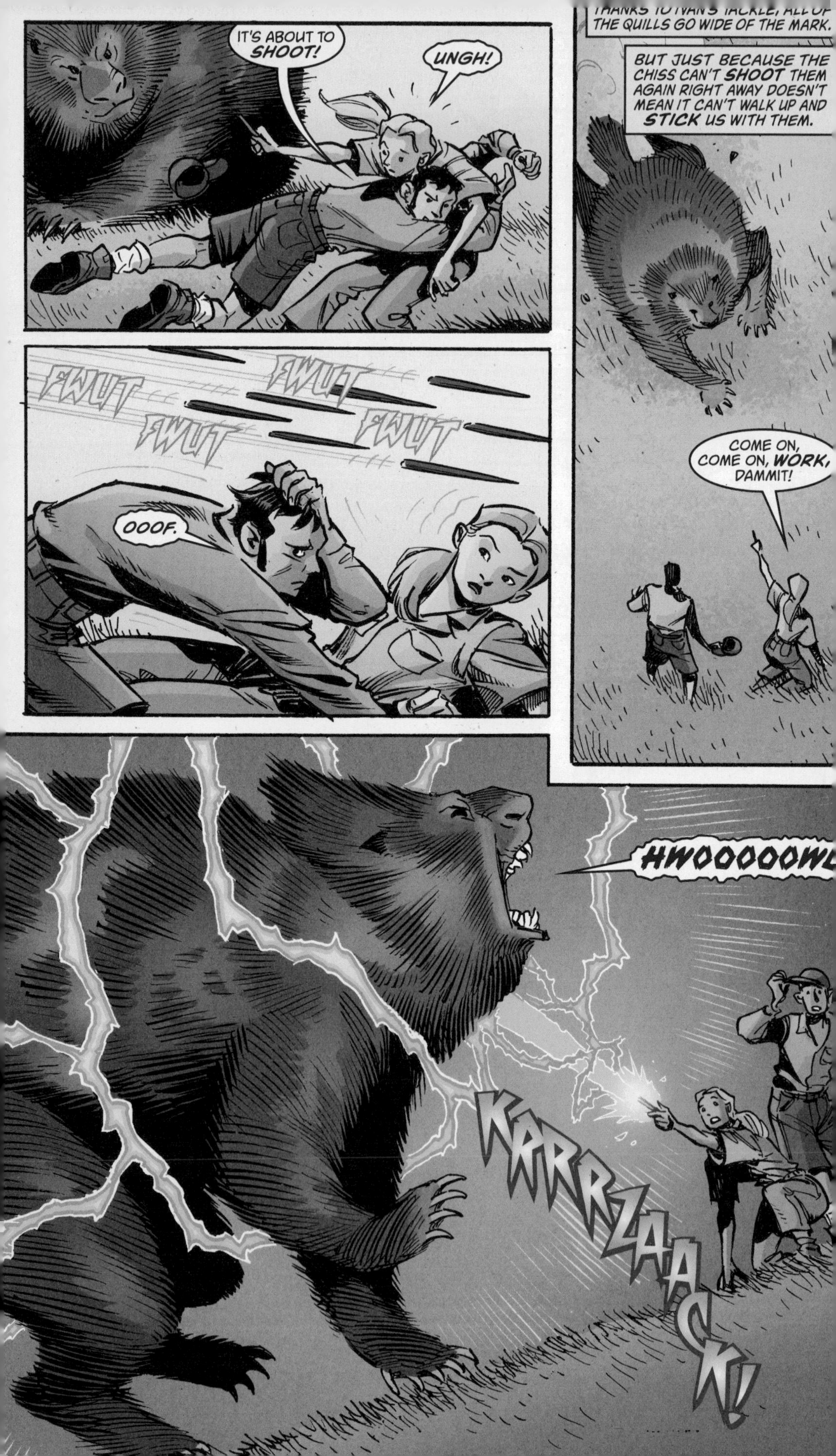
IT'S ABOUT TO SHOOT!
UNGH!
FWUT
FWUT
FWUT
FWUT
OOOF.
THANKS TO IVAN'S TACKLE, ALL OF THE QUILLS GO WIDE OF THE MARK.
BUT JUST BECAUSE THE CHISS CAN'T SHOOT THEM AGAIN RIGHT AWAY DOESN'T MEAN IT CAN'T WALK UP AND STICK US WITH THEM.
COME ON, COME ON, WORK, DAMMIT!
HWOOOOOW
KRRRZAAACK!

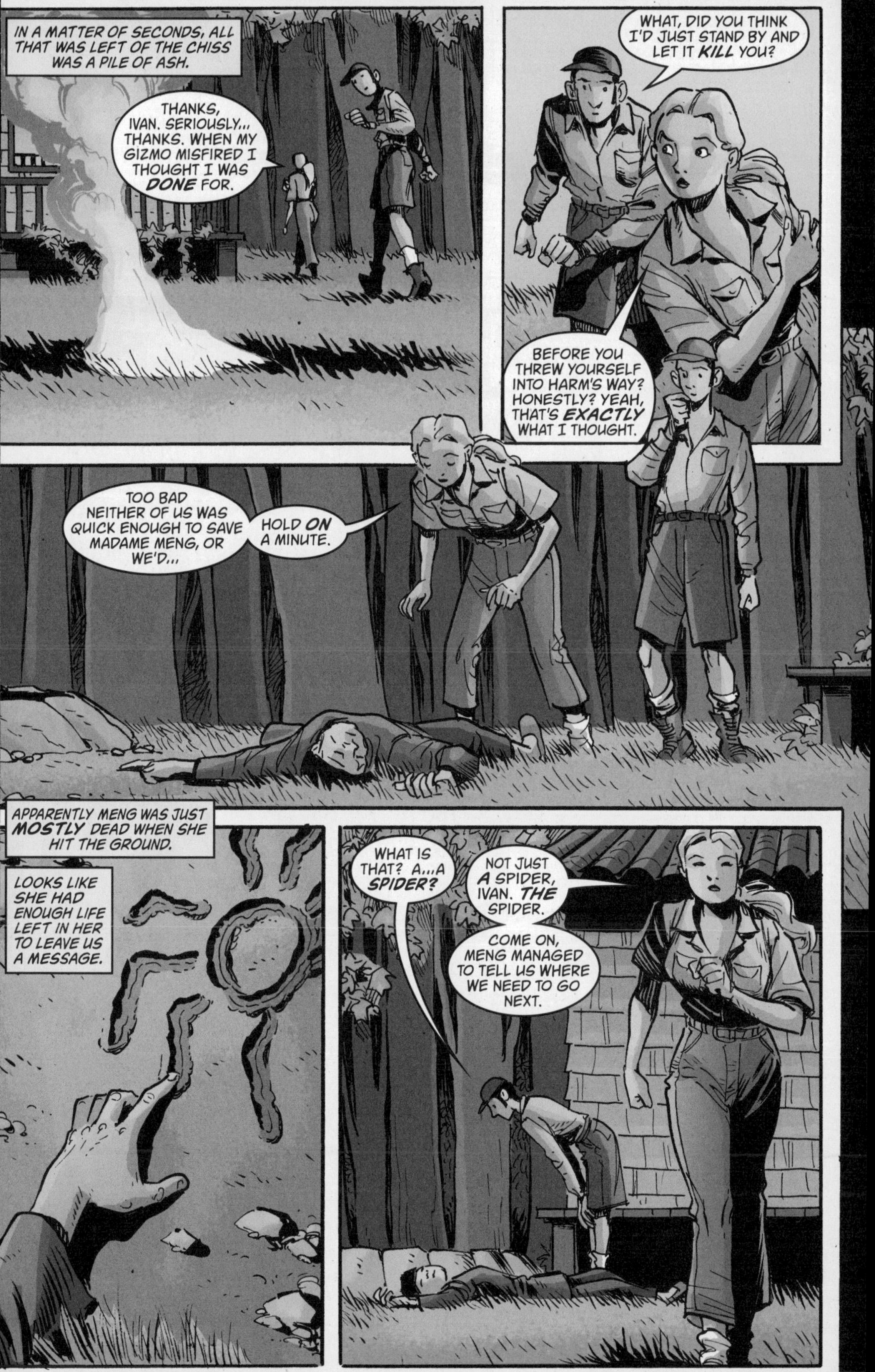
IN A MATTER OF SECONDS, ALL THAT WAS LEFT OF THE CHISS WAS A PILE OF ASH.
THANKS, IVAN. SERIOUSLY... THANKS. WHEN MY GIZMO MISFIRED I THOUGHT I WAS DONE FOR.
WHAT, DID YOU THINK I'D JUST STAND BY AND LET IT KILL YOU?
BEFORE YOU THREW YOURSELF INTO HARM'S WAY? HONESTLY? YEAH, THAT'S EXACTLY WHAT I THOUGHT.
TOO BAD NEITHER OF US WAS QUICK ENOUGH TO SAVE MADAME MENG, OR WE'D...
HOLD ON A MINUTE.
APPARENTLY MENG WAS JUST MOSTLY DEAD WHEN SHE HIT THE GROUND.
LOOKS LIKE SHE HAD ENOUGH LIFE LEFT IN HER TO LEAVE US A MESSAGE.
WHAT IS THAT? A...A SPIDER?
NOT JUST A SPIDER, IVAN. THE SPIDER.
COME ON, MENG MANAGED TO TELL US WHERE WE NEED TO GO NEXT.

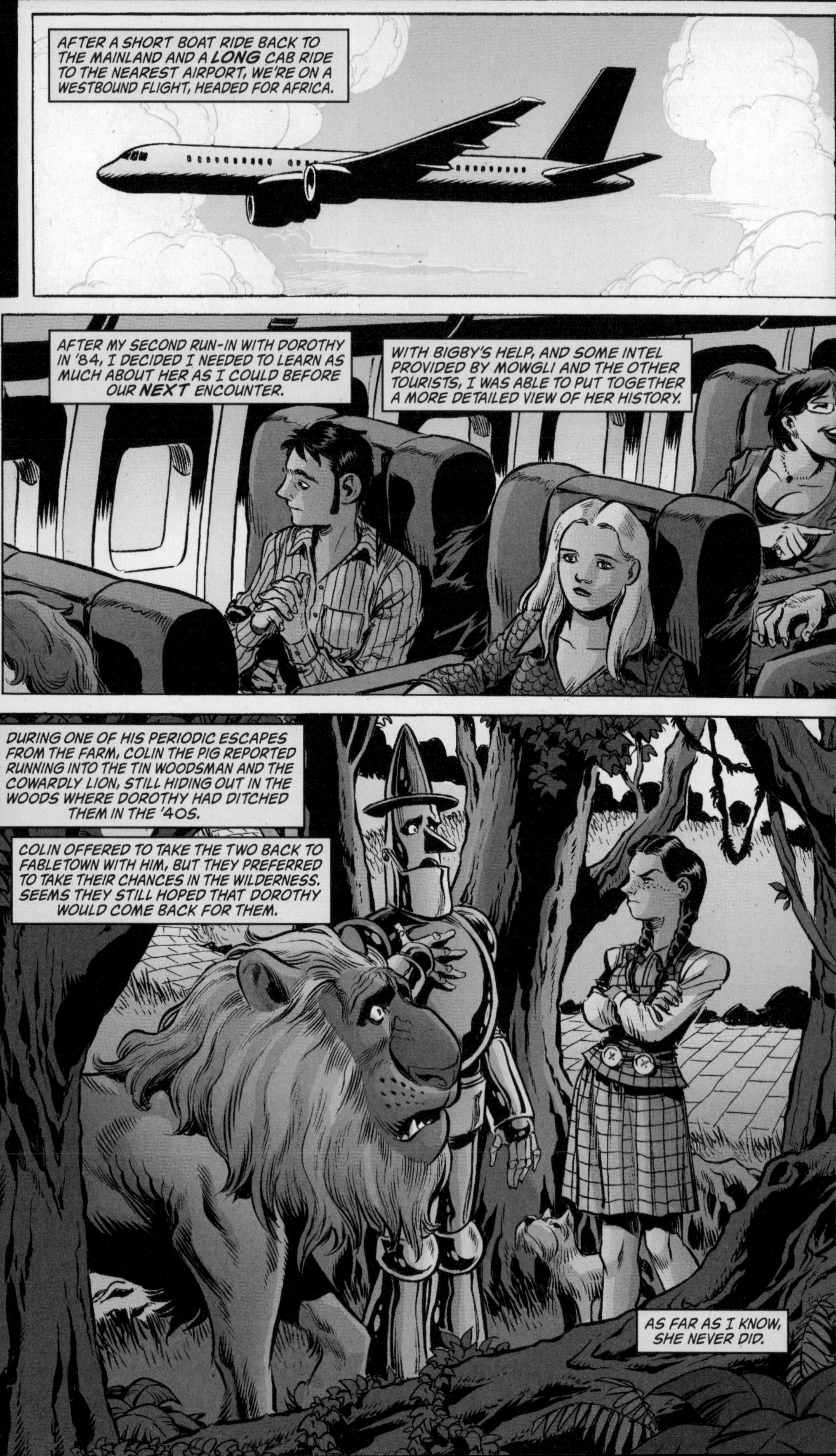
AFTER A SHORT BOAT RIDE BACK TO THE MAINLAND AND A **LONG** CAB RIDE TO THE NEAREST AIRPORT, WE'RE ON A WESTBOUND FLIGHT, HEADED FOR AFRICA.
AFTER MY SECOND RUN-IN WITH DOROTHY IN '84, I DECIDED I NEEDED TO LEARN AS MUCH ABOUT HER AS I COULD BEFORE OUR **NEXT** ENCOUNTER.
WITH BIGBY'S HELP, AND SOME INTEL PROVIDED BY MOWGLI AND THE OTHER TOURISTS, I WAS ABLE TO PUT TOGETHER A MORE DETAILED VIEW OF HER HISTORY.
DURING ONE OF HIS PERIODIC ESCAPES FROM THE FARM, COLIN THE PIG REPORTED RUNNING INTO THE TIN WOODSMAN AND THE COWARDLY LION, STILL HIDING OUT IN THE WOODS WHERE DOROTHY HAD DITCHED THEM IN THE '40S.
COLIN OFFERED TO TAKE THE TWO BACK TO FABLETOWN WITH HIM, BUT THEY PREFERRED TO TAKE THEIR CHANCES IN THE WILDERNESS. SEEMS THEY STILL HOPED THAT DOROTHY WOULD COME BACK FOR THEM.
AS FAR AS I KNOW, SHE NEVER DID.

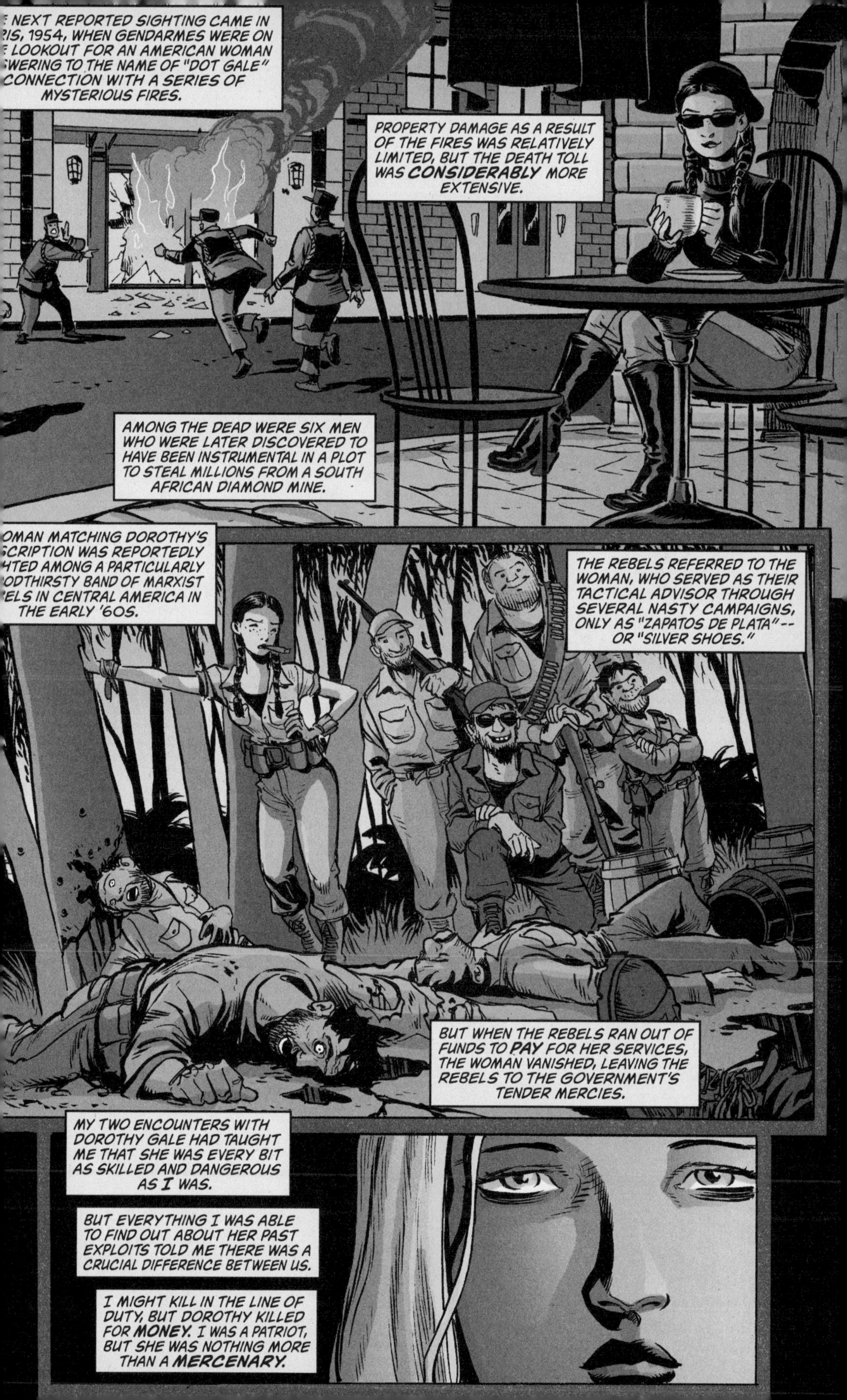

E NEXT REPORTED SIGHTING CAME IN RIS, 1954, WHEN GENDARMES WERE ON E LOOKOUT FOR AN AMERICAN WOMAN SWERING TO THE NAME OF "DOT GALE" CONNECTION WITH A SERIES OF MYSTERIOUS FIRES.
PROPERTY DAMAGE AS A RESULT OF THE FIRES WAS RELATIVELY LIMITED, BUT THE DEATH TOLL WAS CONSIDERABLY MORE EXTENSIVE.
AMONG THE DEAD WERE SIX MEN WHO WERE LATER DISCOVERED TO HAVE BEEN INSTRUMENTAL IN A PLOT TO STEAL MILLIONS FROM A SOUTH AFRICAN DIAMOND MINE.
OMAN MATCHING DOROTHY'S SCRIPTION WAS REPORTEDLY HTED AMONG A PARTICULARLY ODTHIRSTY BAND OF MARXIST ELS IN CENTRAL AMERICA IN THE EARLY '60S.
THE REBELS REFERRED TO THE WOMAN, WHO SERVED AS THEIR TACTICAL ADVISOR THROUGH SEVERAL NASTY CAMPAIGNS, ONLY AS "ZAPATOS DE PLATA"-- OR "SILVER SHOES."
BUT WHEN THE REBELS RAN OUT OF FUNDS TO PAY FOR HER SERVICES, THE WOMAN VANISHED, LEAVING THE REBELS TO THE GOVERNMENT'S TENDER MERCIES.
MY TWO ENCOUNTERS WITH DOROTHY GALE HAD TAUGHT ME THAT SHE WAS EVERY BIT AS SKILLED AND DANGEROUS AS I WAS.
BUT EVERYTHING I WAS ABLE TO FIND OUT ABOUT HER PAST EXPLOITS TOLD ME THERE WAS A CRUCIAL DIFFERENCE BETWEEN US.
I MIGHT KILL IN THE LINE OF DUTY, BUT DOROTHY KILLED FOR MONEY. I WAS A PATRIOT, BUT SHE WAS NOTHING MORE THAN A MERCENARY.

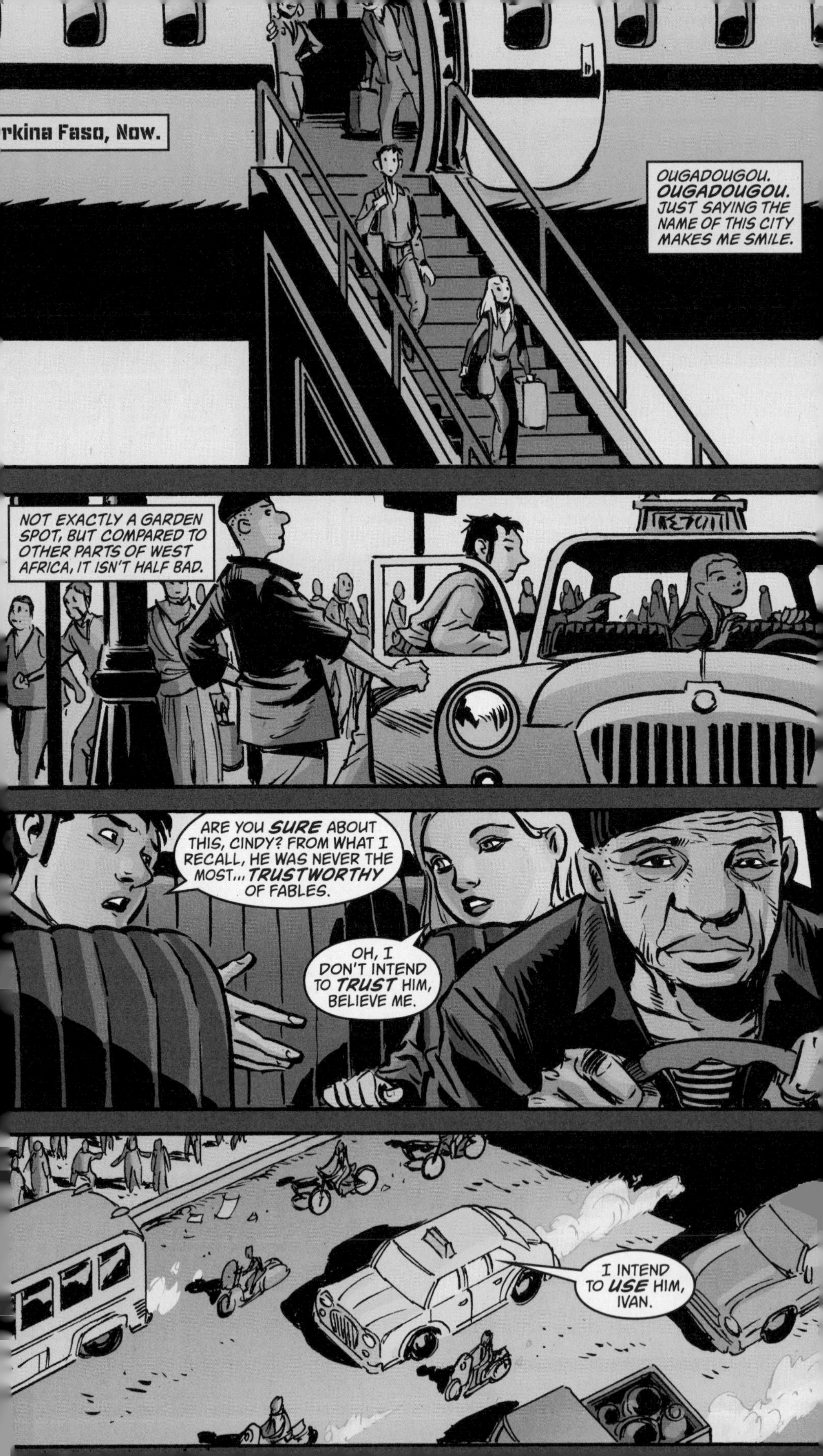
rkina Faso, Now.
OUGADOUGOU. OUGADOUGOU. JUST SAYING THE NAME OF THIS CITY MAKES ME SMILE.
NOT EXACTLY A GARDEN SPOT, BUT COMPARED TO OTHER PARTS OF WEST AFRICA, IT ISN'T HALF BAD.
ARE YOU SURE ABOUT THIS, CINDY? FROM WHAT I RECALL, HE WAS NEVER THE MOST... TRUSTWORTHY OF FABLES.
OH, I DON'T INTEND TO TRUST HIM, BELIEVE ME.
I INTEND TO USE HIM, IVAN.

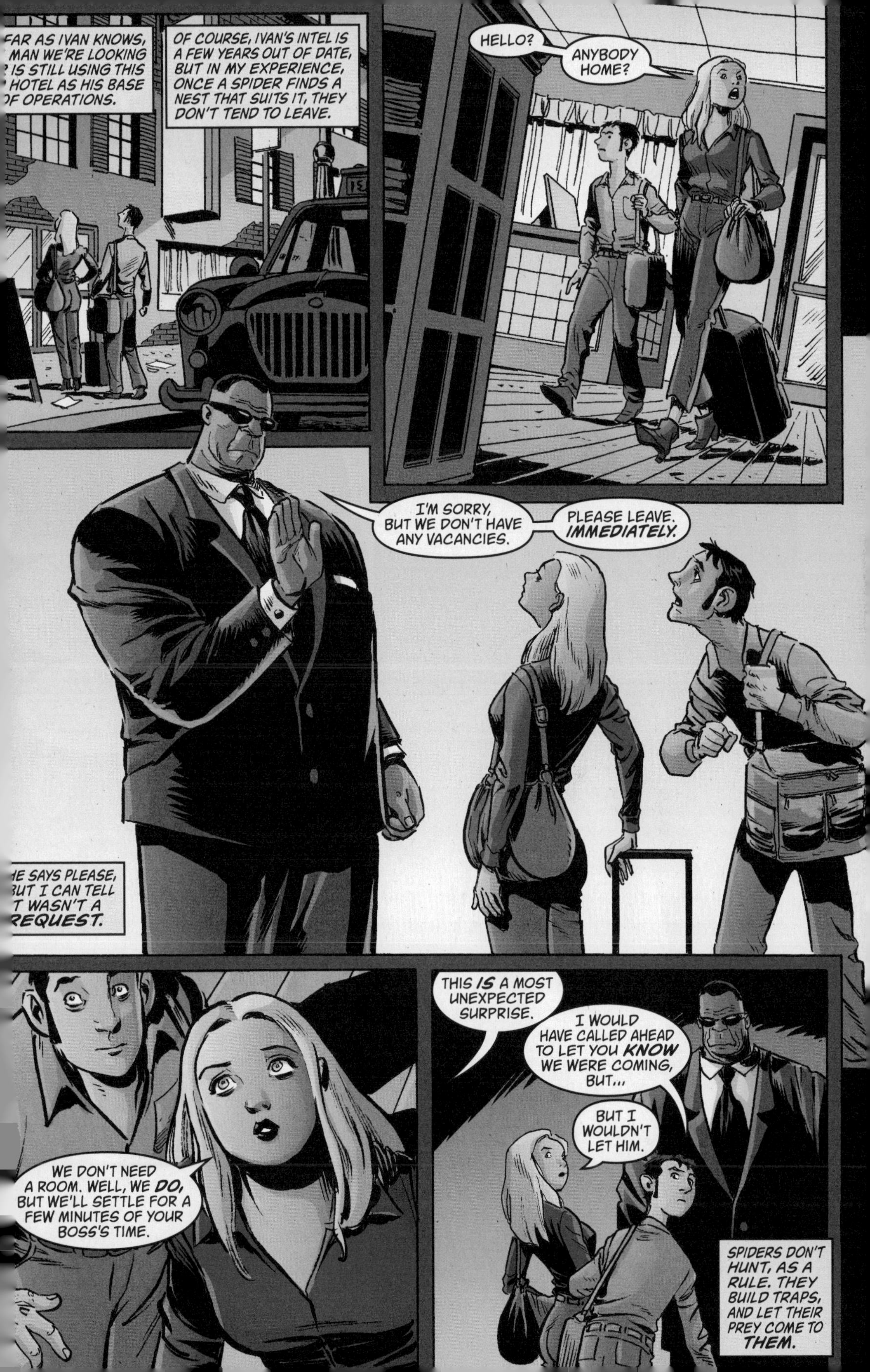
FAR AS IVAN KNOWS, MAN WE'RE LOOKING IS STILL USING THIS HOTEL AS HIS BASE OF OPERATIONS.
OF COURSE, IVAN'S INTEL IS A FEW YEARS OUT OF DATE, BUT IN MY EXPERIENCE, ONCE A SPIDER FINDS A NEST THAT SUITS IT, THEY DON'T TEND TO LEAVE.
HELLO?
ANYBODY HOME?
I'M SORRY, BUT WE DON'T HAVE ANY VACANCIES.
PLEASE LEAVE. IMMEDIATELY.
HE SAYS PLEASE, BUT I CAN TELL T WASN'T A REQUEST.
WE DON'T NEED A ROOM. WELL, WE DO, BUT WE'LL SETTLE FOR A FEW MINUTES OF YOUR BOSS'S TIME.
THIS IS A MOST UNEXPECTED SURPRISE.
I WOULD HAVE CALLED AHEAD TO LET YOU KNOW WE WERE COMING, BUT...
BUT I WOULDN'T LET HIM.
SPIDERS DON'T HUNT, AS A RULE. THEY BUILD TRAPS, AND LET THEIR PREY COME TO THEM.

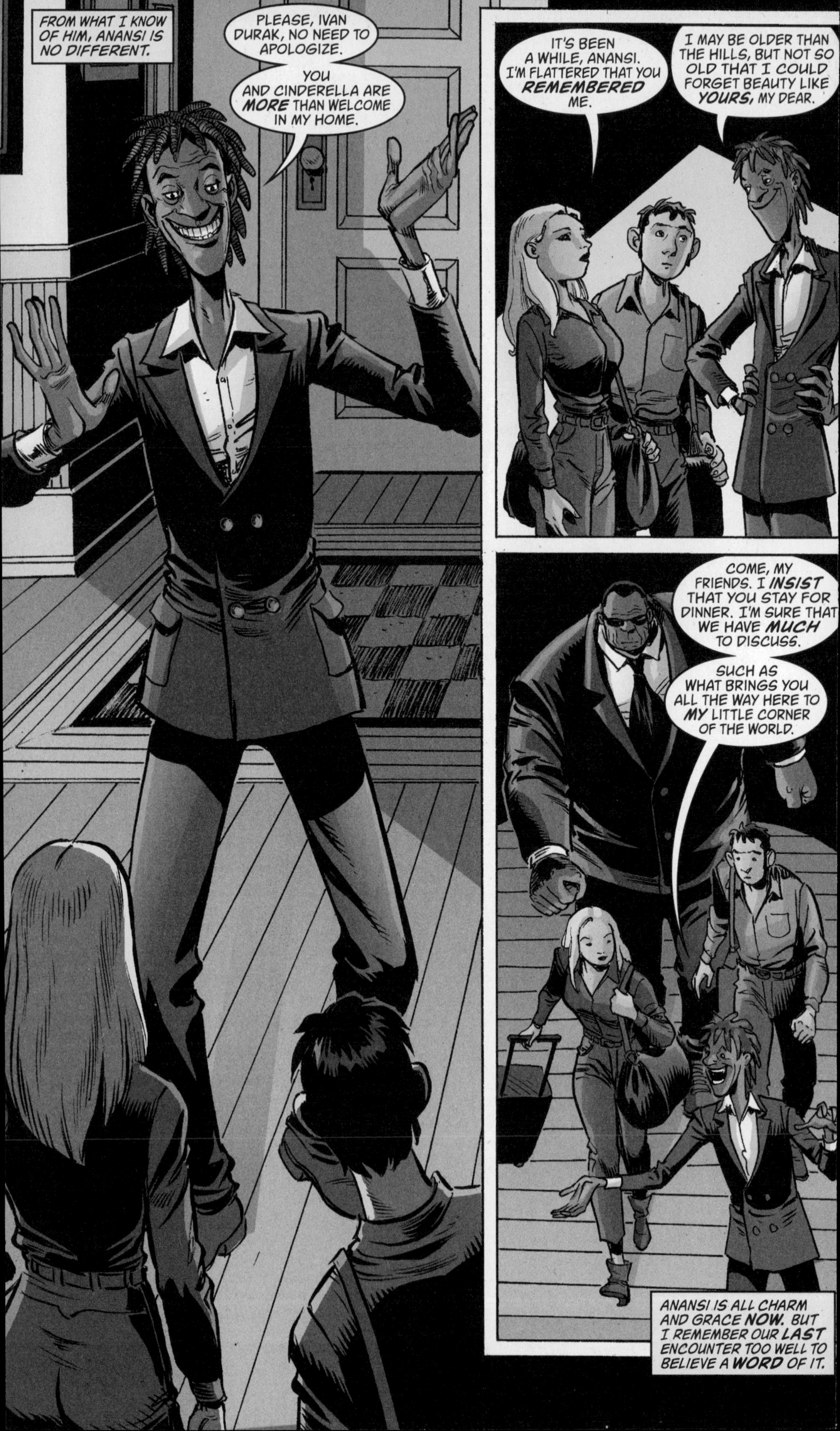
FROM WHAT I KNOW OF HIM, ANANSI IS NO DIFFERENT.
PLEASE, IVAN DURAK, NO NEED TO APOLOGIZE.
YOU AND CINDERELLA ARE MORE THAN WELCOME IN MY HOME.
IT'S BEEN A WHILE, ANANSI. I'M FLATTERED THAT YOU REMEMBERED ME.
I MAY BE OLDER THAN THE HILLS, BUT NOT SO OLD THAT I COULD FORGET BEAUTY LIKE YOURS, MY DEAR.
COME, MY FRIENDS. I INSIST THAT YOU STAY FOR DINNER. I'M SURE THAT WE HAVE MUCH TO DISCUSS.
SUCH AS WHAT BRINGS YOU ALL THE WAY HERE TO MY LITTLE CORNER OF THE WORLD.
ANANSI IS ALL CHARM AND GRACE NOW. BUT I REMEMBER OUR LAST ENCOUNTER TOO WELL TO BELIEVE A WORD OF IT.

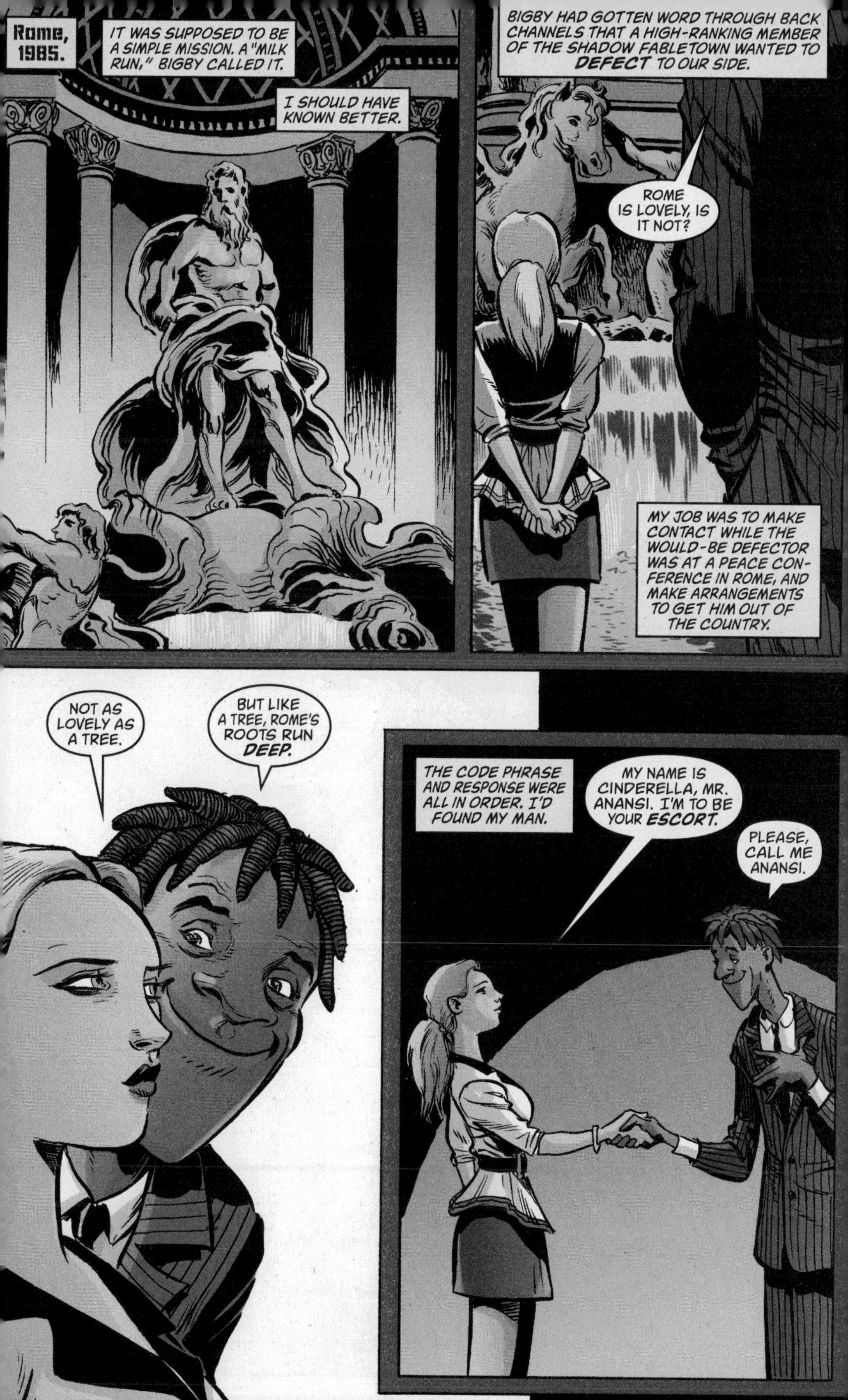
Rome, 1985.
IT WAS SUPPOSED TO BE A SIMPLE MISSION. A "MILK RUN," BIGBY CALLED IT.
I SHOULD HAVE KNOWN BETTER.
BIGBY HAD GOTTEN WORD THROUGH BACK CHANNELS THAT A HIGH-RANKING MEMBER OF THE SHADOW FABLETOWN WANTED TO DEFECT TO OUR SIDE.
ROME IS LOVELY, IS IT NOT?
MY JOB WAS TO MAKE CONTACT WHILE THE WOULD-BE DEFECTOR WAS AT A PEACE CONFERENCE IN ROME, AND MAKE ARRANGEMENTS TO GET HIM OUT OF THE COUNTRY.
NOT AS LOVELY AS A TREE.
BUT LIKE A TREE, ROME'S ROOTS RUN DEEP.
THE CODE PHRASE AND RESPONSE WERE ALL IN ORDER. I'D FOUND MY MAN.
MY NAME IS CINDERELLA, MR. ANANSI. I'M TO BE YOUR ESCORT.
PLEASE, CALL ME ANANSI.

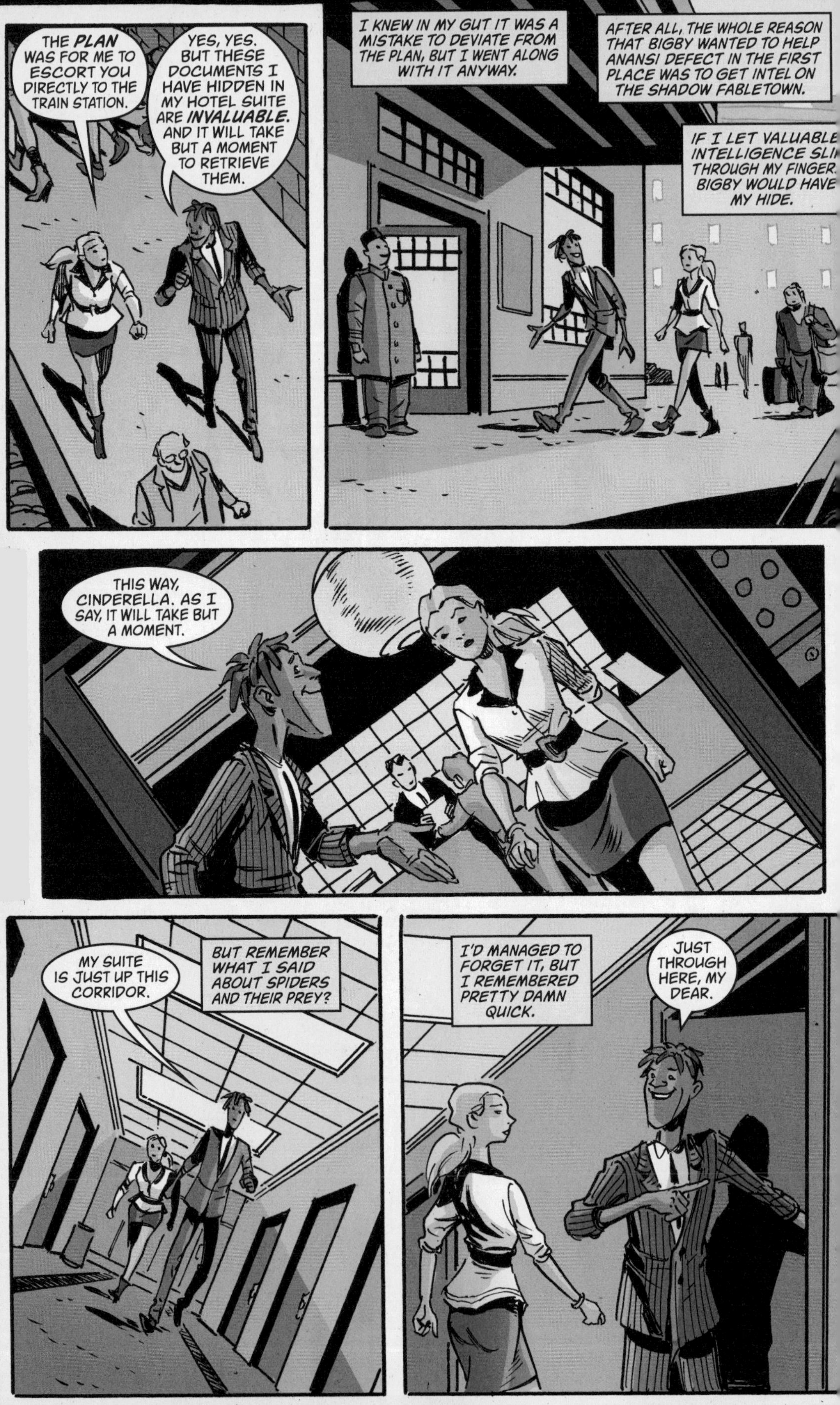
THE PLAN WAS FOR ME TO ESCORT YOU DIRECTLY TO THE TRAIN STATION.
YES, YES. BUT THESE DOCUMENTS I HAVE HIDDEN IN MY HOTEL SUITE ARE INVALUABLE. AND IT WILL TAKE BUT A MOMENT TO RETRIEVE THEM.
I KNEW IN MY GUT IT WAS A MISTAKE TO DEVIATE FROM THE PLAN, BUT I WENT ALONG WITH IT ANYWAY.
AFTER ALL, THE WHOLE REASON THAT BIGBY WANTED TO HELP ANANSI DEFECT IN THE FIRST PLACE WAS TO GET INTEL ON THE SHADOW FABLETOWN.
IF I LET VALUABLE INTELLIGENCE SLI THROUGH MY FINGER BIGBY WOULD HAVE MY HIDE.
THIS WAY, CINDERELLA. AS I SAY, IT WILL TAKE BUT A MOMENT.
MY SUITE IS JUST UP THIS CORRIDOR.
BUT REMEMBER WHAT I SAID ABOUT SPIDERS AND THEIR PREY?
I'D MANAGED TO FORGET IT, BUT I REMEMBERED PRETTY DAMN QUICK.
JUST THROUGH HERE, MY DEAR.

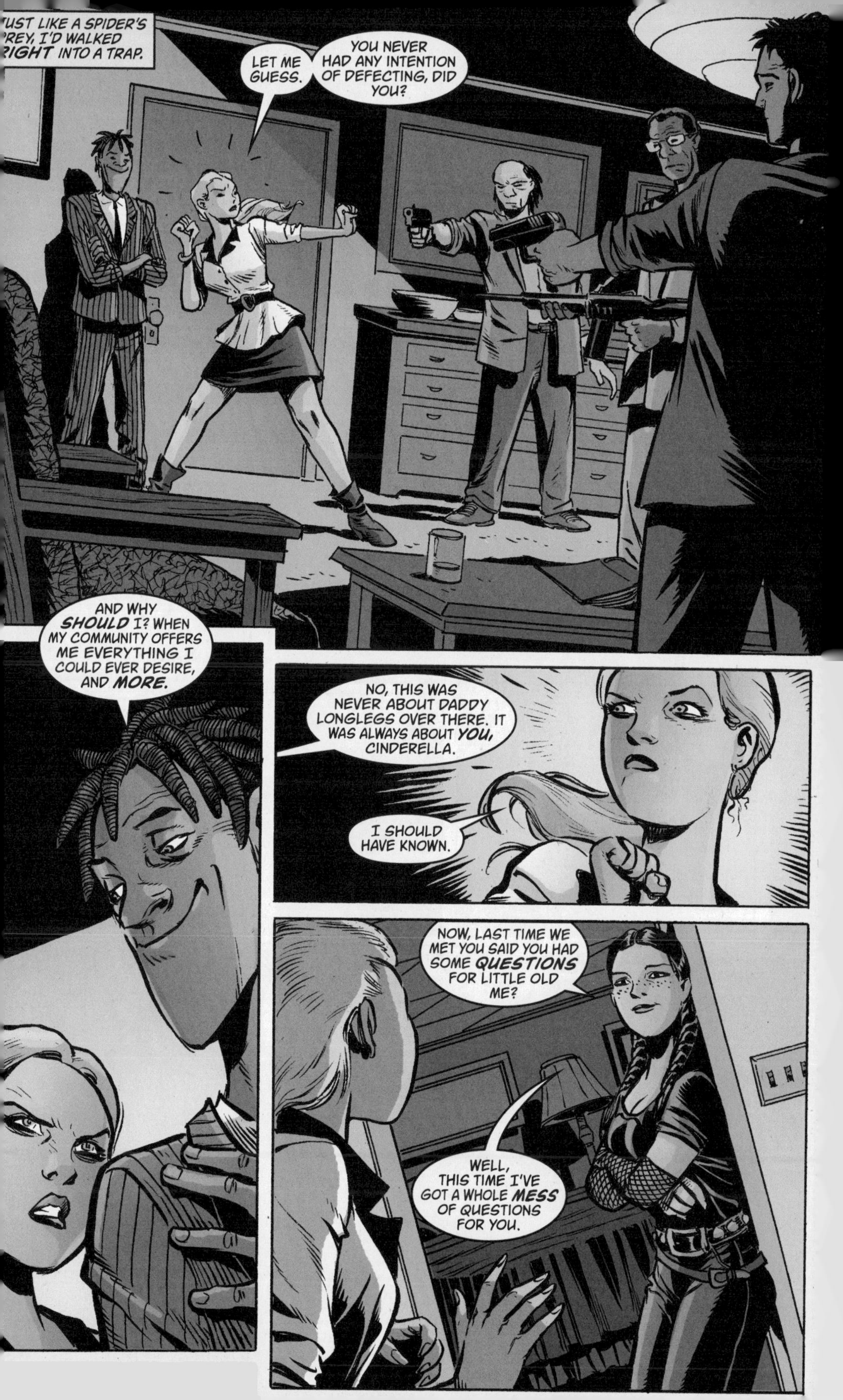

JUST LIKE A SPIDER'S PREY, I'D WALKED RIGHT INTO A TRAP.
LET ME GUESS.
YOU NEVER HAD ANY INTENTION OF DEFECTING, DID YOU?
AND WHY SHOULD I? WHEN MY COMMUNITY OFFERS ME EVERYTHING I COULD EVER DESIRE, AND MORE.
NO, THIS WAS NEVER ABOUT DADDY LONGLEGS OVER THERE. IT WAS ALWAYS ABOUT YOU, CINDERELLA.
I SHOULD HAVE KNOWN.
NOW, LAST TIME WE MET YOU SAID YOU HAD SOME QUESTIONS FOR LITTLE OLD ME?
WELL, THIS TIME I'VE GOT A WHOLE MESS OF QUESTIONS FOR YOU.

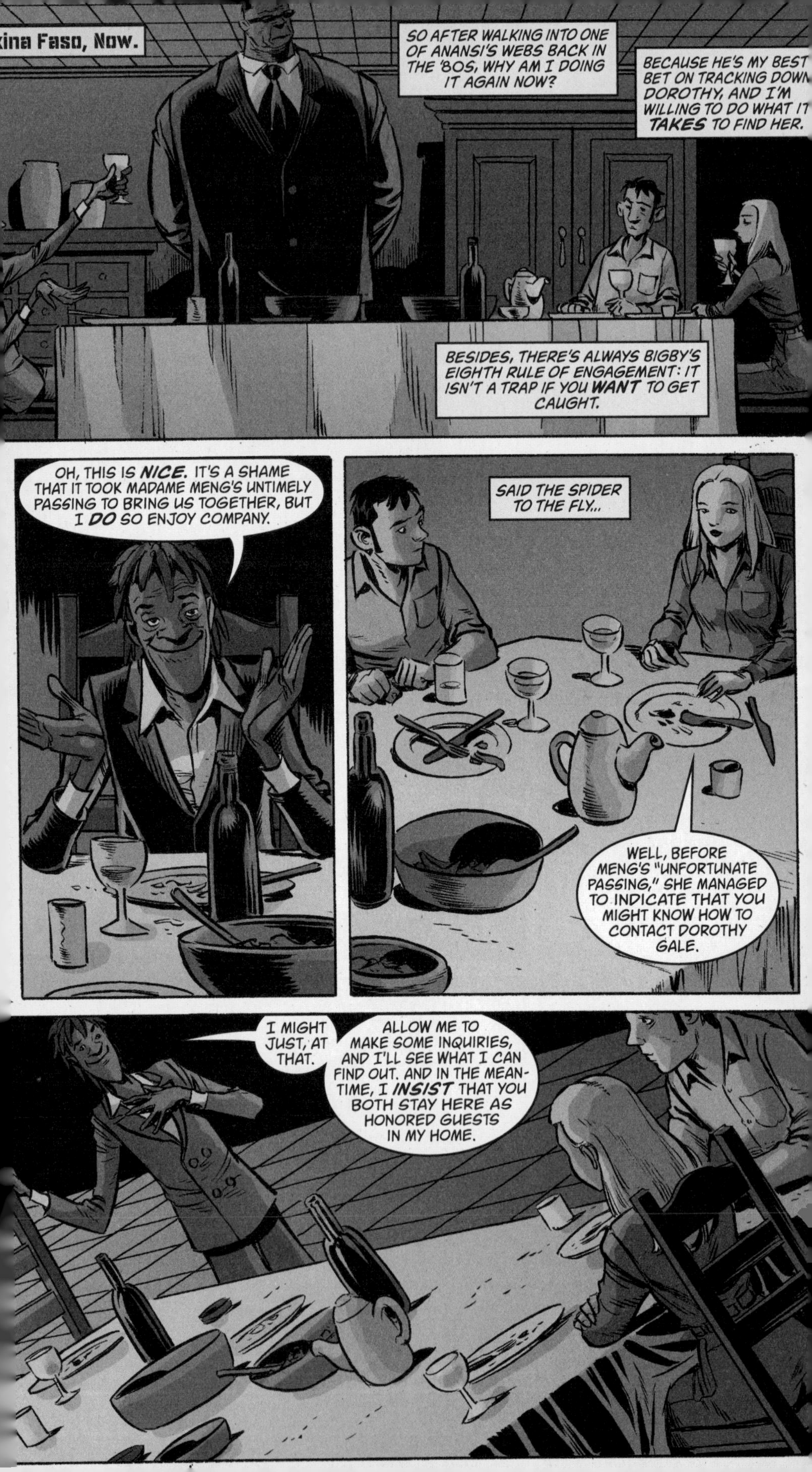
…kina Faso, Now.
SO AFTER WALKING INTO ONE OF ANANSI'S WEBS BACK IN THE '80S, WHY AM I DOING IT AGAIN NOW?
BECAUSE HE'S MY BEST BET ON TRACKING DOWN DOROTHY, AND I'M WILLING TO DO WHAT IT TAKES TO FIND HER.
BESIDES, THERE'S ALWAYS BIGBY'S EIGHTH RULE OF ENGAGEMENT: IT ISN'T A TRAP IF YOU WANT TO GET CAUGHT.
OH, THIS IS NICE. IT'S A SHAME THAT IT TOOK MADAME MENG'S UNTIMELY PASSING TO BRING US TOGETHER, BUT I DO SO ENJOY COMPANY.
SAID THE SPIDER TO THE FLY...
WELL, BEFORE MENG'S "UNFORTUNATE PASSING," SHE MANAGED TO INDICATE THAT YOU MIGHT KNOW HOW TO CONTACT DOROTHY GALE.
I MIGHT JUST, AT THAT.
ALLOW ME TO MAKE SOME INQUIRIES, AND I'LL SEE WHAT I CAN FIND OUT. AND IN THE MEANTIME, I INSIST THAT YOU BOTH STAY HERE AS HONORED GUESTS IN MY HOME.

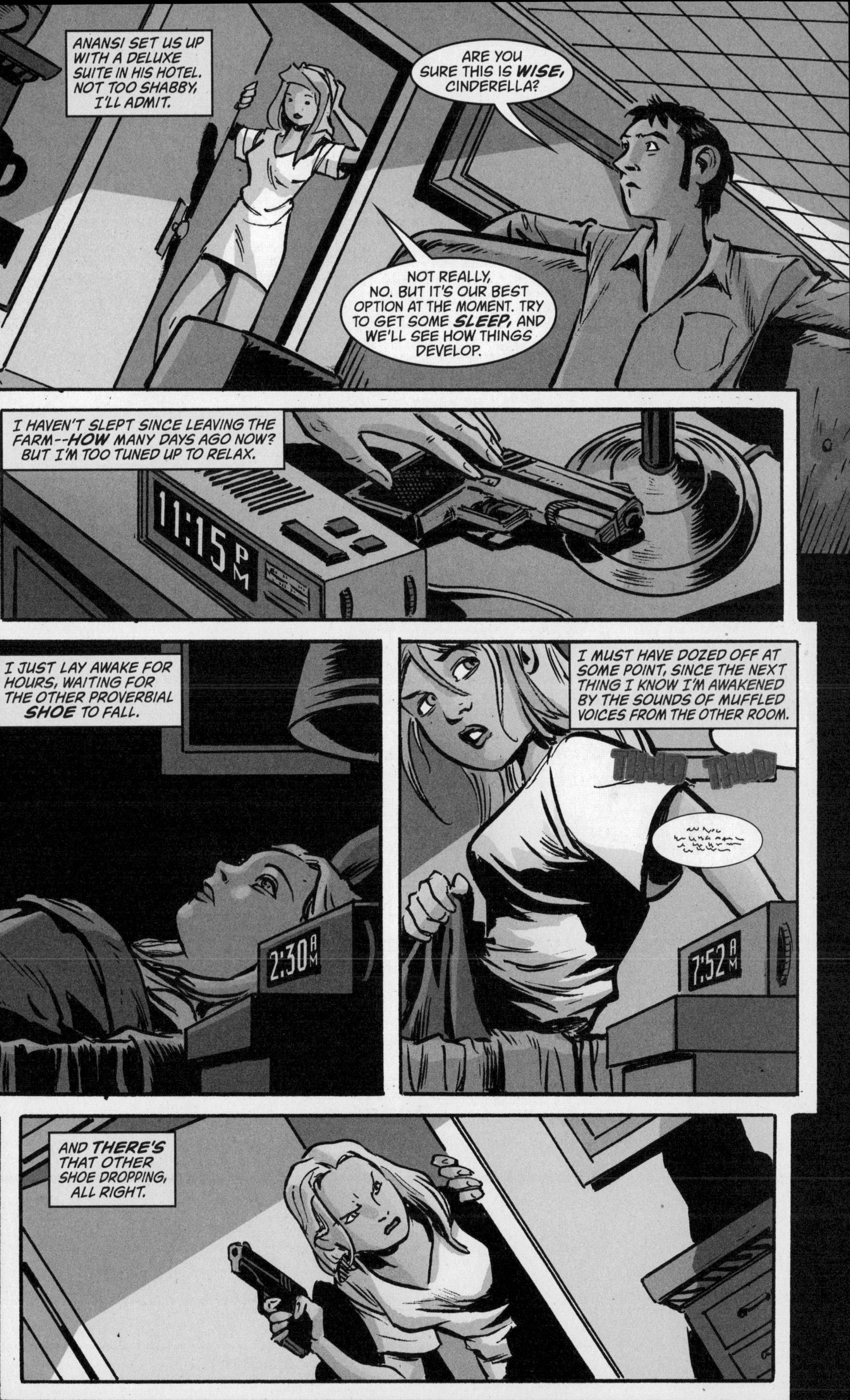
ANANSI SET US UP WITH A DELUXE SUITE IN HIS HOTEL. NOT TOO SHABBY, I'LL ADMIT.
ARE YOU SURE THIS IS WISE, CINDERELLA?
NOT REALLY, NO. BUT IT'S OUR BEST OPTION AT THE MOMENT. TRY TO GET SOME SLEEP, AND WE'LL SEE HOW THINGS DEVELOP.
I HAVEN'T SLEPT SINCE LEAVING THE FARM--HOW MANY DAYS AGO NOW? BUT I'M TOO TUNED UP TO RELAX.
11:15 PM
I JUST LAY AWAKE FOR HOURS, WAITING FOR THE OTHER PROVERBIAL SHOE TO FALL.
2:30 AM
I MUST HAVE DOZED OFF AT SOME POINT, SINCE THE NEXT THING I KNOW I'M AWAKENED BY THE SOUNDS OF MUFFLED VOICES FROM THE OTHER ROOM.
THUD THUD
7:52 AM
AND THERE'S THAT OTHER SHOE DROPPING, ALL RIGHT.

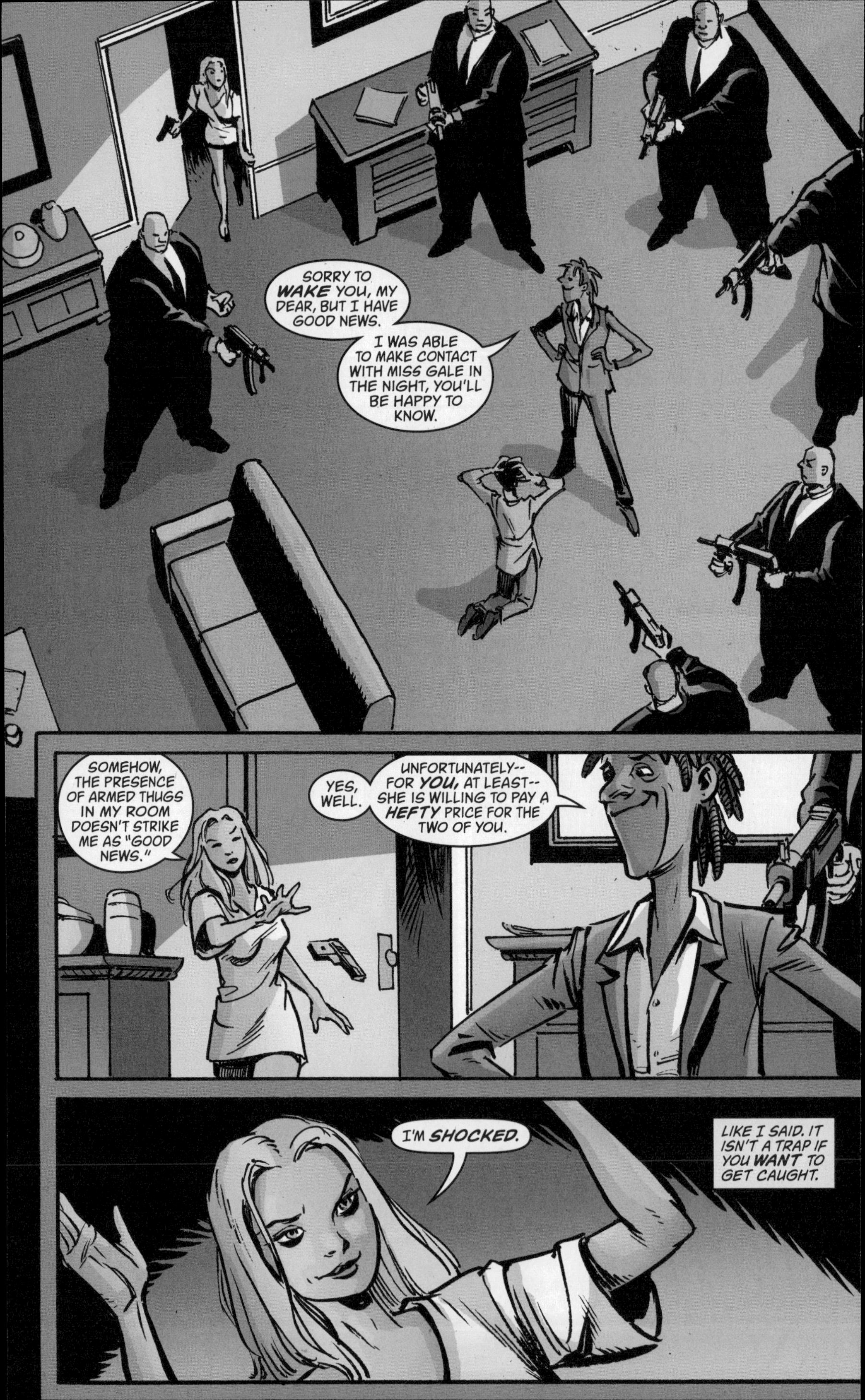
SORRY TO WAKE YOU, MY DEAR, BUT I HAVE GOOD NEWS.
I WAS ABLE TO MAKE CONTACT WITH MISS GALE IN THE NIGHT, YOU'LL BE HAPPY TO KNOW.
SOMEHOW, THE PRESENCE OF ARMED THUGS IN MY ROOM DOESN'T STRIKE ME AS "GOOD NEWS."
YES, WELL.
UNFORTUNATELY-- FOR YOU, AT LEAST-- SHE IS WILLING TO PAY A HEFTY PRICE FOR THE TWO OF YOU.
I'M SHOCKED.
LIKE I SAID. IT ISN'T A TRAP IF YOU WANT TO GET CAUGHT.

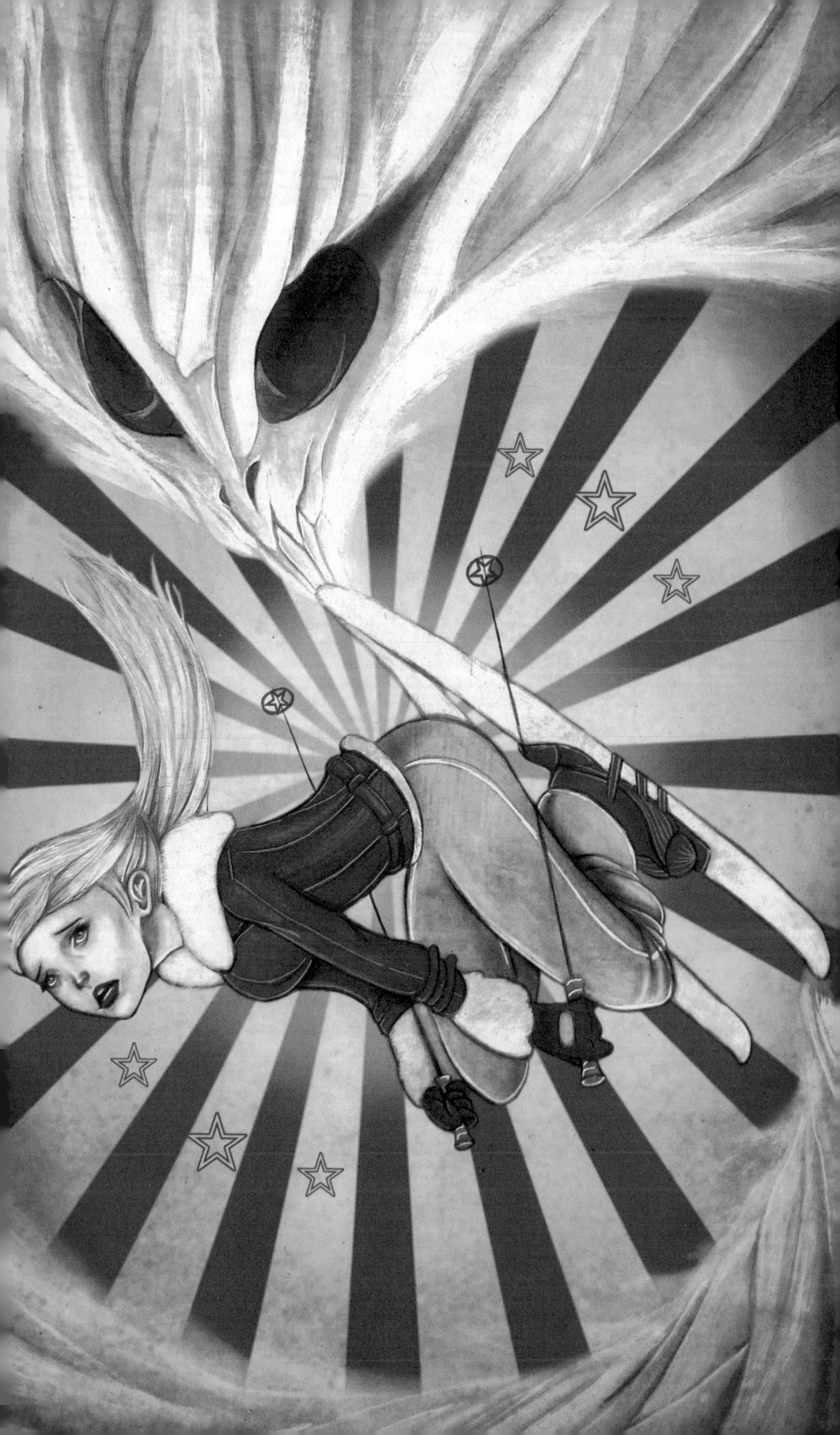

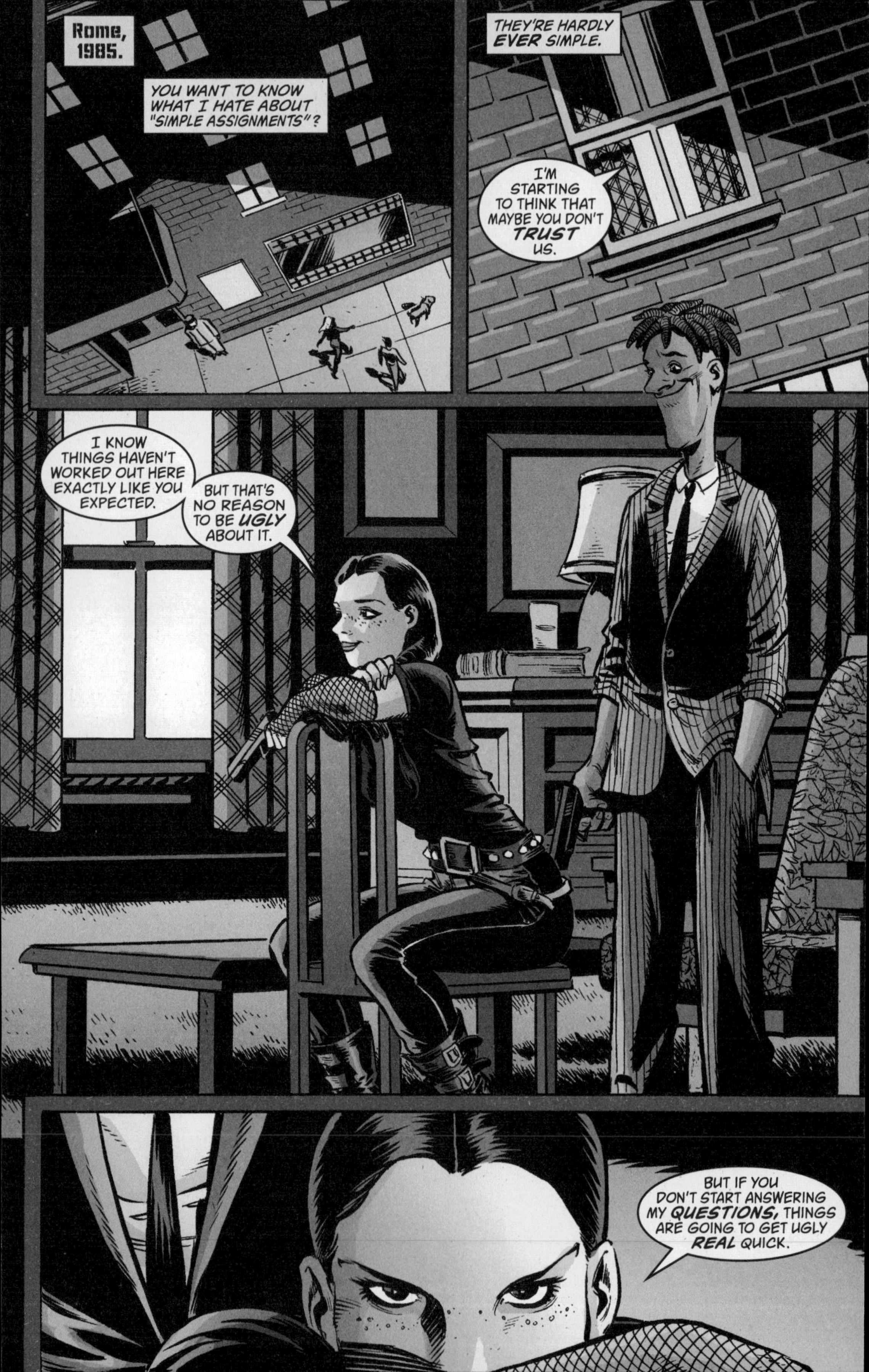
Rome, 1985.
YOU WANT TO KNOW WHAT I HATE ABOUT "SIMPLE ASSIGNMENTS"?
THEY'RE HARDLY EVER SIMPLE.
I'M STARTING TO THINK THAT MAYBE YOU DON'T TRUST US.
I KNOW THINGS HAVEN'T WORKED OUT HERE EXACTLY LIKE YOU EXPECTED.
BUT THAT'S NO REASON TO BE UGLY ABOUT IT.
BUT IF YOU DON'T START ANSWERING MY QUESTIONS, THINGS ARE GOING TO GET UGLY REAL QUICK.

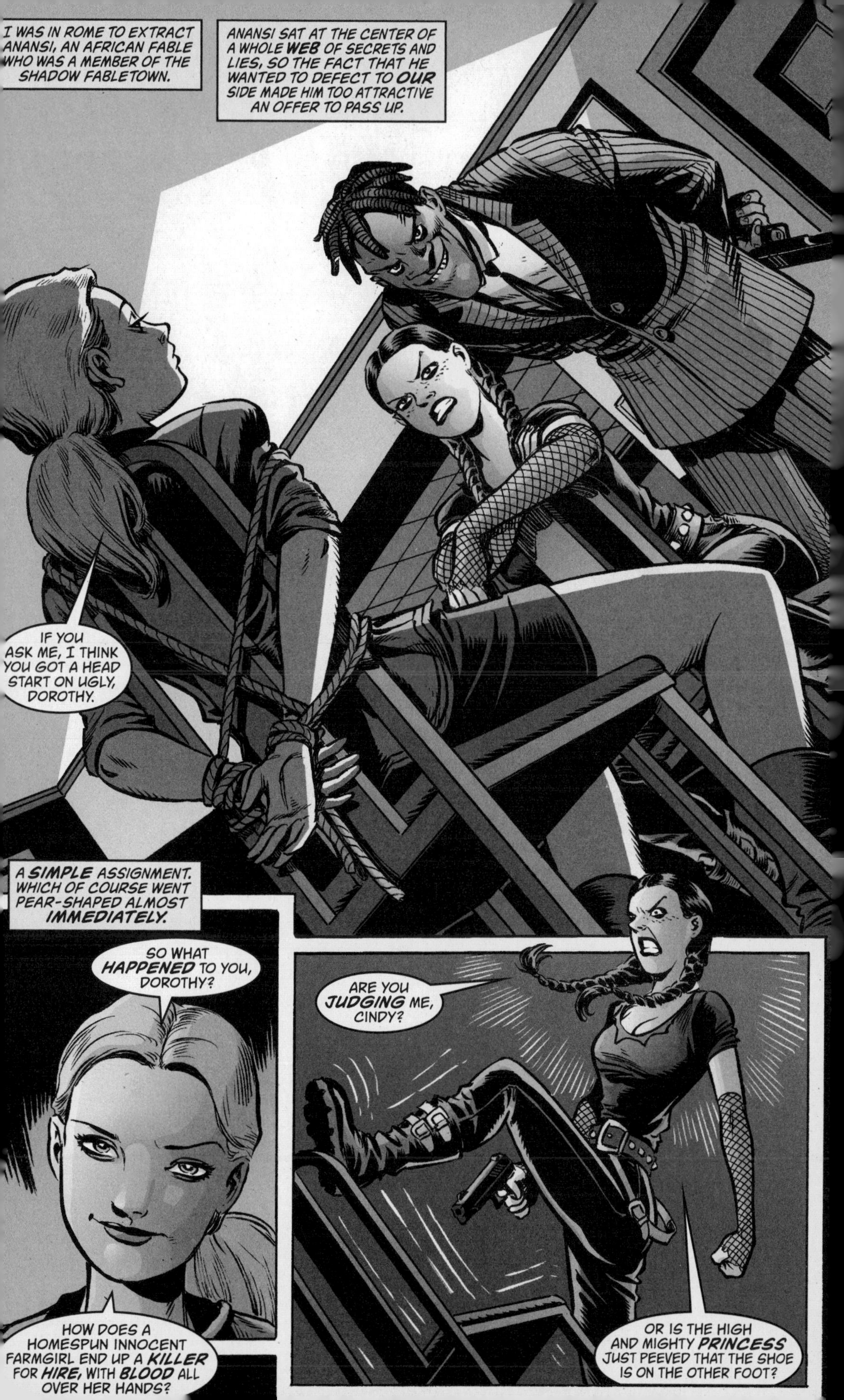
I WAS IN ROME TO EXTRACT ANANSI, AN AFRICAN FABLE WHO WAS A MEMBER OF THE SHADOW FABLETOWN.
ANANSI SAT AT THE CENTER OF A WHOLE WEB OF SECRETS AND LIES, SO THE FACT THAT HE WANTED TO DEFECT TO OUR SIDE MADE HIM TOO ATTRACTIVE AN OFFER TO PASS UP.
IF YOU ASK ME, I THINK YOU GOT A HEAD START ON UGLY, DOROTHY.
A SIMPLE ASSIGNMENT. WHICH OF COURSE WENT PEAR-SHAPED ALMOST IMMEDIATELY.
SO WHAT HAPPENED TO YOU, DOROTHY?
HOW DOES A HOMESPUN INNOCENT FARMGIRL END UP A KILLER FOR HIRE, WITH BLOOD ALL OVER HER HANDS?
ARE YOU JUDGING ME, CINDY?
OR IS THE HIGH AND MIGHTY PRINCESS JUST PEEVED THAT THE SHOE IS ON THE OTHER FOOT?

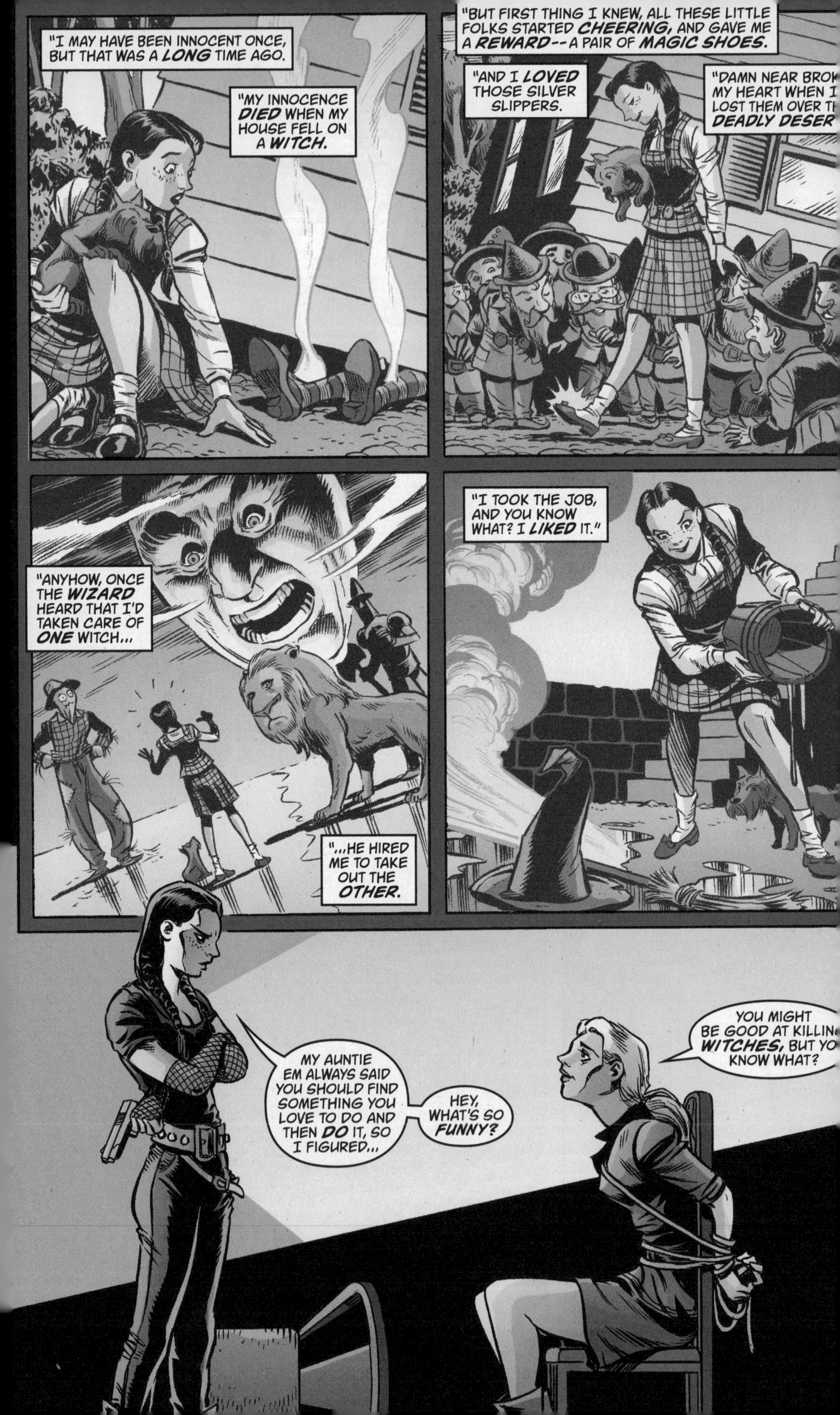

"I MAY HAVE BEEN INNOCENT ONCE, BUT THAT WAS A LONG TIME AGO.
"MY INNOCENCE DIED WHEN MY HOUSE FELL ON A WITCH.
"BUT FIRST THING I KNEW, ALL THESE LITTLE FOLKS STARTED CHEERING, AND GAVE ME A REWARD--A PAIR OF MAGIC SHOES.
"AND I LOVED THOSE SILVER SLIPPERS.
"DAMN NEAR BROK MY HEART WHEN I LOST THEM OVER T DEADLY DESER
"ANYHOW, ONCE THE WIZARD HEARD THAT I'D TAKEN CARE OF ONE WITCH...
"...HE HIRED ME TO TAKE OUT THE OTHER.
"I TOOK THE JOB, AND YOU KNOW WHAT? I LIKED IT."
MY AUNTIE EM ALWAYS SAID YOU SHOULD FIND SOMETHING YOU LOVE TO DO AND THEN DO IT, SO I FIGURED...
HEY, WHAT'S SO FUNNY?
YOU MIGHT BE GOOD AT KILLIN WITCHES, BUT YO KNOW WHAT?

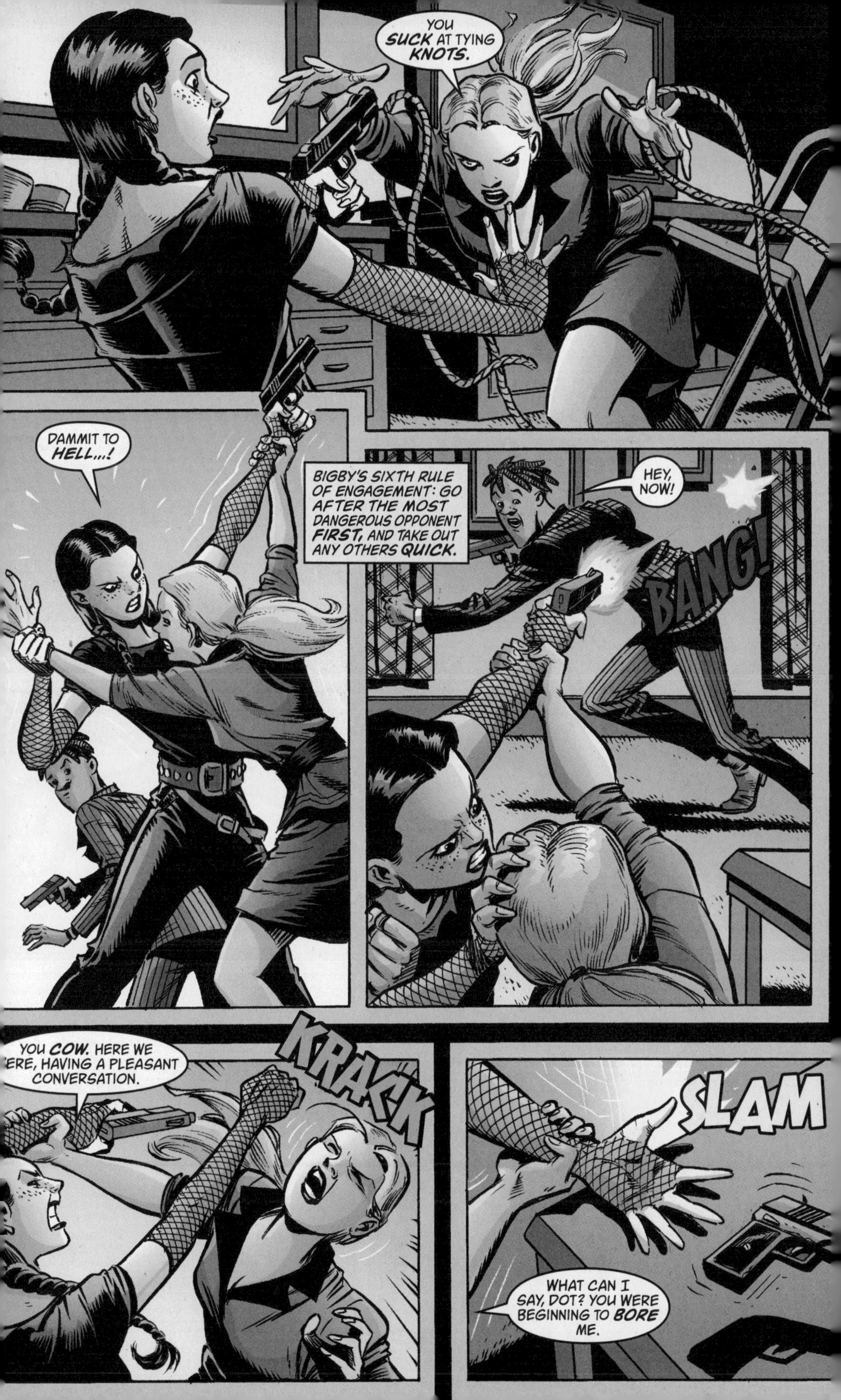

YOU SUCK AT TYING KNOTS.
DAMMIT TO HELL...!
BIGBY'S SIXTH RULE OF ENGAGEMENT: GO AFTER THE MOST DANGEROUS OPPONENT FIRST, AND TAKE OUT ANY OTHERS QUICK.
HEY, NOW!
BANG!
YOU COW. HERE WE ERE, HAVING A PLEASANT CONVERSATION.
KRACK
SLAM
WHAT CAN I SAY, DOT? YOU WERE BEGINNING TO BORE ME.

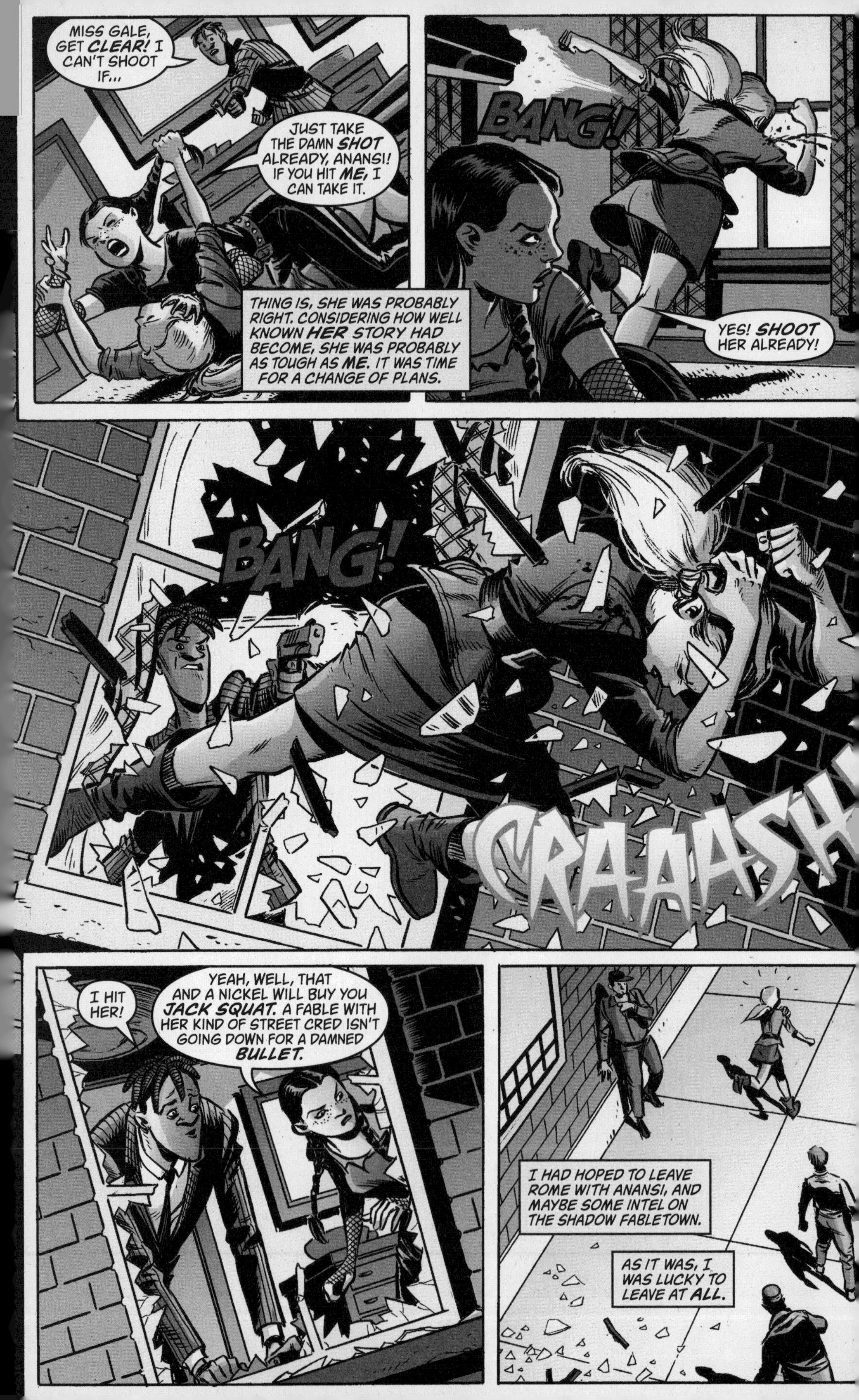
MISS GALE, GET CLEAR! I CAN'T SHOOT IF...
JUST TAKE THE DAMN SHOT ALREADY, ANANSI! IF YOU HIT ME, I CAN TAKE IT.
THING IS, SHE WAS PROBABLY RIGHT. CONSIDERING HOW WELL KNOWN HER STORY HAD BECOME, SHE WAS PROBABLY AS TOUGH AS ME. IT WAS TIME FOR A CHANGE OF PLANS.
BANG!
YES! SHOOT HER ALREADY!
BANG!
CRAAASH
I HIT HER!
YEAH, WELL, THAT AND A NICKEL WILL BUY YOU JACK SQUAT. A FABLE WITH HER KIND OF STREET CRED ISN'T GOING DOWN FOR A DAMNED BULLET.
I HAD HOPED TO LEAVE ROME WITH ANANSI, AND MAYBE SOME INTEL ON THE SHADOW FABLETOWN.
AS IT WAS, I WAS LUCKY TO LEAVE AT ALL.

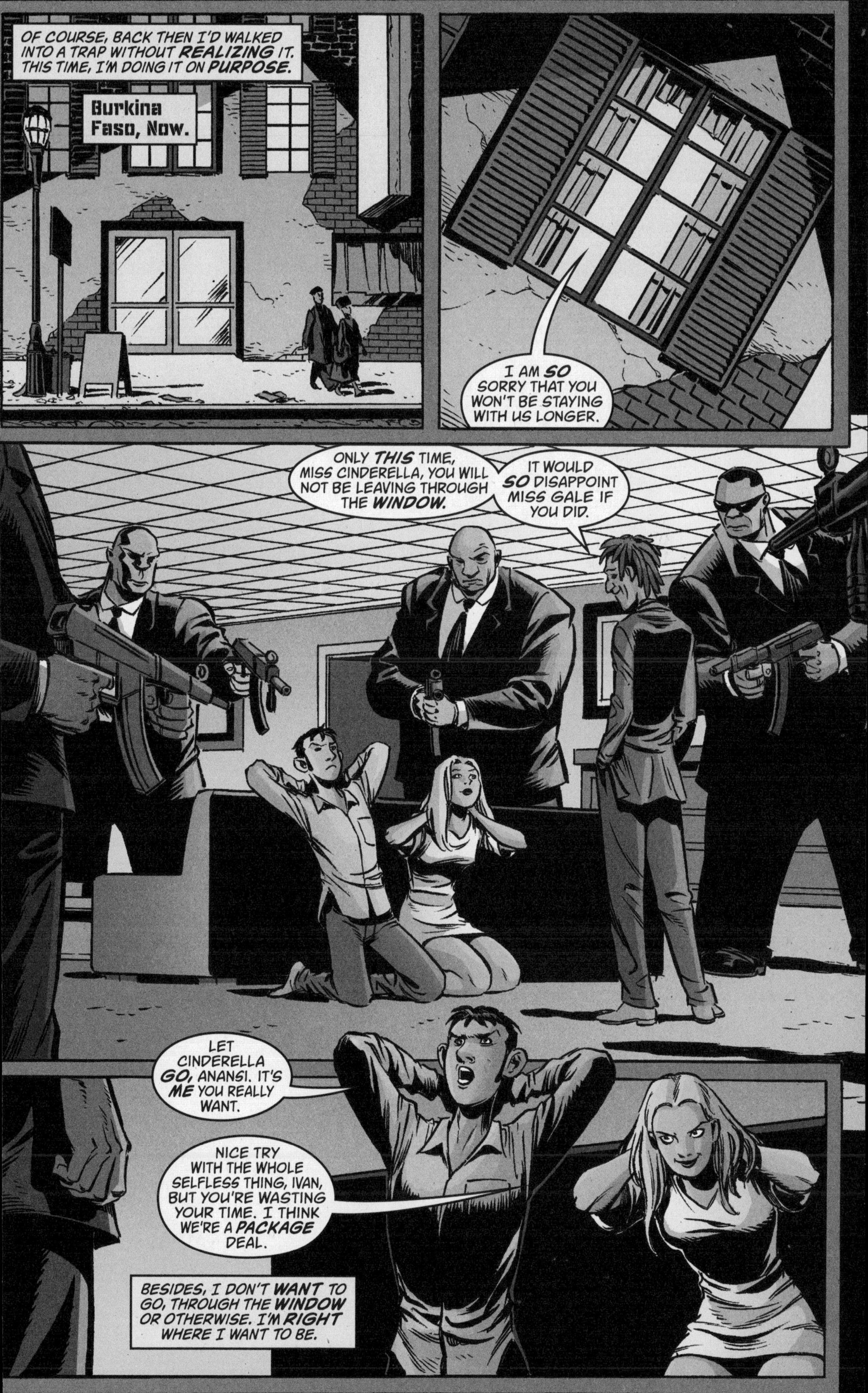
OF COURSE, BACK THEN I'D WALKED INTO A TRAP WITHOUT REALIZING IT. THIS TIME, I'M DOING IT ON PURPOSE.
Burkina Faso, Now.
I AM SO SORRY THAT YOU WON'T BE STAYING WITH US LONGER.
ONLY THIS TIME, MISS CINDERELLA, YOU WILL NOT BE LEAVING THROUGH THE WINDOW.
IT WOULD SO DISAPPOINT MISS GALE IF YOU DID.
LET CINDERELLA GO, ANANSI. IT'S ME YOU REALLY WANT.
NICE TRY WITH THE WHOLE SELFLESS THING, IVAN, BUT YOU'RE WASTING YOUR TIME. I THINK WE'RE A PACKAGE DEAL.
BESIDES, I DON'T WANT TO GO, THROUGH THE WINDOW OR OTHERWISE. I'M RIGHT WHERE I WANT TO BE.

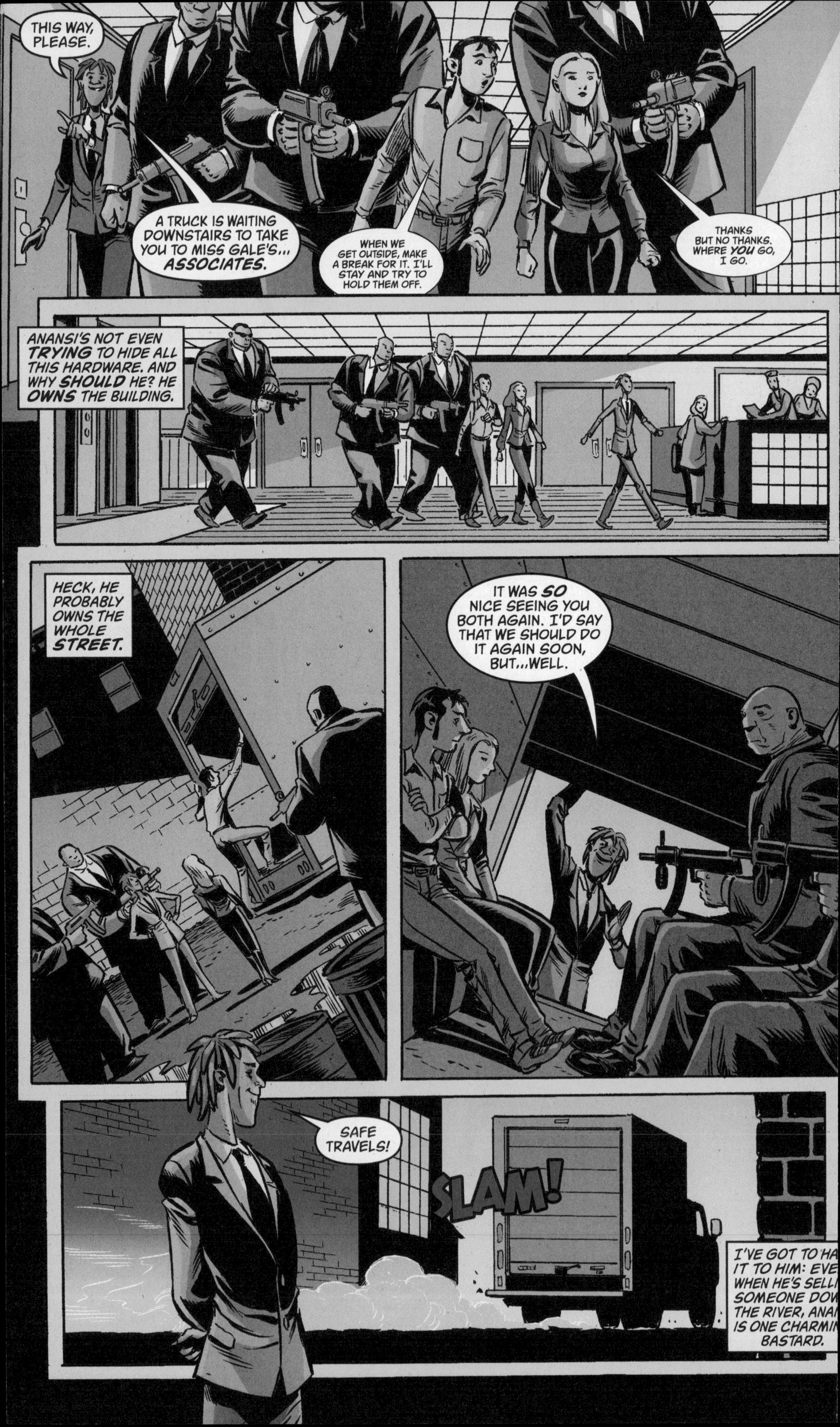
THIS WAY, PLEASE.
A TRUCK IS WAITING DOWNSTAIRS TO TAKE YOU TO MISS GALE'S... ASSOCIATES.
WHEN WE GET OUTSIDE, MAKE A BREAK FOR IT. I'LL STAY AND TRY TO HOLD THEM OFF.
THANKS BUT NO THANKS. WHERE YOU GO, I GO.
ANANSI'S NOT EVEN TRYING TO HIDE ALL THIS HARDWARE. AND WHY SHOULD HE? HE OWNS THE BUILDING.
HECK, HE PROBABLY OWNS THE WHOLE STREET.
IT WAS SO NICE SEEING YOU BOTH AGAIN. I'D SAY THAT WE SHOULD DO IT AGAIN SOON, BUT...WELL.
SAFE TRAVELS!
SLAM!
I'VE GOT TO HA
IT TO HIM: EVE
WHEN HE'S SELL
SOMEONE DOW
THE RIVER, ANA
IS ONE CHARMI
BASTARD.

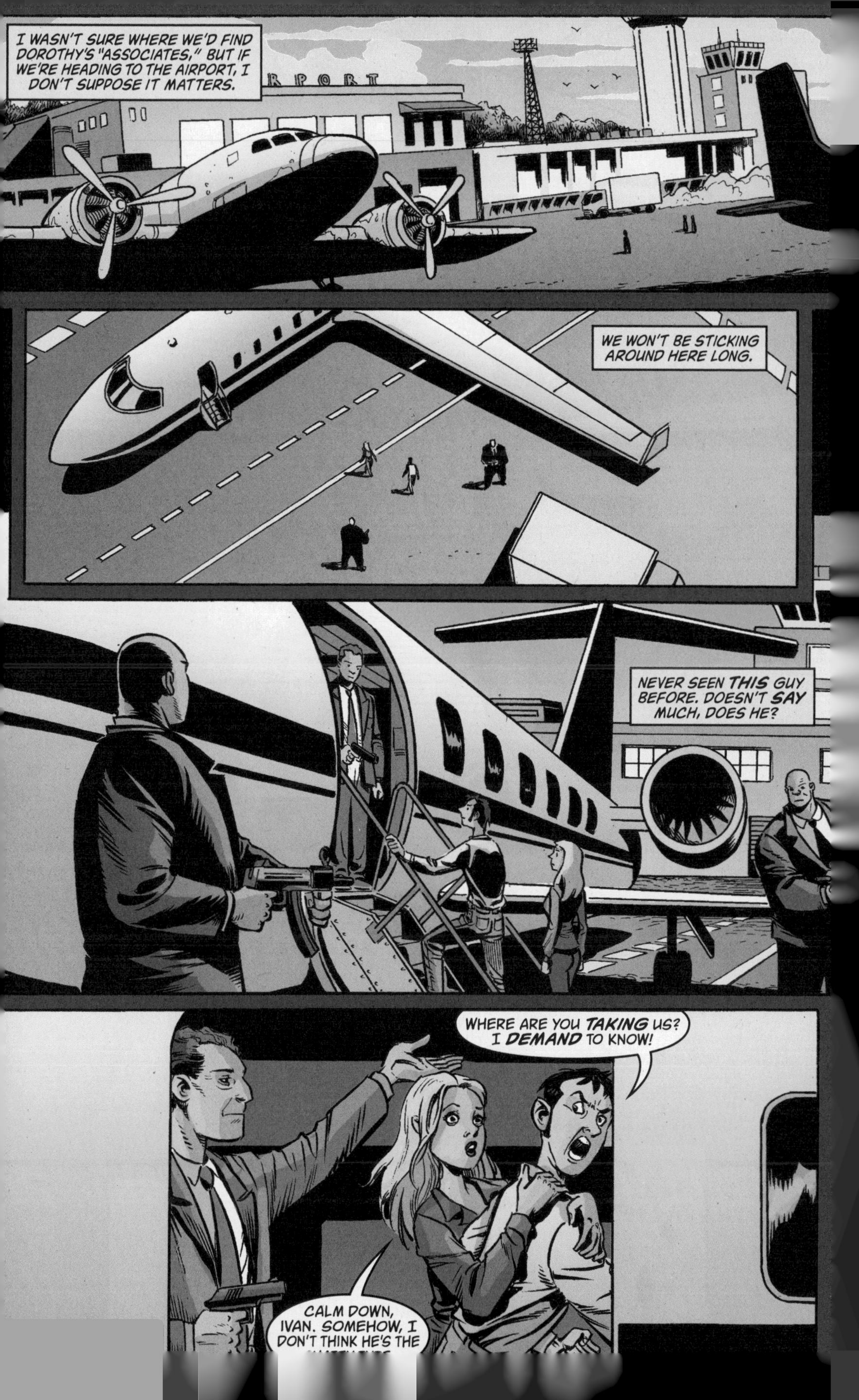
I WASN'T SURE WHERE WE'D FIND DOROTHY'S "ASSOCIATES," BUT IF WE'RE HEADING TO THE AIRPORT, I DON'T SUPPOSE IT MATTERS.
WE WON'T BE STICKING AROUND HERE LONG.
NEVER SEEN THIS GUY BEFORE. DOESN'T SAY MUCH, DOES HE?
WHERE ARE YOU TAKING US? I DEMAND TO KNOW!
CALM DOWN, IVAN. SOMEHOW, I DON'T THINK HE'S THE

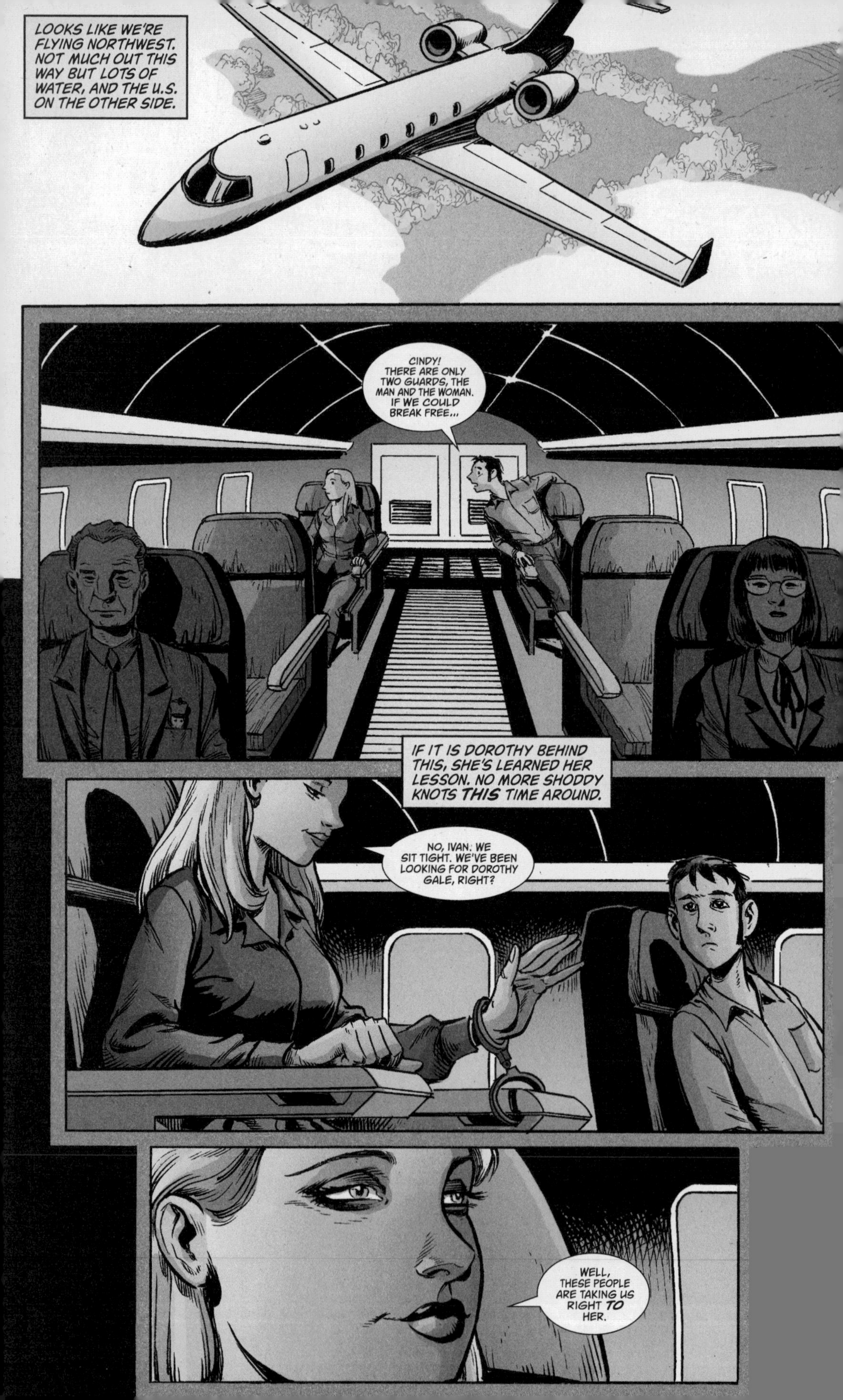
LOOKS LIKE WE'RE FLYING NORTHWEST. NOT MUCH OUT THIS WAY BUT LOTS OF WATER, AND THE U.S. ON THE OTHER SIDE.
CINDY! THERE ARE ONLY TWO GUARDS, THE MAN AND THE WOMAN. IF WE COULD BREAK FREE...
IF IT IS DOROTHY BEHIND THIS, SHE'S LEARNED HER LESSON. NO MORE SHODDY KNOTS *THIS* TIME AROUND.
NO, IVAN. WE SIT TIGHT. WE'VE BEEN LOOKING FOR DOROTHY GALE, RIGHT?
WELL, THESE PEOPLE ARE TAKING US RIGHT *TO* HER.

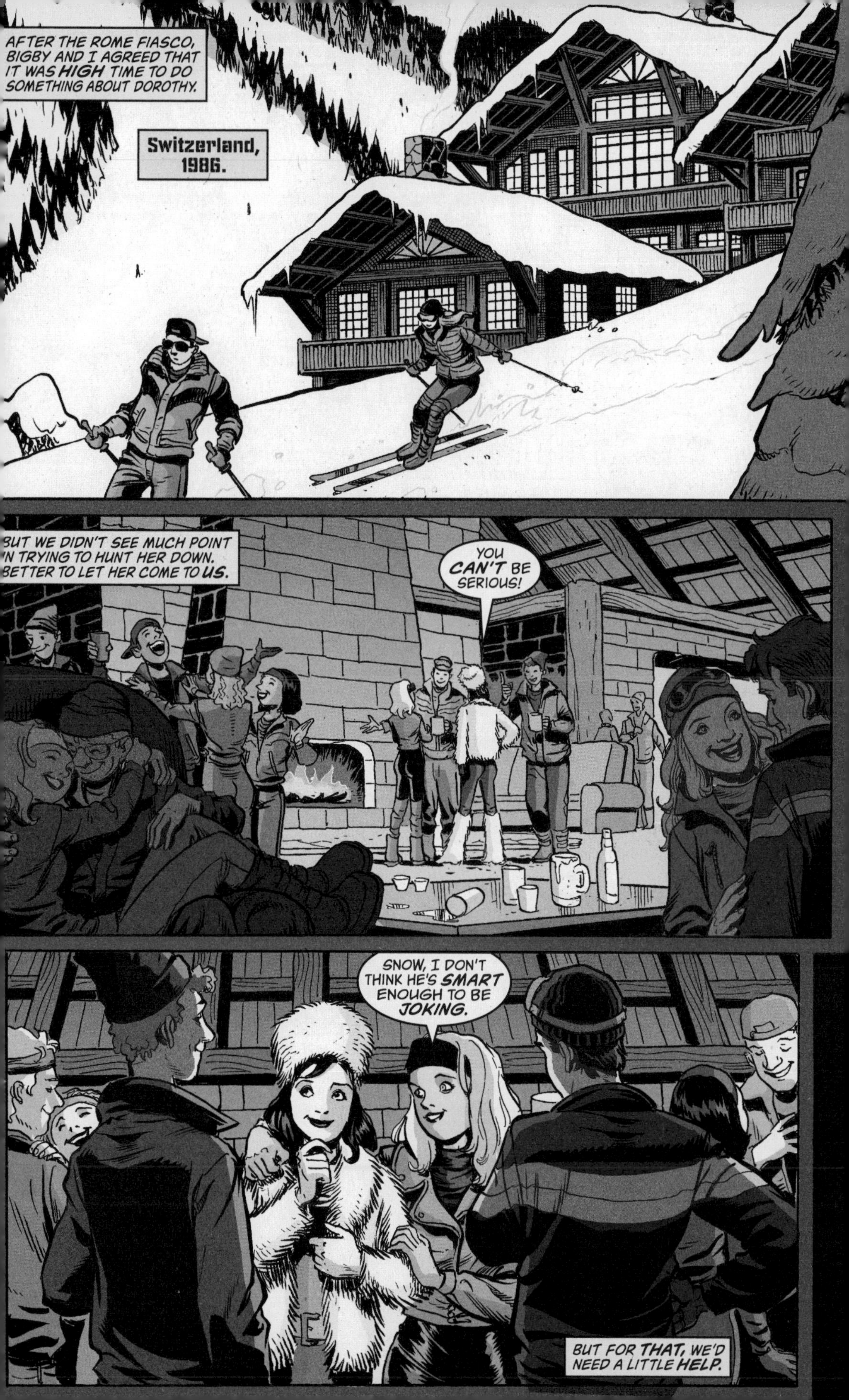
AFTER THE ROME FIASCO, BIGBY AND I AGREED THAT IT WAS HIGH TIME TO DO SOMETHING ABOUT DOROTHY.
Switzerland, 1986.
BUT WE DIDN'T SEE MUCH POINT IN TRYING TO HUNT HER DOWN. BETTER TO LET HER COME TO US.
YOU CAN'T BE SERIOUS!
SNOW, I DON'T THINK HE'S SMART ENOUGH TO BE JOKING.
BUT FOR THAT, WE'D NEED A LITTLE HELP.

BIGBY HAD CONVINCED SNOW WHITE THAT SHE NEEDED A BREAK FROM HER DUTIES AS DEPUTY MAYOR, SINCE SHE HADN'T HAD A VACATION IN *DECADES*.

...HOW COULD SNOW REFUSE?

RUM GIMLET FOR ME.

I'LL HAVE A WHITE WINE SPRITZER.

WHEN HE GOT KING COLE TO *PAY* FOR THE TRIP OUT OF FABLETOWN FUNDS...

YOU KNOW, CINDY, I *STILL* CAN'T FIGURE OUT HOW YOU JUST *HAPPENED* TO BE STAYING IN THE SAME CHALET AS ME.

OH, IT WASN'T AN *ACCIDENT*, SNOW. WHEN I HEARD ABOUT YOUR VACATION I GOT *SO* JEALOUS I COULDN'T STAND IT. SO HERE I AM.

BESIDES, IT'S NOT LIKE CRISPIN CAN'T RUN THE SHOE STORE WHILE I'M AWAY. AND *GAH*, THAT PLACE CAN BE *SO* BORING.

MMM. WELL, I'LL SAY *THIS* FOR YOU, CINDY, YOU'RE *NOTHING* IF NOT CONSISTENT.

LIKE ALMOST EVERY ONE ELSE IN FABLETO SNOW HAD NO IDEA I ANYTHING OTHER T WHAT I SEEMED-- BUBBLEHEADED GADABOUT.

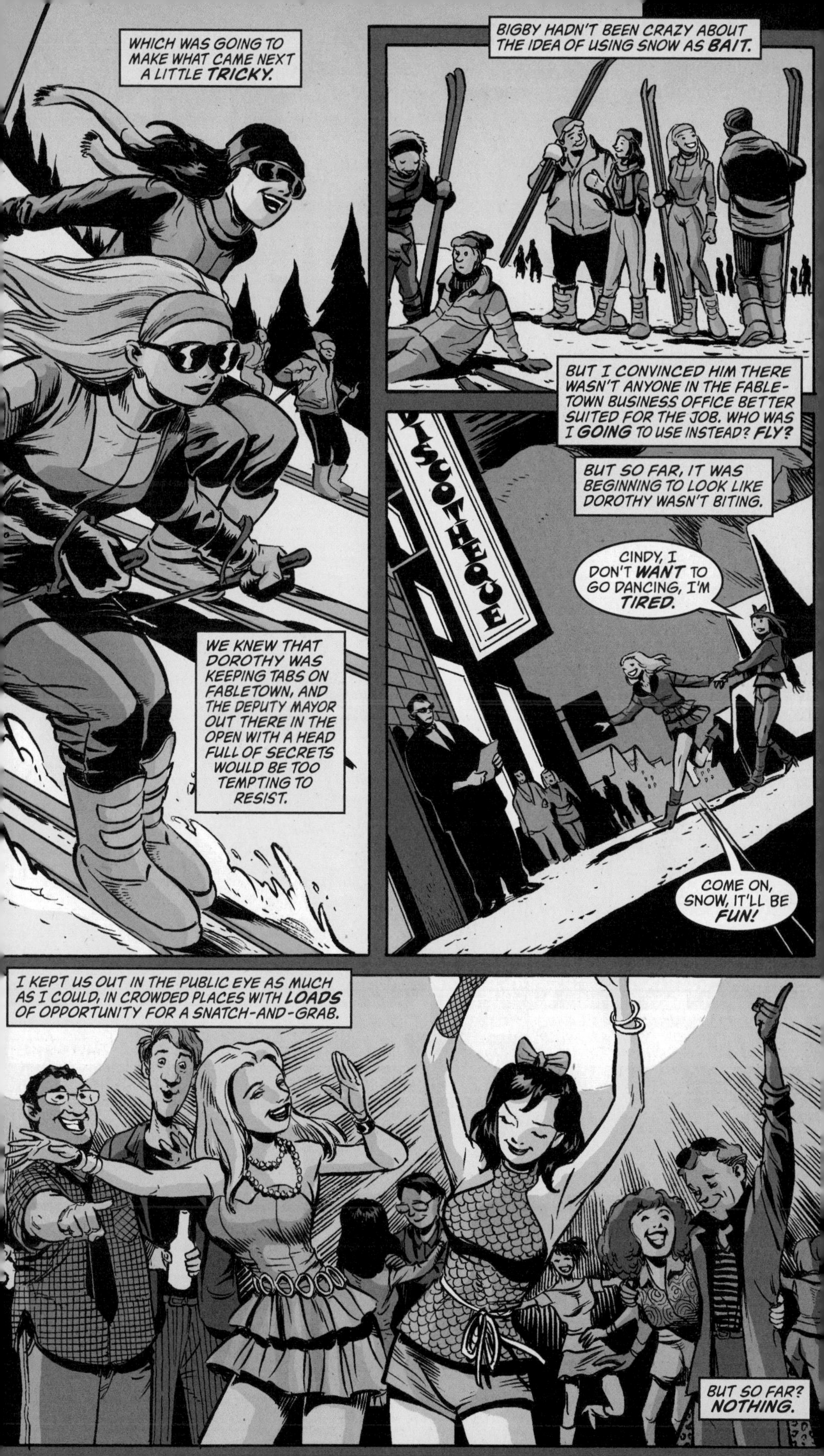
WHICH WAS GOING TO MAKE WHAT CAME NEXT A LITTLE TRICKY.
WE KNEW THAT DOROTHY WAS KEEPING TABS ON FABLETOWN, AND THE DEPUTY MAYOR OUT THERE IN THE OPEN WITH A HEAD FULL OF SECRETS WOULD BE TOO TEMPTING TO RESIST.
BIGBY HADN'T BEEN CRAZY ABOUT THE IDEA OF USING SNOW AS BAIT.
BUT I CONVINCED HIM THERE WASN'T ANYONE IN THE FABLE-TOWN BUSINESS OFFICE BETTER SUITED FOR THE JOB. WHO WAS I GOING TO USE INSTEAD? FLY?
BUT SO FAR, IT WAS BEGINNING TO LOOK LIKE DOROTHY WASN'T BITING.
DISCOTHEQUE
CINDY, I DON'T WANT TO GO DANCING, I'M TIRED.
COME ON, SNOW, IT'LL BE FUN!
I KEPT US OUT IN THE PUBLIC EYE AS MUCH AS I COULD, IN CROWDED PLACES WITH LOADS OF OPPORTUNITY FOR A SNATCH-AND-GRAB.
BUT SO FAR? NOTHING.

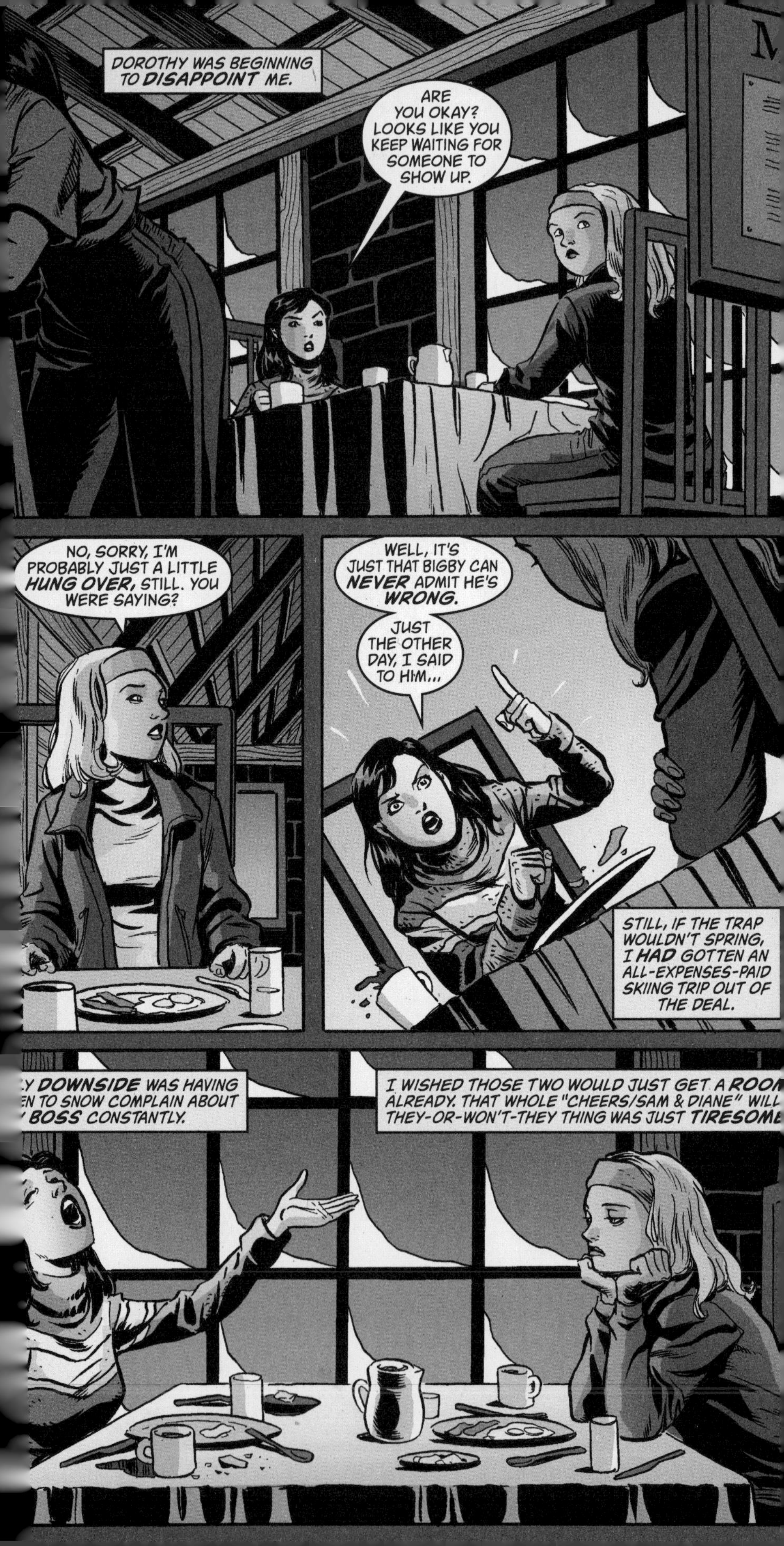

DOROTHY WAS BEGINNING TO **DISAPPOINT** ME.
ARE YOU OKAY? LOOKS LIKE YOU KEEP WAITING FOR SOMEONE TO SHOW UP.
NO, SORRY, I'M PROBABLY JUST A LITTLE **HUNG OVER,** STILL. YOU WERE SAYING?
WELL, IT'S JUST THAT BIGBY CAN **NEVER** ADMIT HE'S **WRONG.**
JUST THE OTHER DAY, I SAID TO HIM...
STILL, IF THE TRAP WOULDN'T SPRING, I **HAD** GOTTEN AN ALL-EXPENSES-PAID SKIING TRIP OUT OF THE DEAL.
Y **DOWNSIDE** WAS HAVING EN TO SNOW COMPLAIN ABOUT Y **BOSS** CONSTANTLY.
I WISHED THOSE TWO WOULD JUST GET A **ROOM** ALREADY. THAT WHOLE "CHEERS/SAM & DIANE" WILL THEY-OR-WON'T-THEY THING WAS JUST **TIRESOME**

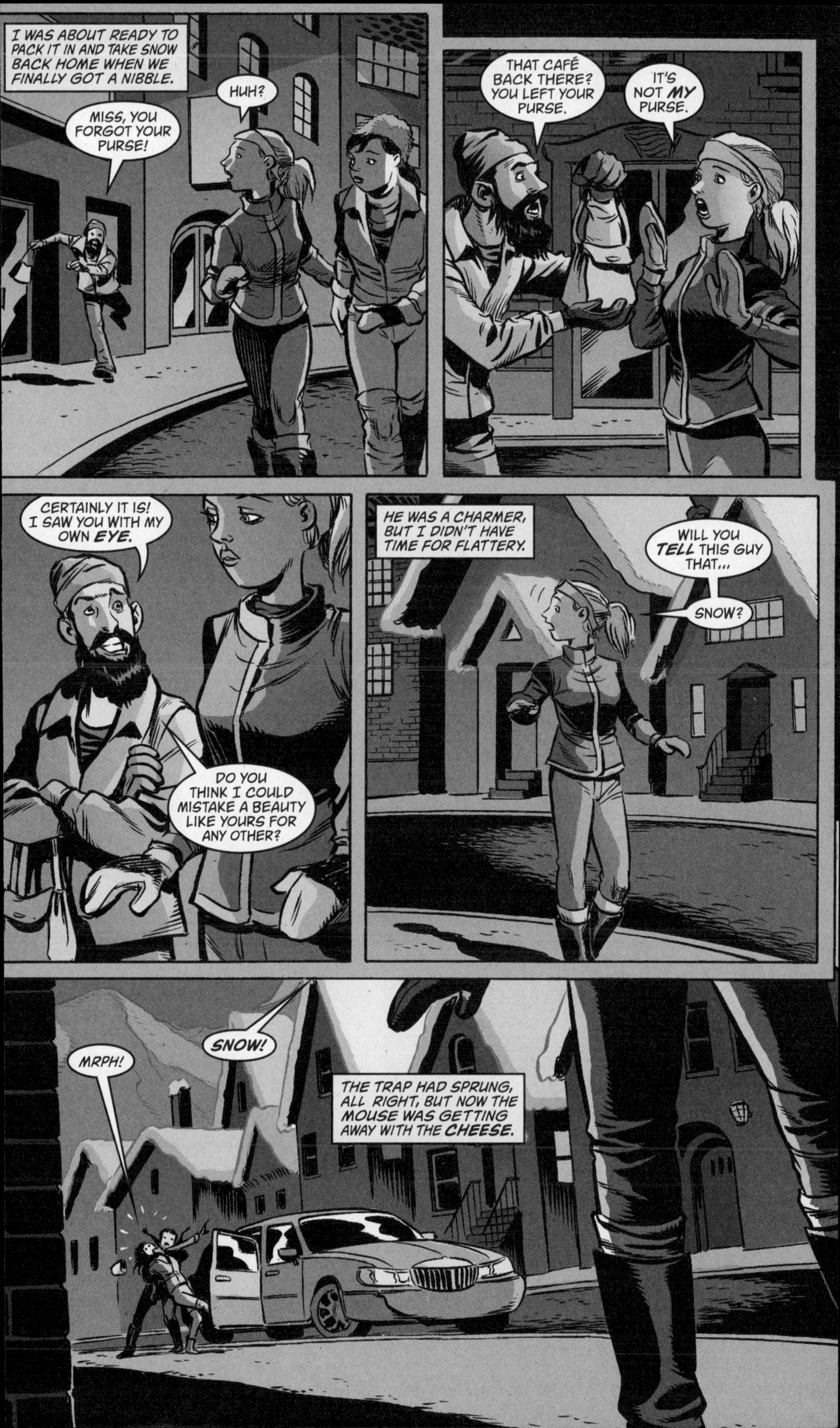
I WAS ABOUT READY TO PACK IT IN AND TAKE SNOW BACK HOME WHEN WE FINALLY GOT A NIBBLE.
MISS, YOU FORGOT YOUR PURSE!
HUH?
THAT CAFÉ BACK THERE? YOU LEFT YOUR PURSE.
IT'S NOT MY PURSE.
CERTAINLY IT IS! I SAW YOU WITH MY OWN EYE.
DO YOU THINK I COULD MISTAKE A BEAUTY LIKE YOURS FOR ANY OTHER?
HE WAS A CHARMER, BUT I DIDN'T HAVE TIME FOR FLATTERY.
WILL YOU TELL THIS GUY THAT...
SNOW?
SNOW!
MRPH!
THE TRAP HAD SPRUNG, ALL RIGHT, BUT NOW THE MOUSE WAS GETTING AWAY WITH THE CHEESE.

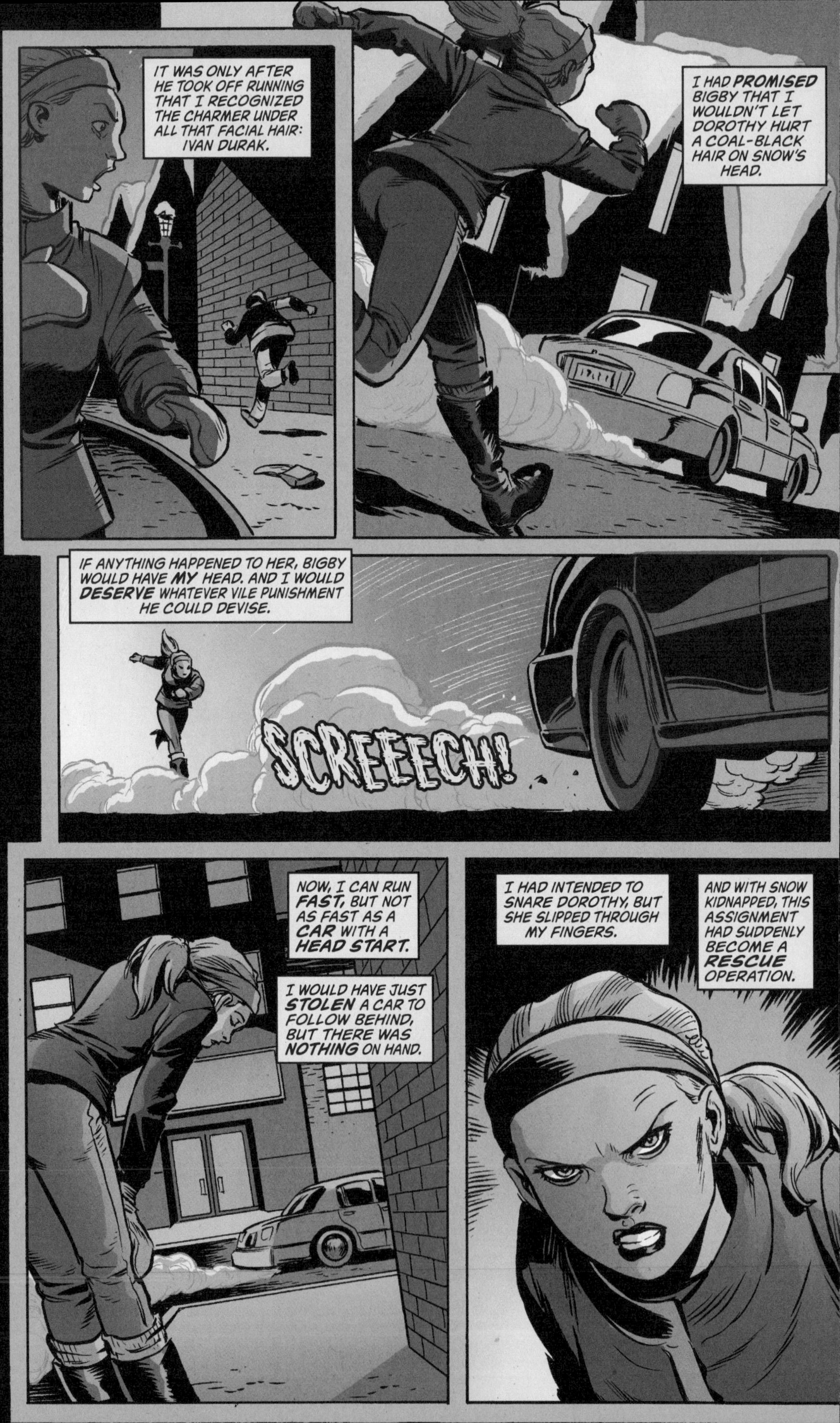

IT WAS ONLY AFTER HE TOOK OFF RUNNING THAT I RECOGNIZED THE CHARMER UNDER ALL THAT FACIAL HAIR: IVAN DURAK.
I HAD PROMISED BIGBY THAT I WOULDN'T LET DOROTHY HURT A COAL-BLACK HAIR ON SNOW'S HEAD.
IF ANYTHING HAPPENED TO HER, BIGBY WOULD HAVE MY HEAD. AND I WOULD DESERVE WHATEVER VILE PUNISHMENT HE COULD DEVISE.
SCREEECH!
NOW, I CAN RUN FAST, BUT NOT AS FAST AS A CAR WITH A HEAD START.
I WOULD HAVE JUST STOLEN A CAR TO FOLLOW BEHIND, BUT THERE WAS NOTHING ON HAND.
I HAD INTENDED TO SNARE DOROTHY, BUT SHE SLIPPED THROUGH MY FINGERS.
AND WITH SNOW KIDNAPPED, THIS ASSIGNMENT HAD SUDDENLY BECOME A RESCUE OPERATION.

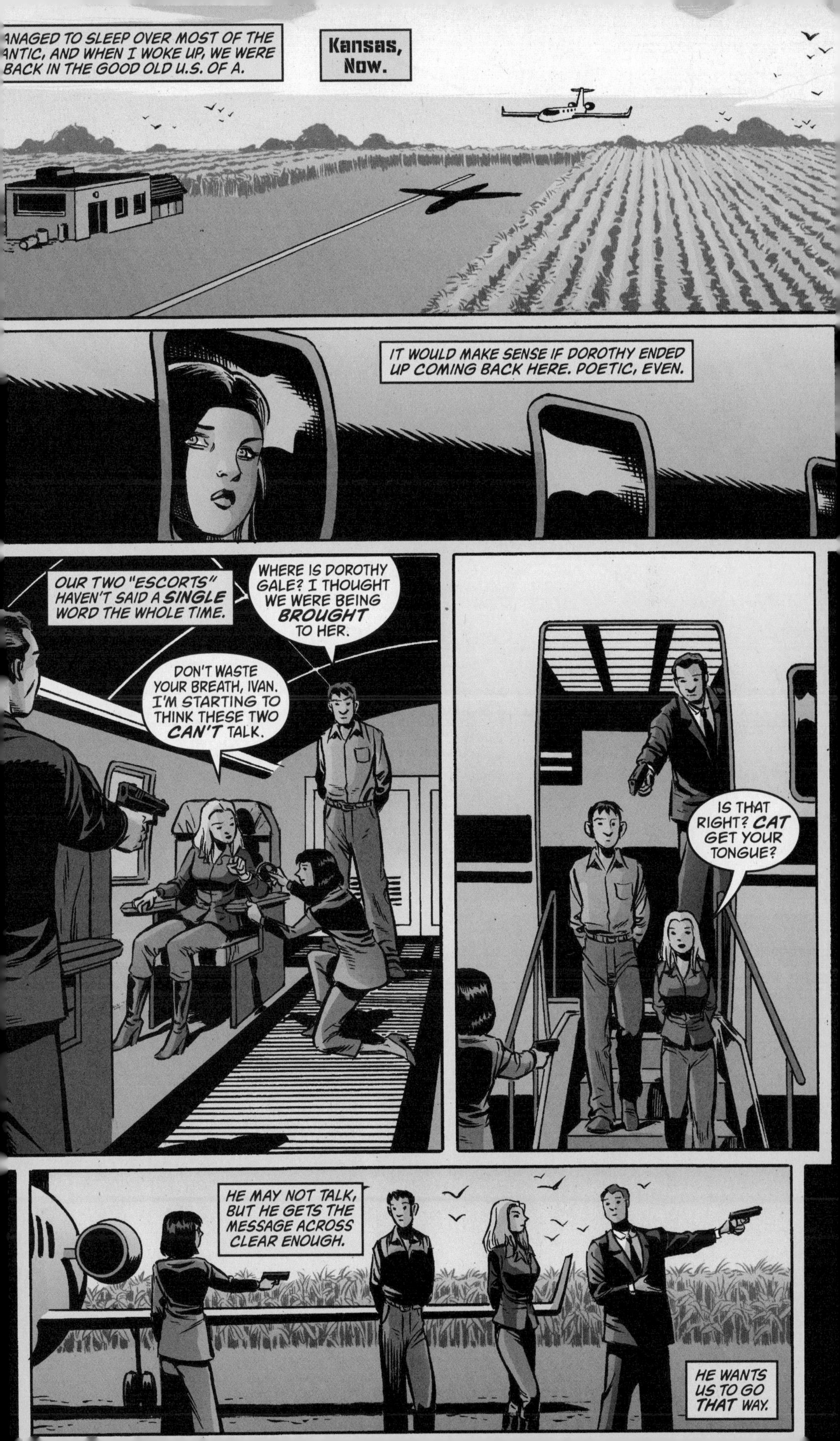

ANAGED TO SLEEP OVER MOST OF THE
ANTIC, AND WHEN I WOKE UP, WE WERE BACK IN THE GOOD OLD U.S. OF A.
Kansas, Now.
IT WOULD MAKE SENSE IF DOROTHY ENDED UP COMING BACK HERE. POETIC, EVEN.
OUR TWO "ESCORTS" HAVEN'T SAID A SINGLE WORD THE WHOLE TIME.
WHERE IS DOROTHY GALE? I THOUGHT WE WERE BEING BROUGHT TO HER.
DON'T WASTE YOUR BREATH, IVAN. I'M STARTING TO THINK THESE TWO CAN'T TALK.
IS THAT RIGHT? CAT GET YOUR TONGUE?
HE MAY NOT TALK, BUT HE GETS THE MESSAGE ACROSS CLEAR ENOUGH.
HE WANTS US TO GO THAT WAY.

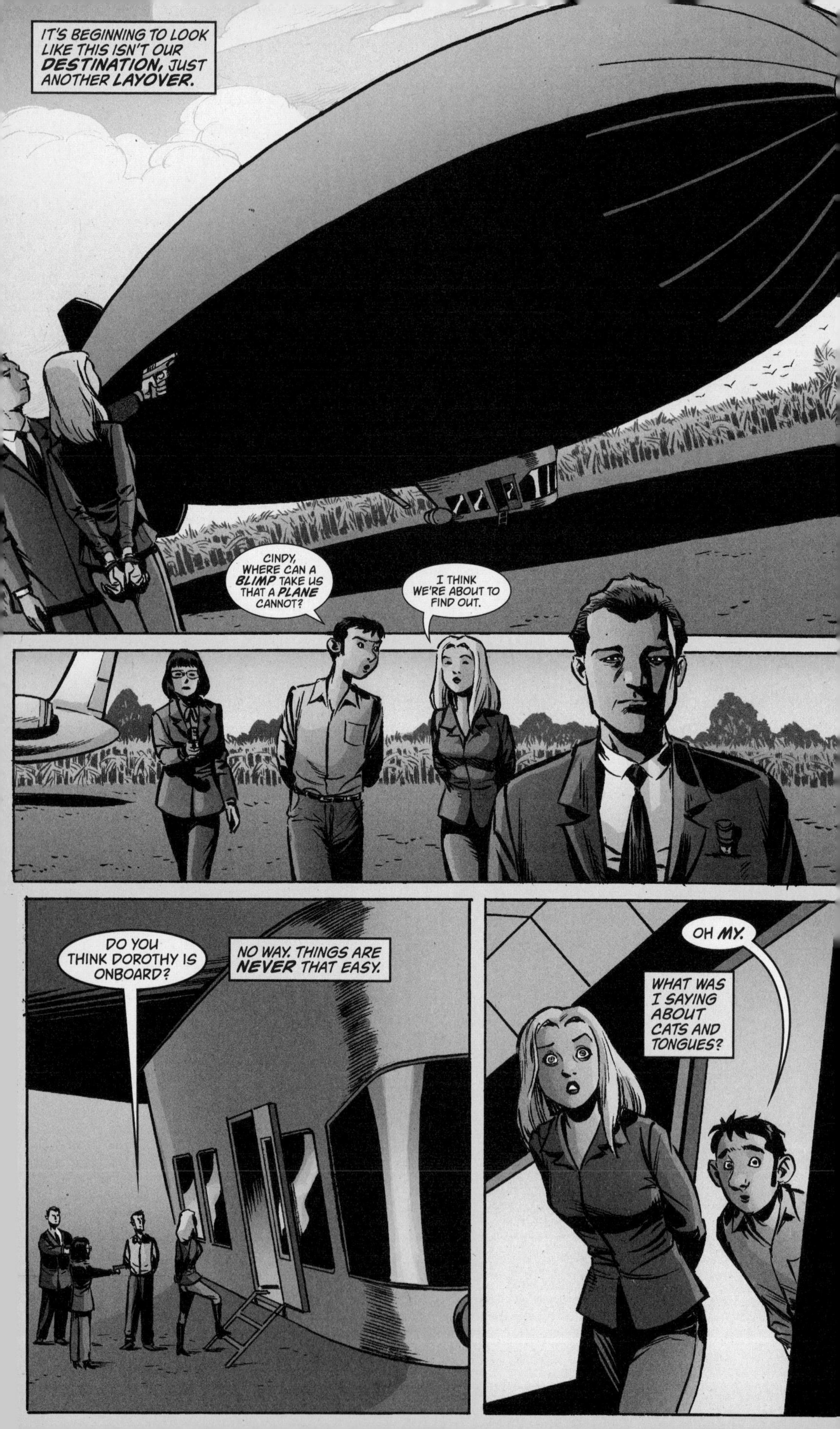
IT'S BEGINNING TO LOOK LIKE THIS ISN'T OUR DESTINATION, JUST ANOTHER LAYOVER.
CINDY, WHERE CAN A BLIMP TAKE US THAT A PLANE CANNOT?
I THINK WE'RE ABOUT TO FIND OUT.
DO YOU THINK DOROTHY IS ONBOARD?
NO WAY. THINGS ARE NEVER THAT EASY.
OH MY.
WHAT WAS I SAYING ABOUT CATS AND TONGUES?

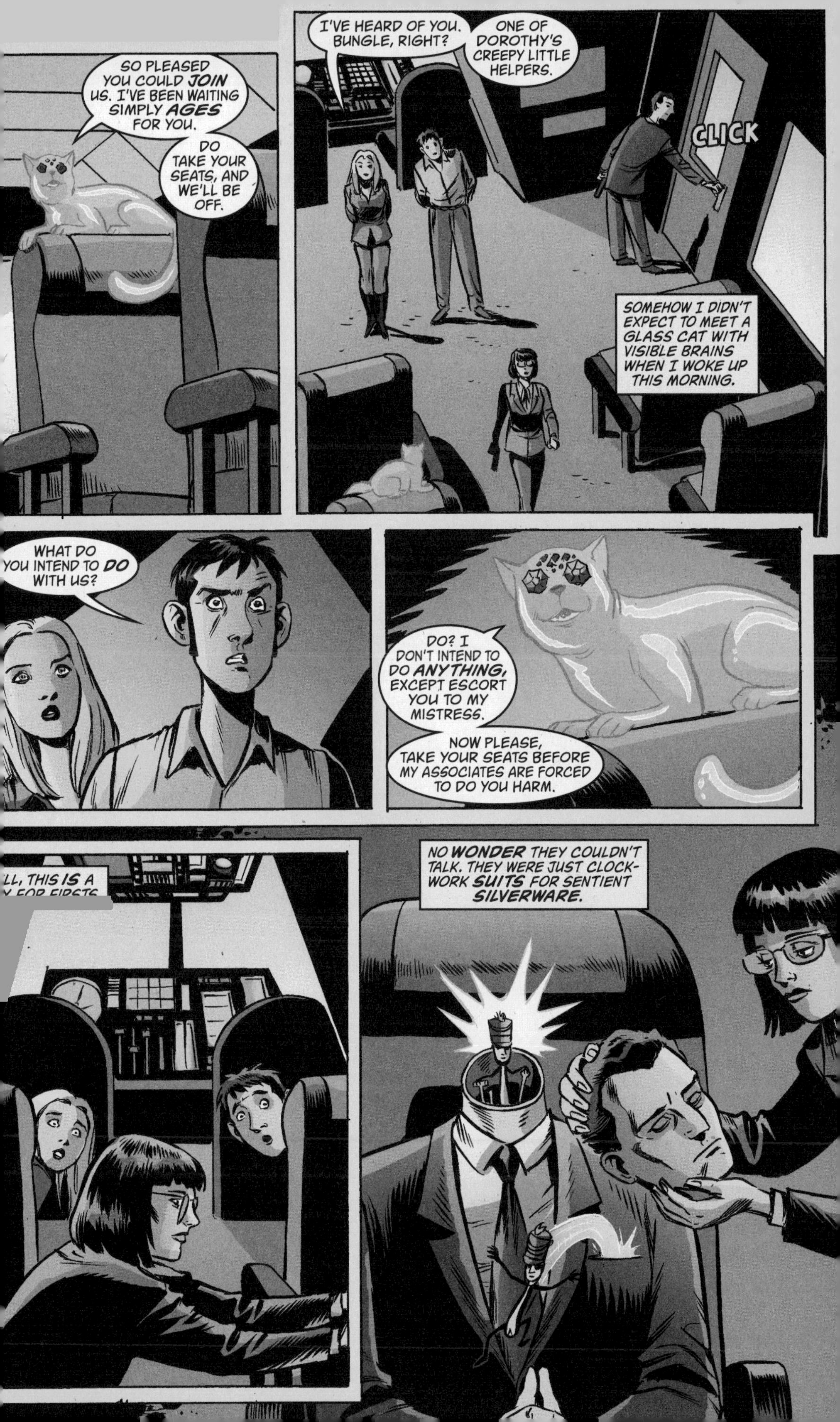
SO PLEASED YOU COULD JOIN US. I'VE BEEN WAITING SIMPLY AGES FOR YOU.
DO TAKE YOUR SEATS, AND WE'LL BE OFF.
I'VE HEARD OF YOU. BUNGLE, RIGHT?
ONE OF DOROTHY'S CREEPY LITTLE HELPERS.
CLICK
SOMEHOW I DIDN'T EXPECT TO MEET A GLASS CAT WITH VISIBLE BRAINS WHEN I WOKE UP THIS MORNING.
WHAT DO YOU INTEND TO DO WITH US?
DO? I DON'T INTEND TO DO ANYTHING, EXCEPT ESCORT YOU TO MY MISTRESS.
NOW PLEASE, TAKE YOUR SEATS BEFORE MY ASSOCIATES ARE FORCED TO DO YOU HARM.
LL, THIS IS A
NO WONDER THEY COULDN'T TALK. THEY WERE JUST CLOCK-WORK SUITS FOR SENTIENT SILVERWARE.

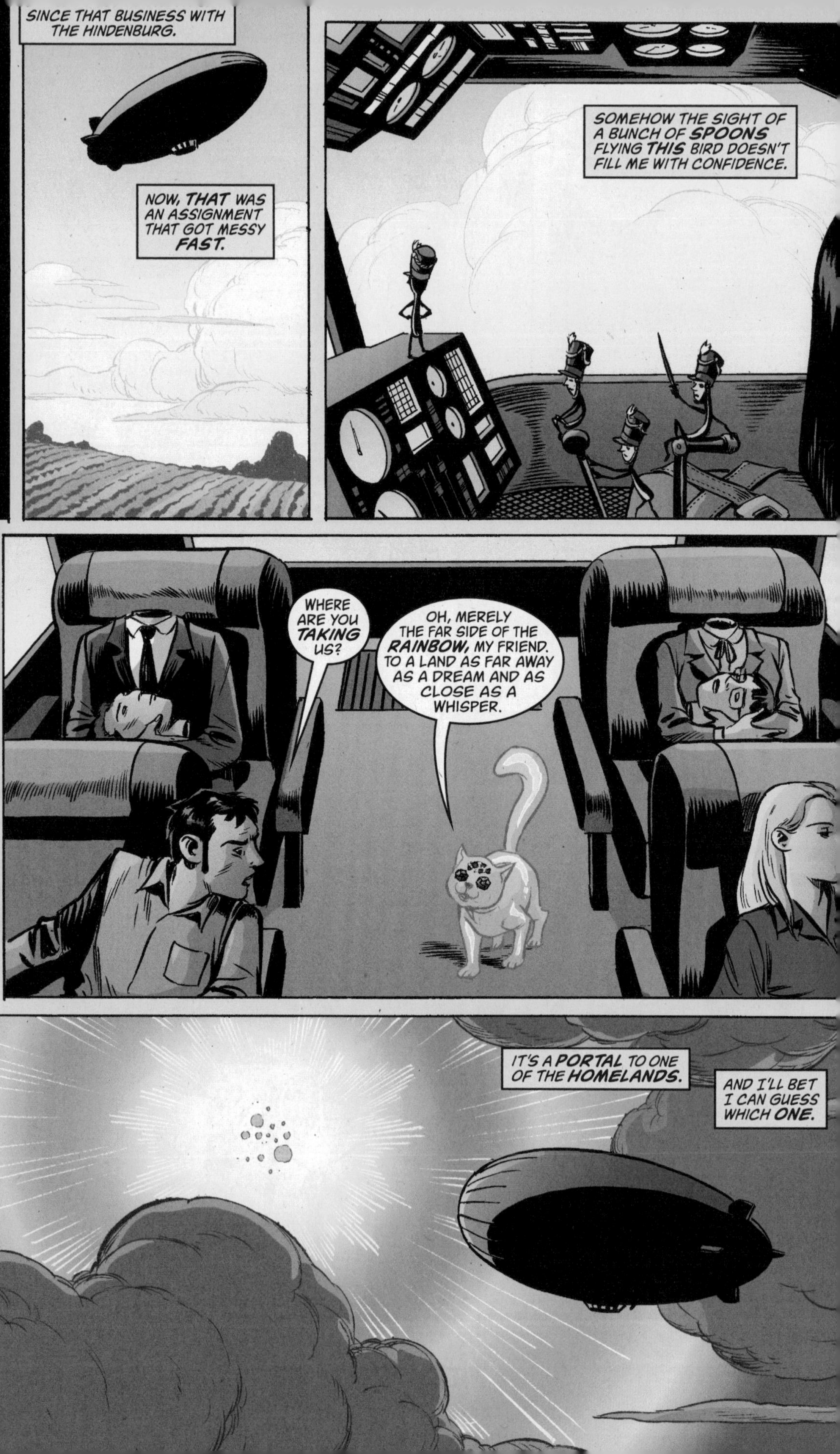
SINCE THAT BUSINESS WITH THE HINDENBURG.
NOW, THAT WAS AN ASSIGNMENT THAT GOT MESSY FAST.
SOMEHOW THE SIGHT OF A BUNCH OF SPOONS FLYING THIS BIRD DOESN'T FILL ME WITH CONFIDENCE.
WHERE ARE YOU TAKING US?
OH, MERELY THE FAR SIDE OF THE RAINBOW, MY FRIEND. TO A LAND AS FAR AWAY AS A DREAM AND AS CLOSE AS A WHISPER.
IT'S A PORTAL TO ONE OF THE HOMELANDS.
AND I'LL BET I CAN GUESS WHICH ONE.

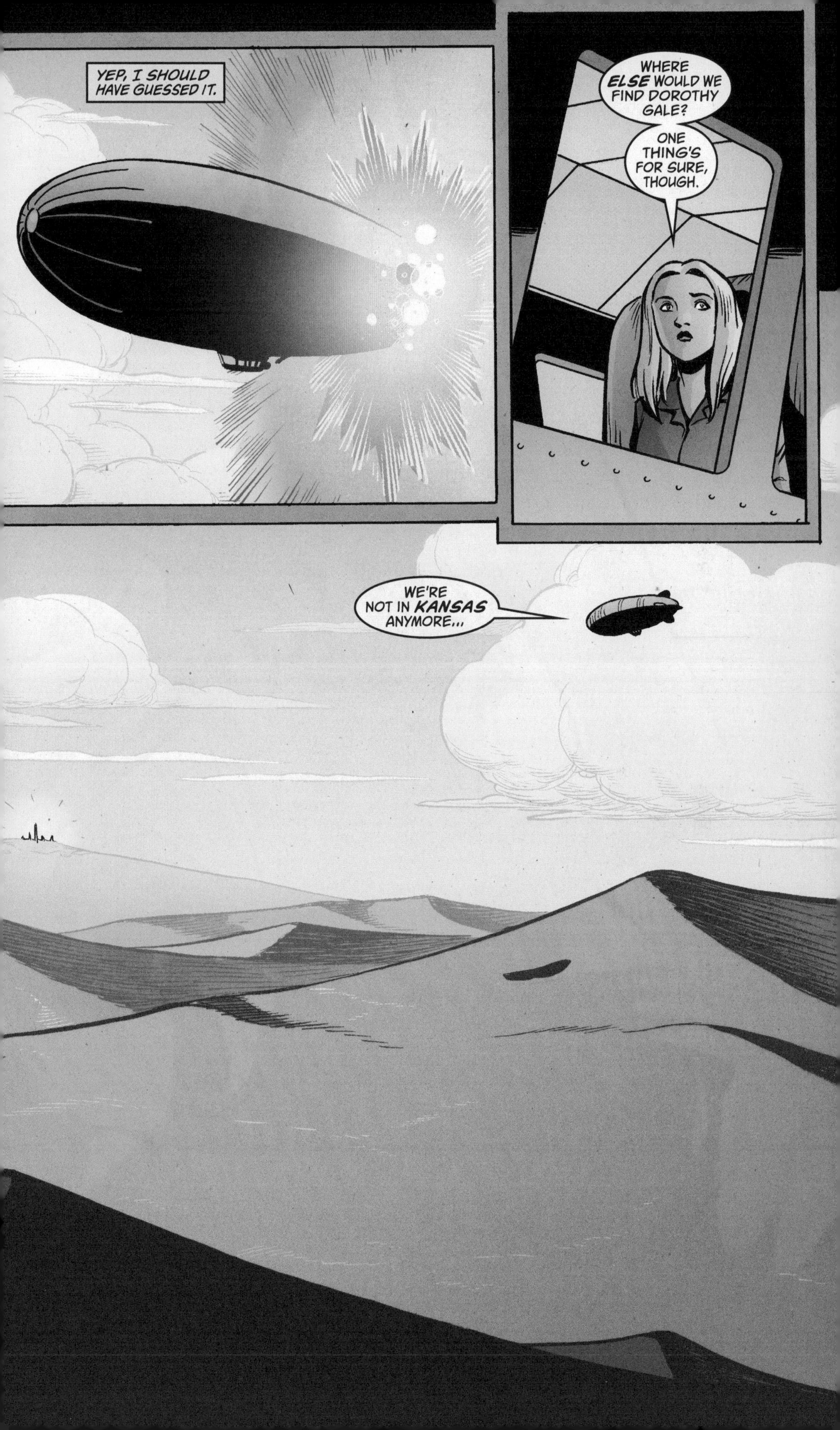
YEP, I SHOULD HAVE GUESSED IT.
WHERE ELSE WOULD WE FIND DOROTHY GALE?
ONE THING'S FOR SURE, THOUGH.
WE'RE NOT IN KANSAS ANYMORE...

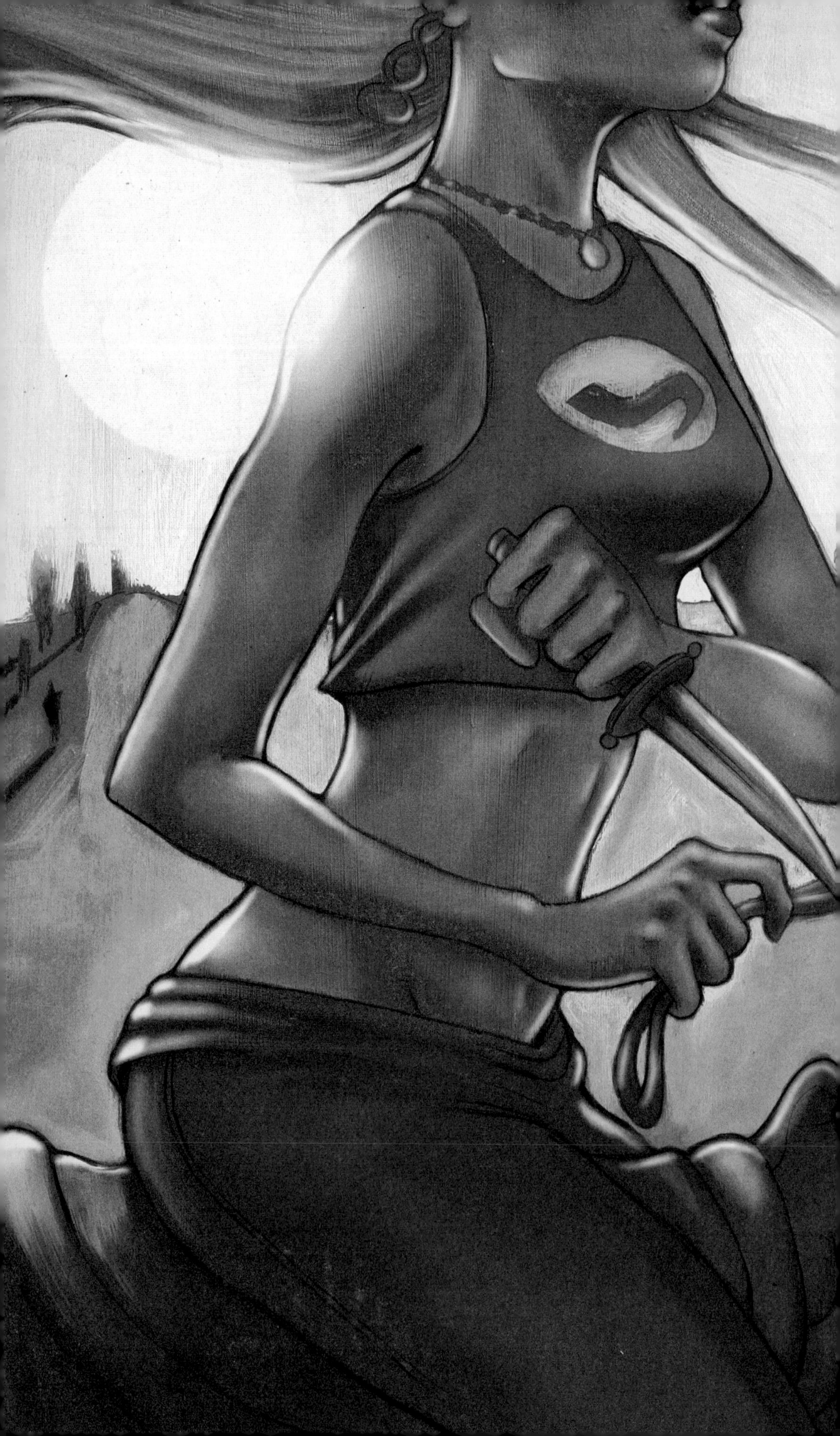

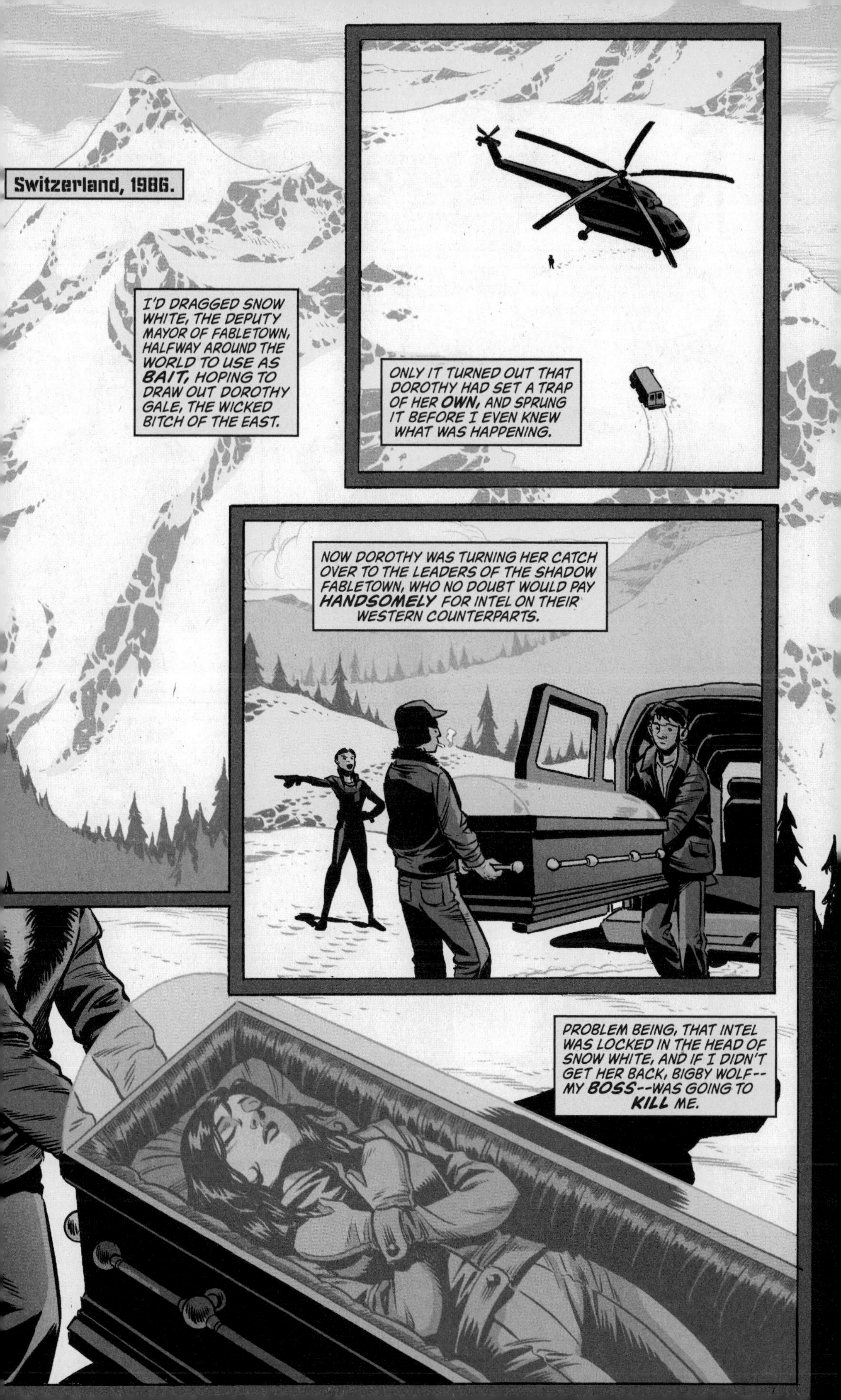
Switzerland, 1986.
I'D DRAGGED SNOW WHITE, THE DEPUTY MAYOR OF FABLETOWN, HALFWAY AROUND THE WORLD TO USE AS BAIT, HOPING TO DRAW OUT DOROTHY GALE, THE WICKED BITCH OF THE EAST.
ONLY IT TURNED OUT THAT DOROTHY HAD SET A TRAP OF HER OWN, AND SPRUNG IT BEFORE I EVEN KNEW WHAT WAS HAPPENING.
NOW DOROTHY WAS TURNING HER CATCH OVER TO THE LEADERS OF THE SHADOW FABLETOWN, WHO NO DOUBT WOULD PAY HANDSOMELY FOR INTEL ON THEIR WESTERN COUNTERPARTS.
PROBLEM BEING, THAT INTEL WAS LOCKED IN THE HEAD OF SNOW WHITE, AND IF I DIDN'T GET HER BACK, BIGBY WOLF-- MY BOSS--WAS GOING TO KILL ME.

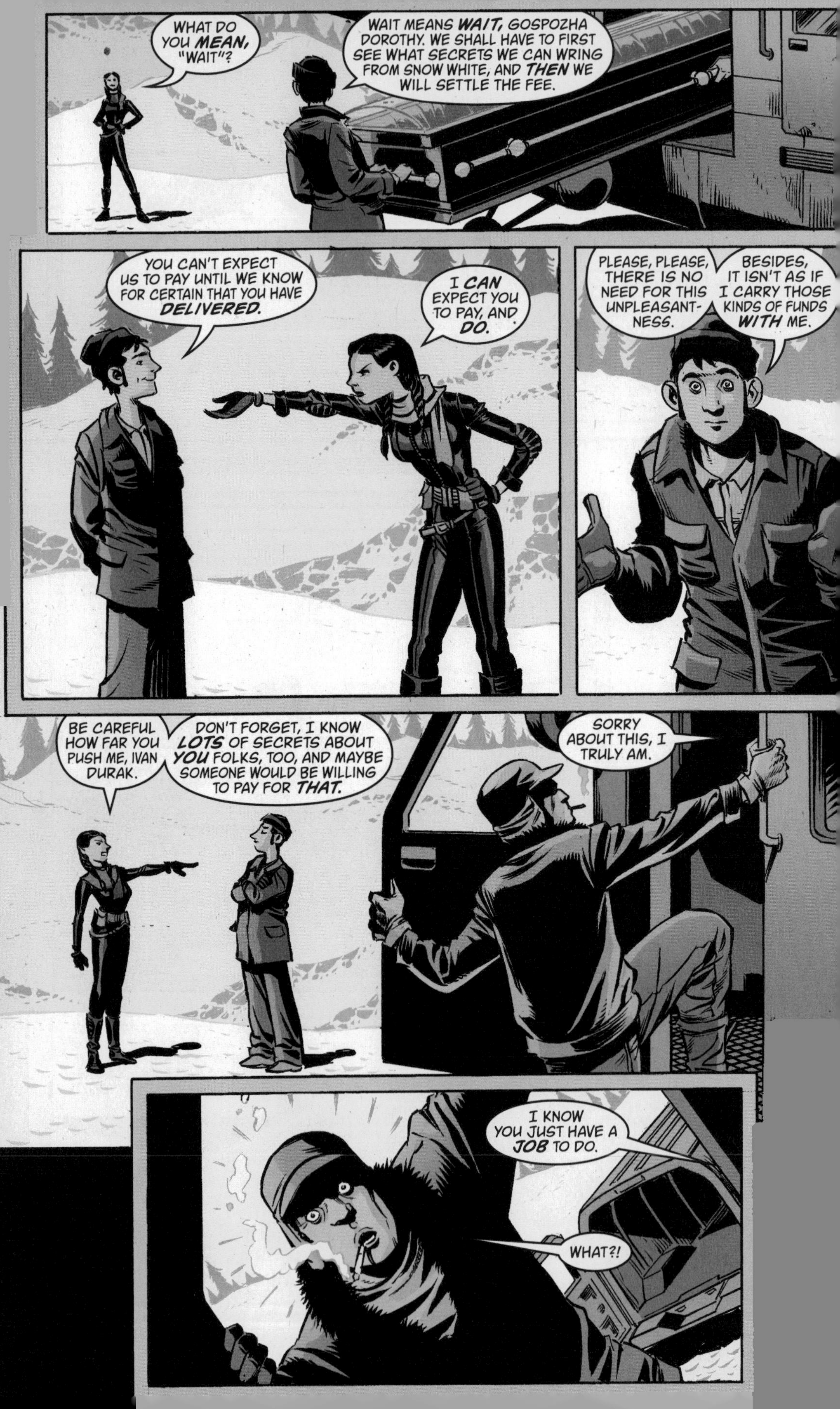
WHAT DO YOU MEAN, "WAIT"?
WAIT MEANS WAIT, GOSPOZHA DOROTHY. WE SHALL HAVE TO FIRST SEE WHAT SECRETS WE CAN WRING FROM SNOW WHITE, AND THEN WE WILL SETTLE THE FEE.
YOU CAN'T EXPECT US TO PAY UNTIL WE KNOW FOR CERTAIN THAT YOU HAVE DELIVERED.
I CAN EXPECT YOU TO PAY, AND DO.
PLEASE, PLEASE, THERE IS NO NEED FOR THIS UNPLEASANT-NESS.
BESIDES, IT ISN'T AS IF I CARRY THOSE KINDS OF FUNDS WITH ME.
BE CAREFUL HOW FAR YOU PUSH ME, IVAN DURAK.
DON'T FORGET, I KNOW LOTS OF SECRETS ABOUT YOU FOLKS, TOO, AND MAYBE SOMEONE WOULD BE WILLING TO PAY FOR THAT.
SORRY ABOUT THIS, I TRULY AM.
I KNOW YOU JUST HAVE A JOB TO DO.
WHAT?!

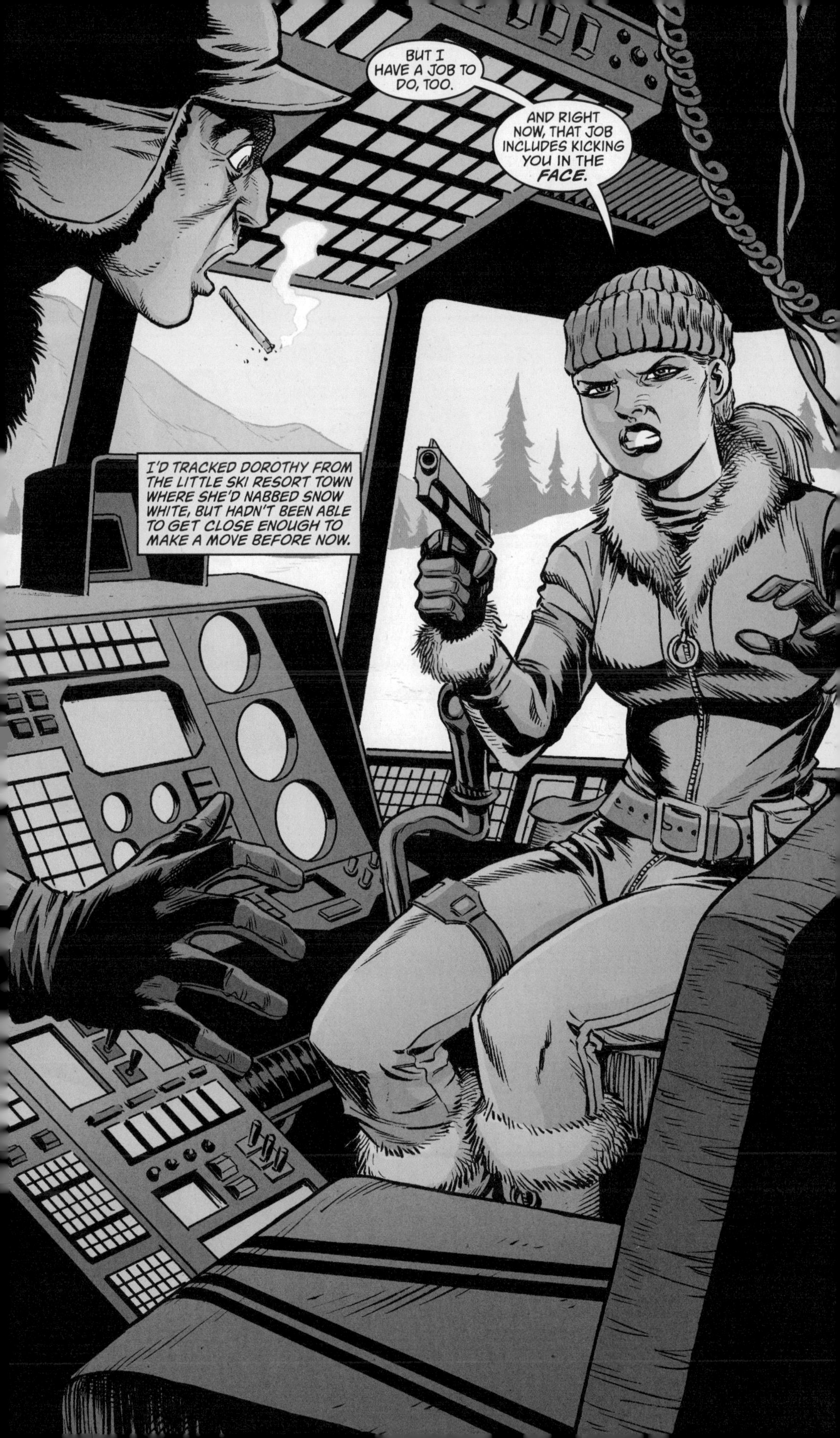
BUT I HAVE A JOB TO DO, TOO.
AND RIGHT NOW, THAT JOB INCLUDES KICKING YOU IN THE *FACE.*
I'D TRACKED DOROTHY FROM THE LITTLE SKI RESORT TOWN WHERE SHE'D NABBED SNOW WHITE, BUT HADN'T BEEN ABLE TO GET CLOSE ENOUGH TO MAKE A MOVE BEFORE NOW.

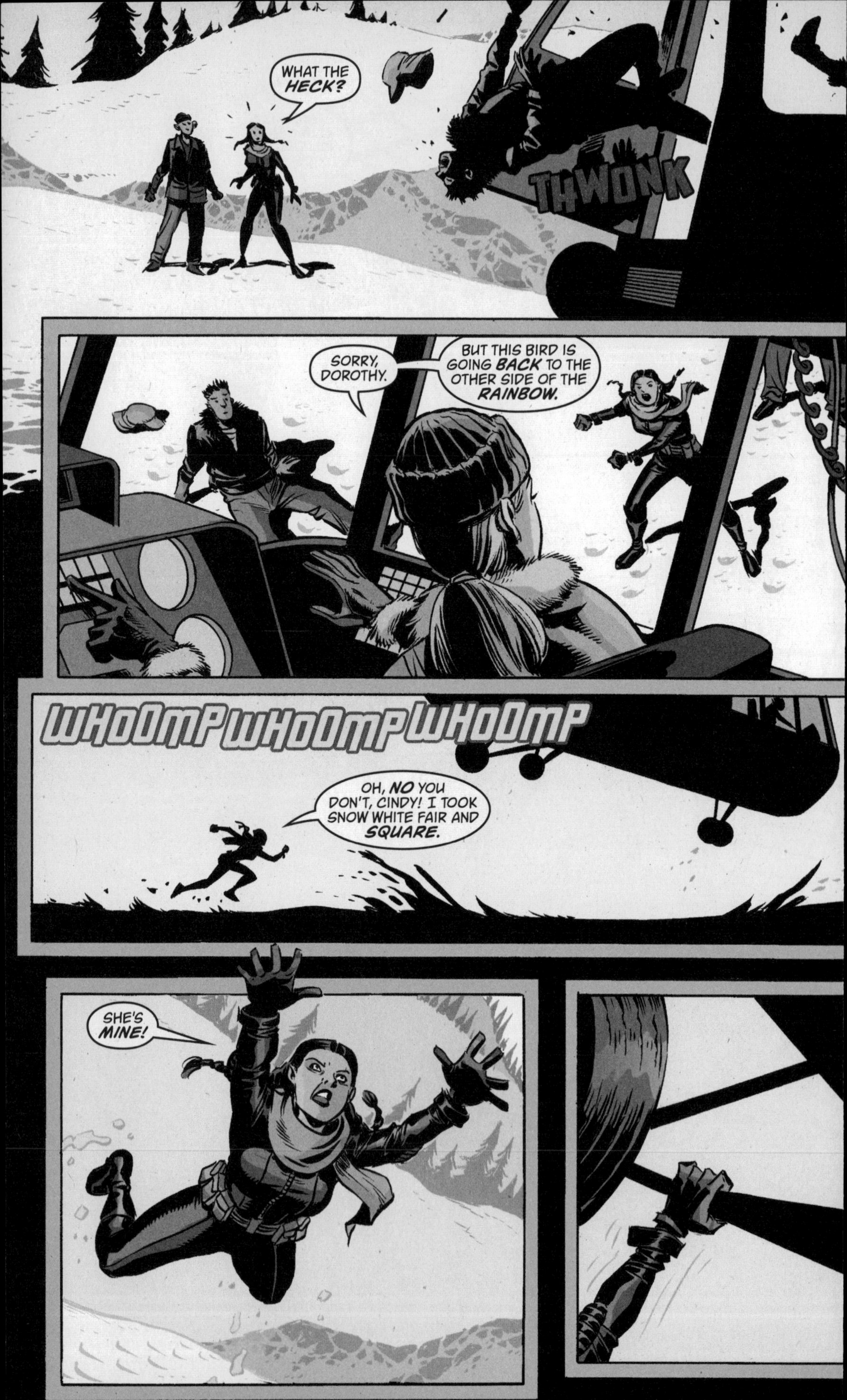
WHAT THE HECK?
THWONK
SORRY, DOROTHY.
BUT THIS BIRD IS GOING BACK TO THE OTHER SIDE OF THE RAINBOW.
WHOOMP WHOOMP WHOOMP
OH, NO YOU DON'T, CINDY! I TOOK SNOW WHITE FAIR AND SQUARE.
SHE'S MINE!

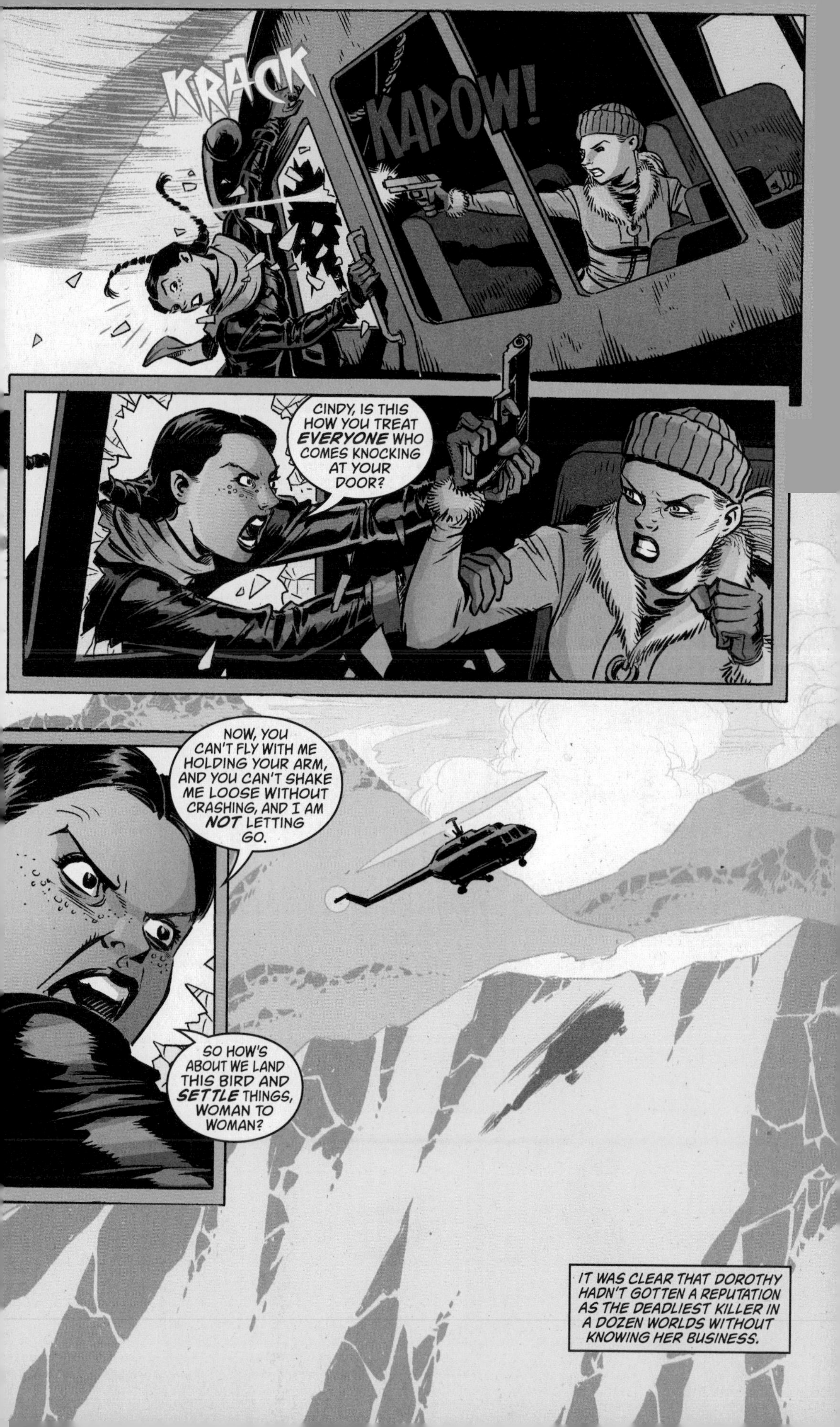
KRACK
KAPOW!
CINDY, IS THIS HOW YOU TREAT EVERYONE WHO COMES KNOCKING AT YOUR DOOR?
NOW, YOU CAN'T FLY WITH ME HOLDING YOUR ARM, AND YOU CAN'T SHAKE ME LOOSE WITHOUT CRASHING, AND I AM NOT LETTING GO.
SO HOW'S ABOUT WE LAND THIS BIRD AND SETTLE THINGS, WOMAN TO WOMAN?
IT WAS CLEAR THAT DOROTHY HADN'T GOTTEN A REPUTATION AS THE DEADLIEST KILLER IN A DOZEN WORLDS WITHOUT KNOWING HER BUSINESS.

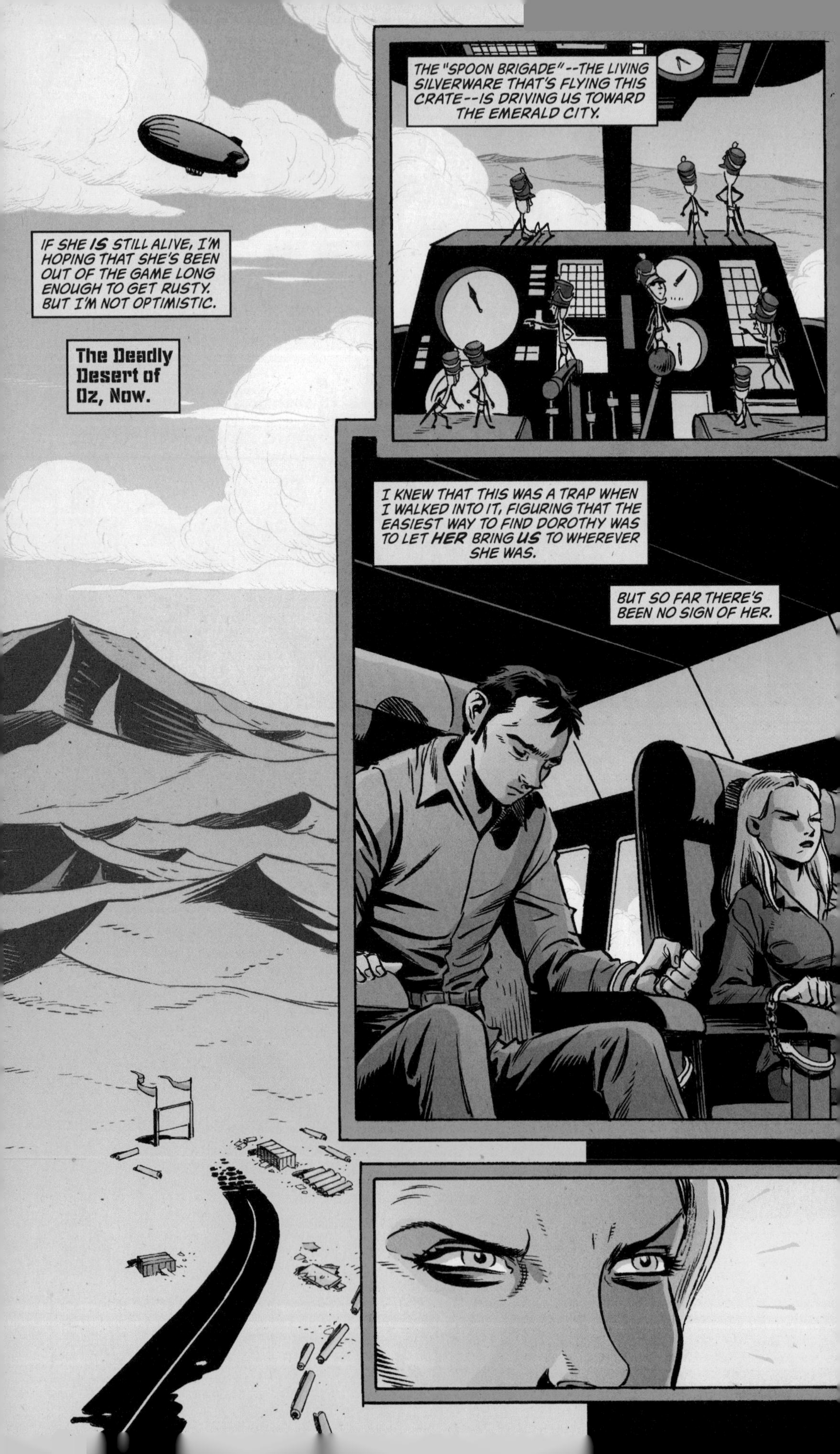

IF SHE IS STILL ALIVE, I'M HOPING THAT SHE'S BEEN OUT OF THE GAME LONG ENOUGH TO GET RUSTY. BUT I'M NOT OPTIMISTIC.
The Deadly Desert of Oz, Now.
THE "SPOON BRIGADE"--THE LIVING SILVERWARE THAT'S FLYING THIS CRATE--IS DRIVING US TOWARD THE EMERALD CITY.
I KNEW THAT THIS WAS A TRAP WHEN I WALKED INTO IT, FIGURING THAT THE EASIEST WAY TO FIND DOROTHY WAS TO LET HER BRING US TO WHEREVER SHE WAS.
BUT SO FAR THERE'S BEEN NO SIGN OF HER.

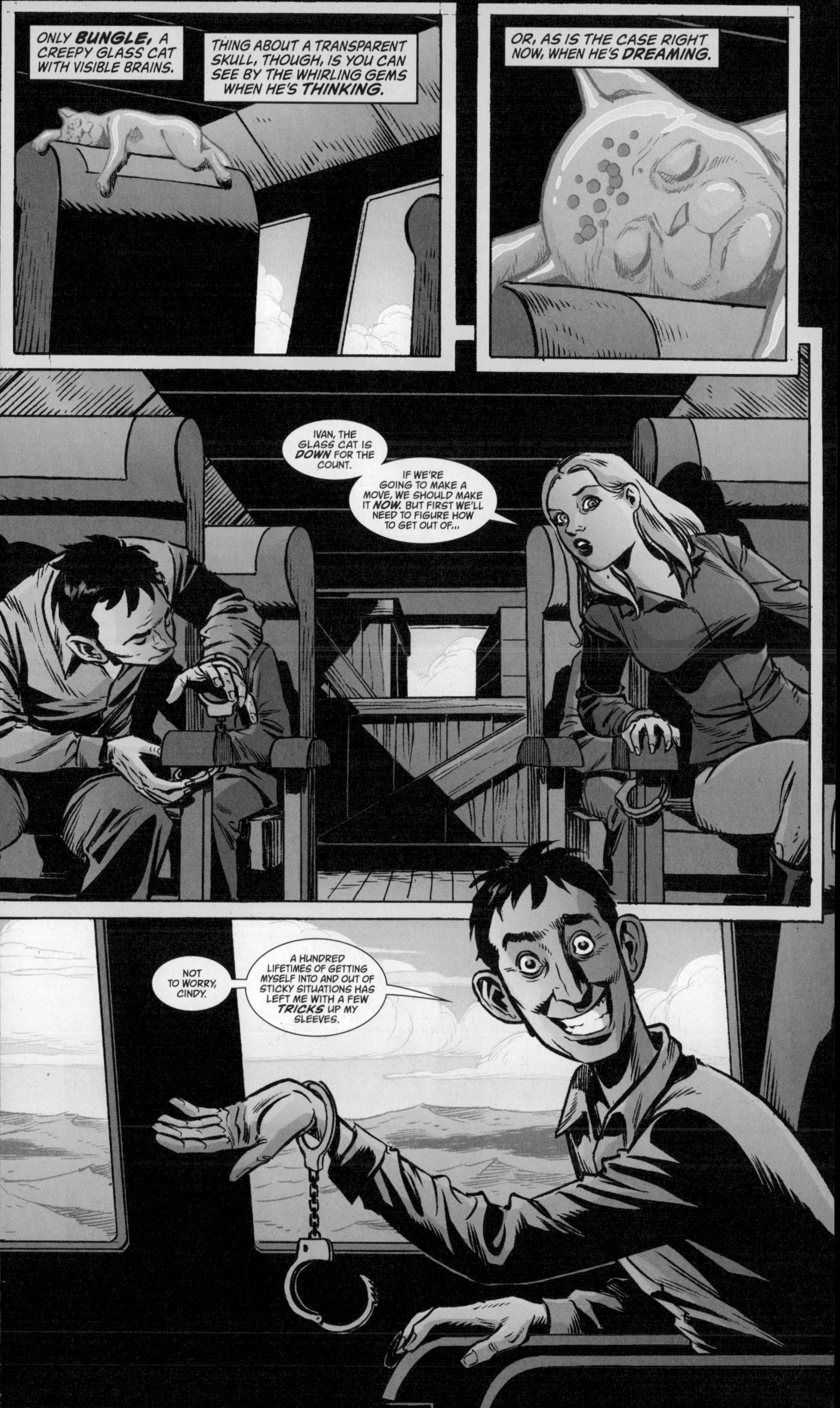
ONLY **BUNGLE,** A CREEPY GLASS CAT WITH VISIBLE BRAINS.
THING ABOUT A TRANSPARENT SKULL, THOUGH, IS YOU CAN SEE BY THE WHIRLING GEMS WHEN HE'S **THINKING.**
OR, AS IS THE CASE RIGHT NOW, WHEN HE'S **DREAMING.**
IVAN, THE GLASS CAT IS **DOWN** FOR THE COUNT.
IF WE'RE GOING TO MAKE A MOVE, WE SHOULD MAKE IT **NOW.** BUT FIRST WE'LL NEED TO FIGURE HOW TO GET OUT OF...
NOT TO WORRY, CINDY.
A HUNDRED LIFETIMES OF GETTING MYSELF INTO AND OUT OF STICKY SITUATIONS HAS LEFT ME WITH A FEW **TRICKS** UP MY SLEEVES.

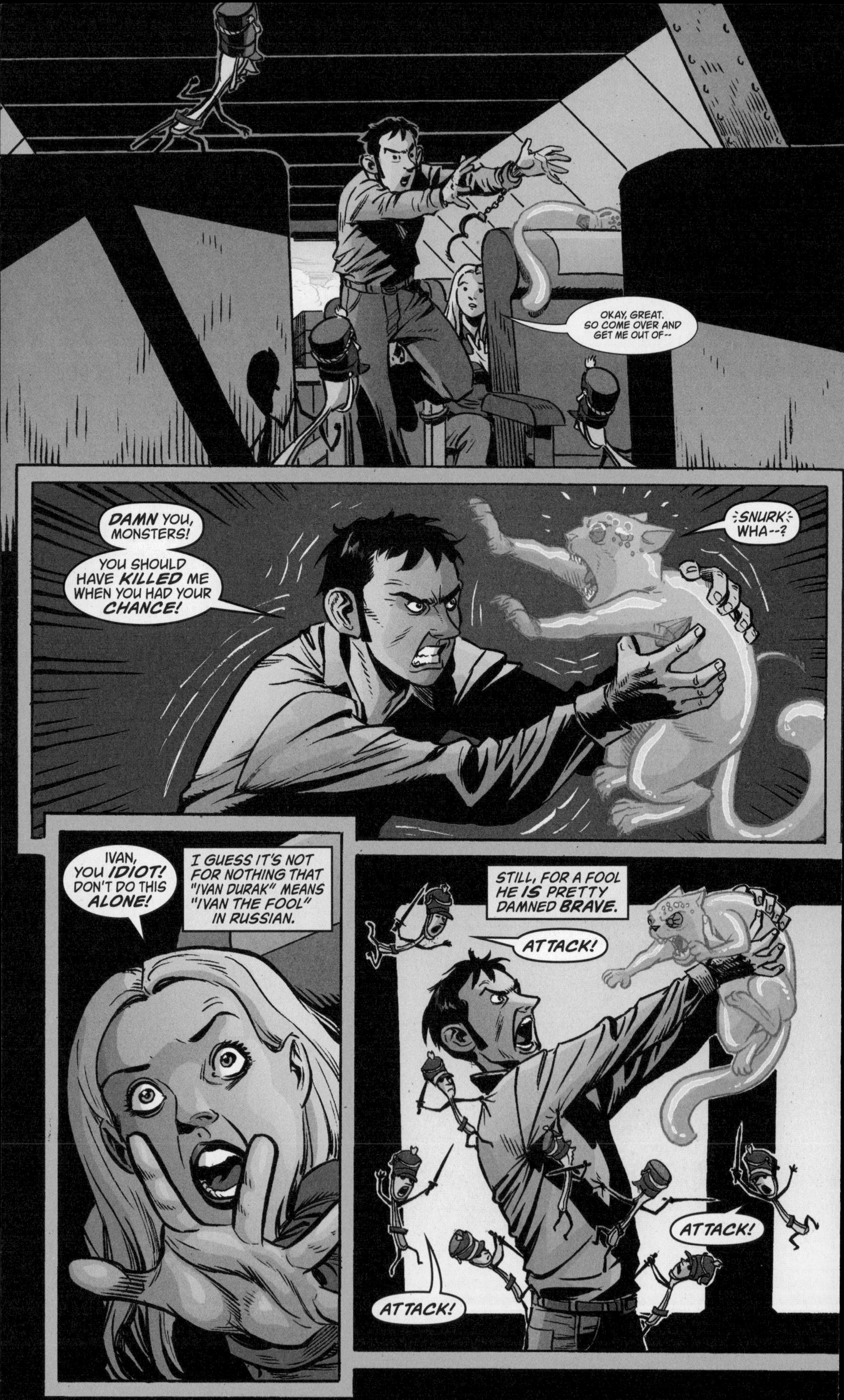

OKAY, GREAT. SO COME OVER AND GET ME OUT OF--
DAMN YOU, MONSTERS!
YOU SHOULD HAVE KILLED ME WHEN YOU HAD YOUR CHANCE!
SNURK WHA--?
IVAN, YOU IDIOT! DON'T DO THIS ALONE!
I GUESS IT'S NOT FOR NOTHING THAT "IVAN DURAK" MEANS "IVAN THE FOOL" IN RUSSIAN.
STILL, FOR A FOOL HE IS PRETTY DAMNED BRAVE.
ATTACK!
ATTACK!
ATTACK!

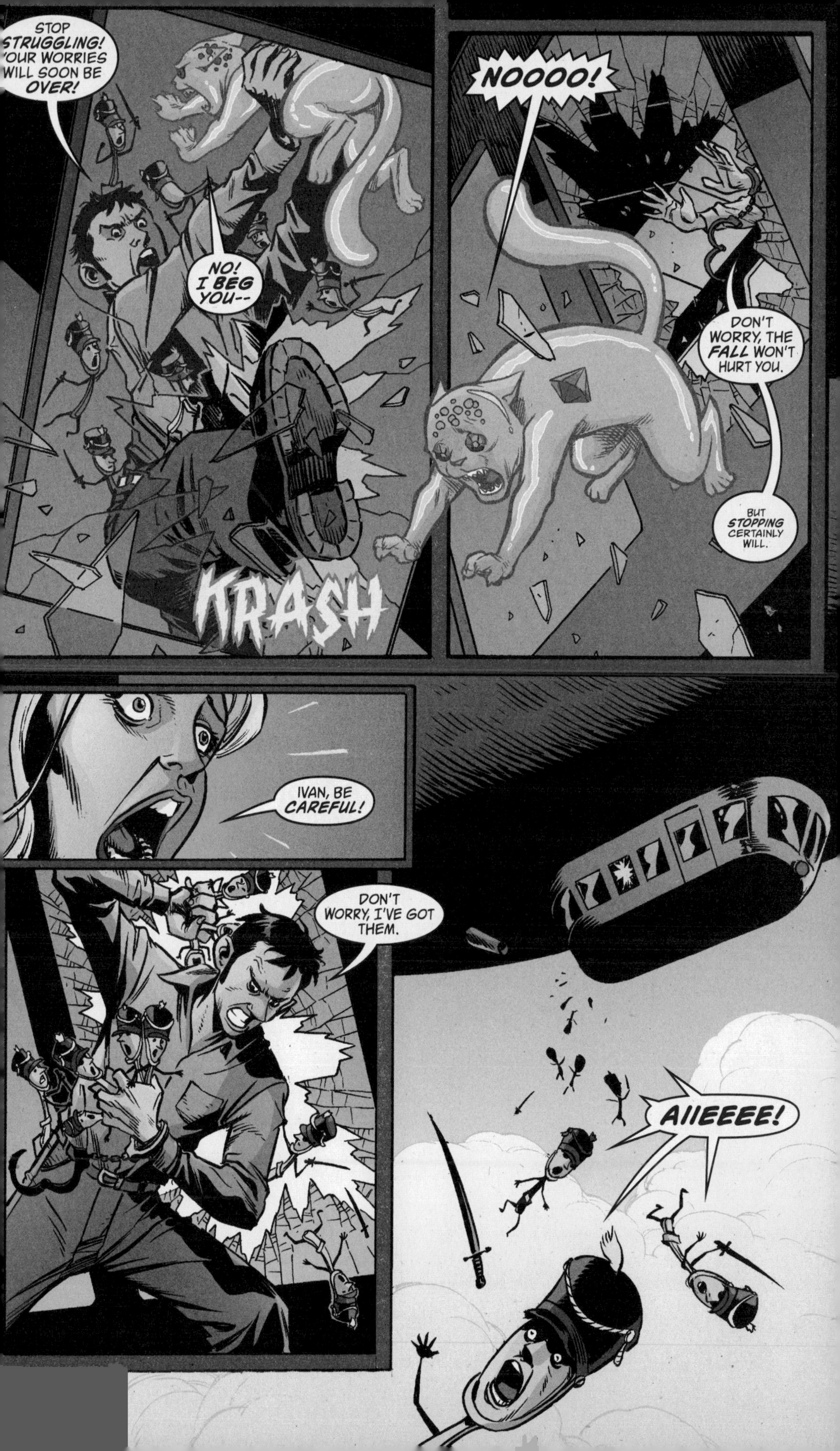
STOP STRUGGLING! YOUR WORRIES WILL SOON BE OVER!
NO! I BEG YOU--
KRASH
NOOOO!
DON'T WORRY, THE FALL WON'T HURT YOU.
BUT STOPPING CERTAINLY WILL.
IVAN, BE CAREFUL!
DON'T WORRY, I'VE GOT THEM.
AIIEEEE!

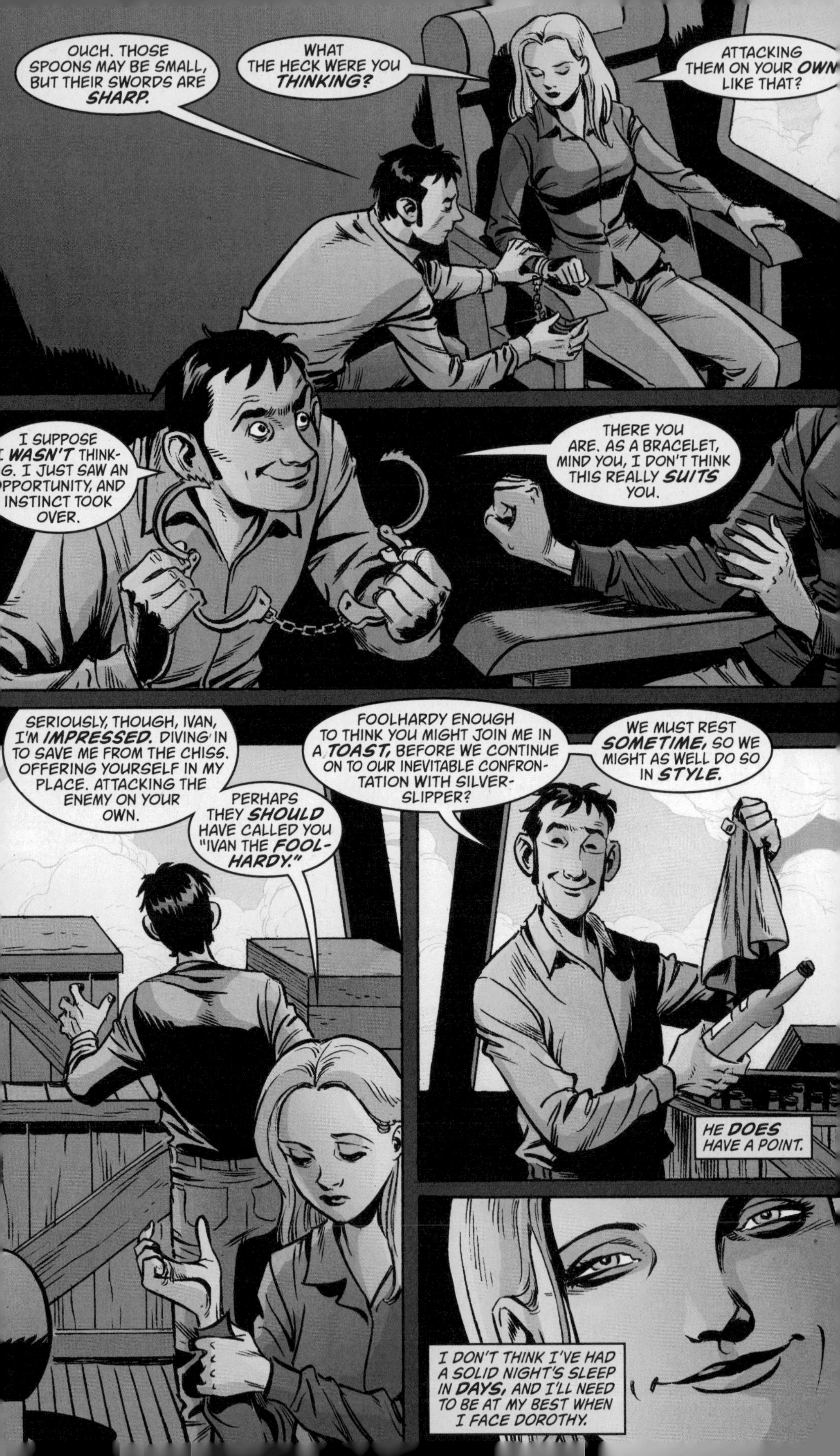
OUCH. THOSE SPOONS MAY BE SMALL, BUT THEIR SWORDS ARE SHARP.
WHAT THE HECK WERE YOU THINKING?
ATTACKING THEM ON YOUR OWN LIKE THAT?
I SUPPOSE I WASN'T THINKING. I JUST SAW AN OPPORTUNITY, AND INSTINCT TOOK OVER.
THERE YOU ARE. AS A BRACELET, MIND YOU, I DON'T THINK THIS REALLY SUITS YOU.
SERIOUSLY, THOUGH, IVAN, I'M IMPRESSED. DIVING IN TO SAVE ME FROM THE CHISS. OFFERING YOURSELF IN MY PLACE. ATTACKING THE ENEMY ON YOUR OWN.
PERHAPS THEY SHOULD HAVE CALLED YOU "IVAN THE FOOLHARDY."
FOOLHARDY ENOUGH TO THINK YOU MIGHT JOIN ME IN A TOAST, BEFORE WE CONTINUE ON TO OUR INEVITABLE CONFRONTATION WITH SILVERSLIPPER?
WE MUST REST SOMETIME, SO WE MIGHT AS WELL DO SO IN STYLE.
HE DOES HAVE A POINT.
I DON'T THINK I'VE HAD A SOLID NIGHT'S SLEEP IN DAYS, AND I'LL NEED TO BE AT MY BEST WHEN I FACE DOROTHY.

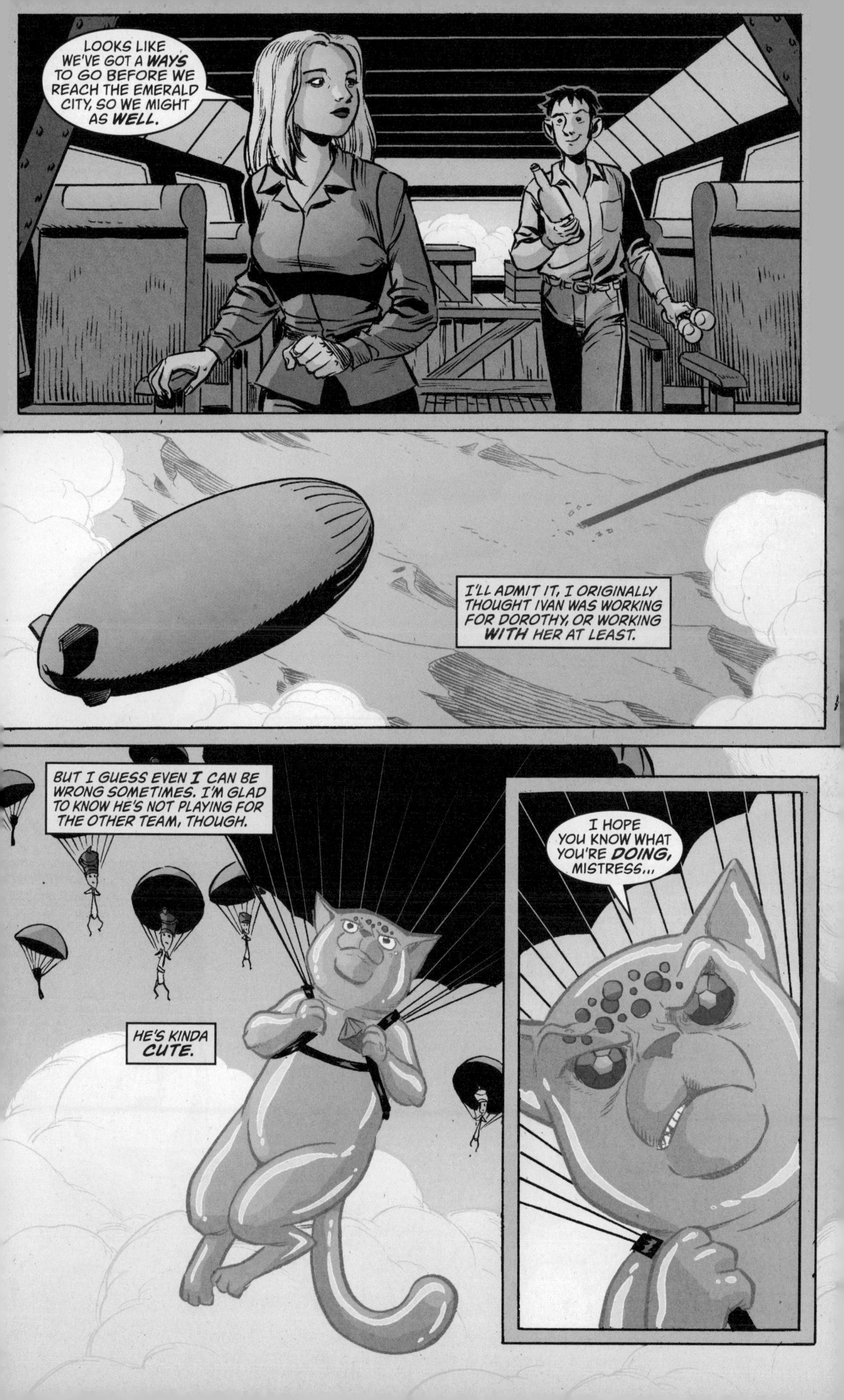
LOOKS LIKE WE'VE GOT A WAYS TO GO BEFORE WE REACH THE EMERALD CITY, SO WE MIGHT AS WELL.
I'LL ADMIT IT, I ORIGINALLY THOUGHT IVAN WAS WORKING FOR DOROTHY, OR WORKING WITH HER AT LEAST.
BUT I GUESS EVEN I CAN BE WRONG SOMETIMES. I'M GLAD TO KNOW HE'S NOT PLAYING FOR THE OTHER TEAM, THOUGH.
HE'S KINDA CUTE.
I HOPE YOU KNOW WHAT YOU'RE DOING, MISTRESS...

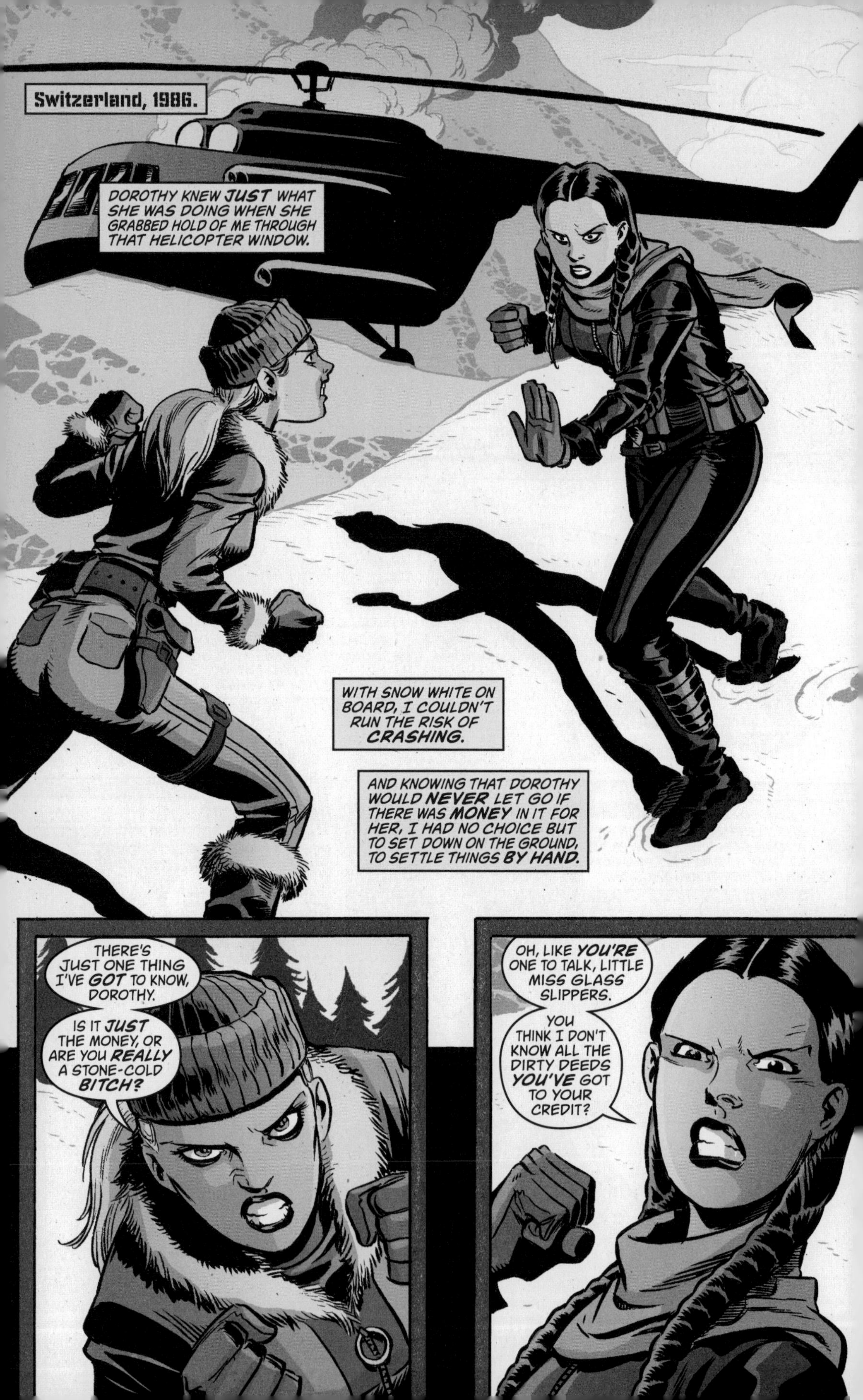

Switzerland, 1986.
DOROTHY KNEW JUST WHAT SHE WAS DOING WHEN SHE GRABBED HOLD OF ME THROUGH THAT HELICOPTER WINDOW.
WITH SNOW WHITE ON BOARD, I COULDN'T RUN THE RISK OF CRASHING.
AND KNOWING THAT DOROTHY WOULD NEVER LET GO IF THERE WAS MONEY IN IT FOR HER, I HAD NO CHOICE BUT TO SET DOWN ON THE GROUND, TO SETTLE THINGS BY HAND.
THERE'S JUST ONE THING I'VE GOT TO KNOW, DOROTHY.
IS IT JUST THE MONEY, OR ARE YOU REALLY A STONE-COLD BITCH?
OH, LIKE YOU'RE ONE TO TALK, LITTLE MISS GLASS SLIPPERS.
YOU THINK I DON'T KNOW ALL THE DIRTY DEEDS YOU'VE GOT TO YOUR CREDIT?

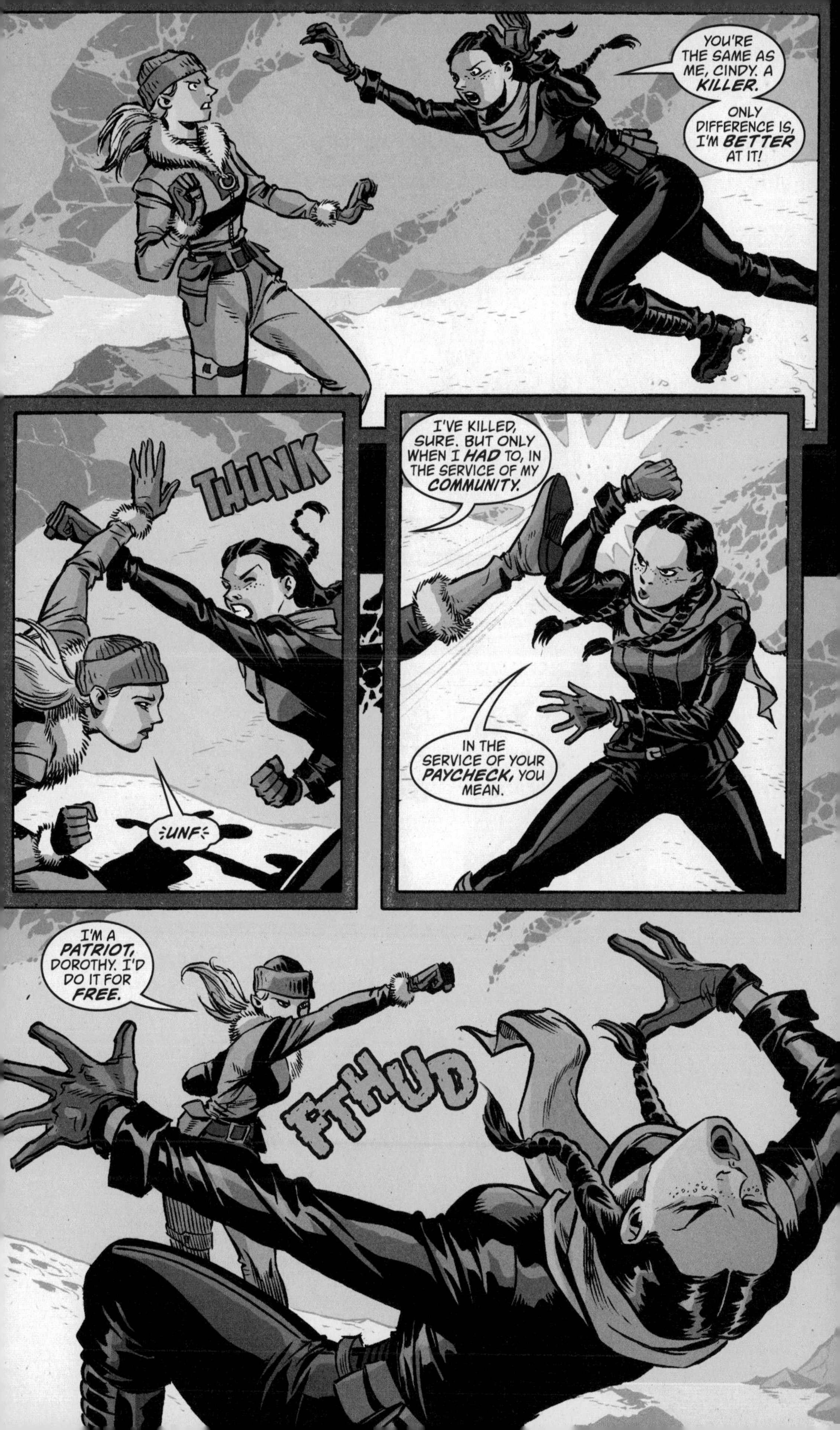

YOU'RE THE SAME AS ME, CINDY. A KILLER.
ONLY DIFFERENCE IS, I'M BETTER AT IT!
THUNK
UNF
I'VE KILLED, SURE. BUT ONLY WHEN I HAD TO, IN THE SERVICE OF MY COMMUNITY.
IN THE SERVICE OF YOUR PAYCHECK, YOU MEAN.
I'M A PATRIOT, DOROTHY. I'D DO IT FOR FREE.
FTHUD

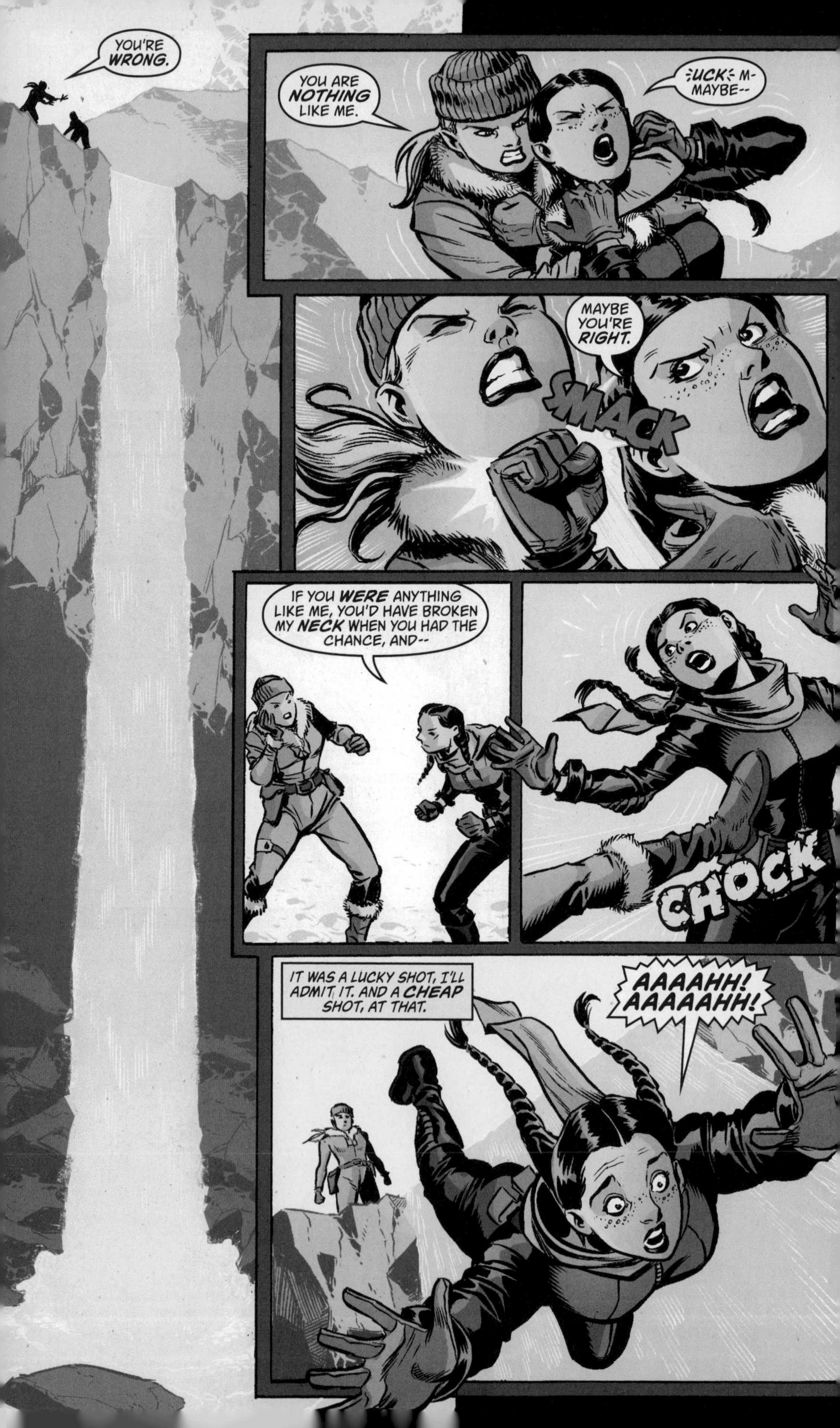

YOU'RE WRONG.
YOU ARE NOTHING LIKE ME.
-UCK- M-MAYBE--
MAYBE YOU'RE RIGHT.
SMACK
IF YOU WERE ANYTHING LIKE ME, YOU'D HAVE BROKEN MY NECK WHEN YOU HAD THE CHANCE, AND--
CHOCK
IT WAS A LUCKY SHOT, I'LL ADMIT IT. AND A CHEAP SHOT, AT THAT.
AAAAHH! AAAAAHH!

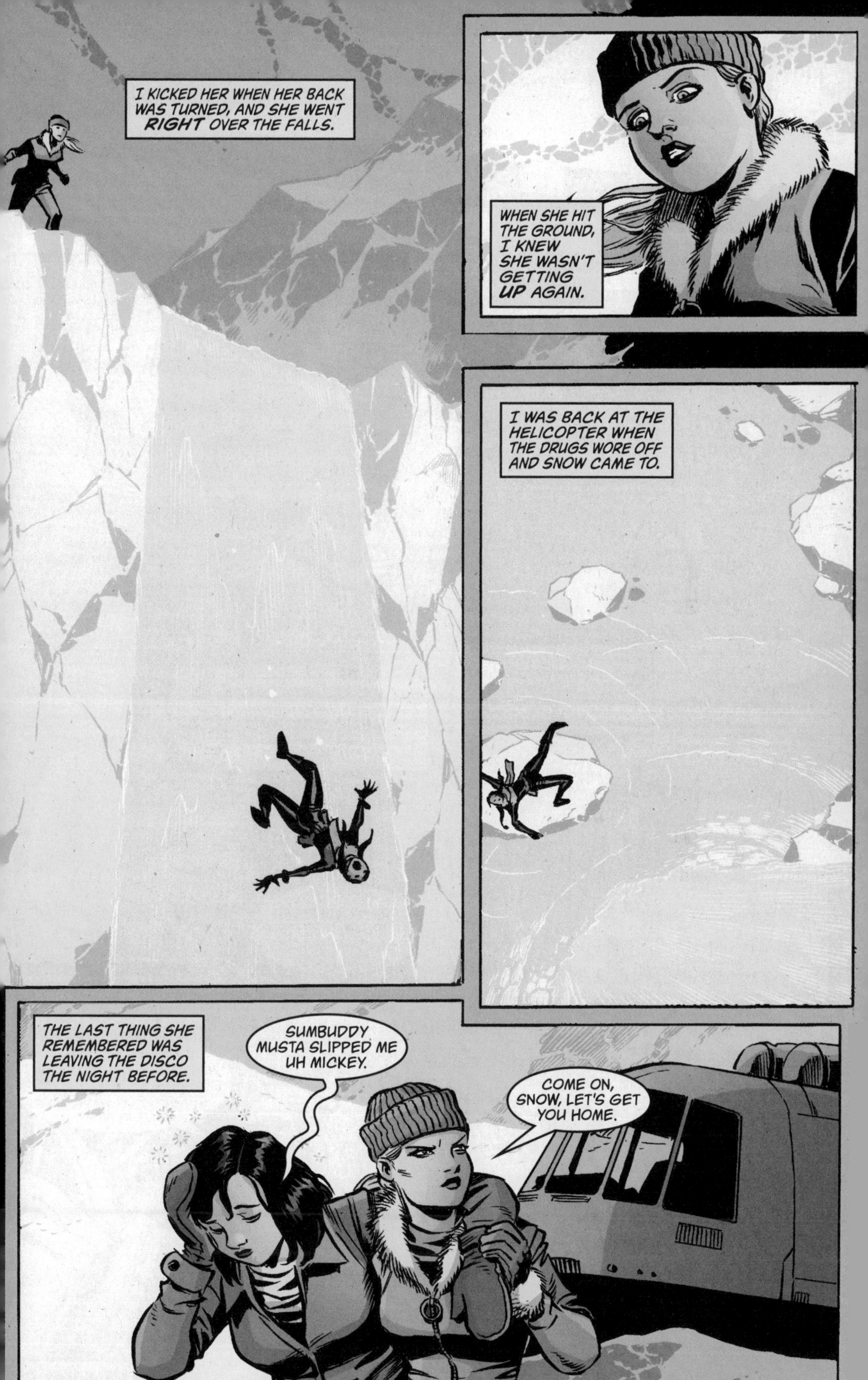
I KICKED HER WHEN HER BACK WAS TURNED, AND SHE WENT **RIGHT** OVER THE FALLS.
WHEN SHE HIT THE GROUND, I KNEW SHE WASN'T GETTING **UP** AGAIN.
I WAS BACK AT THE HELICOPTER WHEN THE DRUGS WORE OFF AND SNOW CAME TO.
THE LAST THING SHE REMEMBERED WAS LEAVING THE DISCO THE NIGHT BEFORE.
SUMBUDDY MUSTA SLIPPED ME UH MICKEY.
COME ON, SNOW, LET'S GET YOU HOME.

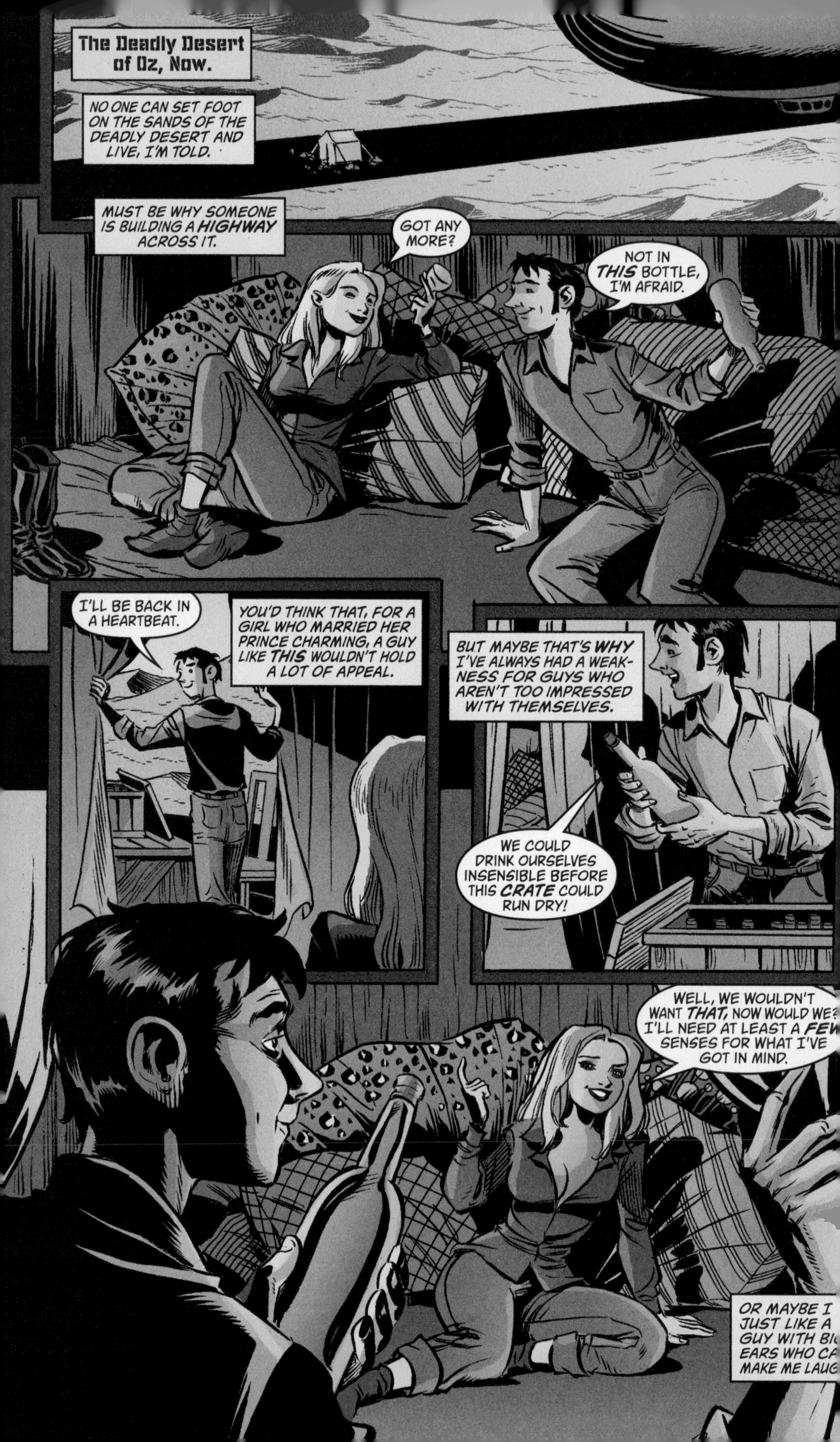
The Deadly Desert of Oz, Now.
NO ONE CAN SET FOOT ON THE SANDS OF THE DEADLY DESERT AND LIVE, I'M TOLD.
MUST BE WHY SOMEONE IS BUILDING A HIGHWAY ACROSS IT.
GOT ANY MORE?
NOT IN THIS BOTTLE, I'M AFRAID.
I'LL BE BACK IN A HEARTBEAT.
YOU'D THINK THAT, FOR A GIRL WHO MARRIED HER PRINCE CHARMING, A GUY LIKE THIS WOULDN'T HOLD A LOT OF APPEAL.
BUT MAYBE THAT'S WHY I'VE ALWAYS HAD A WEAKNESS FOR GUYS WHO AREN'T TOO IMPRESSED WITH THEMSELVES.
WE COULD DRINK OURSELVES INSENSIBLE BEFORE THIS CRATE COULD RUN DRY!
WELL, WE WOULDN'T WANT THAT, NOW WOULD WE? I'LL NEED AT LEAST A FEW SENSES FOR WHAT I'VE GOT IN MIND.
OR MAYBE I JUST LIKE A GUY WITH BI EARS WHO CA MAKE ME LAUG

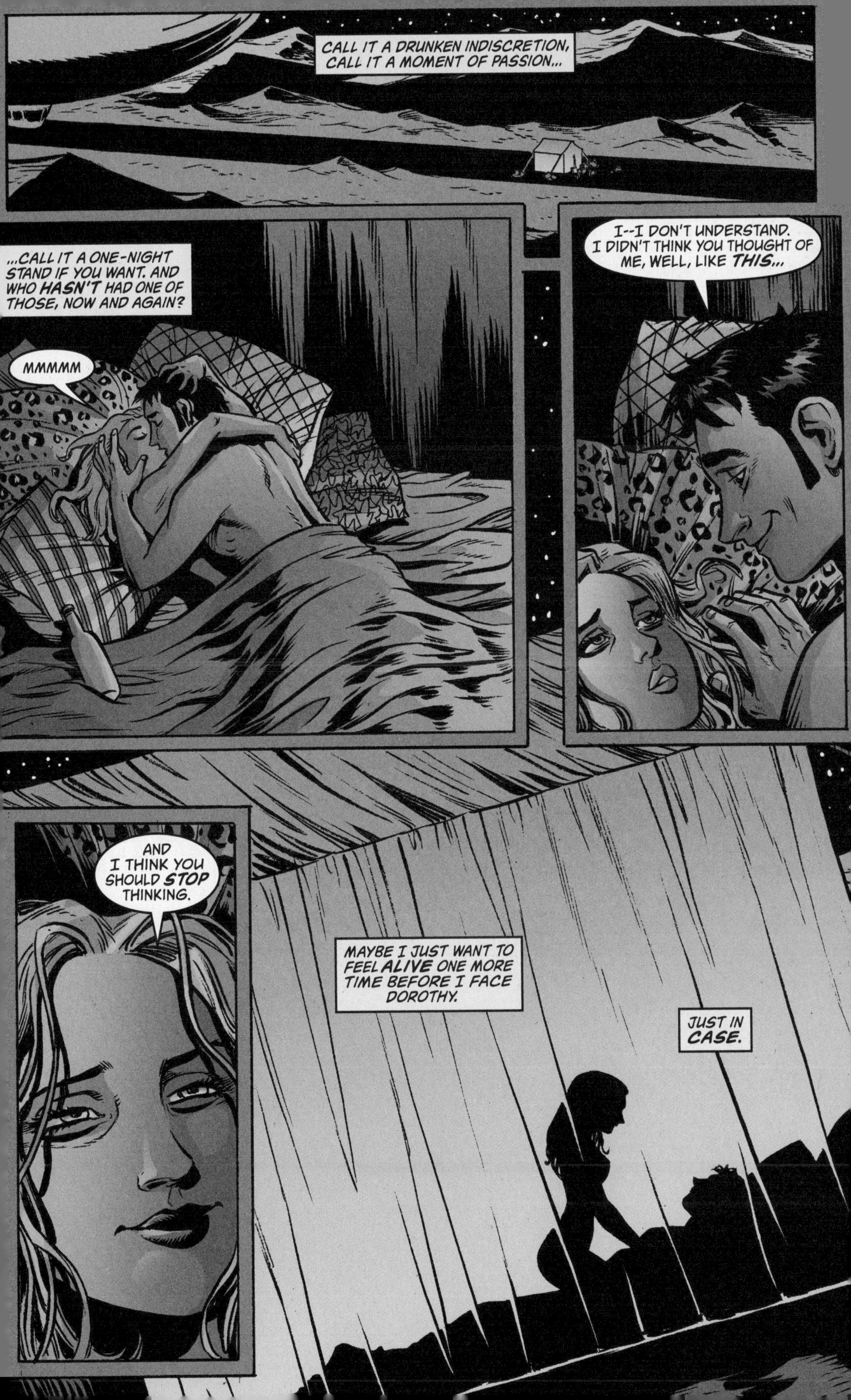

CALL IT A DRUNKEN INDISCRETION, CALL IT A MOMENT OF PASSION...
...CALL IT A ONE-NIGHT STAND IF YOU WANT. AND WHO HASN'T HAD ONE OF THOSE, NOW AND AGAIN?
MMMMM
I--I DON'T UNDERSTAND. I DIDN'T THINK YOU THOUGHT OF ME, WELL, LIKE THIS...
AND I THINK YOU SHOULD STOP THINKING.
MAYBE I JUST WANT TO FEEL ALIVE ONE MORE TIME BEFORE I FACE DOROTHY.
JUST IN CASE.

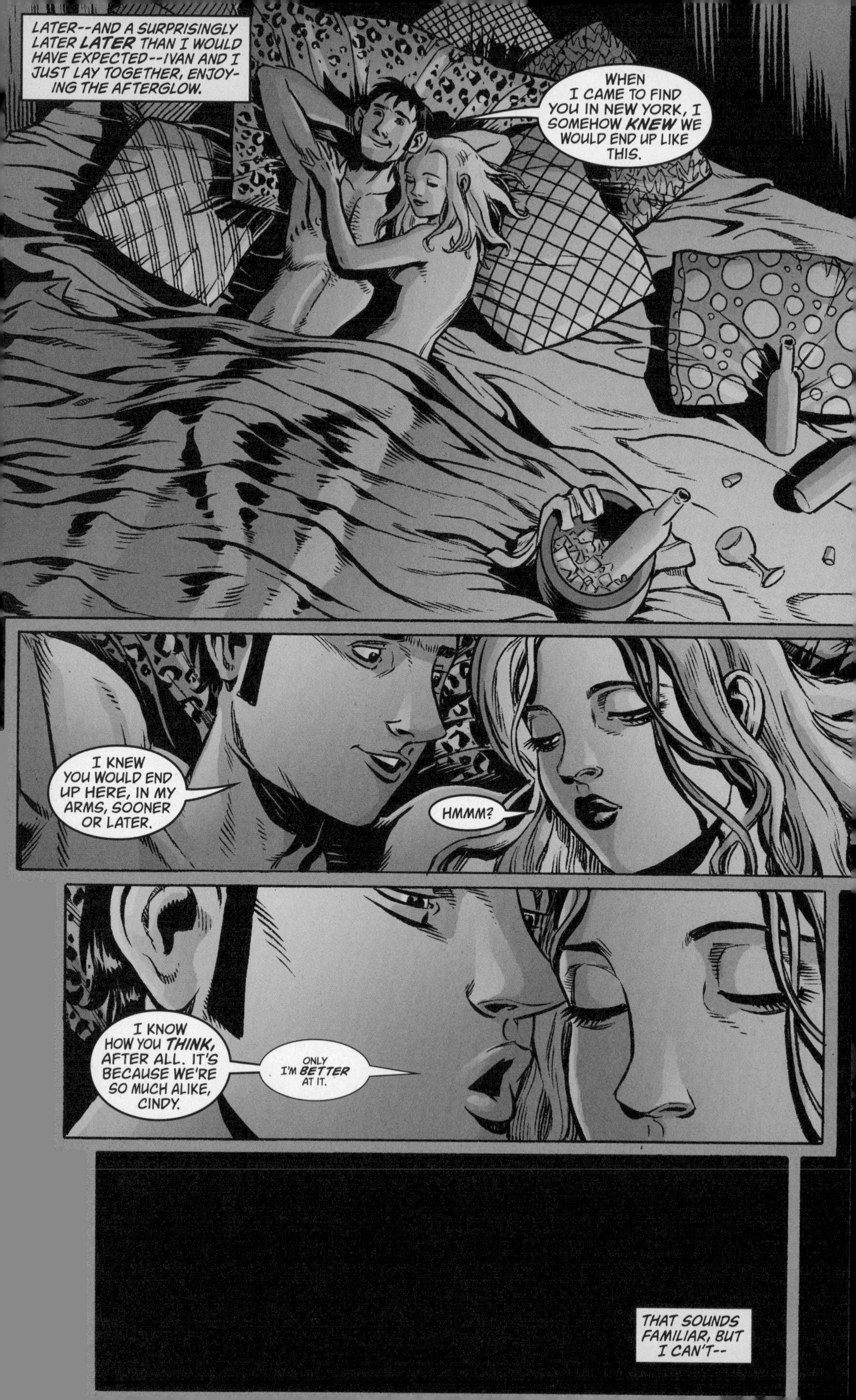
LATER--AND A SURPRISINGLY LATER LATER THAN I WOULD HAVE EXPECTED--IVAN AND I JUST LAY TOGETHER, ENJOYING THE AFTERGLOW.
WHEN I CAME TO FIND YOU IN NEW YORK, I SOMEHOW KNEW WE WOULD END UP LIKE THIS.
I KNEW YOU WOULD END UP HERE, IN MY ARMS, SOONER OR LATER.
HMMM?
I KNOW HOW YOU THINK, AFTER ALL. IT'S BECAUSE WE'RE SO MUCH ALIKE, CINDY.
ONLY I'M BETTER AT IT.
THAT SOUNDS FAMILIAR, BUT I CAN'T--

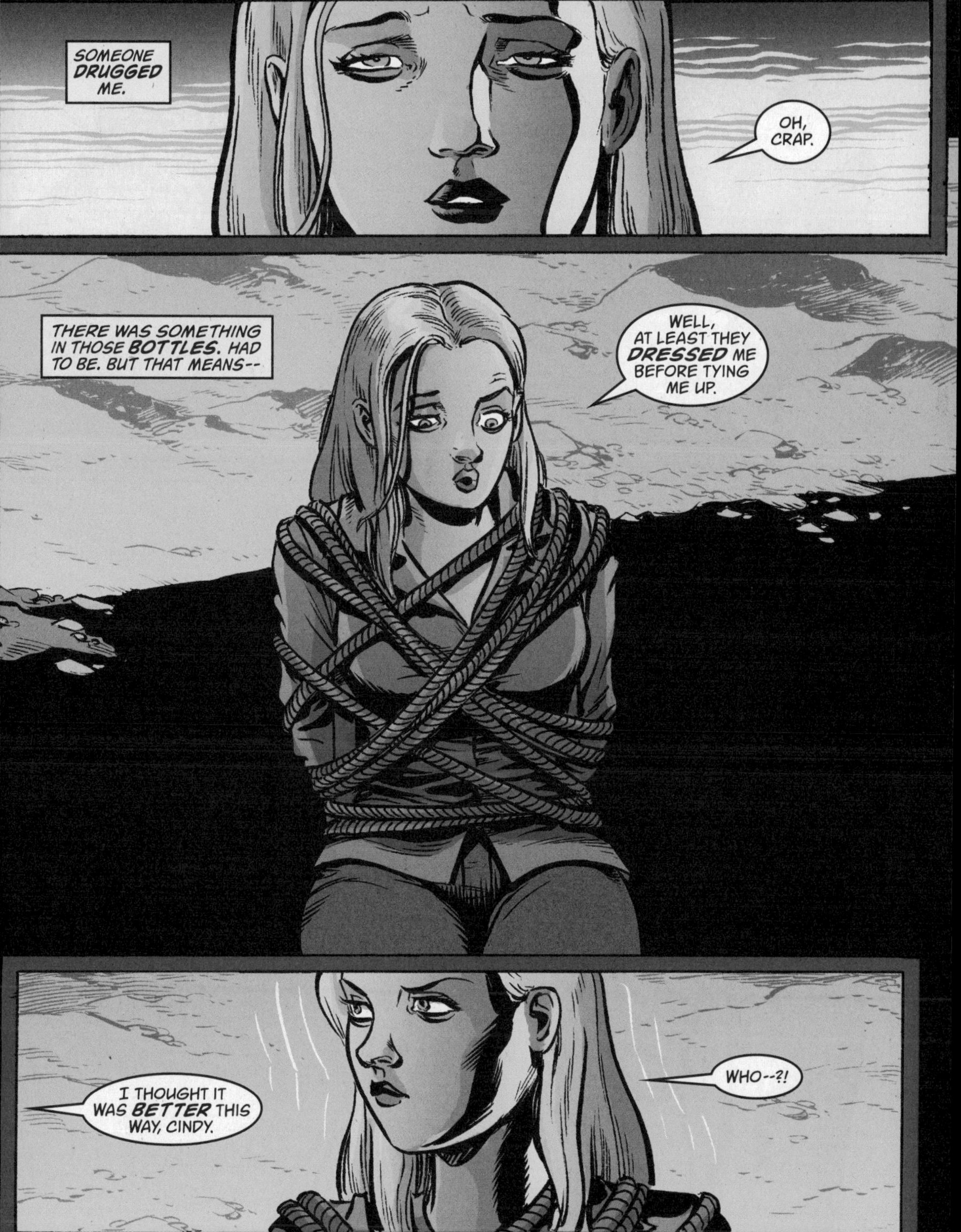
SOMEONE DRUGGED ME.
OH, CRAP.
THERE WAS SOMETHING IN THOSE BOTTLES. HAD TO BE. BUT THAT MEANS--
WELL, AT LEAST THEY DRESSED ME BEFORE TYING ME UP.
I THOUGHT IT WAS BETTER THIS WAY, CINDY.
WHO--?!

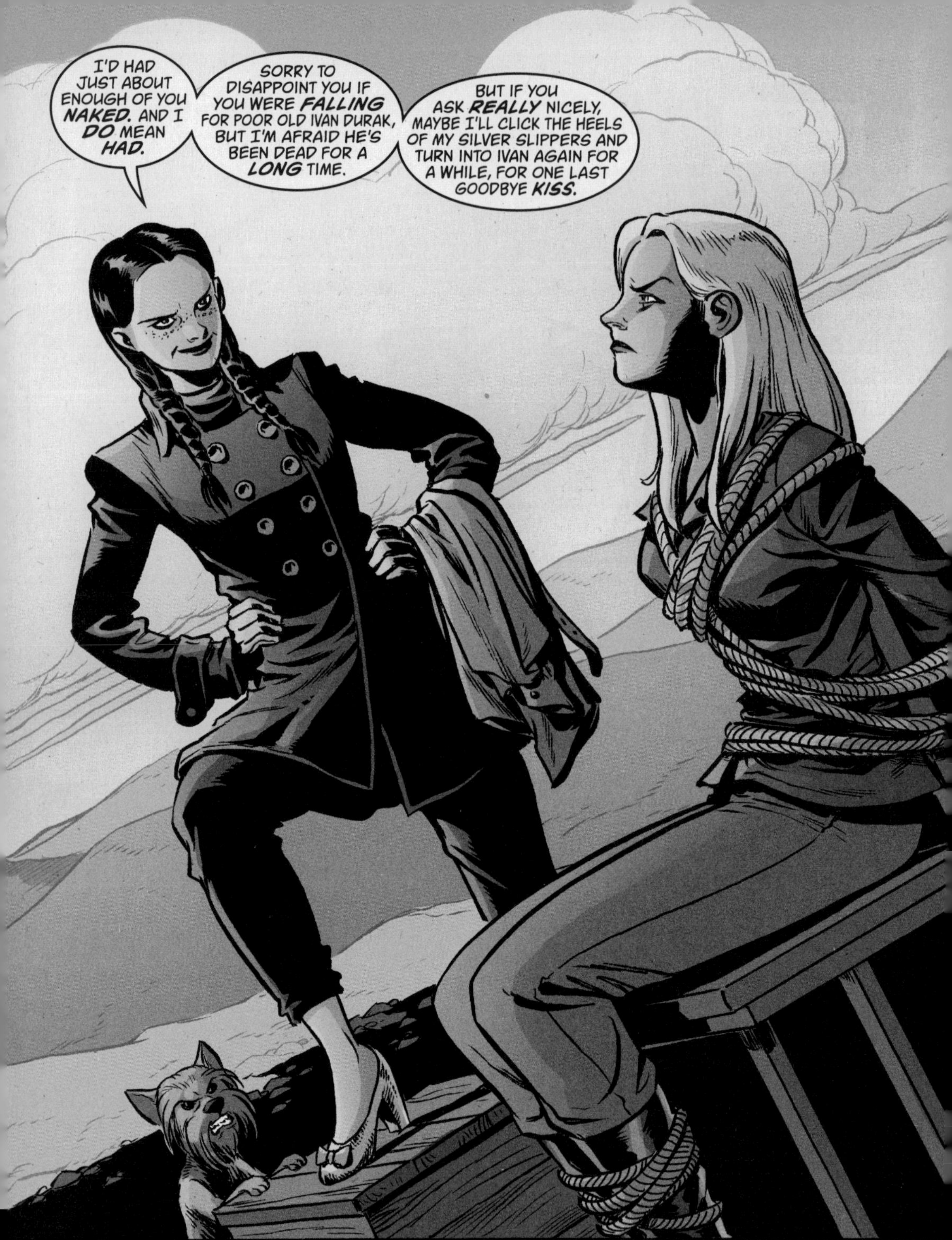
I'D HAD JUST ABOUT ENOUGH OF YOU NAKED. AND I DO MEAN HAD.
SORRY TO DISAPPOINT YOU IF YOU WERE FALLING FOR POOR OLD IVAN DURAK, BUT I'M AFRAID HE'S BEEN DEAD FOR A LONG TIME.
BUT IF YOU ASK REALLY NICELY, MAYBE I'LL CLICK THE HEELS OF MY SILVER SLIPPERS AND TURN INTO IVAN AGAIN FOR A WHILE, FOR ONE LAST GOODBYE KISS.

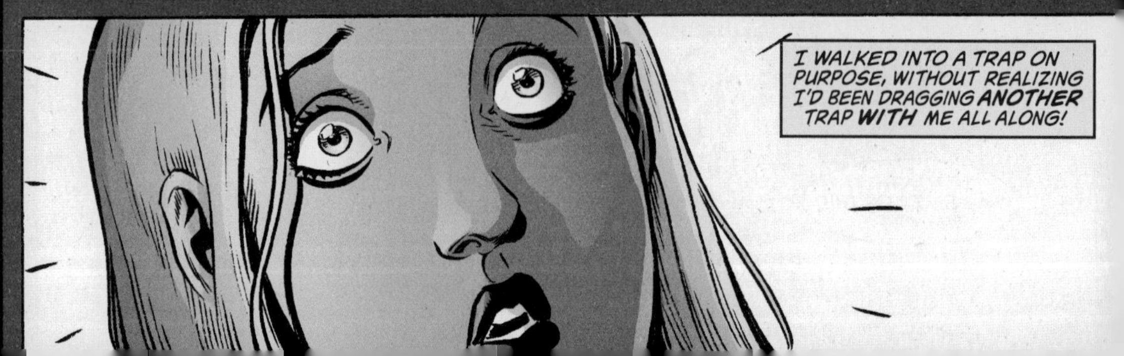
I WALKED INTO A TRAP ON PURPOSE, WITHOUT REALIZING I'D BEEN DRAGGING ANOTHER TRAP WITH ME ALL ALONG!

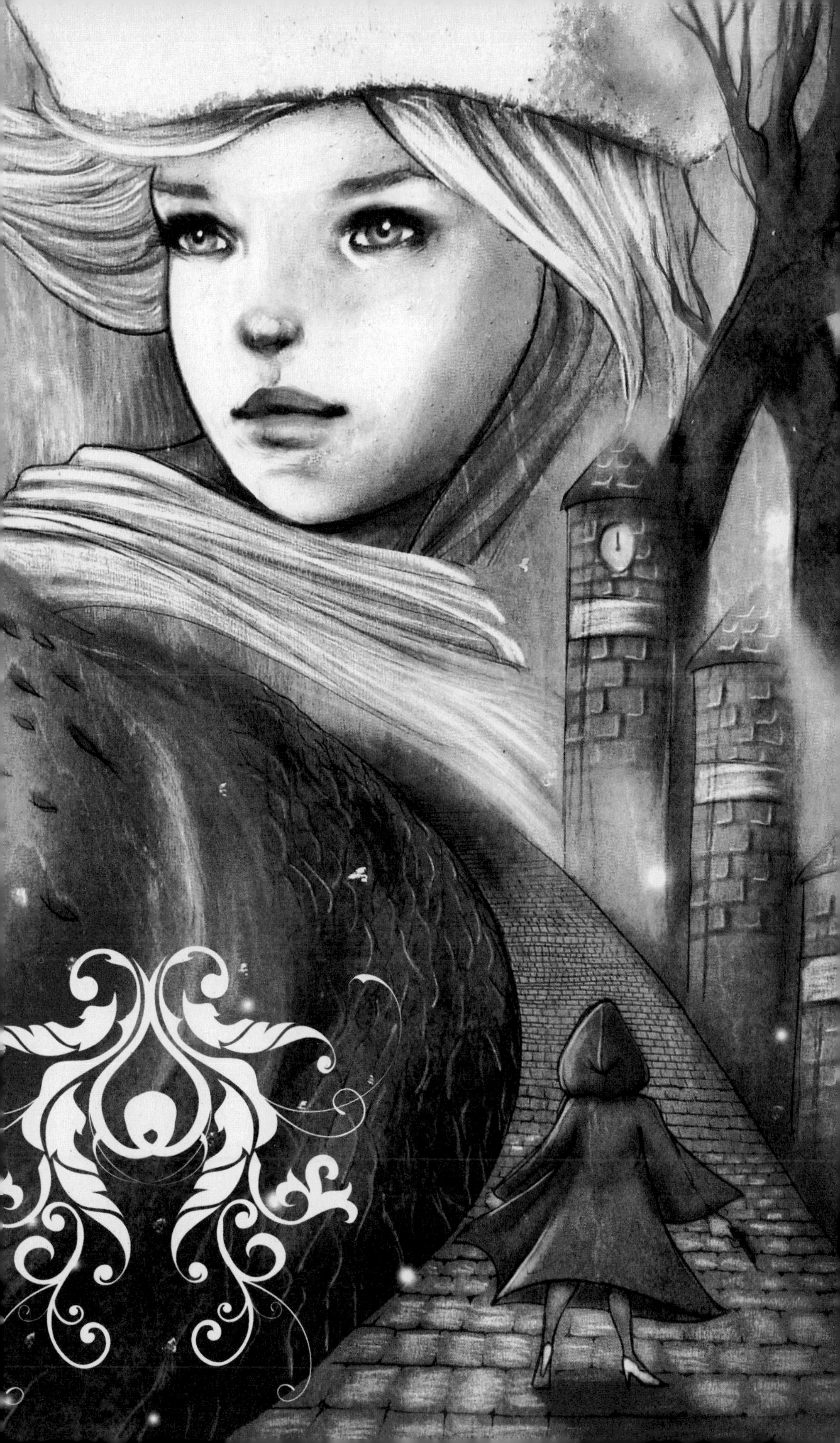

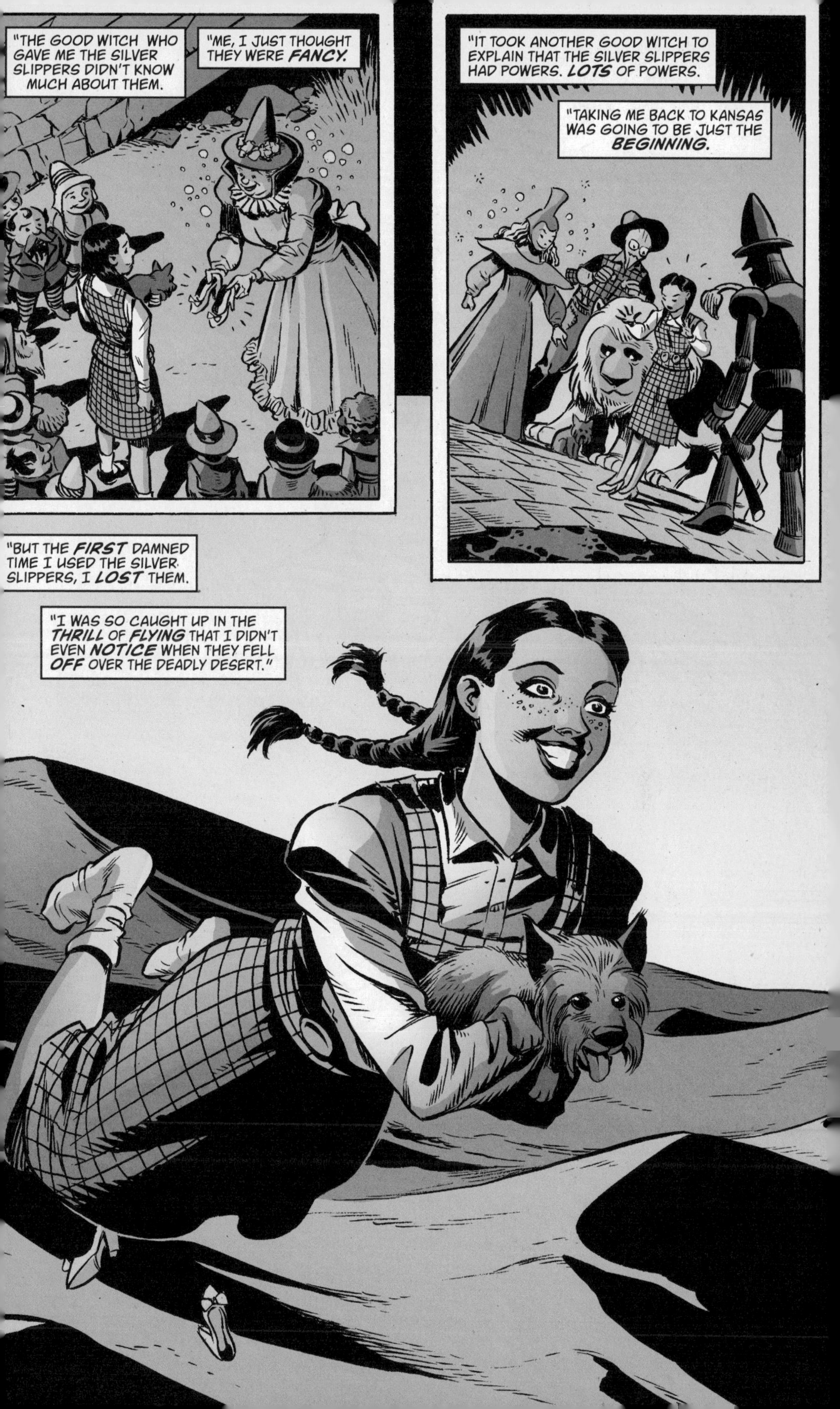
"THE GOOD WITCH WHO GAVE ME THE SILVER SLIPPERS DIDN'T KNOW MUCH ABOUT THEM.
"ME, I JUST THOUGHT THEY WERE FANCY.
"IT TOOK ANOTHER GOOD WITCH TO EXPLAIN THAT THE SILVER SLIPPERS HAD POWERS. LOTS OF POWERS.
"TAKING ME BACK TO KANSAS WAS GOING TO BE JUST THE BEGINNING.
"BUT THE FIRST DAMNED TIME I USED THE SILVER SLIPPERS, I LOST THEM.
"I WAS SO CAUGHT UP IN THE THRILL OF FLYING THAT I DIDN'T EVEN NOTICE WHEN THEY FELL OFF OVER THE DEADLY DESERT."

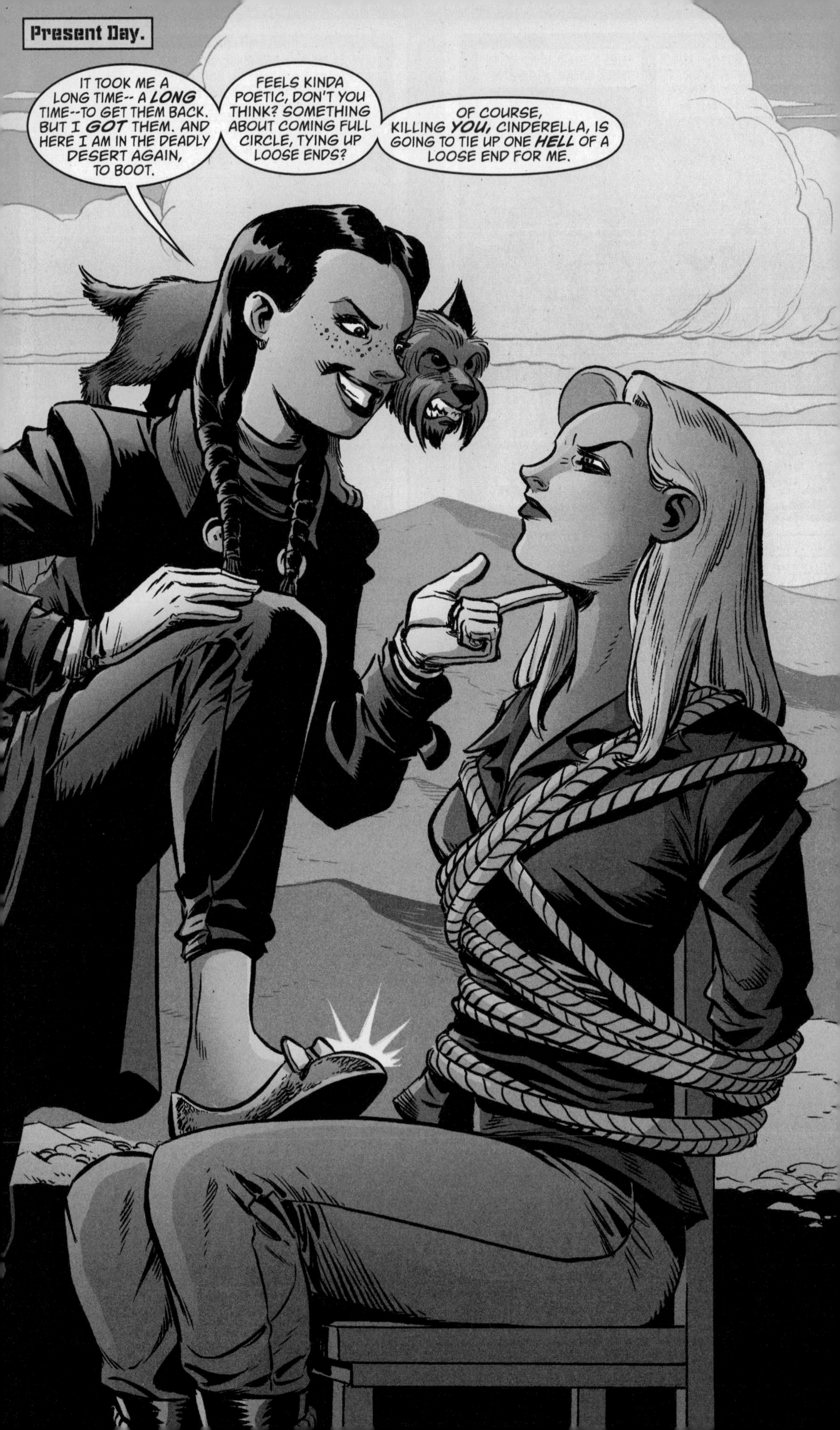
Present Day.
IT TOOK ME A LONG TIME-- A LONG TIME--TO GET THEM BACK. BUT I GOT THEM. AND HERE I AM IN THE DEADLY DESERT AGAIN, TO BOOT.
FEELS KINDA POETIC, DON'T YOU THINK? SOMETHING ABOUT COMING FULL CIRCLE, TYING UP LOOSE ENDS?
OF COURSE, KILLING YOU, CINDERELLA, IS GOING TO TIE UP ONE HELL OF A LOOSE END FOR ME.

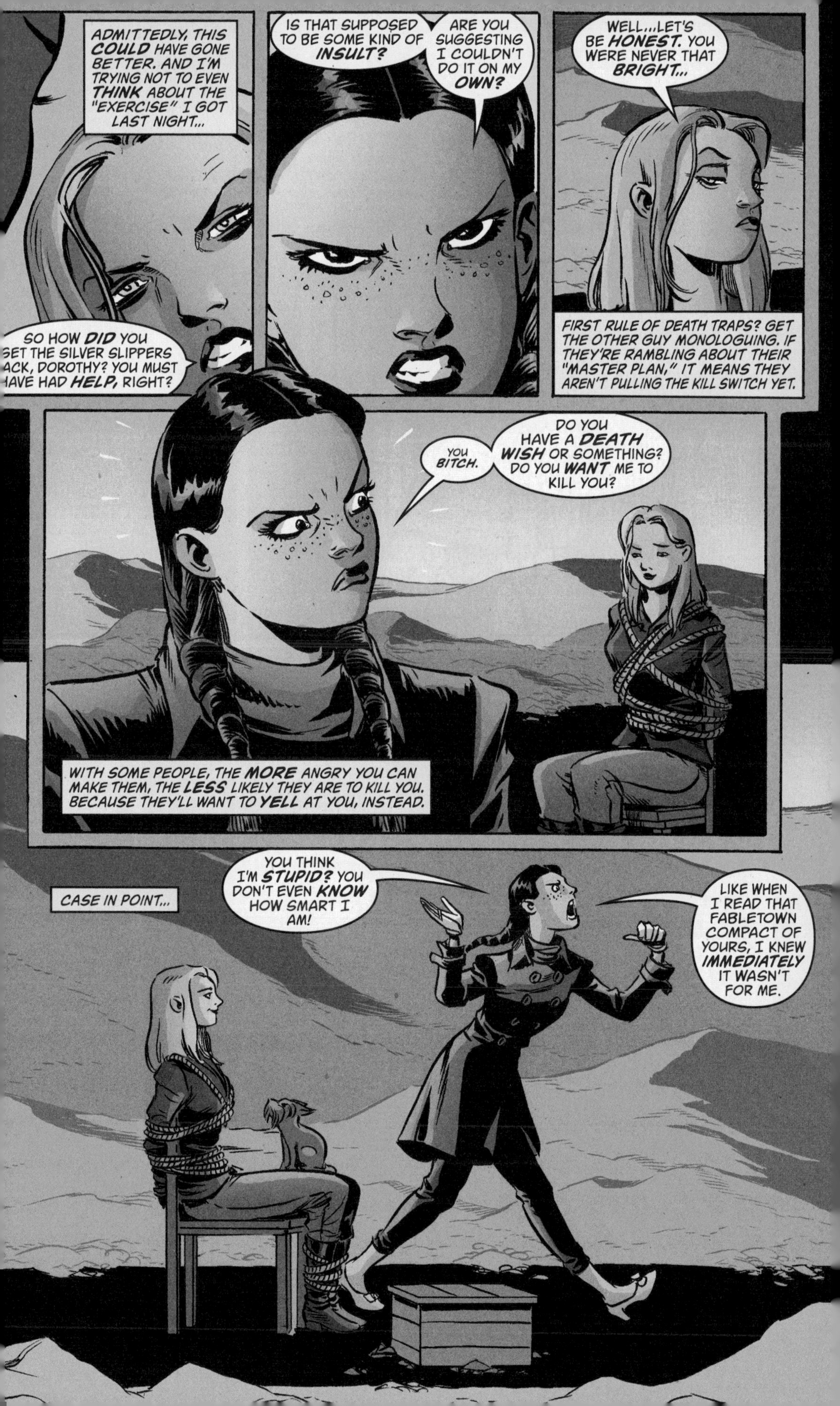

ADMITTEDLY, THIS COULD HAVE GONE BETTER. AND I'M TRYING NOT TO EVEN THINK ABOUT THE "EXERCISE" I GOT LAST NIGHT...
SO HOW DID YOU GET THE SILVER SLIPPERS BACK, DOROTHY? YOU MUST HAVE HAD HELP, RIGHT?
IS THAT SUPPOSED TO BE SOME KIND OF INSULT?
ARE YOU SUGGESTING I COULDN'T DO IT ON MY OWN?
WELL...LET'S BE HONEST. YOU WERE NEVER THAT BRIGHT...
FIRST RULE OF DEATH TRAPS? GET THE OTHER GUY MONOLOGUING. IF THEY'RE RAMBLING ABOUT THEIR "MASTER PLAN," IT MEANS THEY AREN'T PULLING THE KILL SWITCH YET.
YOU BITCH.
DO YOU HAVE A DEATH WISH OR SOMETHING? DO YOU WANT ME TO KILL YOU?
WITH SOME PEOPLE, THE MORE ANGRY YOU CAN MAKE THEM, THE LESS LIKELY THEY ARE TO KILL YOU. BECAUSE THEY'LL WANT TO YELL AT YOU, INSTEAD.
CASE IN POINT...
YOU THINK I'M STUPID? YOU DON'T EVEN KNOW HOW SMART I AM!
LIKE WHEN I READ THAT FABLETOWN COMPACT OF YOURS, I KNEW IMMEDIATELY IT WASN'T FOR ME.

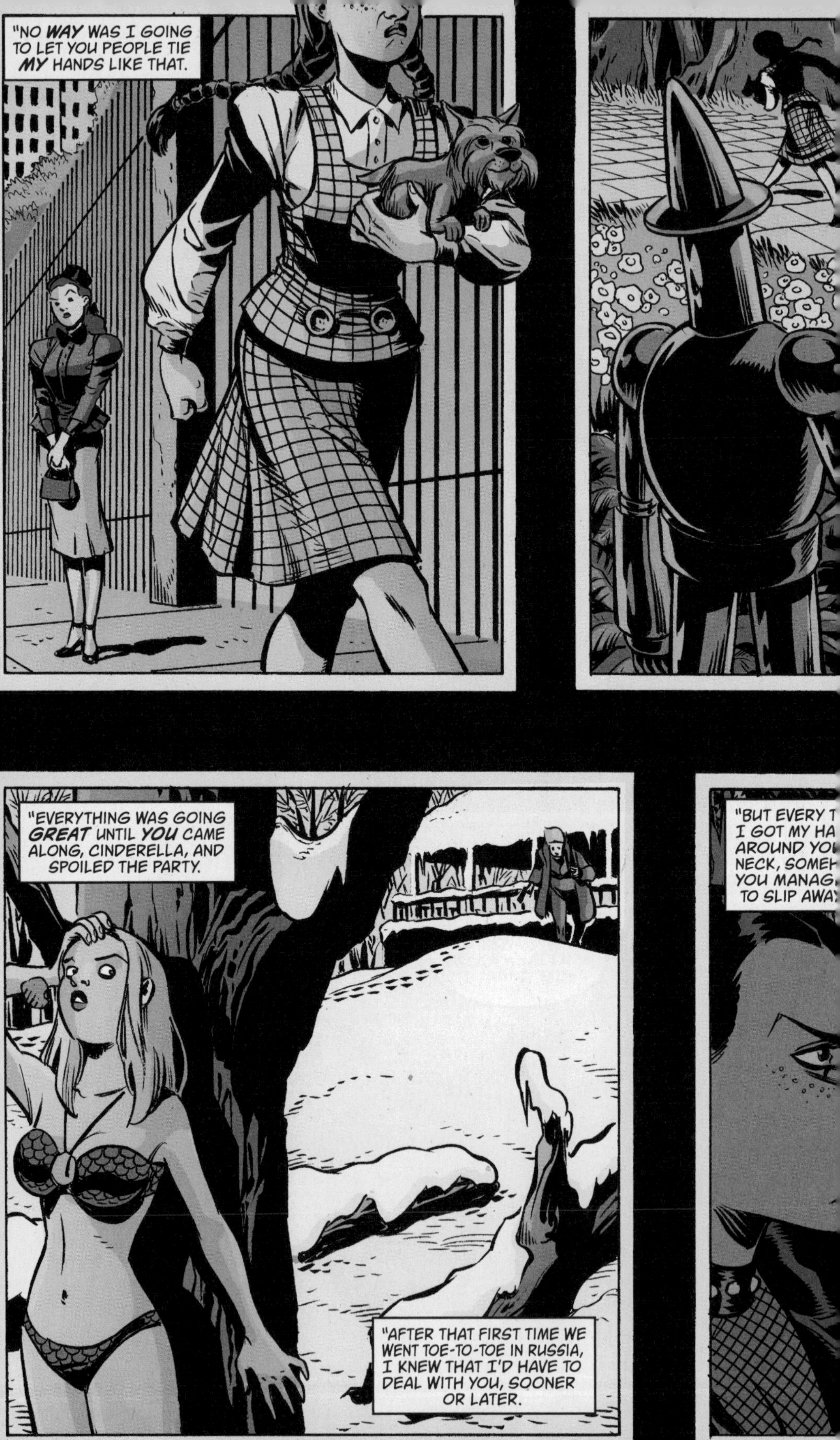
"NO WAY WAS I GOING TO LET YOU PEOPLE TIE MY HANDS LIKE THAT.
"EVERYTHING WAS GOING GREAT UNTIL YOU CAME ALONG, CINDERELLA, AND SPOILED THE PARTY.
"AFTER THAT FIRST TIME WE WENT TOE-TO-TOE IN RUSSIA, I KNEW THAT I'D HAVE TO DEAL WITH YOU, SOONER OR LATER.
"BUT EVERY T
I GOT MY HA
AROUND YO
NECK, SOMEH
YOU MANAG
TO SLIP AWA

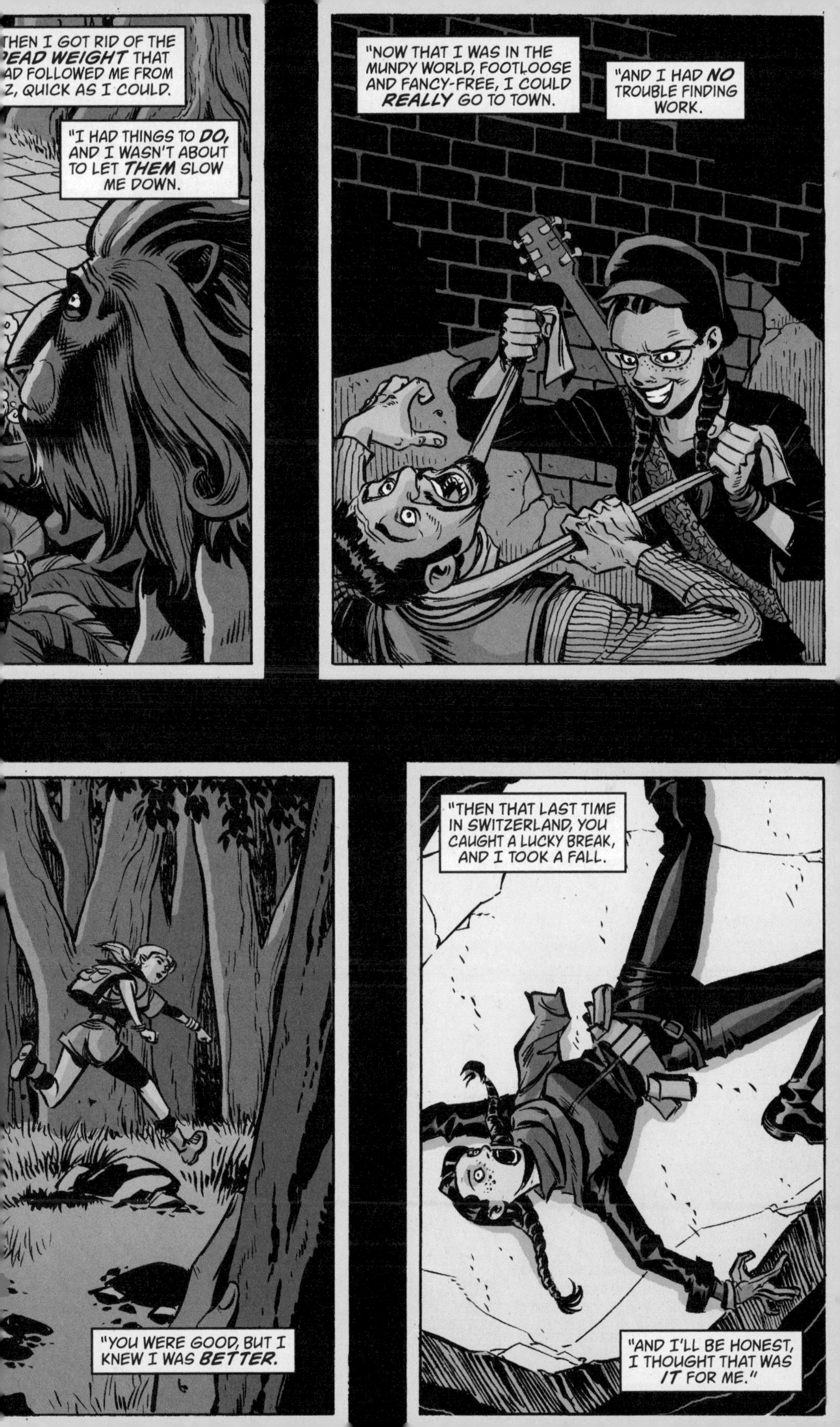

THEN I GOT RID OF THE DEAD WEIGHT THAT HAD FOLLOWED ME FROM OZ, QUICK AS I COULD.
"I HAD THINGS TO DO, AND I WASN'T ABOUT TO LET THEM SLOW ME DOWN.
"NOW THAT I WAS IN THE MUNDY WORLD, FOOTLOOSE AND FANCY-FREE, I COULD REALLY GO TO TOWN.
"AND I HAD NO TROUBLE FINDING WORK.
"YOU WERE GOOD, BUT I KNEW I WAS BETTER.
"THEN THAT LAST TIME IN SWITZERLAND, YOU CAUGHT A LUCKY BREAK, AND I TOOK A FALL.
"AND I'LL BE HONEST, I THOUGHT THAT WAS IT FOR ME."

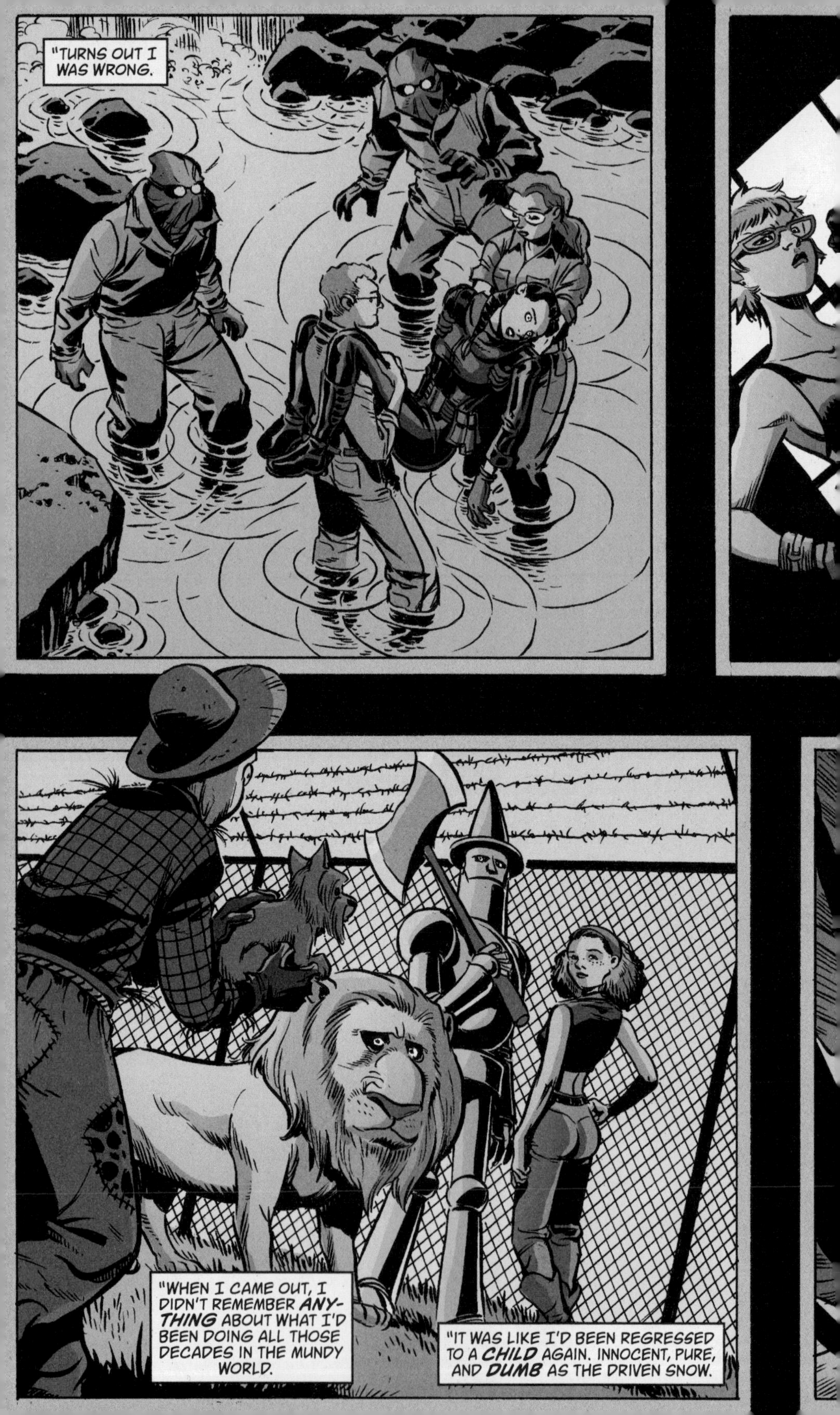
"TURNS OUT I WAS WRONG.
"WHEN I CAME OUT, I DIDN'T REMEMBER ANY-THING ABOUT WHAT I'D BEEN DOING ALL THOSE DECADES IN THE MUNDY WORLD.
"IT WAS LIKE I'D BEEN REGRESSED TO A CHILD AGAIN. INNOCENT, PURE, AND DUMB AS THE DRIVEN SNOW.

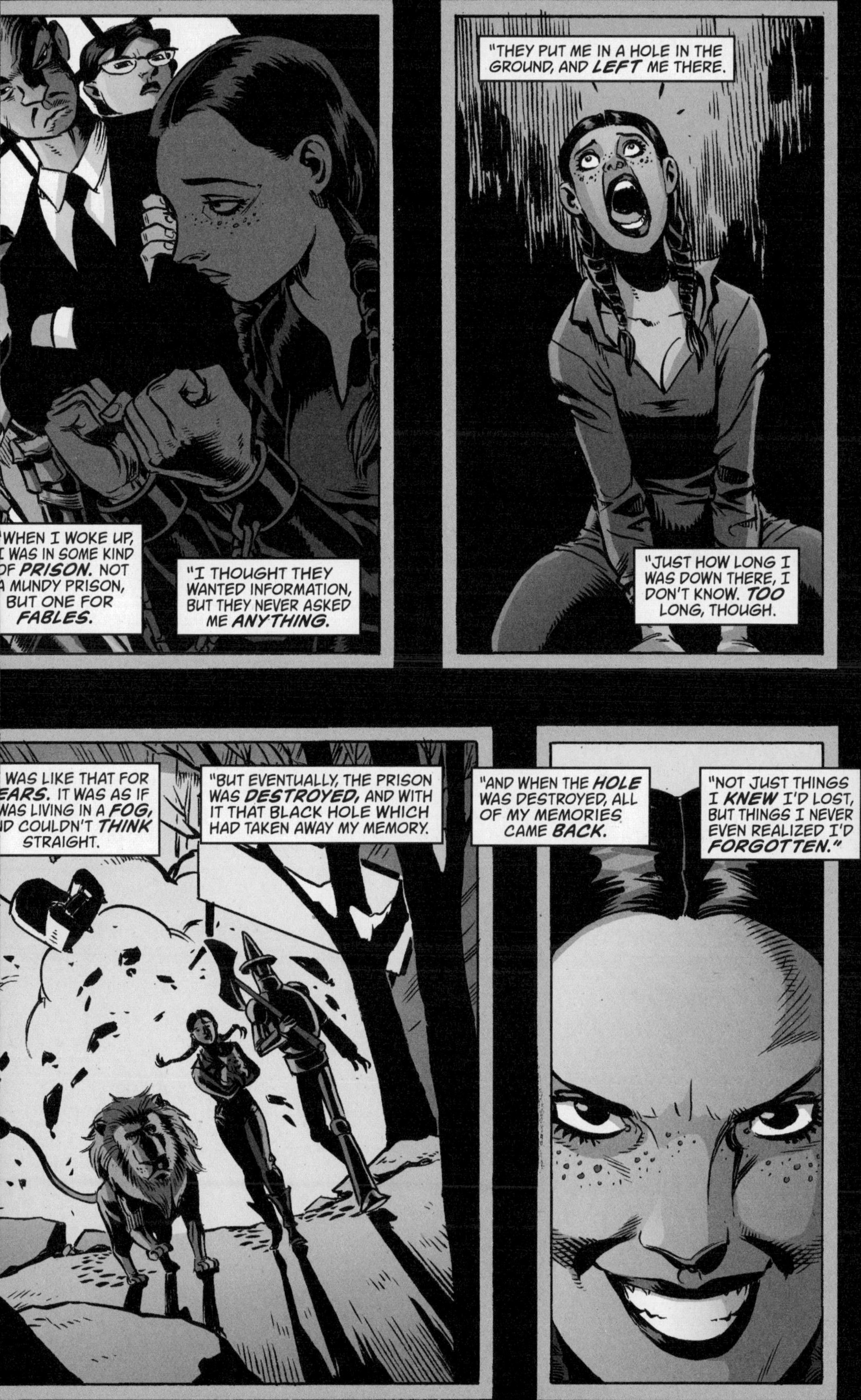
"WHEN I WOKE UP, I WAS IN SOME KIND OF PRISON. NOT A MUNDY PRISON, BUT ONE FOR FABLES.
"I THOUGHT THEY WANTED INFORMATION, BUT THEY NEVER ASKED ME ANYTHING.
"THEY PUT ME IN A HOLE IN THE GROUND, AND LEFT ME THERE.
"JUST HOW LONG I WAS DOWN THERE, I DON'T KNOW. TOO LONG, THOUGH.
WAS LIKE THAT FOR EARS. IT WAS AS IF WAS LIVING IN A FOG, D COULDN'T THINK STRAIGHT.
"BUT EVENTUALLY, THE PRISON WAS DESTROYED, AND WITH IT THAT BLACK HOLE WHICH HAD TAKEN AWAY MY MEMORY.
"AND WHEN THE HOLE WAS DESTROYED, ALL OF MY MEMORIES CAME BACK.
"NOT JUST THINGS I KNEW I'D LOST, BUT THINGS I NEVER EVEN REALIZED I'D FORGOTTEN."

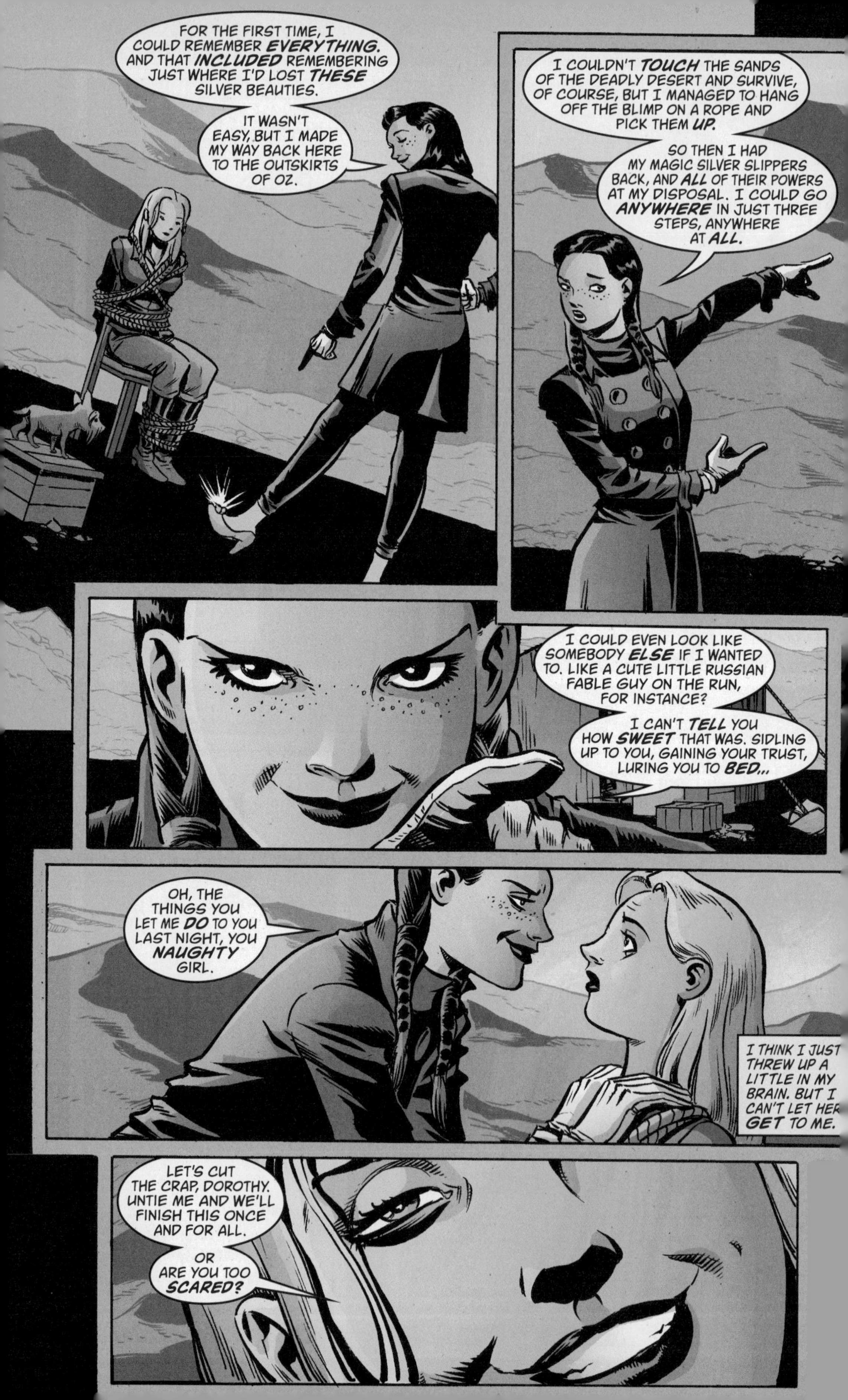

FOR THE FIRST TIME, I COULD REMEMBER EVERYTHING. AND THAT INCLUDED REMEMBERING JUST WHERE I'D LOST THESE SILVER BEAUTIES.
IT WASN'T EASY, BUT I MADE MY WAY BACK HERE TO THE OUTSKIRTS OF OZ.
I COULDN'T TOUCH THE SANDS OF THE DEADLY DESERT AND SURVIVE, OF COURSE, BUT I MANAGED TO HANG OFF THE BLIMP ON A ROPE AND PICK THEM UP.
SO THEN I HAD MY MAGIC SILVER SLIPPERS BACK, AND ALL OF THEIR POWERS AT MY DISPOSAL. I COULD GO ANYWHERE IN JUST THREE STEPS, ANYWHERE AT ALL.
I COULD EVEN LOOK LIKE SOMEBODY ELSE IF I WANTED TO. LIKE A CUTE LITTLE RUSSIAN FABLE GUY ON THE RUN, FOR INSTANCE?
I CAN'T TELL YOU HOW SWEET THAT WAS. SIDLING UP TO YOU, GAINING YOUR TRUST, LURING YOU TO BED...
OH, THE THINGS YOU LET ME DO TO YOU LAST NIGHT, YOU NAUGHTY GIRL.
I THINK I JUST THREW UP A LITTLE IN MY BRAIN. BUT I CAN'T LET HER GET TO ME.
LET'S CUT THE CRAP, DOROTHY. UNTIE ME AND WE'LL FINISH THIS ONCE AND FOR ALL.
OR ARE YOU TOO SCARED?

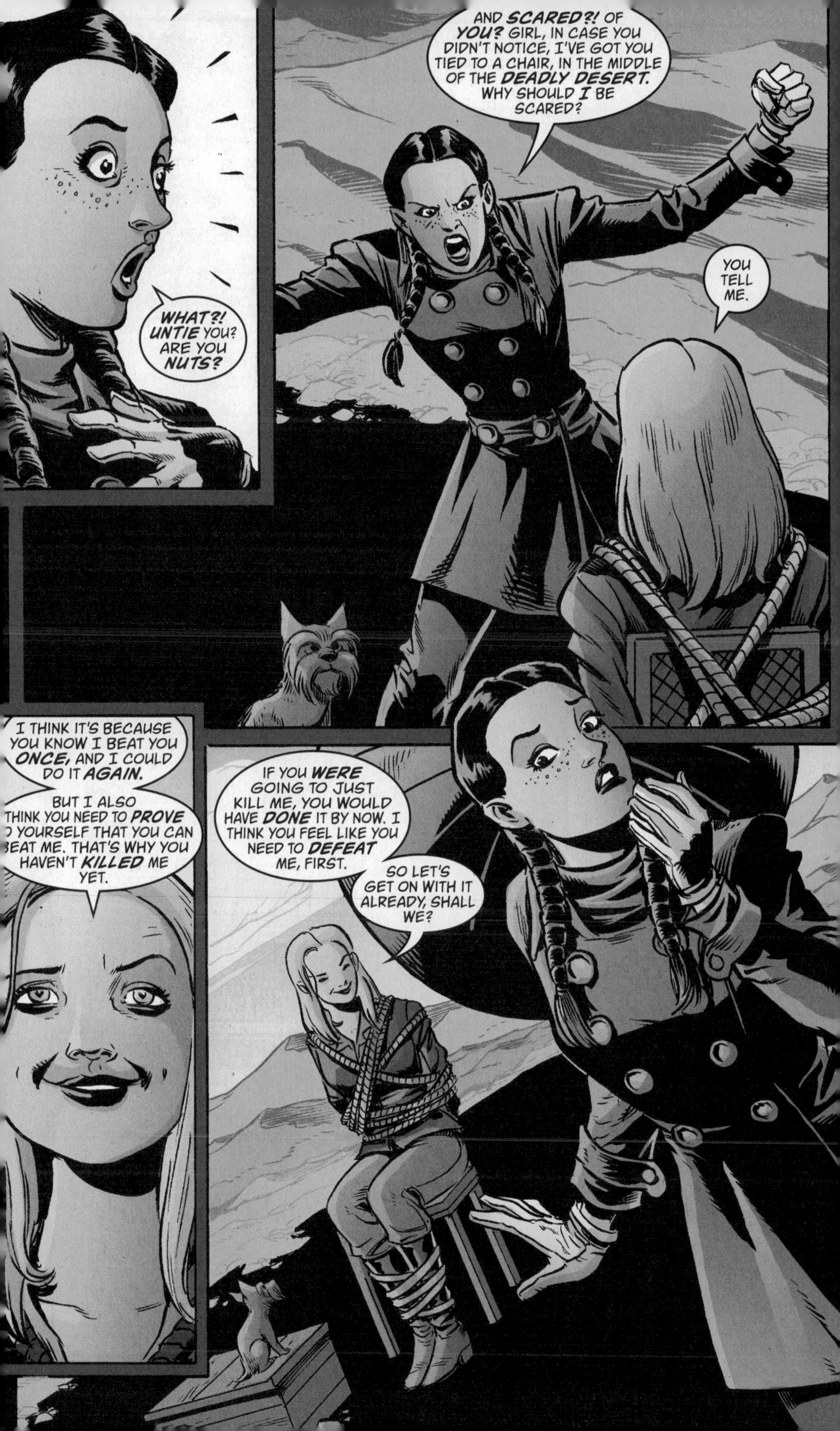
WHAT?! UNTIE YOU? ARE YOU NUTS?
AND SCARED?! OF YOU? GIRL, IN CASE YOU DIDN'T NOTICE, I'VE GOT YOU TIED TO A CHAIR, IN THE MIDDLE OF THE DEADLY DESERT. WHY SHOULD I BE SCARED?
YOU TELL ME.
I THINK IT'S BECAUSE YOU KNOW I BEAT YOU ONCE, AND I COULD DO IT AGAIN.
BUT I ALSO THINK YOU NEED TO PROVE TO YOURSELF THAT YOU CAN BEAT ME. THAT'S WHY YOU HAVEN'T KILLED ME YET.
IF YOU WERE GOING TO JUST KILL ME, YOU WOULD HAVE DONE IT BY NOW. I THINK YOU FEEL LIKE YOU NEED TO DEFEAT ME, FIRST.
SO LET'S GET ON WITH IT ALREADY, SHALL WE?

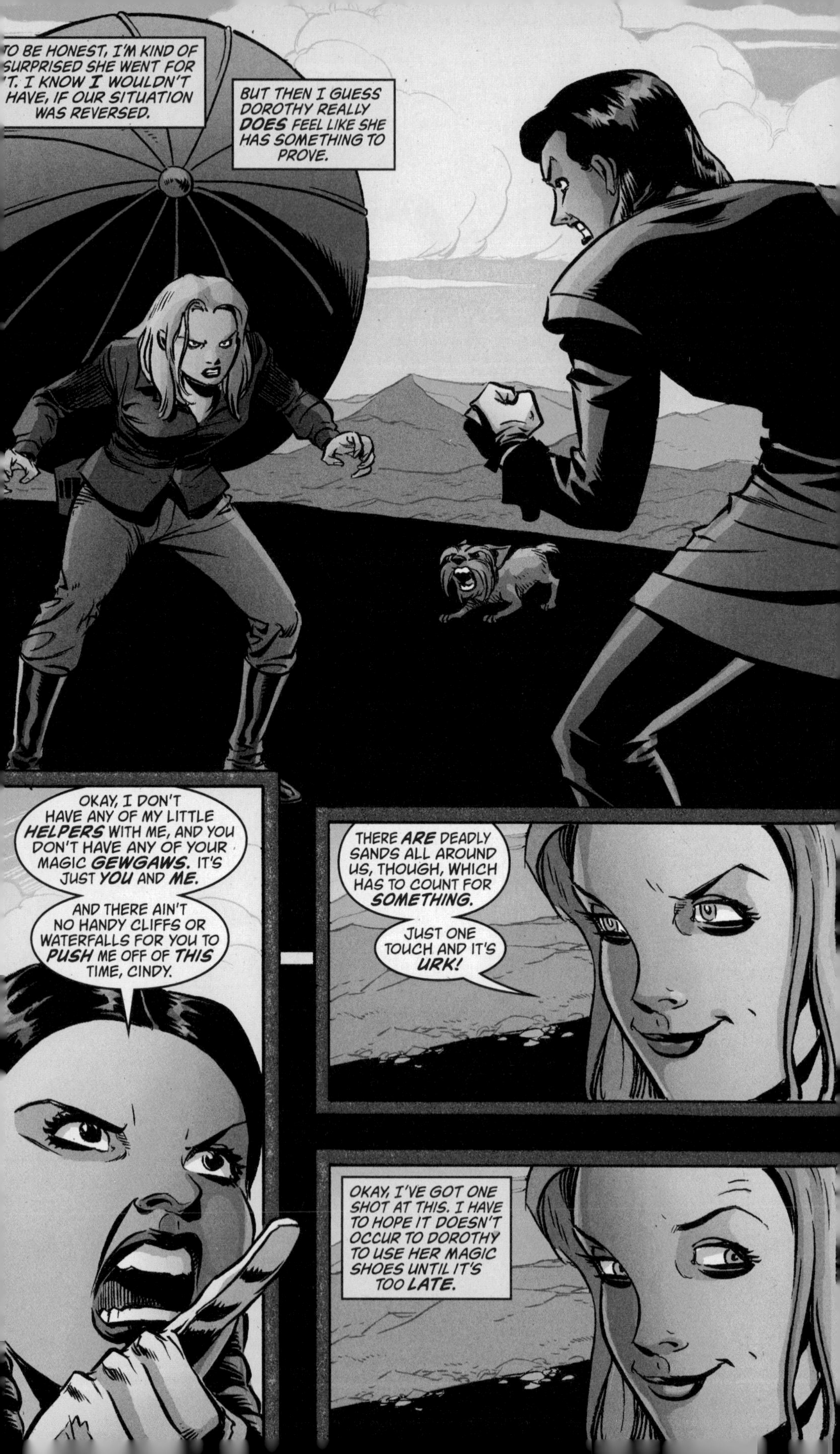
TO BE HONEST, I'M KIND OF SURPRISED SHE WENT FOR IT. I KNOW I WOULDN'T HAVE, IF OUR SITUATION WAS REVERSED.
BUT THEN I GUESS DOROTHY REALLY DOES FEEL LIKE SHE HAS SOMETHING TO PROVE.
OKAY, I DON'T HAVE ANY OF MY LITTLE HELPERS WITH ME, AND YOU DON'T HAVE ANY OF YOUR MAGIC GEWGAWS. IT'S JUST YOU AND ME.
AND THERE AIN'T NO HANDY CLIFFS OR WATERFALLS FOR YOU TO PUSH ME OFF OF THIS TIME, CINDY.
THERE ARE DEADLY SANDS ALL AROUND US, THOUGH, WHICH HAS TO COUNT FOR SOMETHING.
JUST ONE TOUCH AND IT'S URK!
OKAY, I'VE GOT ONE SHOT AT THIS. I HAVE TO HOPE IT DOESN'T OCCUR TO DOROTHY TO USE HER MAGIC SHOES UNTIL IT'S TOO LATE.

OKAY, DOROTHY, SEE YOU LATER!

W-WHAT?!

DOROTHY MIGHT HAVE A CHIP ON HER SHOULDER, BUT ME? I'VE GOT NOTHING TO PROVE.

COME BACK HERE!!

:OOF!:

SLAM!

:UNF!:

OF COURSE THERE ISN'T ANYTHING I CAN USE AS A WEAPON IN HERE, I

WELL, DISCRETION IS THE BETTER PART OF VALOR.

THUD THUD THUD

THIS ISN'T OVER, YOU BITCH! COME OUT HERE AND FIGHT LIKE A GIRL!

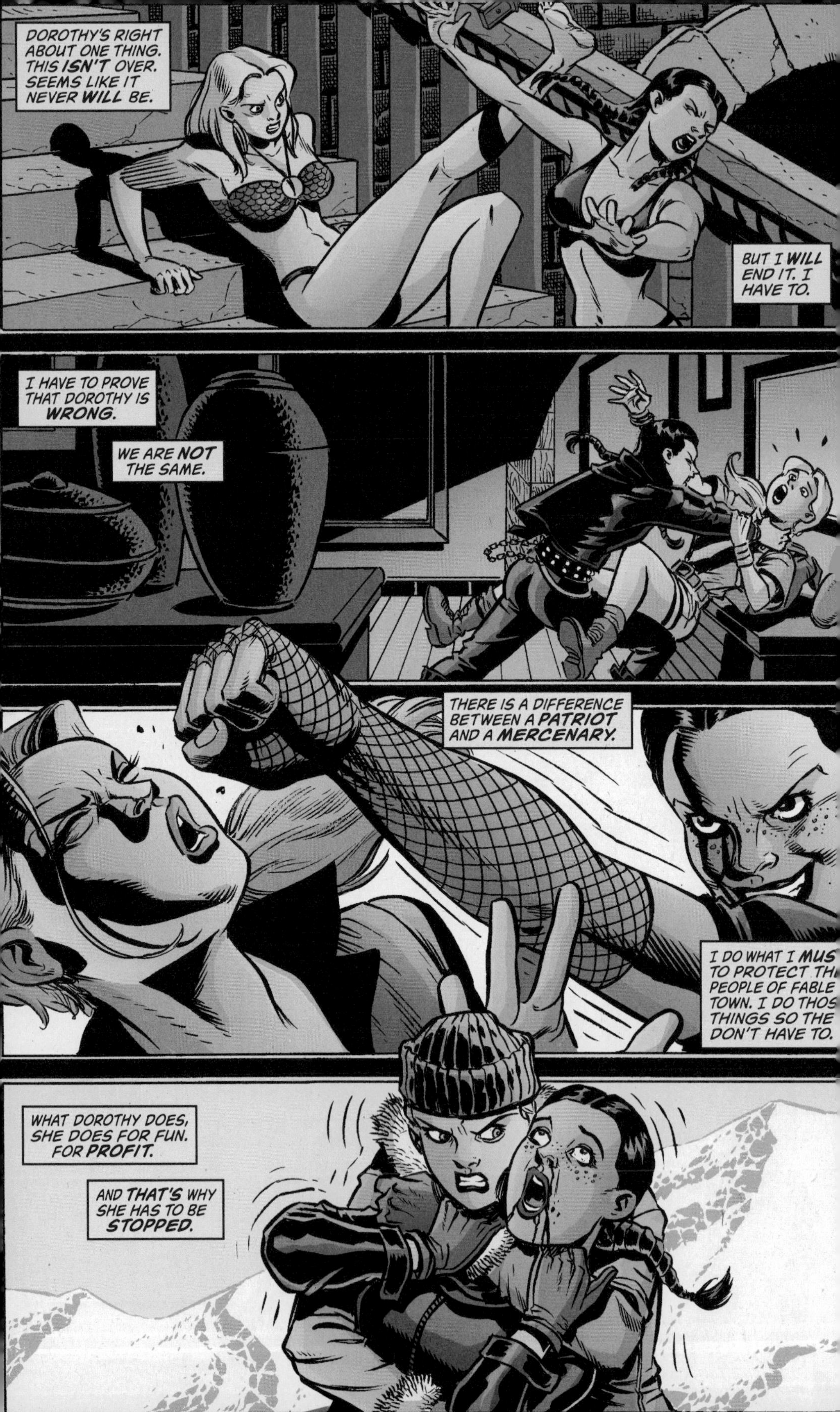
DOROTHY'S RIGHT ABOUT ONE THING. THIS ISN'T OVER. SEEMS LIKE IT NEVER WILL BE.
BUT I WILL END IT. I HAVE TO.
I HAVE TO PROVE THAT DOROTHY IS WRONG.
WE ARE NOT THE SAME.
THERE IS A DIFFERENCE BETWEEN A PATRIOT AND A MERCENARY.
I DO WHAT I MUS TO PROTECT TH PEOPLE OF FABLE TOWN. I DO THOS THINGS SO THE DON'T HAVE TO.
WHAT DOROTHY DOES, SHE DOES FOR FUN. FOR PROFIT.
AND THAT'S WHY SHE HAS TO BE STOPPED.

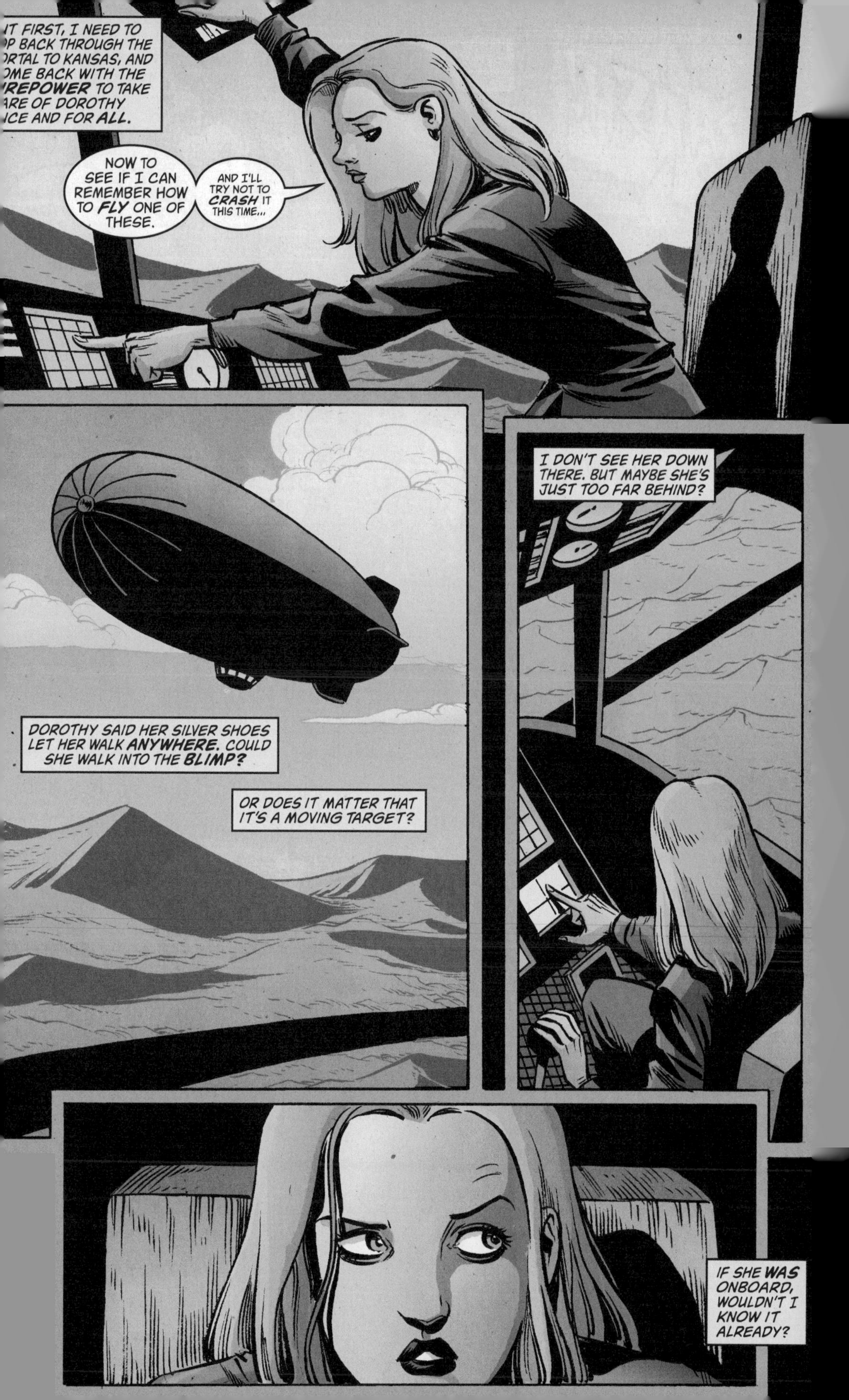

IT FIRST, I NEED TO
P BACK THROUGH THE
RTAL TO KANSAS, AND
OME BACK WITH THE
REPOWER TO TAKE
ARE OF DOROTHY
ICE AND FOR ALL.
NOW TO SEE IF I CAN REMEMBER HOW TO FLY ONE OF THESE.
AND I'LL TRY NOT TO CRASH IT THIS TIME...
DOROTHY SAID HER SILVER SHOES LET HER WALK ANYWHERE. COULD SHE WALK INTO THE BLIMP?
OR DOES IT MATTER THAT IT'S A MOVING TARGET?
I DON'T SEE HER DOWN THERE. BUT MAYBE SHE'S JUST TOO FAR BEHIND?
IF SHE WAS ONBOARD, WOULDN'T I KNOW IT ALREADY?

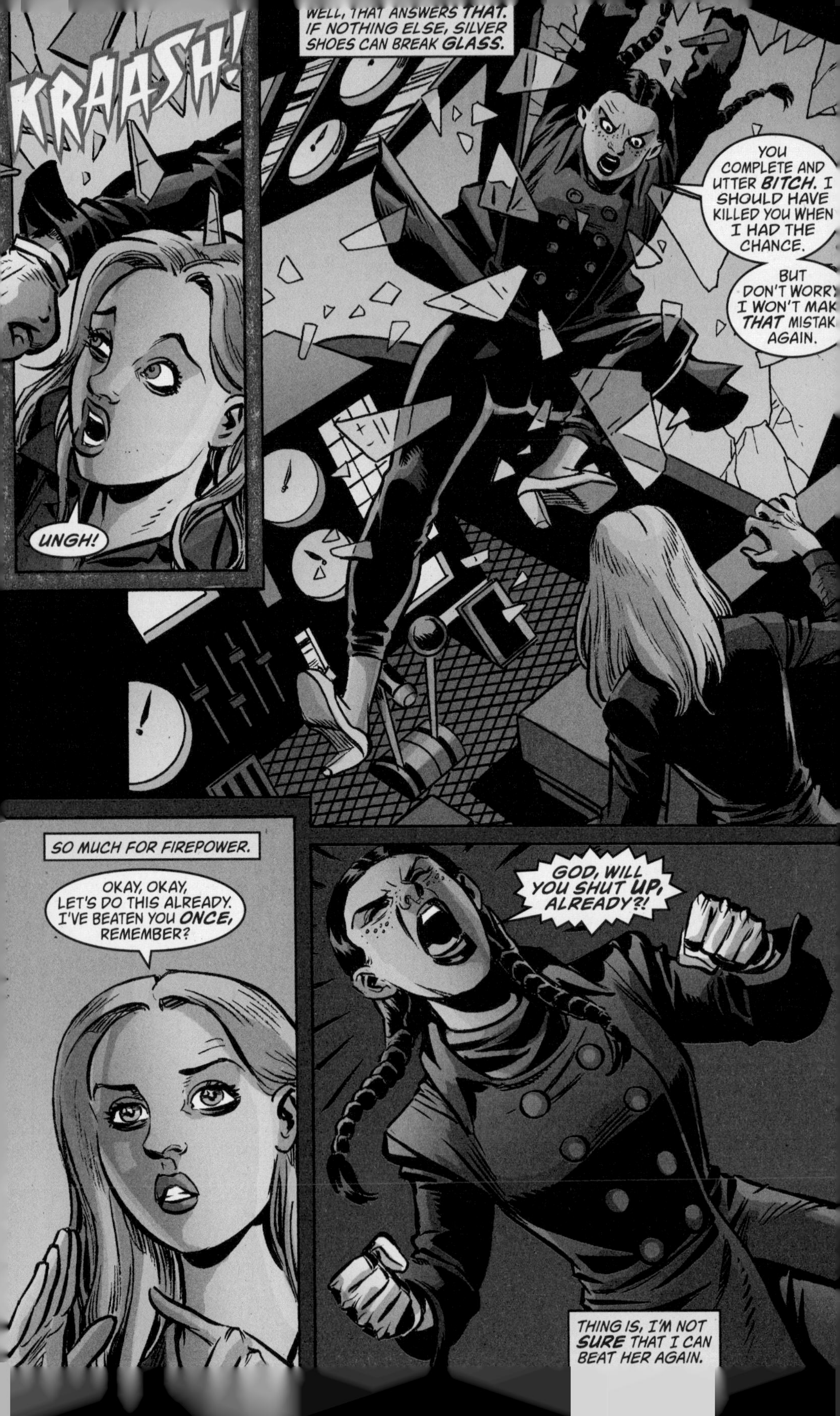
KRAASH!
UNGH!
WELL, THAT ANSWERS THAT. IF NOTHING ELSE, SILVER SHOES CAN BREAK GLASS.
YOU COMPLETE AND UTTER BITCH. I SHOULD HAVE KILLED YOU WHEN I HAD THE CHANCE.
BUT DON'T WORRY I WON'T MAK THAT MISTAK AGAIN.
SO MUCH FOR FIREPOWER.
OKAY, OKAY, LET'S DO THIS ALREADY. I'VE BEATEN YOU ONCE, REMEMBER?
GOD, WILL YOU SHUT UP, ALREADY?!
THING IS, I'M NOT SURE THAT I CAN BEAT HER AGAIN.

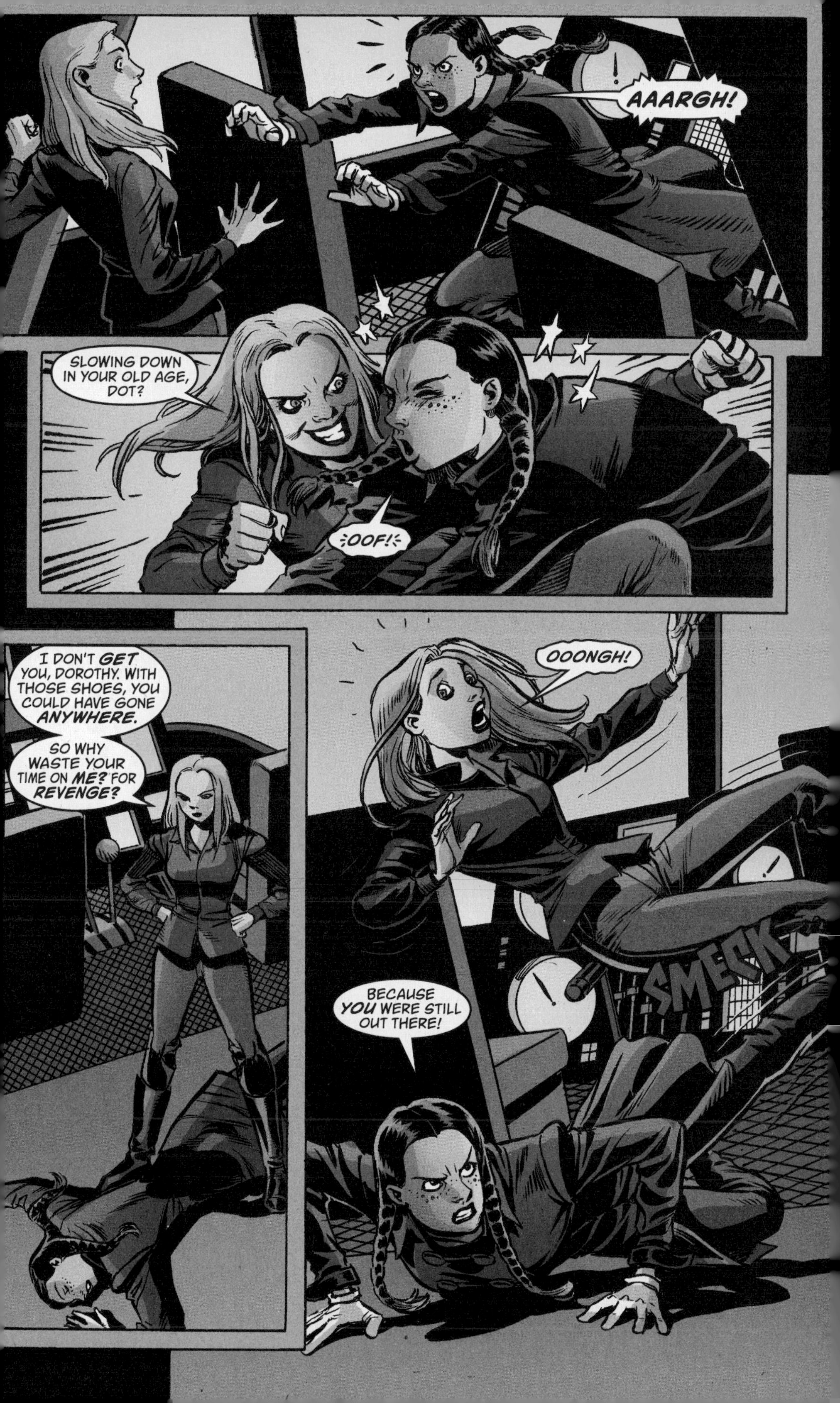
AAARGH!
SLOWING DOWN IN YOUR OLD AGE, DOT?
OOF!
I DON'T GET YOU, DOROTHY. WITH THOSE SHOES, YOU COULD HAVE GONE ANYWHERE.
SO WHY WASTE YOUR TIME ON ME? FOR REVENGE?
OOONGH!
BECAUSE YOU WERE STILL OUT THERE!
SMECK

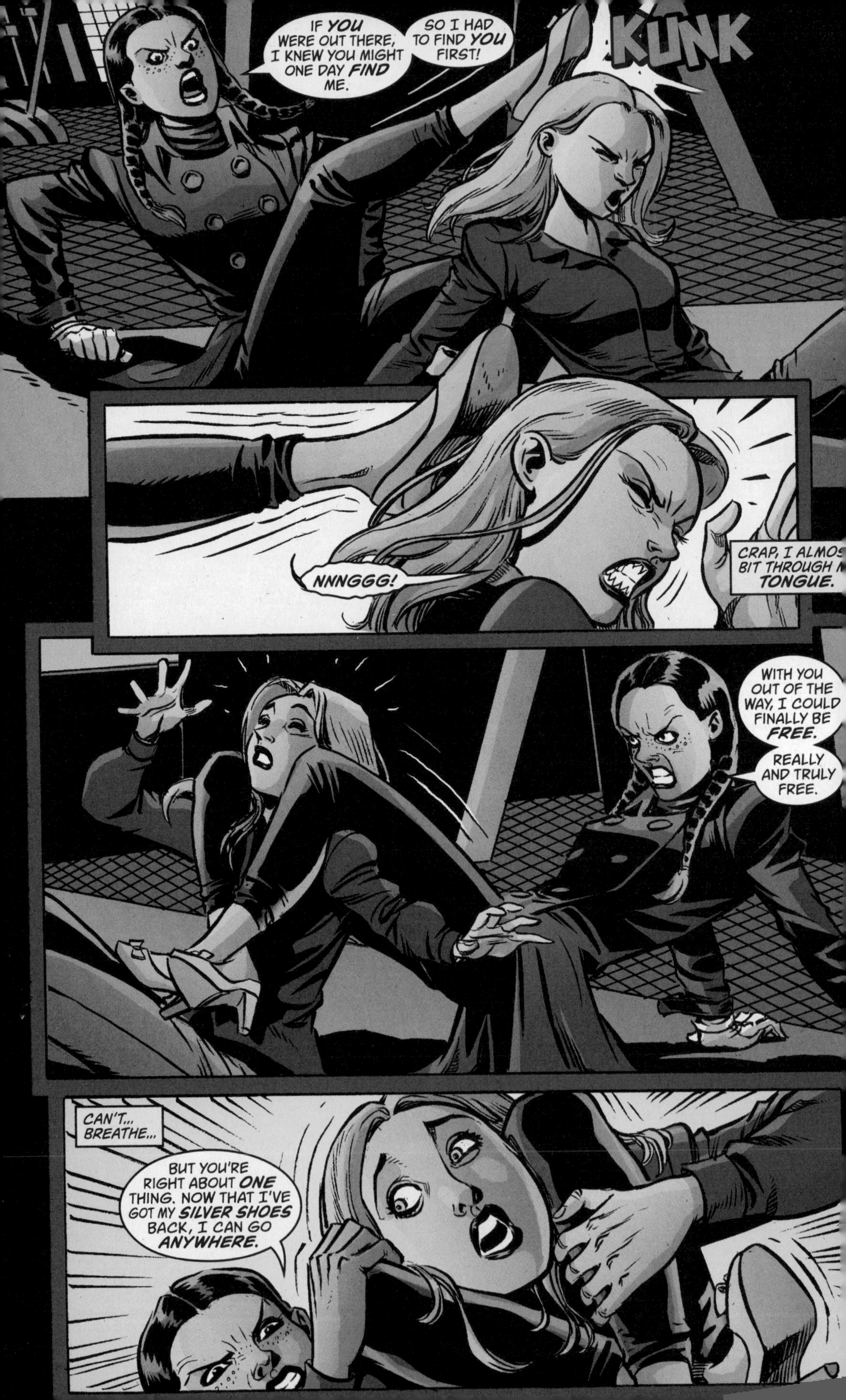
IF YOU WERE OUT THERE, I KNEW YOU MIGHT ONE DAY FIND ME.
SO I HAD TO FIND YOU FIRST!
KUNK
NNNGGG!
CRAP, I ALMOS BIT THROUGH M TONGUE.
WITH YOU OUT OF THE WAY, I COULD FINALLY BE FREE.
REALLY AND TRULY FREE.
CAN'T... BREATHE...
BUT YOU'RE RIGHT ABOUT ONE THING. NOW THAT I'VE GOT MY SILVER SHOES BACK, I CAN GO ANYWHERE.

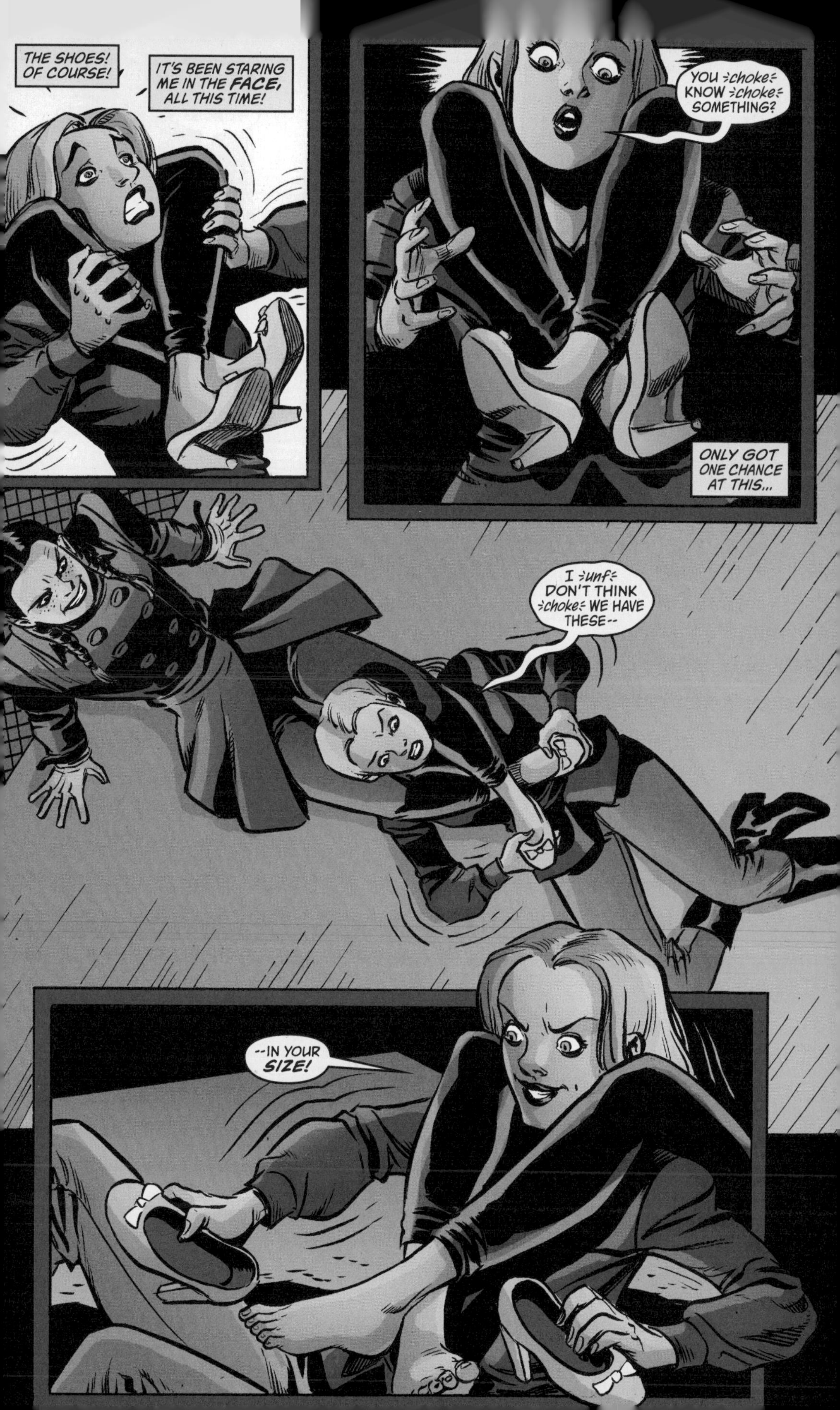

THE SHOES! OF COURSE!
IT'S BEEN STARING ME IN THE FACE, ALL THIS TIME!
YOU choke KNOW choke SOMETHING?
ONLY GOT ONE CHANCE AT THIS...
I unf DON'T THINK choke WE HAVE THESE--
--IN YOUR SIZE!

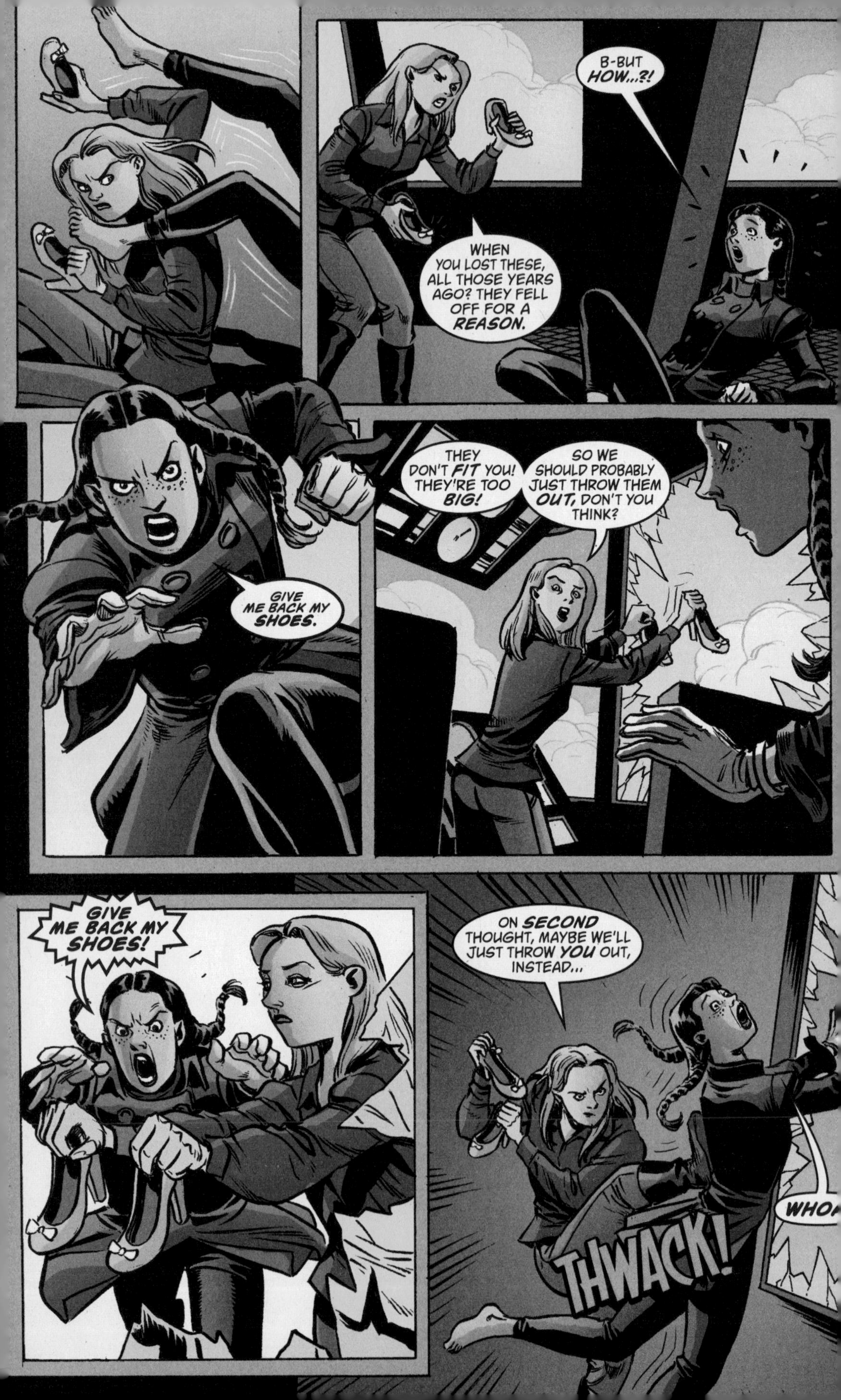

B-BUT HOW...?!
WHEN YOU LOST THESE, ALL THOSE YEARS AGO? THEY FELL OFF FOR A REASON.
GIVE ME BACK MY SHOES.
THEY DON'T FIT YOU! THEY'RE TOO BIG!
SO WE SHOULD PROBABLY JUST THROW THEM OUT, DON'T YOU THINK?
GIVE ME BACK MY SHOES!
ON SECOND THOUGHT, MAYBE WE'LL JUST THROW YOU OUT, INSTEAD...
THWACK!

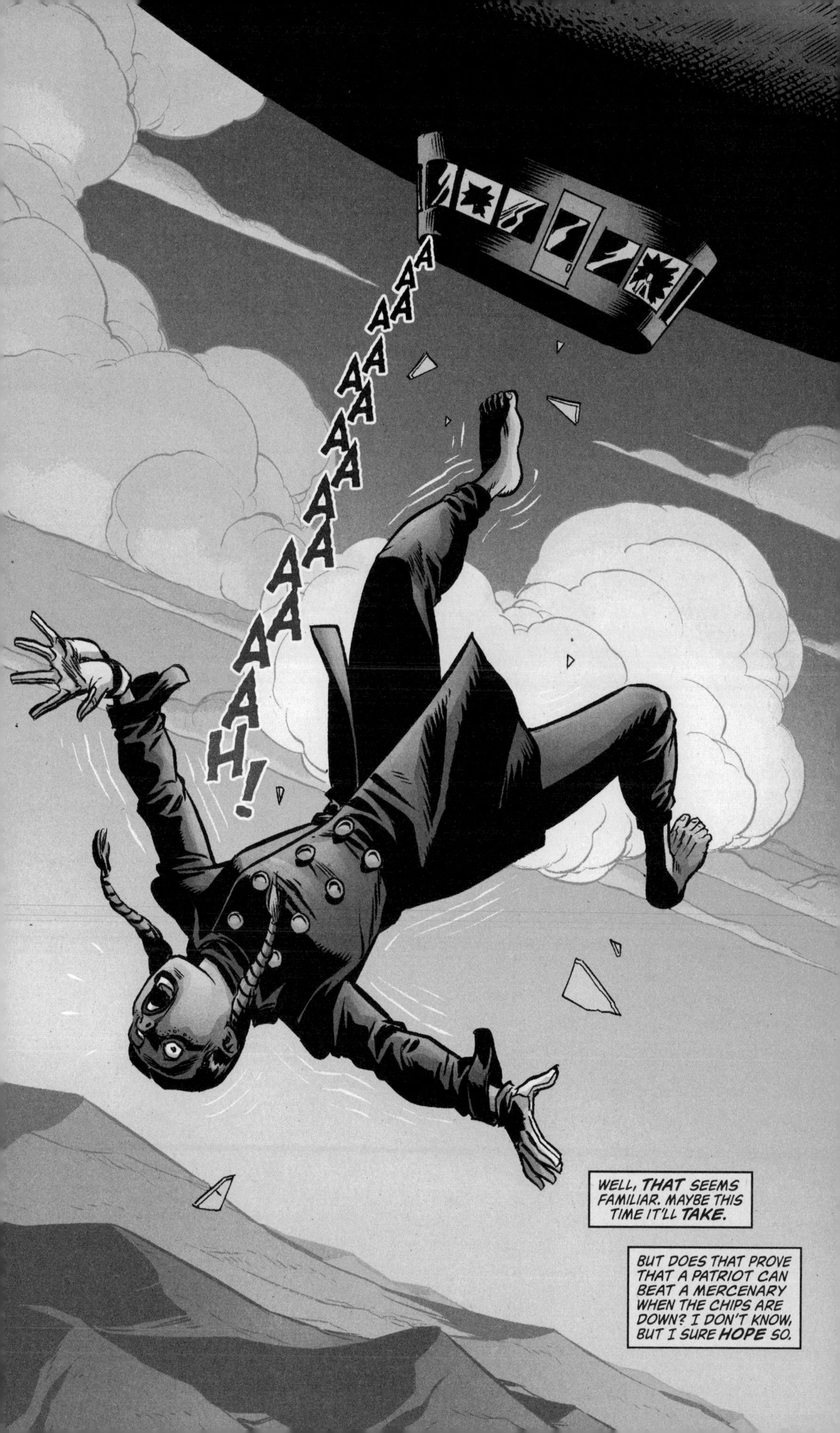
AAAAAAAAAAAAAAAAH!
WELL, THAT SEEMS FAMILIAR. MAYBE THIS TIME IT'LL TAKE.
BUT DOES THAT PROVE THAT A PATRIOT CAN BEAT A MERCENARY WHEN THE CHIPS ARE DOWN? I DON'T KNOW, BUT I SURE HOPE SO.

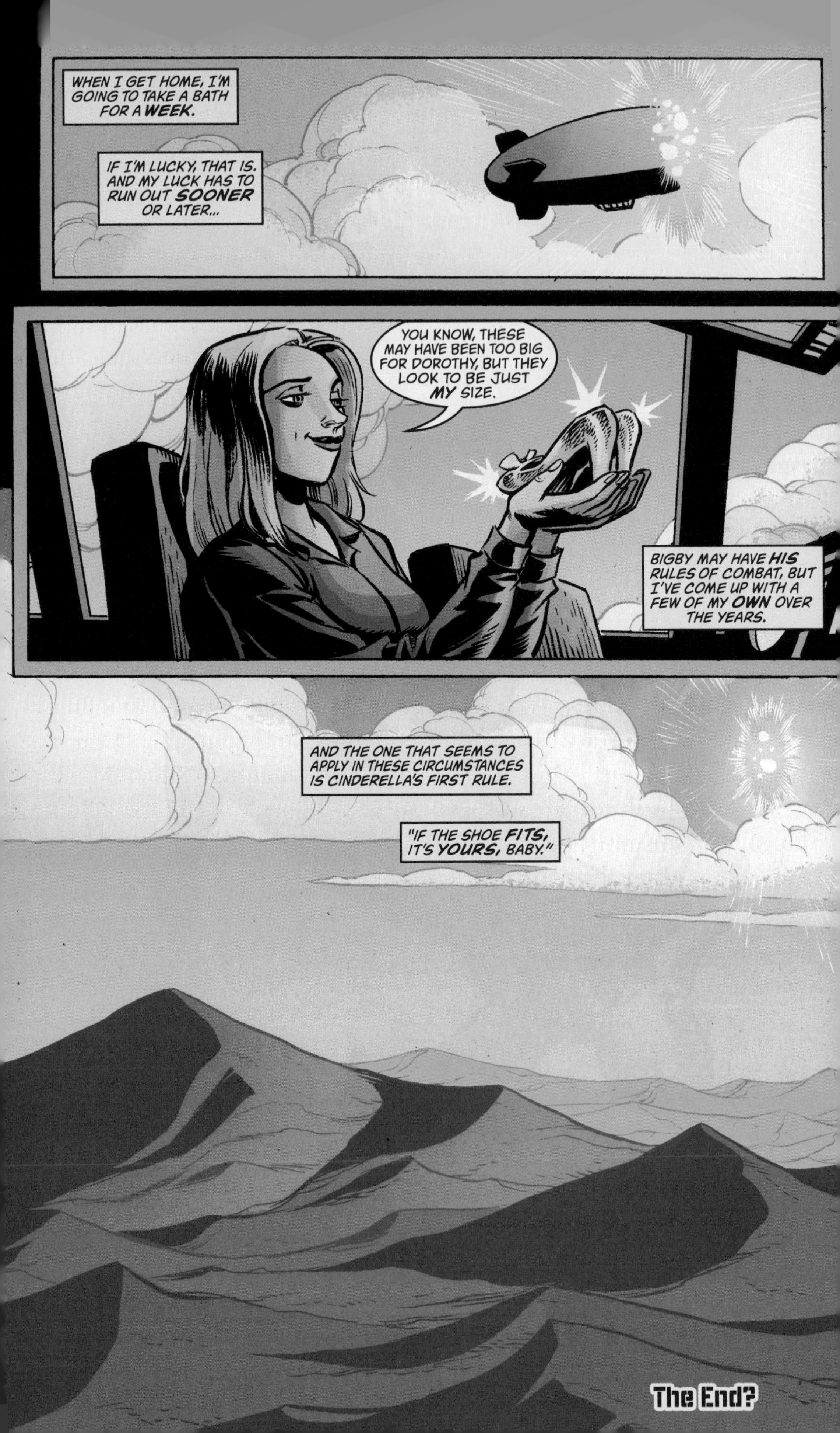
WHEN I GET HOME, I'M GOING TO TAKE A BATH FOR A WEEK.
IF I'M LUCKY, THAT IS. AND MY LUCK HAS TO RUN OUT SOONER OR LATER...
YOU KNOW, THESE MAY HAVE BEEN TOO BIG FOR DOROTHY, BUT THEY LOOK TO BE JUST MY SIZE.
BIGBY MAY HAVE HIS RULES OF COMBAT, BUT I'VE COME UP WITH A FEW OF MY OWN OVER THE YEARS.
AND THE ONE THAT SEEMS TO APPLY IN THESE CIRCUMSTANCES IS CINDERELLA'S FIRST RULE.
"IF THE SHOE FITS, IT'S YOURS, BABY."
The End?

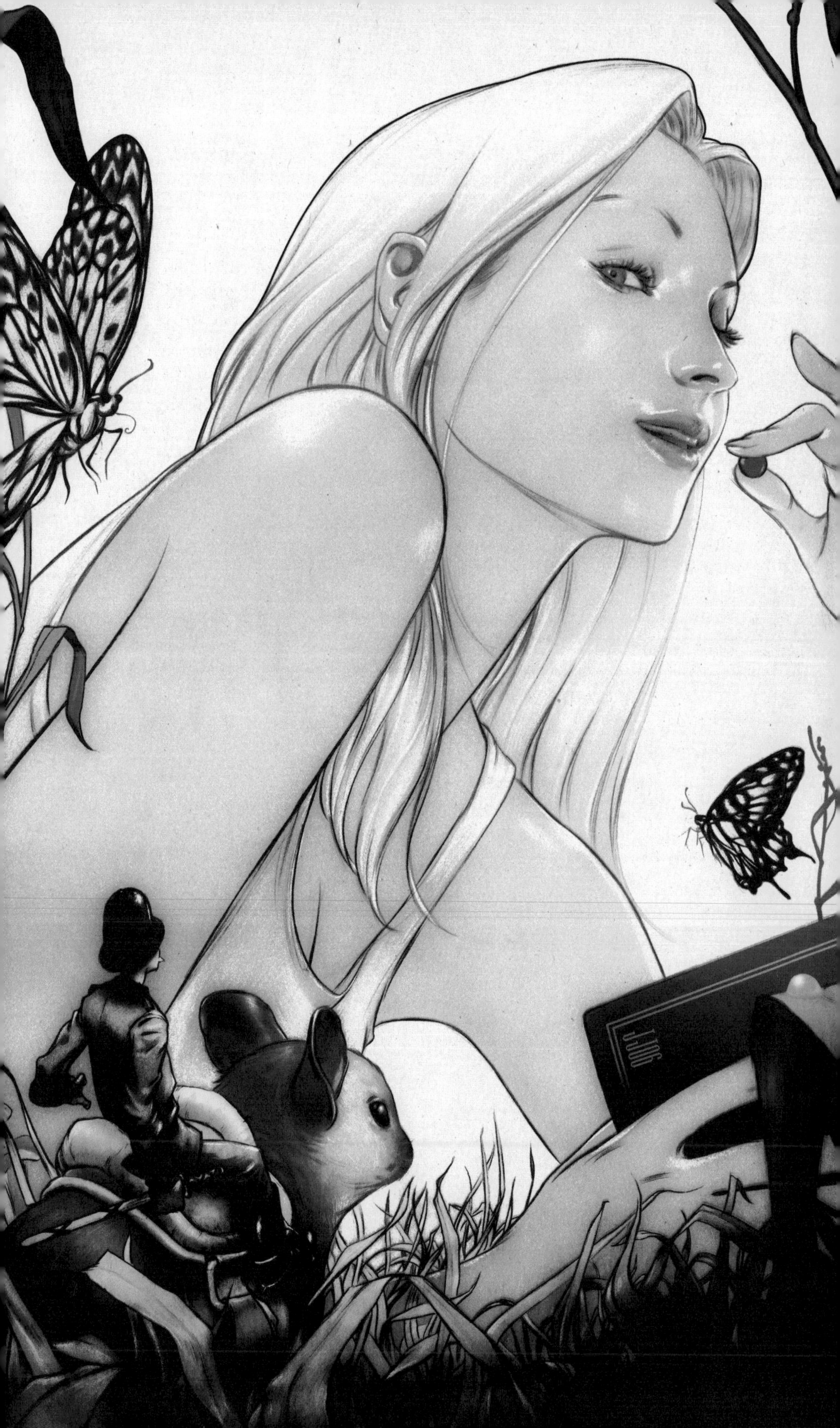

And now, from the pages
of FABLES #51, comes
an earlier tale, set as the
Fables prepare to wage
war with the Adversary,
and featuring Cinderella
as Fabletown's newest
diplomat.

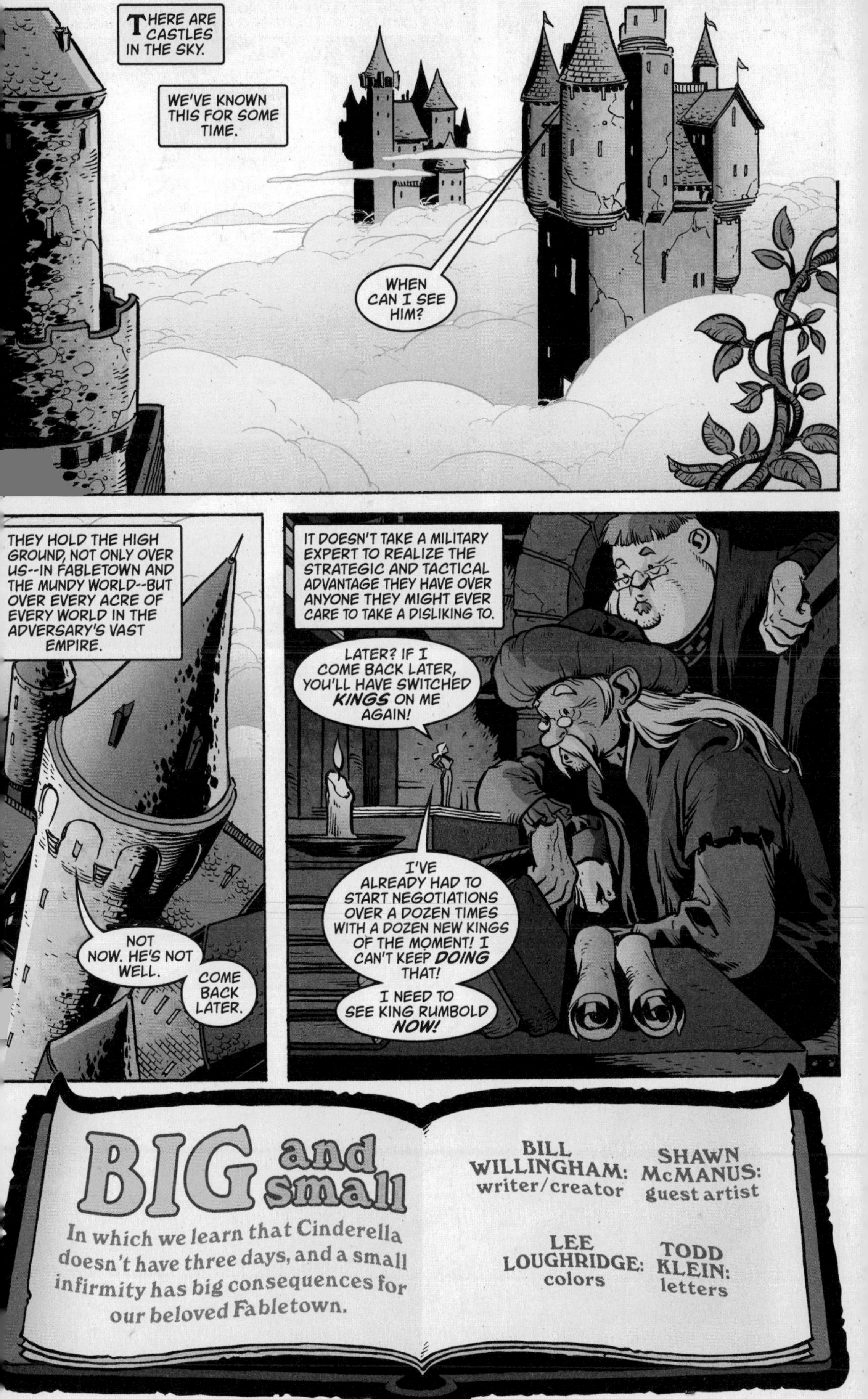

THERE ARE CASTLES IN THE SKY.
WE'VE KNOWN THIS FOR SOME TIME.
WHEN CAN I SEE HIM?
THEY HOLD THE HIGH GROUND, NOT ONLY OVER US--IN FABLETOWN AND THE MUNDY WORLD--BUT OVER EVERY ACRE OF EVERY WORLD IN THE ADVERSARY'S VAST EMPIRE.
NOT NOW. HE'S NOT WELL.
COME BACK LATER.
IT DOESN'T TAKE A MILITARY EXPERT TO REALIZE THE STRATEGIC AND TACTICAL ADVANTAGE THEY HAVE OVER ANYONE THEY MIGHT EVER CARE TO TAKE A DISLIKING TO.
LATER? IF I COME BACK LATER, YOU'LL HAVE SWITCHED KINGS ON ME AGAIN!
I'VE ALREADY HAD TO START NEGOTIATIONS OVER A DOZEN TIMES WITH A DOZEN NEW KINGS OF THE MOMENT! I CAN'T KEEP DOING THAT!
I NEED TO SEE KING RUMBOLD NOW!
BIG and small
In which we learn that Cinderella doesn't have three days, and a small infirmity has big consequences for our beloved Fabletown.
BILL WILLINGHAM: writer/creator
SHAWN McMANUS: guest artist
LEE LOUGHRIDGE: colors
TODD KLEIN: letters

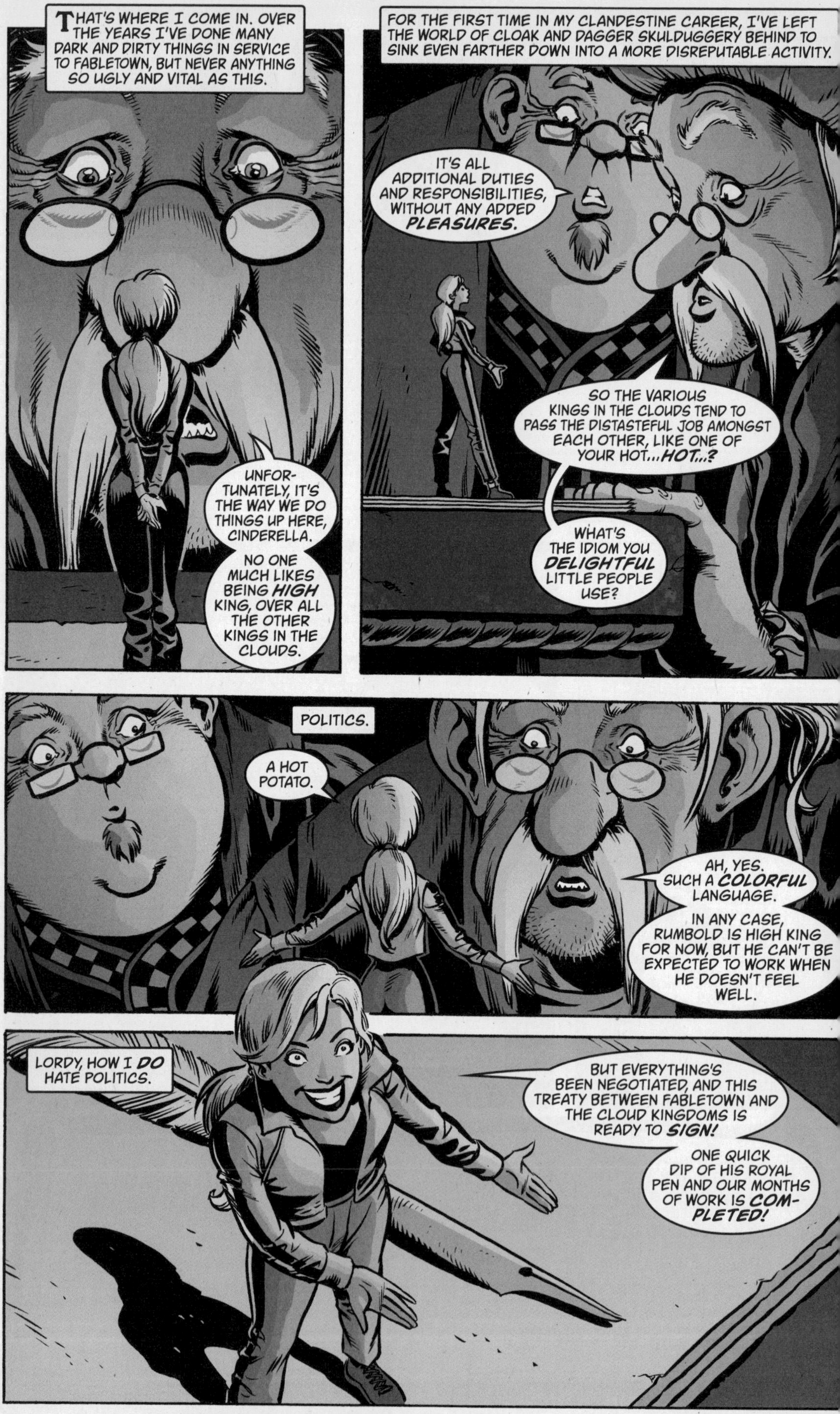
THAT'S WHERE I COME IN. OVER THE YEARS I'VE DONE MANY DARK AND DIRTY THINGS IN SERVICE TO FABLETOWN, BUT NEVER ANYTHING SO UGLY AND VITAL AS THIS.
UNFORTUNATELY, IT'S THE WAY WE DO THINGS UP HERE, CINDERELLA.
NO ONE MUCH LIKES BEING HIGH KING, OVER ALL THE OTHER KINGS IN THE CLOUDS.
FOR THE FIRST TIME IN MY CLANDESTINE CAREER, I'VE LEFT THE WORLD OF CLOAK AND DAGGER SKULDUGGERY BEHIND TO SINK EVEN FARTHER DOWN INTO A MORE DISREPUTABLE ACTIVITY.
IT'S ALL ADDITIONAL DUTIES AND RESPONSIBILITIES, WITHOUT ANY ADDED PLEASURES.
SO THE VARIOUS KINGS IN THE CLOUDS TEND TO PASS THE DISTASTEFUL JOB AMONGST EACH OTHER, LIKE ONE OF YOUR HOT...HOT...?
WHAT'S THE IDIOM YOU DELIGHTFUL LITTLE PEOPLE USE?
POLITICS.
A HOT POTATO.
AH, YES. SUCH A COLORFUL LANGUAGE.
IN ANY CASE, RUMBOLD IS HIGH KING FOR NOW, BUT HE CAN'T BE EXPECTED TO WORK WHEN HE DOESN'T FEEL WELL.
LORDY, HOW I DO HATE POLITICS.
BUT EVERYTHING'S BEEN NEGOTIATED, AND THIS TREATY BETWEEN FABLETOWN AND THE CLOUD KINGDOMS IS READY TO SIGN!
ONE QUICK DIP OF HIS ROYAL PEN AND OUR MONTHS OF WORK IS COMPLETED!

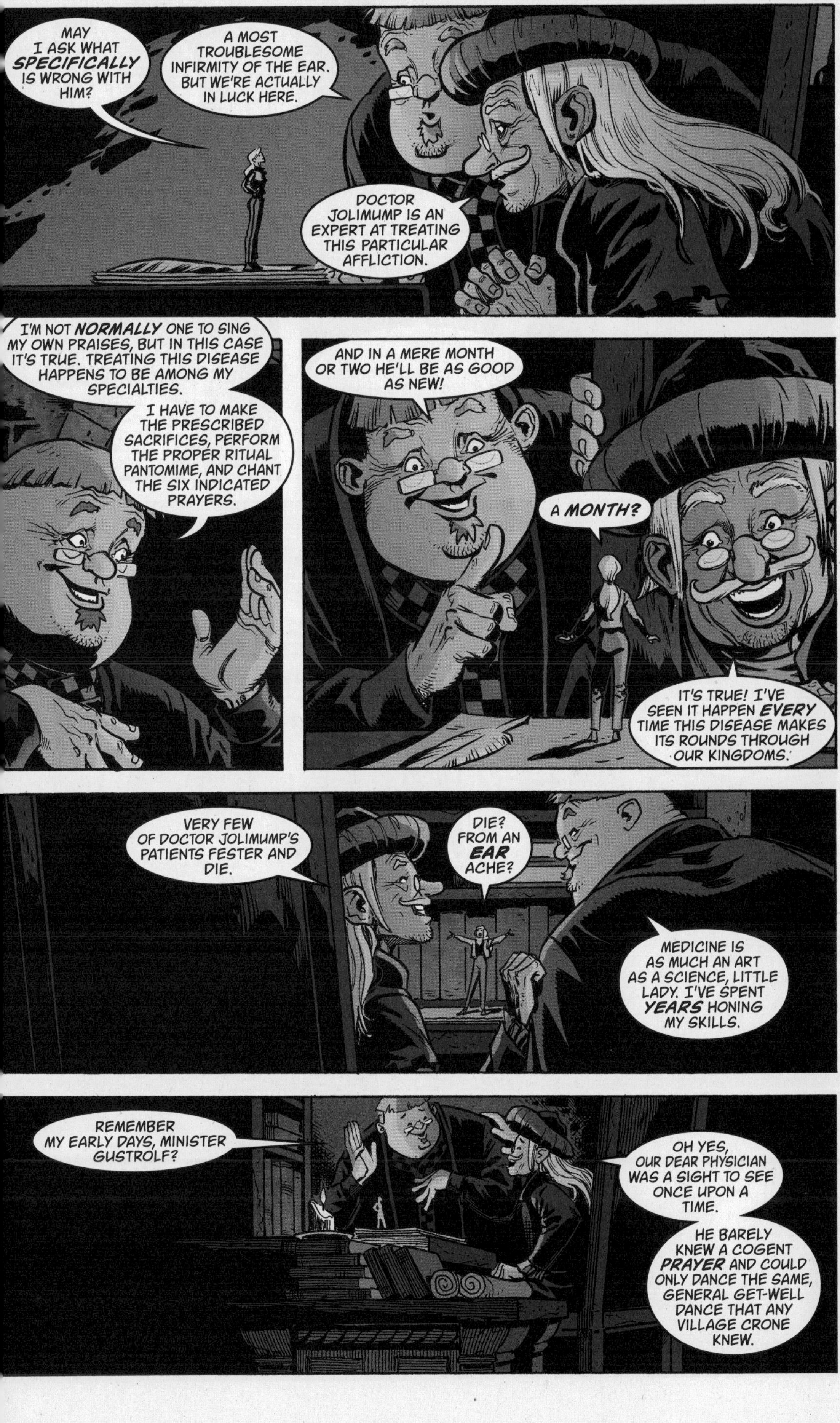

MAY I ASK WHAT SPECIFICALLY IS WRONG WITH HIM?
A MOST TROUBLESOME INFIRMITY OF THE EAR. BUT WE'RE ACTUALLY IN LUCK HERE.
DOCTOR JOLIMUMP IS AN EXPERT AT TREATING THIS PARTICULAR AFFLICTION.
I'M NOT NORMALLY ONE TO SING MY OWN PRAISES, BUT IN THIS CASE IT'S TRUE. TREATING THIS DISEASE HAPPENS TO BE AMONG MY SPECIALTIES.
I HAVE TO MAKE THE PRESCRIBED SACRIFICES, PERFORM THE PROPER RITUAL PANTOMIME, AND CHANT THE SIX INDICATED PRAYERS.
AND IN A MERE MONTH OR TWO HE'LL BE AS GOOD AS NEW!
A MONTH?
IT'S TRUE! I'VE SEEN IT HAPPEN EVERY TIME THIS DISEASE MAKES ITS ROUNDS THROUGH OUR KINGDOMS.
VERY FEW OF DOCTOR JOLIMUMP'S PATIENTS FESTER AND DIE.
DIE? FROM AN EAR ACHE?
MEDICINE IS AS MUCH AN ART AS A SCIENCE, LITTLE LADY. I'VE SPENT YEARS HONING MY SKILLS.
REMEMBER MY EARLY DAYS, MINISTER GUSTROLF?
OH YES, OUR DEAR PHYSICIAN WAS A SIGHT TO SEE ONCE UPON A TIME.
HE BARELY KNEW A COGENT PRAYER AND COULD ONLY DANCE THE SAME, GENERAL GET-WELL DANCE THAT ANY VILLAGE CRONE KNEW.

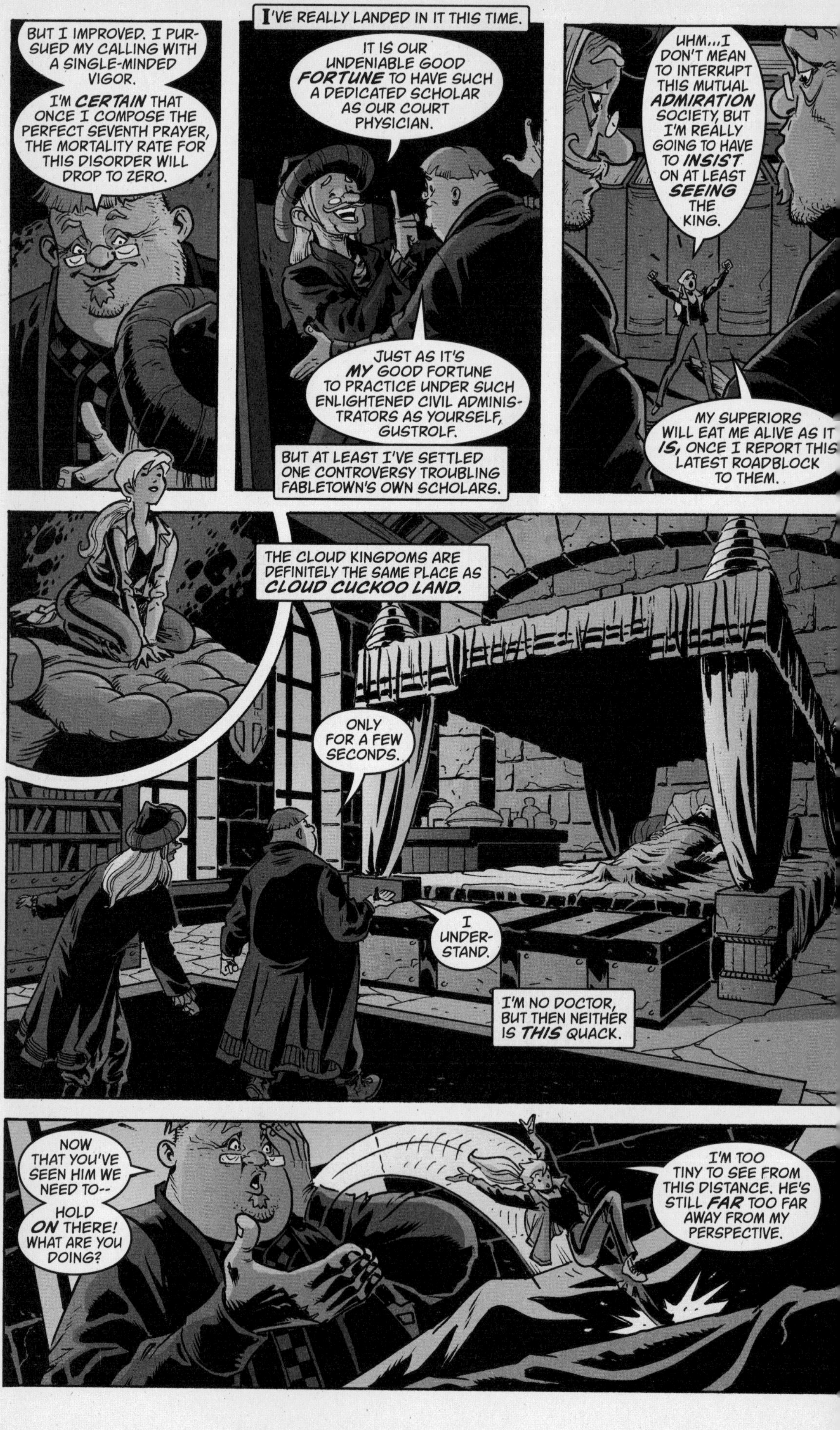

BUT I IMPROVED. I PURSUED MY CALLING WITH A SINGLE-MINDED VIGOR.
I'M CERTAIN THAT ONCE I COMPOSE THE PERFECT SEVENTH PRAYER, THE MORTALITY RATE FOR THIS DISORDER WILL DROP TO ZERO.
I'VE REALLY LANDED IN IT THIS TIME.
IT IS OUR UNDENIABLE GOOD FORTUNE TO HAVE SUCH A DEDICATED SCHOLAR AS OUR COURT PHYSICIAN.
JUST AS IT'S MY GOOD FORTUNE TO PRACTICE UNDER SUCH ENLIGHTENED CIVIL ADMINISTRATORS AS YOURSELF, GUSTROLF.
BUT AT LEAST I'VE SETTLED ONE CONTROVERSY TROUBLING FABLETOWN'S OWN SCHOLARS.
UHM...I DON'T MEAN TO INTERRUPT THIS MUTUAL ADMIRATION SOCIETY, BUT I'M REALLY GOING TO HAVE TO INSIST ON AT LEAST SEEING THE KING.
MY SUPERIORS WILL EAT ME ALIVE AS IT IS, ONCE I REPORT THIS LATEST ROADBLOCK TO THEM.
THE CLOUD KINGDOMS ARE DEFINITELY THE SAME PLACE AS CLOUD CUCKOO LAND.
ONLY FOR A FEW SECONDS.
I UNDERSTAND.
I'M NO DOCTOR, BUT THEN NEITHER IS THIS QUACK.
NOW THAT YOU'VE SEEN HIM WE NEED TO--
HOLD ON THERE! WHAT ARE YOU DOING?
I'M TOO TINY TO SEE FROM THIS DISTANCE. HE'S STILL FAR TOO FAR AWAY FROM MY PERSPECTIVE.

THAT I AM IS A MODERN GIRL LIVING IN A MODERN WORLD. I'VE ABSORBED SOME BASIC SCIENCE THROUGH SIMPLE CULTURAL OSMOSIS.

I NEED A CLOSER LOOK.

ENOUGH TO KNOW A CURE FOR A SIMPLE EARACHE THAT TAKES A MONTH OR MORE IS NO CURE AT ALL.

EWWWW!

I SMELL PUS.

THIS IS OUTRAGEOUS!

I *MUST* INSIST THAT YOU LEAVE!

WHAT'S ALL THIS SCREAMING WHILE I'M TRYING TO SLEEP?

YIKES!

IT'S JUST ME, YOUR HIGHNESS-- YOUR *HUMBLE* LITTLE AMBASSADOR FROM FABLETOWN.

NOW LISTEN HERE, KING RUMBOLD. I APOLOGIZE FOR MY UNCOURTLY CANDOR, BUT I SUSPECT I WON'T HAVE TIME FOR THE USUAL DIPLOMATIC NICETIES.

I KNOW A *REAL* DOCTOR WHO CAN CURE WHAT AILS YOU. IN RETURN, YOU HAVE TO PROMISE ME THAT YOU WON'T HAND OVER YOUR KING-SHIP WHILE I GO FETCH HIM.

BUT--

I'VE NEVER SEEN DOCTOR JOLIMUMP SO ANGRY.

I HAVE THAT EFFECT ON *MOST* MEN. HE'LL GET OVER IT.

ARE YOU SURE YOU CAN MAKE IT BACK BEFORE KING RUMBOLD TRANSFERS HIS POWER? THE NEXT ONE IN LINE IS KING PINEHEART WHO'S *PROUDLY* ILLITERATE.

YOU'D HAVE TO WAIT FOR AN ENTIRE NEW KING AGAIN FOR ANY CHANCE TO GET YOUR TREATY SIGNED.

OH *JOY.*

MY LIFE GETS BETTER ALL THE TIME.

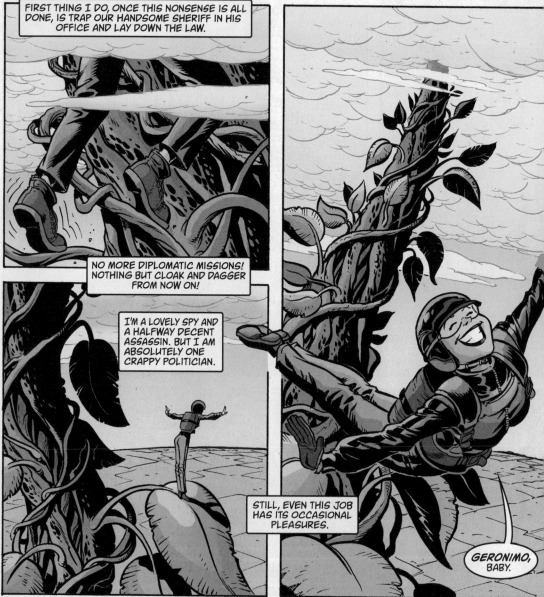

FIRST THING I DO, ONCE THIS NONSENSE IS ALL DONE, IS TRAP OUR HANDSOME SHERIFF IN HIS OFFICE AND LAY DOWN THE LAW.

NO MORE DIPLOMATIC MISSIONS! NOTHING BUT CLOAK AND DAGGER FROM NOW ON!

I'M A LOVELY SPY AND A HALFWAY DECENT ASSASSIN. BUT I AM ABSOLUTELY ONE CRAPPY POLITICIAN.

STILL, EVEN THIS JOB HAS ITS OCCASIONAL PLEASURES.

GERONIMO, BABY.

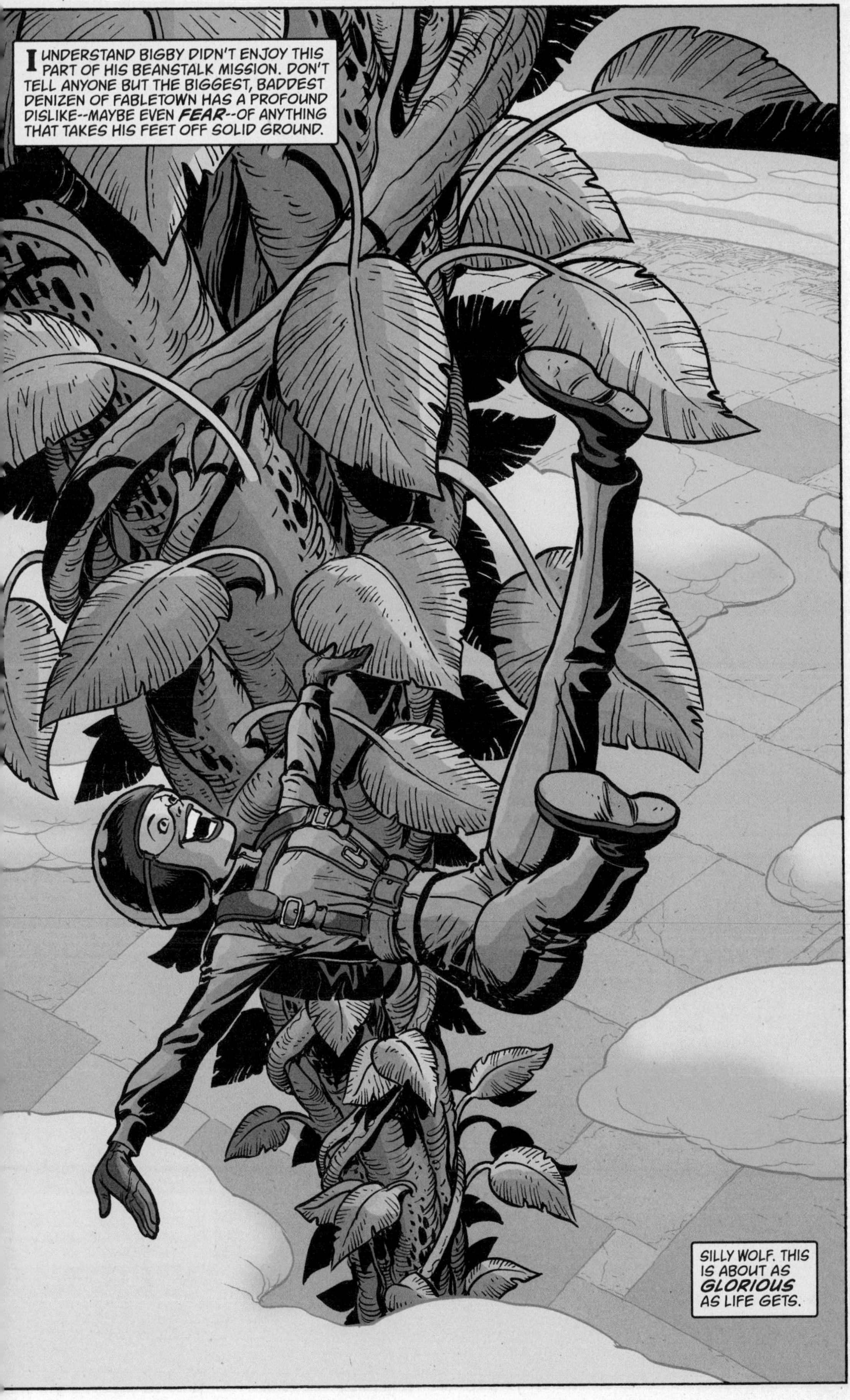
I UNDERSTAND BIGBY DIDN'T ENJOY THIS PART OF HIS BEANSTALK MISSION. DON'T TELL ANYONE BUT THE BIGGEST, BADDEST DENIZEN OF FABLETOWN HAS A PROFOUND DISLIKE--MAYBE EVEN FEAR--OF ANYTHING THAT TAKES HIS FEET OFF SOLID GROUND.
SILLY WOLF. THIS IS ABOUT AS GLORIOUS AS LIFE GETS.

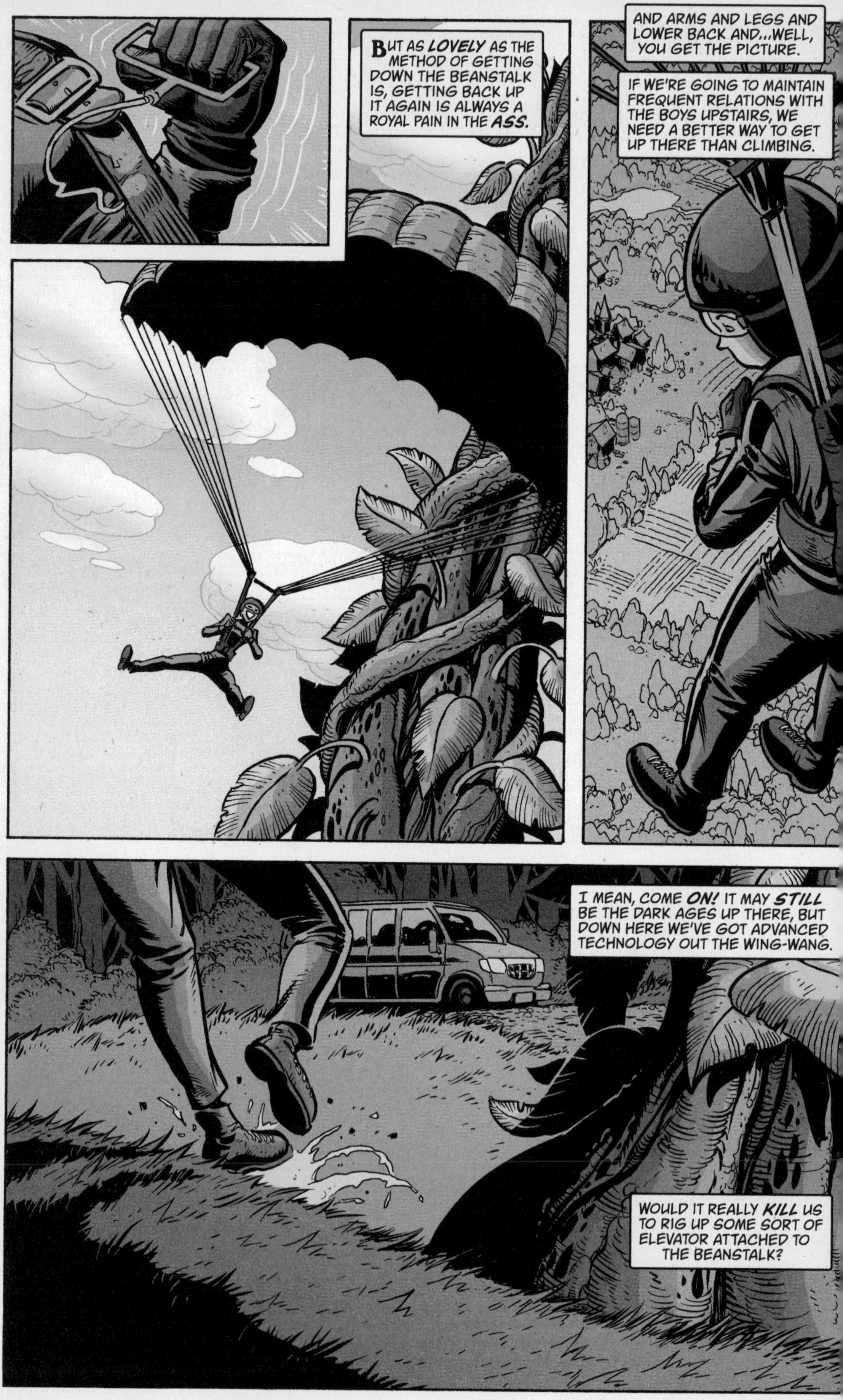
BUT AS LOVELY AS THE METHOD OF GETTING DOWN THE BEANSTALK IS, GETTING BACK UP IT AGAIN IS ALWAYS A ROYAL PAIN IN THE ASS.
AND ARMS AND LEGS AND LOWER BACK AND...WELL, YOU GET THE PICTURE.
IF WE'RE GOING TO MAINTAIN FREQUENT RELATIONS WITH THE BOYS UPSTAIRS, WE NEED A BETTER WAY TO GET UP THERE THAN CLIMBING.
I MEAN, COME ON! IT MAY STILL BE THE DARK AGES UP THERE, BUT DOWN HERE WE'VE GOT ADVANCED TECHNOLOGY OUT THE WING-WANG.
WOULD IT REALLY KILL US TO RIG UP SOME SORT OF ELEVATOR ATTACHED TO THE BEANSTALK?

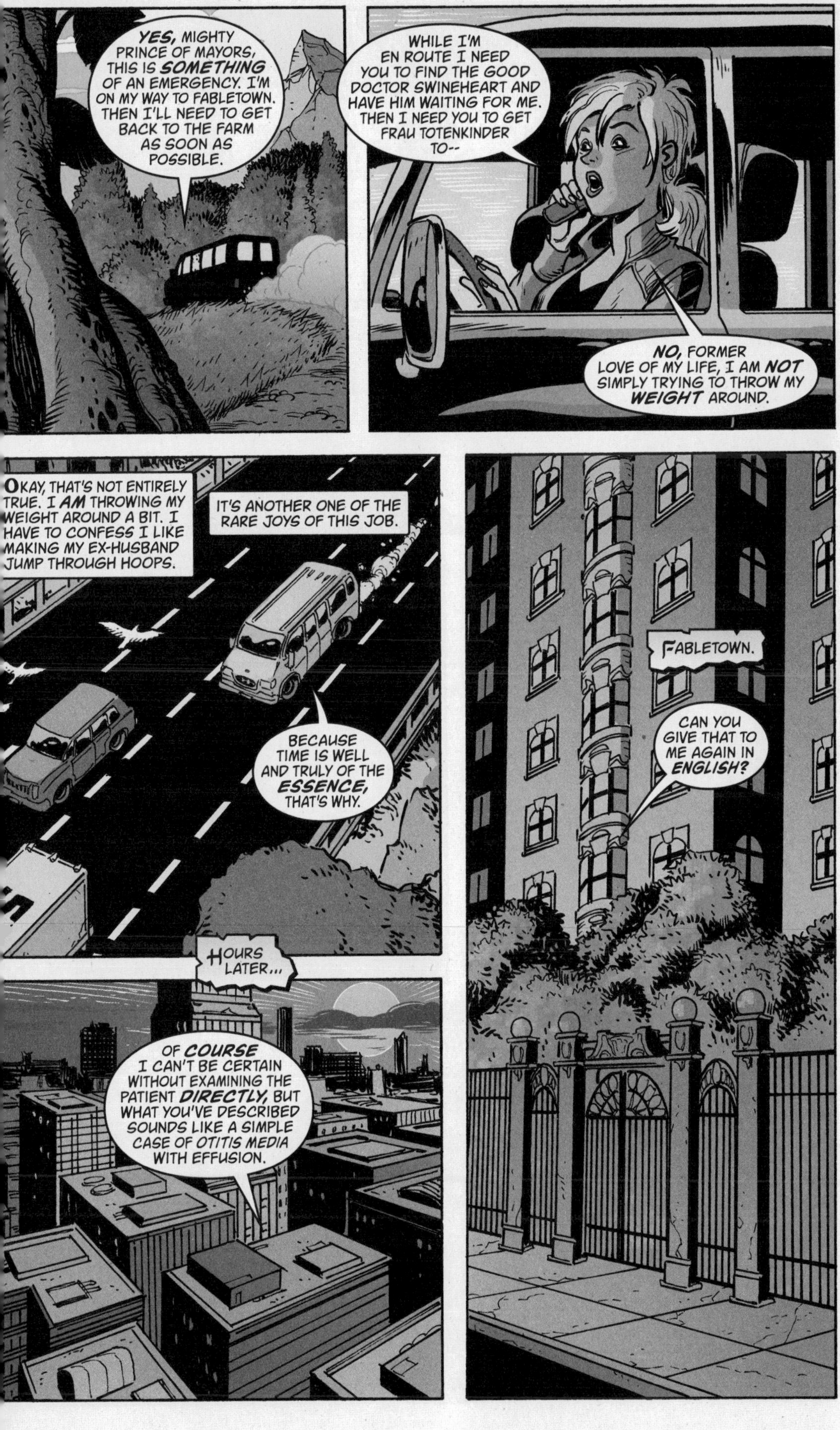
YES, MIGHTY PRINCE OF MAYORS, THIS IS SOMETHING OF AN EMERGENCY. I'M ON MY WAY TO FABLETOWN. THEN I'LL NEED TO GET BACK TO THE FARM AS SOON AS POSSIBLE.
WHILE I'M EN ROUTE I NEED YOU TO FIND THE GOOD DOCTOR SWINEHEART AND HAVE HIM WAITING FOR ME. THEN I NEED YOU TO GET FRAU TOTENKINDER TO--
NO, FORMER LOVE OF MY LIFE, I AM NOT SIMPLY TRYING TO THROW MY WEIGHT AROUND.
OKAY, THAT'S NOT ENTIRELY TRUE. I AM THROWING MY WEIGHT AROUND A BIT. I HAVE TO CONFESS I LIKE MAKING MY EX-HUSBAND JUMP THROUGH HOOPS.
IT'S ANOTHER ONE OF THE RARE JOYS OF THIS JOB.
BECAUSE TIME IS WELL AND TRULY OF THE ESSENCE, THAT'S WHY.
HOURS LATER...
OF COURSE I CAN'T BE CERTAIN WITHOUT EXAMINING THE PATIENT DIRECTLY, BUT WHAT YOU'VE DESCRIBED SOUNDS LIKE A SIMPLE CASE OF OTITIS MEDIA WITH EFFUSION.
FABLETOWN.
CAN YOU GIVE THAT TO ME AGAIN IN ENGLISH?

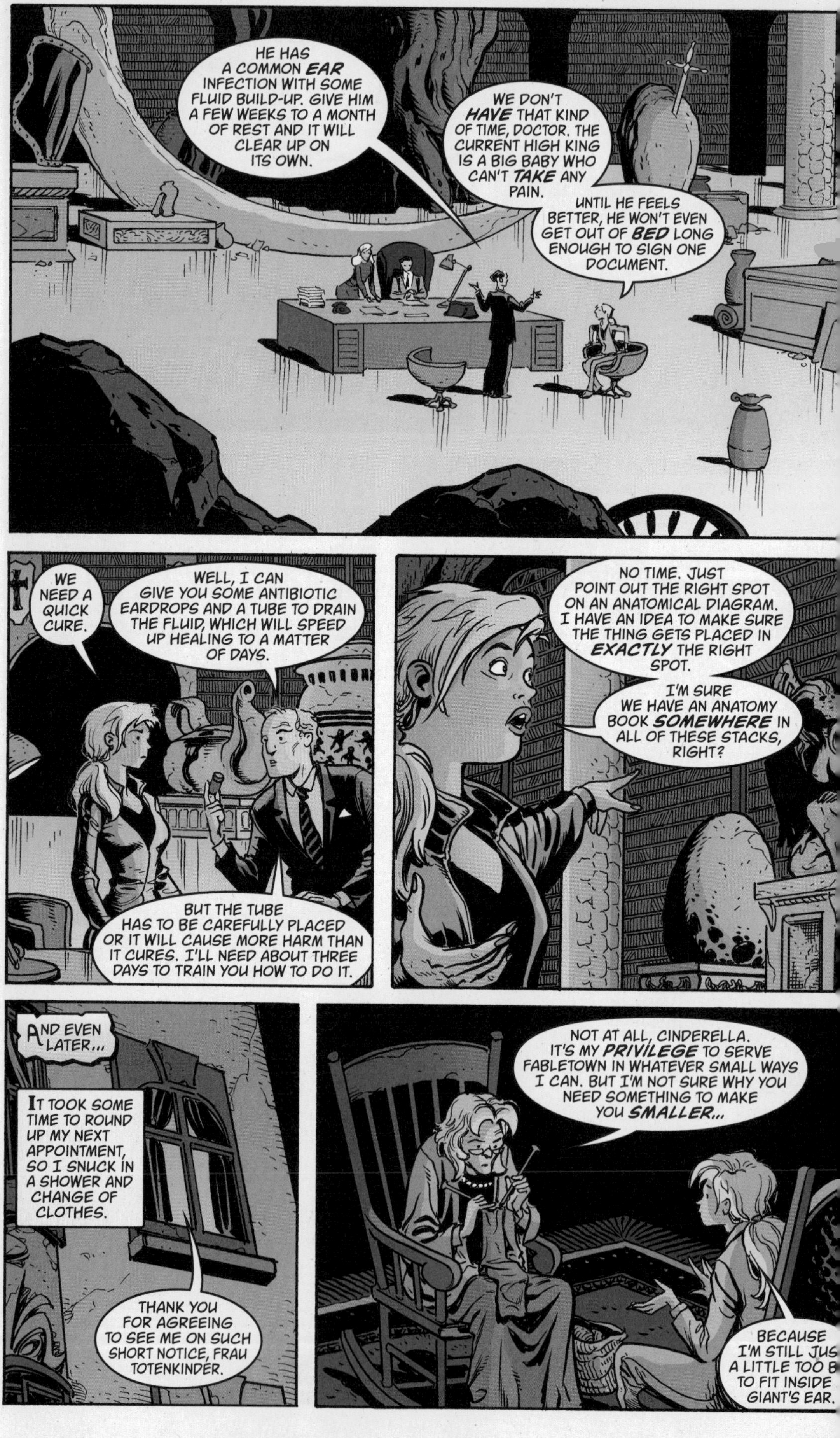
HE HAS A COMMON EAR INFECTION WITH SOME FLUID BUILD-UP. GIVE HIM A FEW WEEKS TO A MONTH OF REST AND IT WILL CLEAR UP ON ITS OWN.
WE DON'T HAVE THAT KIND OF TIME, DOCTOR. THE CURRENT HIGH KING IS A BIG BABY WHO CAN'T TAKE ANY PAIN.
UNTIL HE FEELS BETTER, HE WON'T EVEN GET OUT OF BED LONG ENOUGH TO SIGN ONE DOCUMENT.
WE NEED A QUICK CURE.
WELL, I CAN GIVE YOU SOME ANTIBIOTIC EARDROPS AND A TUBE TO DRAIN THE FLUID, WHICH WILL SPEED UP HEALING TO A MATTER OF DAYS.
BUT THE TUBE HAS TO BE CAREFULLY PLACED OR IT WILL CAUSE MORE HARM THAN IT CURES. I'LL NEED ABOUT THREE DAYS TO TRAIN YOU HOW TO DO IT.
NO TIME. JUST POINT OUT THE RIGHT SPOT ON AN ANATOMICAL DIAGRAM. I HAVE AN IDEA TO MAKE SURE THE THING GETS PLACED IN EXACTLY THE RIGHT SPOT.
I'M SURE WE HAVE AN ANATOMY BOOK SOMEWHERE IN ALL OF THESE STACKS, RIGHT?
AND EVEN LATER...
IT TOOK SOME TIME TO ROUND UP MY NEXT APPOINTMENT, SO I SNUCK IN A SHOWER AND CHANGE OF CLOTHES.
THANK YOU FOR AGREEING TO SEE ME ON SUCH SHORT NOTICE, FRAU TOTENKINDER.
NOT AT ALL, CINDERELLA. IT'S MY PRIVILEGE TO SERVE FABLETOWN IN WHATEVER SMALL WAYS I CAN. BUT I'M NOT SURE WHY YOU NEED SOMETHING TO MAKE YOU SMALLER...
BECAUSE I'M STILL JUS A LITTLE TOO B TO FIT INSIDE GIANT'S EAR.

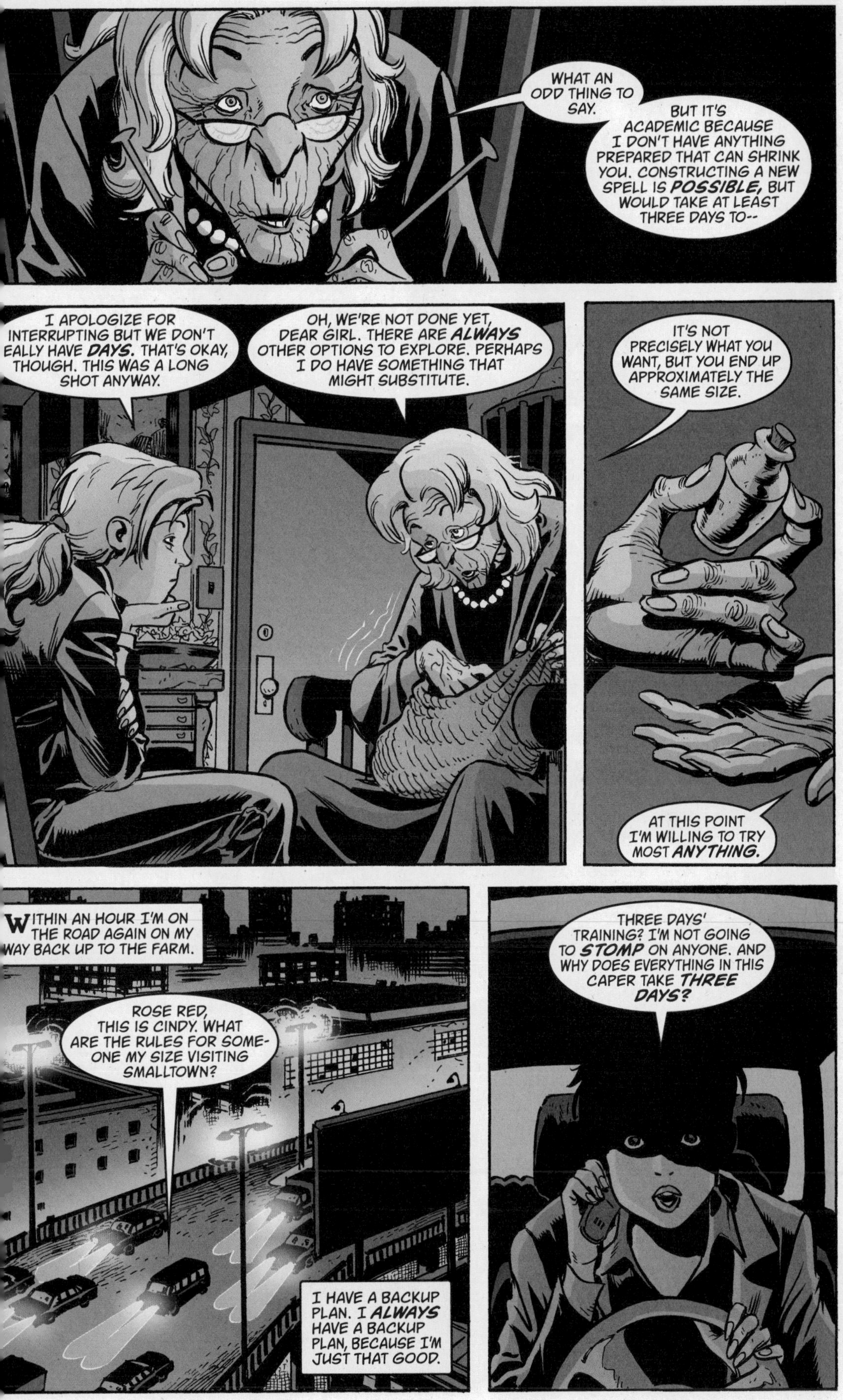
WHAT AN ODD THING TO SAY.
BUT IT'S ACADEMIC BECAUSE I DON'T HAVE ANYTHING PREPARED THAT CAN SHRINK YOU. CONSTRUCTING A NEW SPELL IS POSSIBLE, BUT WOULD TAKE AT LEAST THREE DAYS TO--
I APOLOGIZE FOR INTERRUPTING BUT WE DON'T EALLY HAVE DAYS. THAT'S OKAY, THOUGH. THIS WAS A LONG SHOT ANYWAY.
OH, WE'RE NOT DONE YET, DEAR GIRL. THERE ARE ALWAYS OTHER OPTIONS TO EXPLORE. PERHAPS I DO HAVE SOMETHING THAT MIGHT SUBSTITUTE.
IT'S NOT PRECISELY WHAT YOU WANT, BUT YOU END UP APPROXIMATELY THE SAME SIZE.
AT THIS POINT I'M WILLING TO TRY MOST ANYTHING.
WITHIN AN HOUR I'M ON THE ROAD AGAIN ON MY WAY BACK UP TO THE FARM.
ROSE RED, THIS IS CINDY. WHAT ARE THE RULES FOR SOME-ONE MY SIZE VISITING SMALLTOWN?
I HAVE A BACKUP PLAN. I ALWAYS HAVE A BACKUP PLAN, BECAUSE I'M JUST THAT GOOD.
THREE DAYS' TRAINING? I'M NOT GOING TO STOMP ON ANYONE. AND WHY DOES EVERYTHING IN THIS CAPER TAKE THREE DAYS?

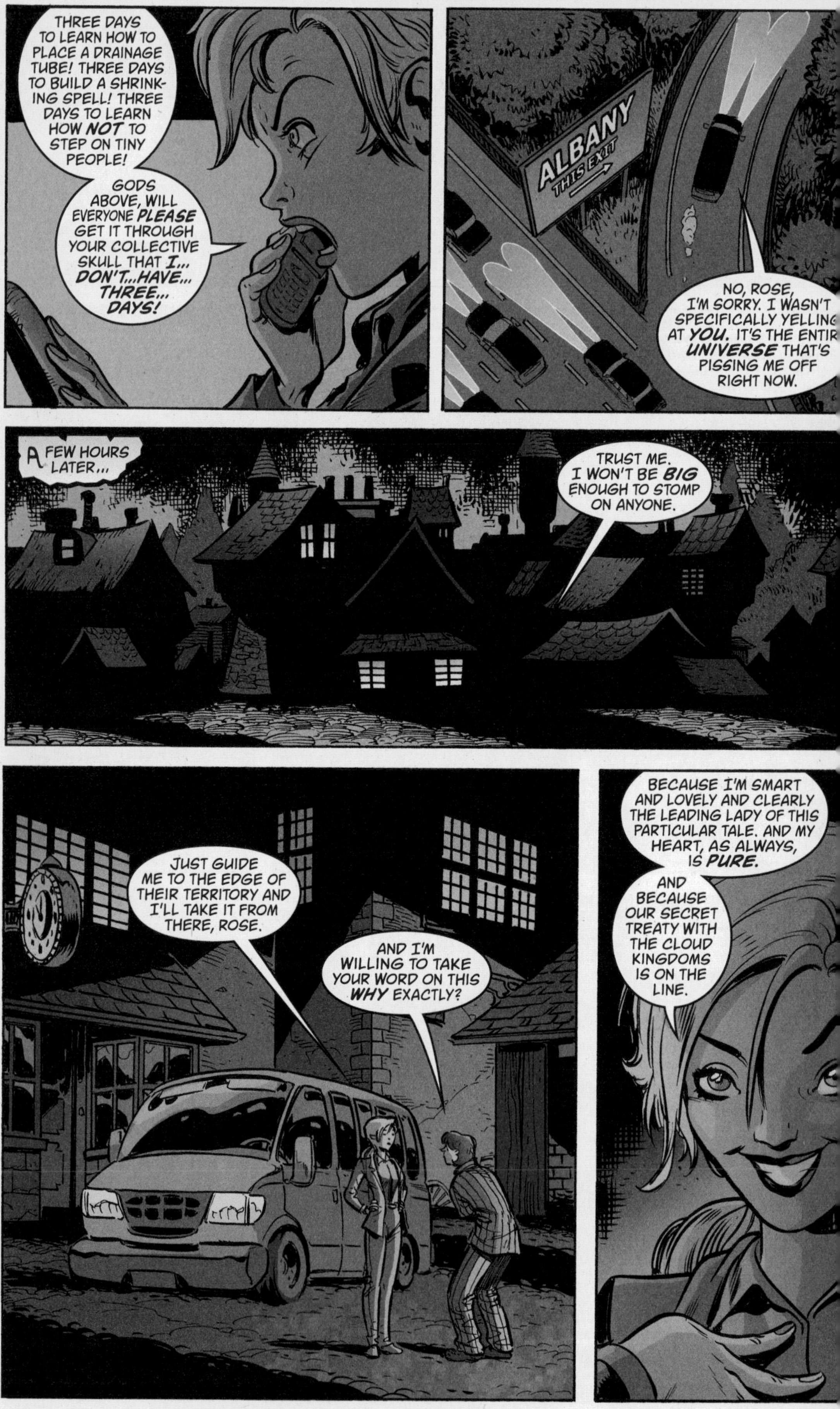

THREE DAYS TO LEARN HOW TO PLACE A DRAINAGE TUBE! THREE DAYS TO BUILD A SHRINKING SPELL! THREE DAYS TO LEARN HOW NOT TO STEP ON TINY PEOPLE!
GODS ABOVE, WILL EVERYONE PLEASE GET IT THROUGH YOUR COLLECTIVE SKULL THAT I... DON'T...HAVE... THREE... DAYS!
ALBANY THIS EXIT
NO, ROSE, I'M SORRY. I WASN'T SPECIFICALLY YELLING AT YOU. IT'S THE ENTIR UNIVERSE THAT'S PISSING ME OFF RIGHT NOW.
A FEW HOURS LATER...
TRUST ME. I WON'T BE BIG ENOUGH TO STOMP ON ANYONE.
JUST GUIDE ME TO THE EDGE OF THEIR TERRITORY AND I'LL TAKE IT FROM THERE, ROSE.
AND I'M WILLING TO TAKE YOUR WORD ON THIS WHY EXACTLY?
BECAUSE I'M SMART AND LOVELY AND CLEARLY THE LEADING LADY OF THIS PARTICULAR TALE. AND MY HEART, AS ALWAYS, IS PURE.
AND BECAUSE OUR SECRET TREATY WITH THE CLOUD KINGDOMS IS ON THE LINE.

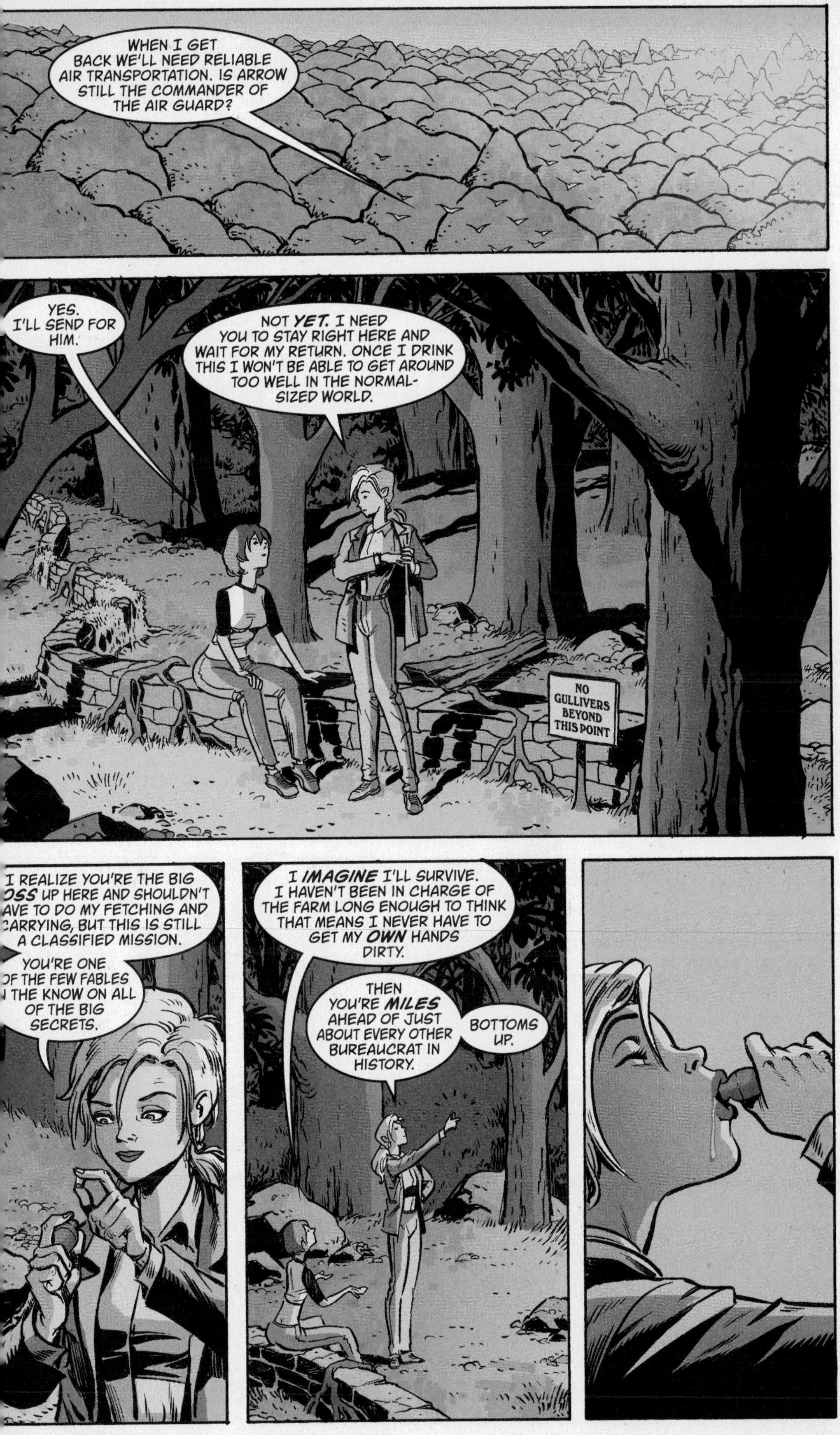
WHEN I GET BACK WE'LL NEED RELIABLE AIR TRANSPORTATION. IS ARROW STILL THE COMMANDER OF THE AIR GUARD?
YES. I'LL SEND FOR HIM.
NOT YET. I NEED YOU TO STAY RIGHT HERE AND WAIT FOR MY RETURN. ONCE I DRINK THIS I WON'T BE ABLE TO GET AROUND TOO WELL IN THE NORMAL-SIZED WORLD.
NO GULLIVERS BEYOND THIS POINT
I REALIZE YOU'RE THE BIG OSS UP HERE AND SHOULDN'T AVE TO DO MY FETCHING AND ARRYING, BUT THIS IS STILL A CLASSIFIED MISSION.
YOU'RE ONE F THE FEW FABLES THE KNOW ON ALL OF THE BIG SECRETS.
I IMAGINE I'LL SURVIVE. I HAVEN'T BEEN IN CHARGE OF THE FARM LONG ENOUGH TO THINK THAT MEANS I NEVER HAVE TO GET MY OWN HANDS DIRTY.
THEN YOU'RE MILES AHEAD OF JUST ABOUT EVERY OTHER BUREAUCRAT IN HISTORY.
BOTTOMS UP.

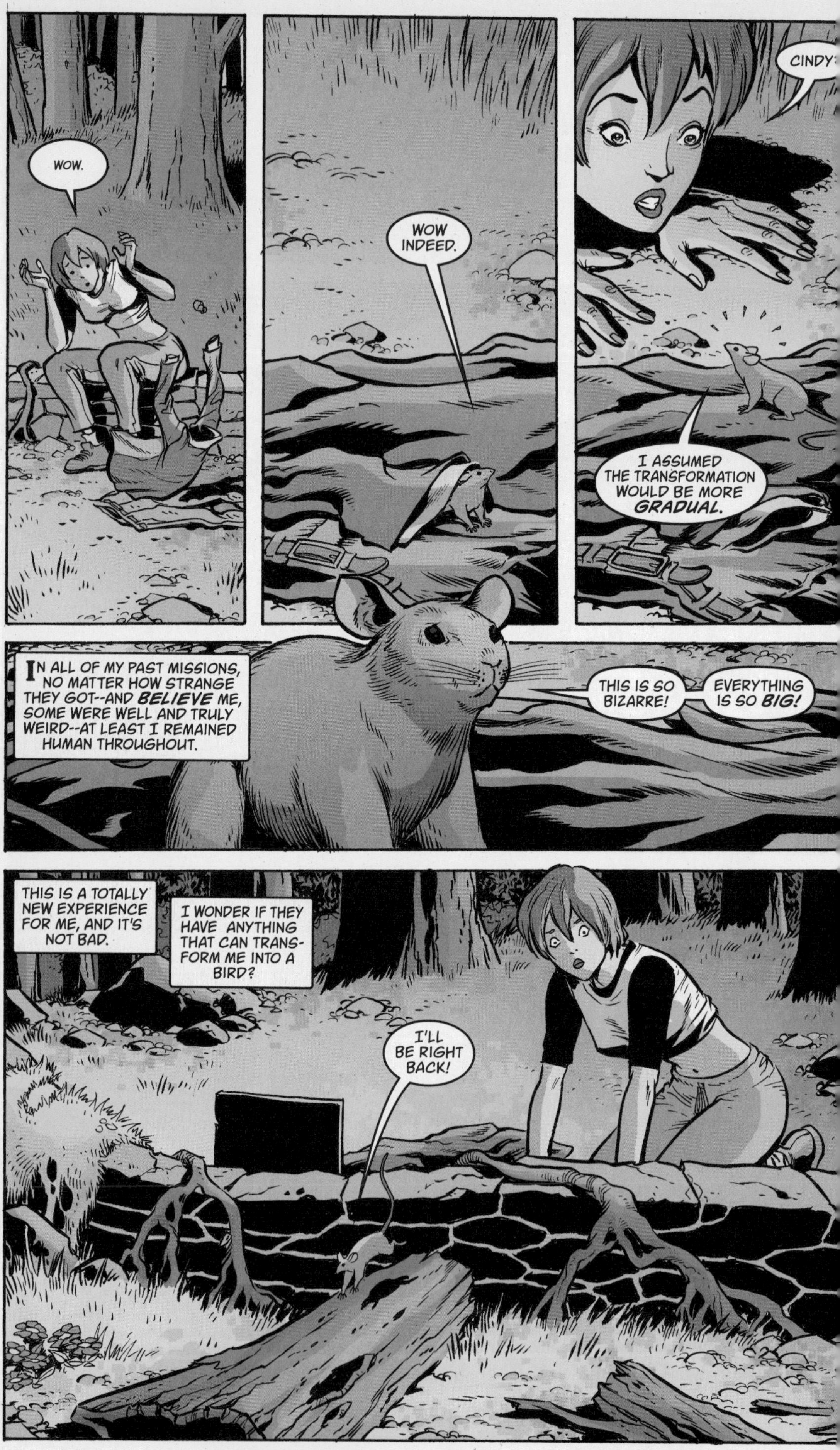
WOW.
WOW INDEED.
CINDY?
I ASSUMED THE TRANSFORMATION WOULD BE MORE GRADUAL.
IN ALL OF MY PAST MISSIONS, NO MATTER HOW STRANGE THEY GOT--AND BELIEVE ME, SOME WERE WELL AND TRULY WEIRD--AT LEAST I REMAINED HUMAN THROUGHOUT.
THIS IS SO BIZARRE!
EVERYTHING IS SO BIG!
THIS IS A TOTALLY NEW EXPERIENCE FOR ME, AND IT'S NOT BAD.
I WONDER IF THEY HAVE ANYTHING THAT CAN TRANSFORM ME INTO A BIRD?
I'LL BE RIGHT BACK!

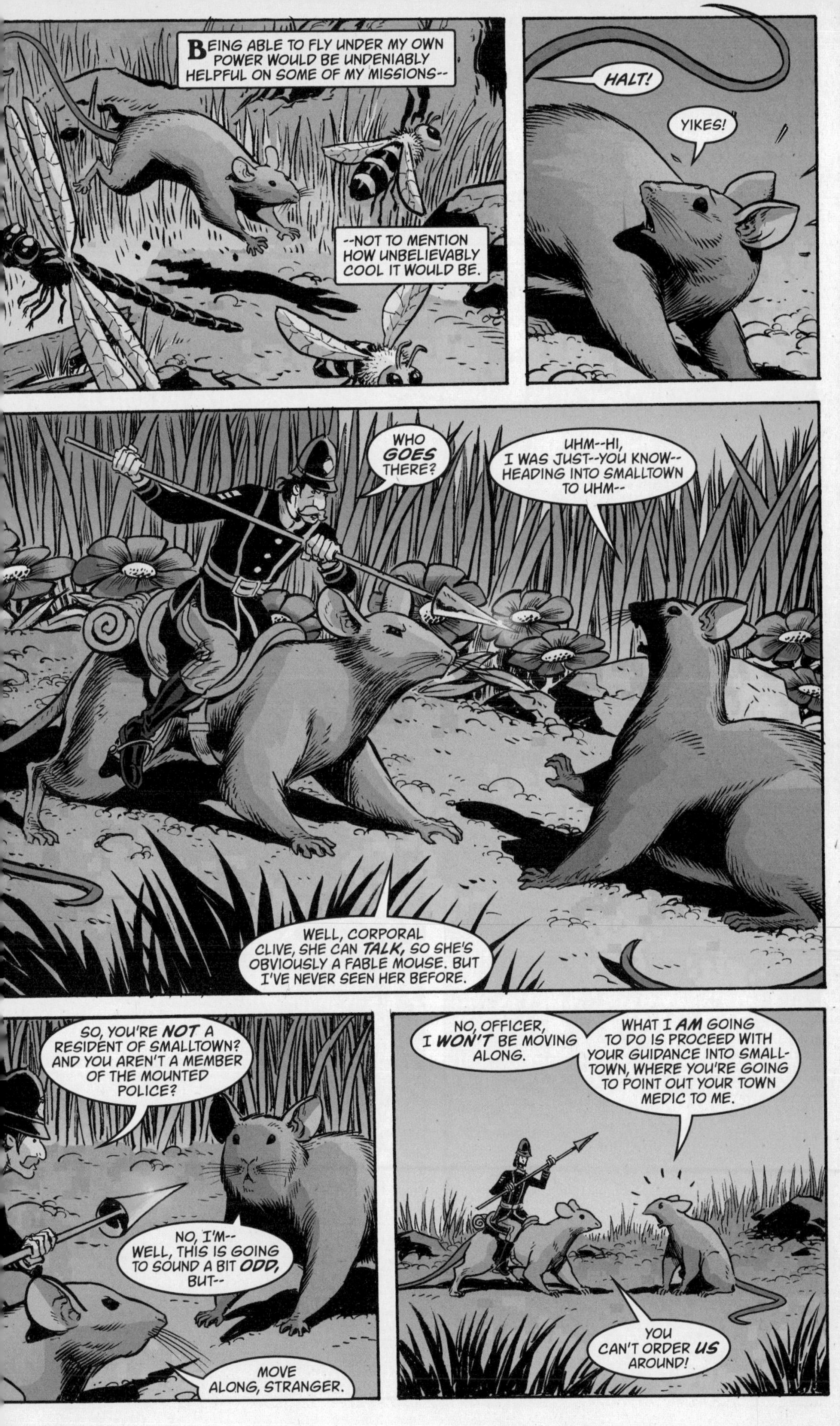
BEING ABLE TO FLY UNDER MY OWN POWER WOULD BE UNDENIABLY HELPFUL ON SOME OF MY MISSIONS--
--NOT TO MENTION HOW UNBELIEVABLY COOL IT WOULD BE.
HALT!
YIKES!
WHO GOES THERE?
UHM--HI, I WAS JUST--YOU KNOW--HEADING INTO SMALLTOWN TO UHM--
WELL, CORPORAL CLIVE, SHE CAN TALK, SO SHE'S OBVIOUSLY A FABLE MOUSE. BUT I'VE NEVER SEEN HER BEFORE.
SO, YOU'RE NOT A RESIDENT OF SMALLTOWN? AND YOU AREN'T A MEMBER OF THE MOUNTED POLICE?
NO, I'M--WELL, THIS IS GOING TO SOUND A BIT ODD, BUT--
MOVE ALONG, STRANGER.
NO, OFFICER, I WON'T BE MOVING ALONG.
WHAT I AM GOING TO DO IS PROCEED WITH YOUR GUIDANCE INTO SMALL-TOWN, WHERE YOU'RE GOING TO POINT OUT YOUR TOWN MEDIC TO ME.
YOU CAN'T ORDER US AROUND!

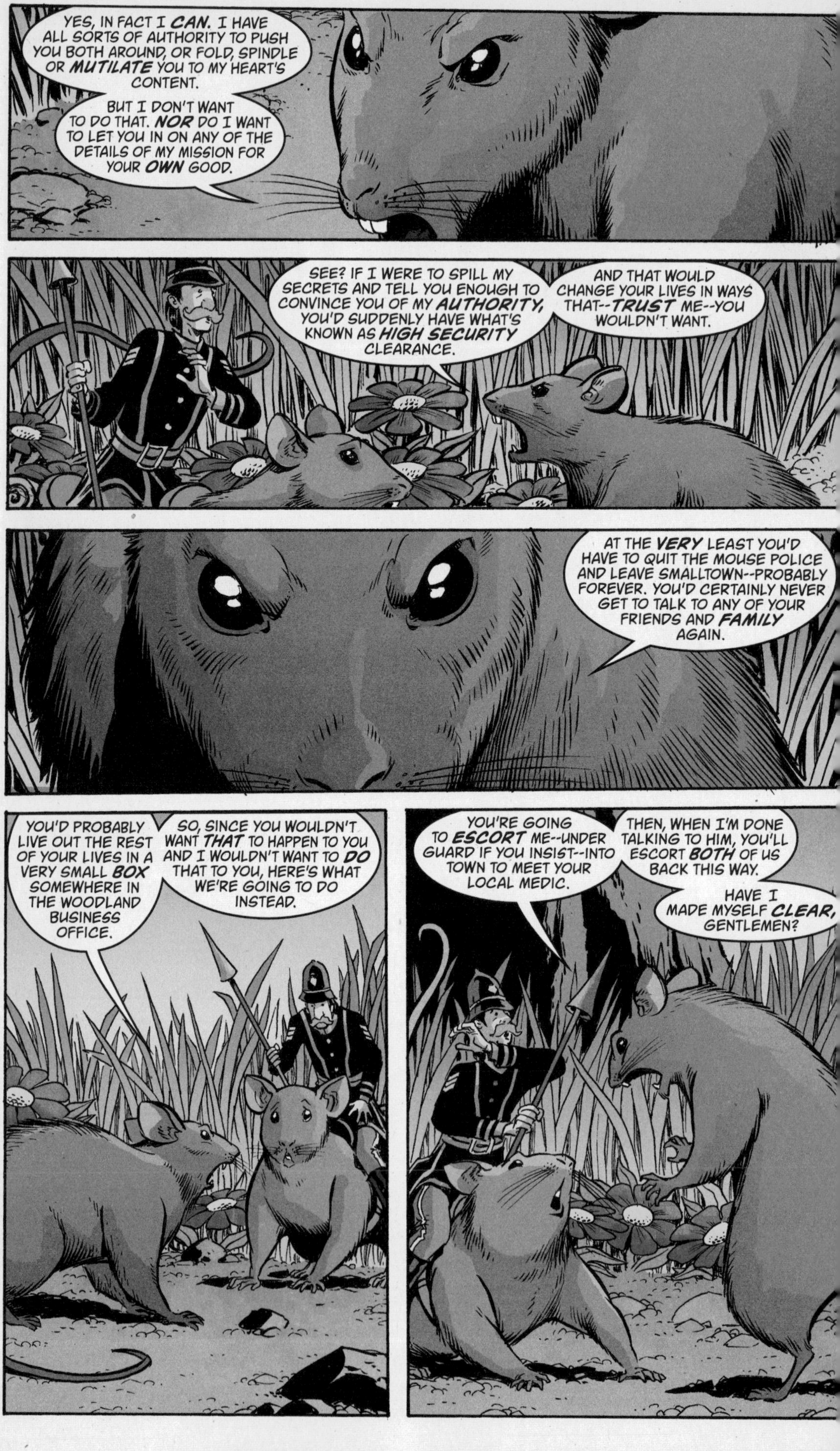
YES, IN FACT I CAN. I HAVE ALL SORTS OF AUTHORITY TO PUSH YOU BOTH AROUND, OR FOLD, SPINDLE OR MUTILATE YOU TO MY HEART'S CONTENT.
BUT I DON'T WANT TO DO THAT. NOR DO I WANT TO LET YOU IN ON ANY OF THE DETAILS OF MY MISSION FOR YOUR OWN GOOD.
SEE? IF I WERE TO SPILL MY SECRETS AND TELL YOU ENOUGH TO CONVINCE YOU OF MY AUTHORITY, YOU'D SUDDENLY HAVE WHAT'S KNOWN AS HIGH SECURITY CLEARANCE.
AND THAT WOULD CHANGE YOUR LIVES IN WAYS THAT--TRUST ME--YOU WOULDN'T WANT.
AT THE VERY LEAST YOU'D HAVE TO QUIT THE MOUSE POLICE AND LEAVE SMALLTOWN--PROBABLY FOREVER. YOU'D CERTAINLY NEVER GET TO TALK TO ANY OF YOUR FRIENDS AND FAMILY AGAIN.
YOU'D PROBABLY LIVE OUT THE REST OF YOUR LIVES IN A VERY SMALL BOX SOMEWHERE IN THE WOODLAND BUSINESS OFFICE.
SO, SINCE YOU WOULDN'T WANT THAT TO HAPPEN TO YOU AND I WOULDN'T WANT TO DO THAT TO YOU, HERE'S WHAT WE'RE GOING TO DO INSTEAD.
YOU'RE GOING TO ESCORT ME--UNDER GUARD IF YOU INSIST--INTO TOWN TO MEET YOUR LOCAL MEDIC.
THEN, WHEN I'M DONE TALKING TO HIM, YOU'LL ESCORT BOTH OF US BACK THIS WAY.
HAVE I MADE MYSELF CLEAR, GENTLEMEN?

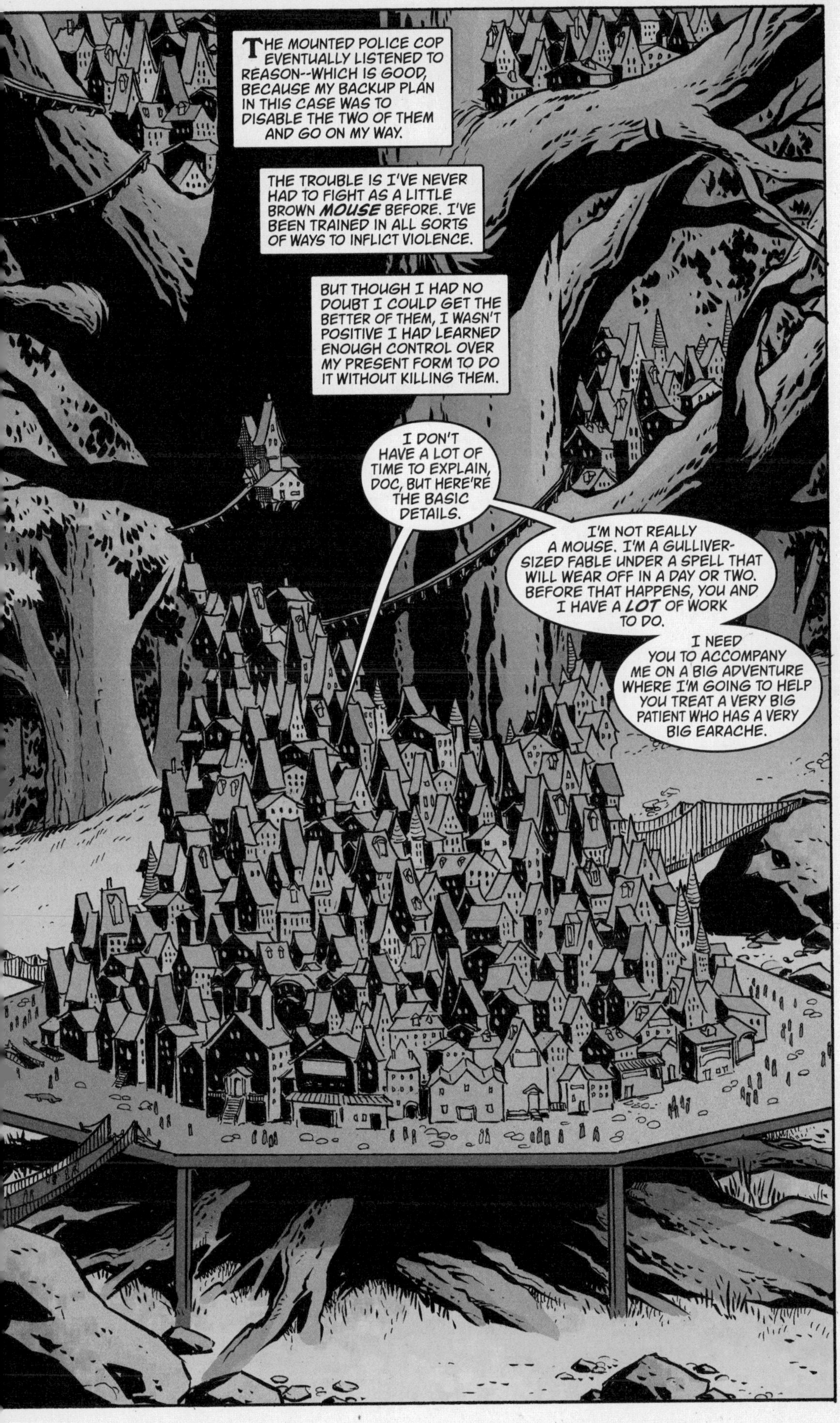
THE MOUNTED POLICE COP EVENTUALLY LISTENED TO REASON--WHICH IS GOOD, BECAUSE MY BACKUP PLAN IN THIS CASE WAS TO DISABLE THE TWO OF THEM AND GO ON MY WAY.
THE TROUBLE IS I'VE NEVER HAD TO FIGHT AS A LITTLE BROWN *MOUSE* BEFORE. I'VE BEEN TRAINED IN ALL SORTS OF WAYS TO INFLICT VIOLENCE.
BUT THOUGH I HAD NO DOUBT I COULD GET THE BETTER OF THEM, I WASN'T POSITIVE I HAD LEARNED ENOUGH CONTROL OVER MY PRESENT FORM TO DO IT WITHOUT KILLING THEM.
I DON'T HAVE A LOT OF TIME TO EXPLAIN, DOC, BUT HERE'RE THE BASIC DETAILS.
I'M NOT REALLY A MOUSE. I'M A GULLIVER-SIZED FABLE UNDER A SPELL THAT WILL WEAR OFF IN A DAY OR TWO. BEFORE THAT HAPPENS, YOU AND I HAVE A *LOT* OF WORK TO DO.
I NEED YOU TO ACCOMPANY ME ON A BIG ADVENTURE WHERE I'M GOING TO HELP YOU TREAT A VERY BIG PATIENT WHO HAS A VERY BIG EARACHE.

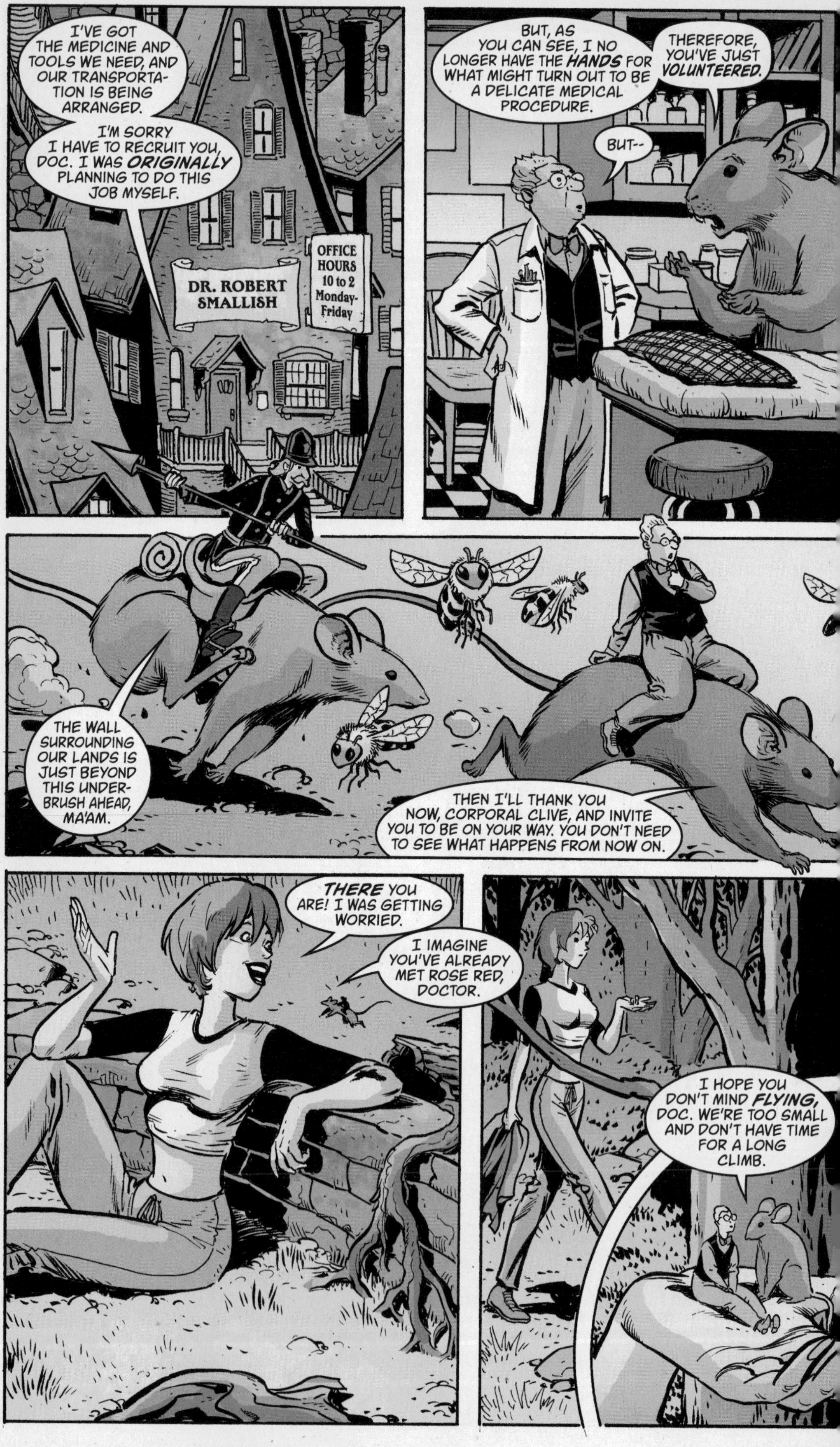
I'VE GOT THE MEDICINE AND TOOLS WE NEED, AND OUR TRANSPORTATION IS BEING ARRANGED.
I'M SORRY I HAVE TO RECRUIT YOU, DOC. I WAS ORIGINALLY PLANNING TO DO THIS JOB MYSELF.
DR. ROBERT SMALLISH
OFFICE HOURS 10 to 2 Monday-Friday
BUT, AS YOU CAN SEE, I NO LONGER HAVE THE HANDS FOR WHAT MIGHT TURN OUT TO BE A DELICATE MEDICAL PROCEDURE.
THEREFORE, YOU'VE JUST VOLUNTEERED.
BUT--
THE WALL SURROUNDING OUR LANDS IS JUST BEYOND THIS UNDER-BRUSH AHEAD, MA'AM.
THEN I'LL THANK YOU NOW, CORPORAL CLIVE, AND INVITE YOU TO BE ON YOUR WAY. YOU DON'T NEED TO SEE WHAT HAPPENS FROM NOW ON.
THERE YOU ARE! I WAS GETTING WORRIED.
I IMAGINE YOU'VE ALREADY MET ROSE RED, DOCTOR.
I HOPE YOU DON'T MIND FLYING, DOC. WE'RE TOO SMALL AND DON'T HAVE TIME FOR A LONG CLIMB.

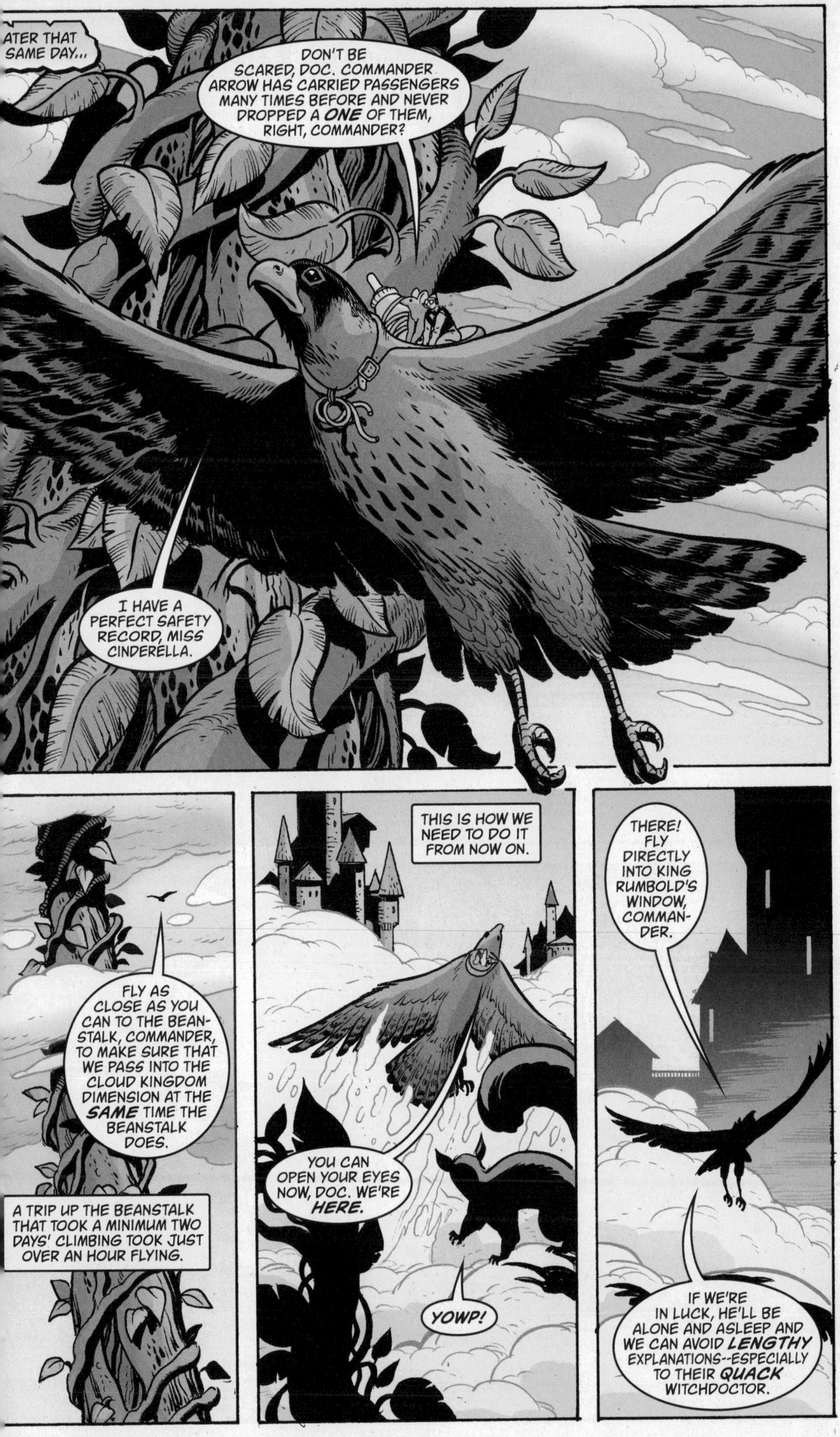
ATER THAT SAME DAY...
DON'T BE SCARED, DOC. COMMANDER ARROW HAS CARRIED PASSENGERS MANY TIMES BEFORE AND NEVER DROPPED A ONE OF THEM, RIGHT, COMMANDER?
I HAVE A PERFECT SAFETY RECORD, MISS CINDERELLA.
FLY AS CLOSE AS YOU CAN TO THE BEAN-STALK, COMMANDER, TO MAKE SURE THAT WE PASS INTO THE CLOUD KINGDOM DIMENSION AT THE SAME TIME THE BEANSTALK DOES.
A TRIP UP THE BEANSTALK THAT TOOK A MINIMUM TWO DAYS' CLIMBING TOOK JUST OVER AN HOUR FLYING.
THIS IS HOW WE NEED TO DO IT FROM NOW ON.
YOU CAN OPEN YOUR EYES NOW, DOC. WE'RE HERE.
YOWP!
THERE! FLY DIRECTLY INTO KING RUMBOLD'S WINDOW, COMMAN-DER.
IF WE'RE IN LUCK, HE'LL BE ALONE AND ASLEEP AND WE CAN AVOID LENGTHY EXPLANATIONS--ESPECIALLY TO THEIR QUACK WITCHDOCTOR.

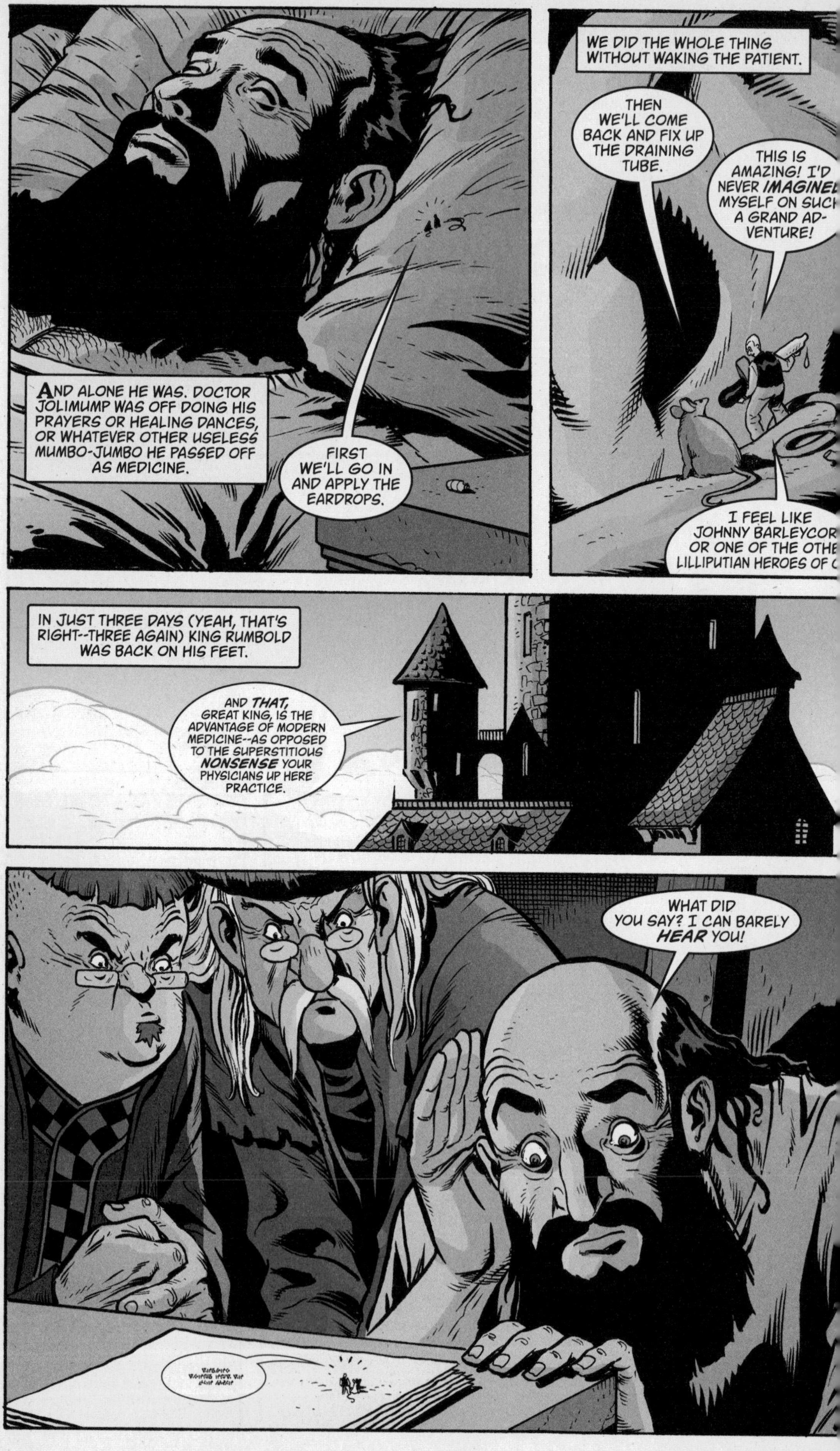
AND ALONE HE WAS. DOCTOR JOLIMUMP WAS OFF DOING HIS PRAYERS OR HEALING DANCES, OR WHATEVER OTHER USELESS MUMBO-JUMBO HE PASSED OFF AS MEDICINE.
FIRST WE'LL GO IN AND APPLY THE EARDROPS.
WE DID THE WHOLE THING WITHOUT WAKING THE PATIENT.
THEN WE'LL COME BACK AND FIX UP THE DRAINING TUBE.
THIS IS AMAZING! I'D NEVER IMAGINE MYSELF ON SUC A GRAND AD-VENTURE!
I FEEL LIKE JOHNNY BARLEYCOR OR ONE OF THE OTHE LILLIPUTIAN HEROES OF
IN JUST THREE DAYS (YEAH, THAT'S RIGHT--THREE AGAIN) KING RUMBOLD WAS BACK ON HIS FEET.
AND THAT, GREAT KING, IS THE ADVANTAGE OF MODERN MEDICINE--AS OPPOSED TO THE SUPERSTITIOUS NONSENSE YOUR PHYSICIANS UP HERE PRACTICE.
WHAT DID YOU SAY? I CAN BARELY HEAR YOU!

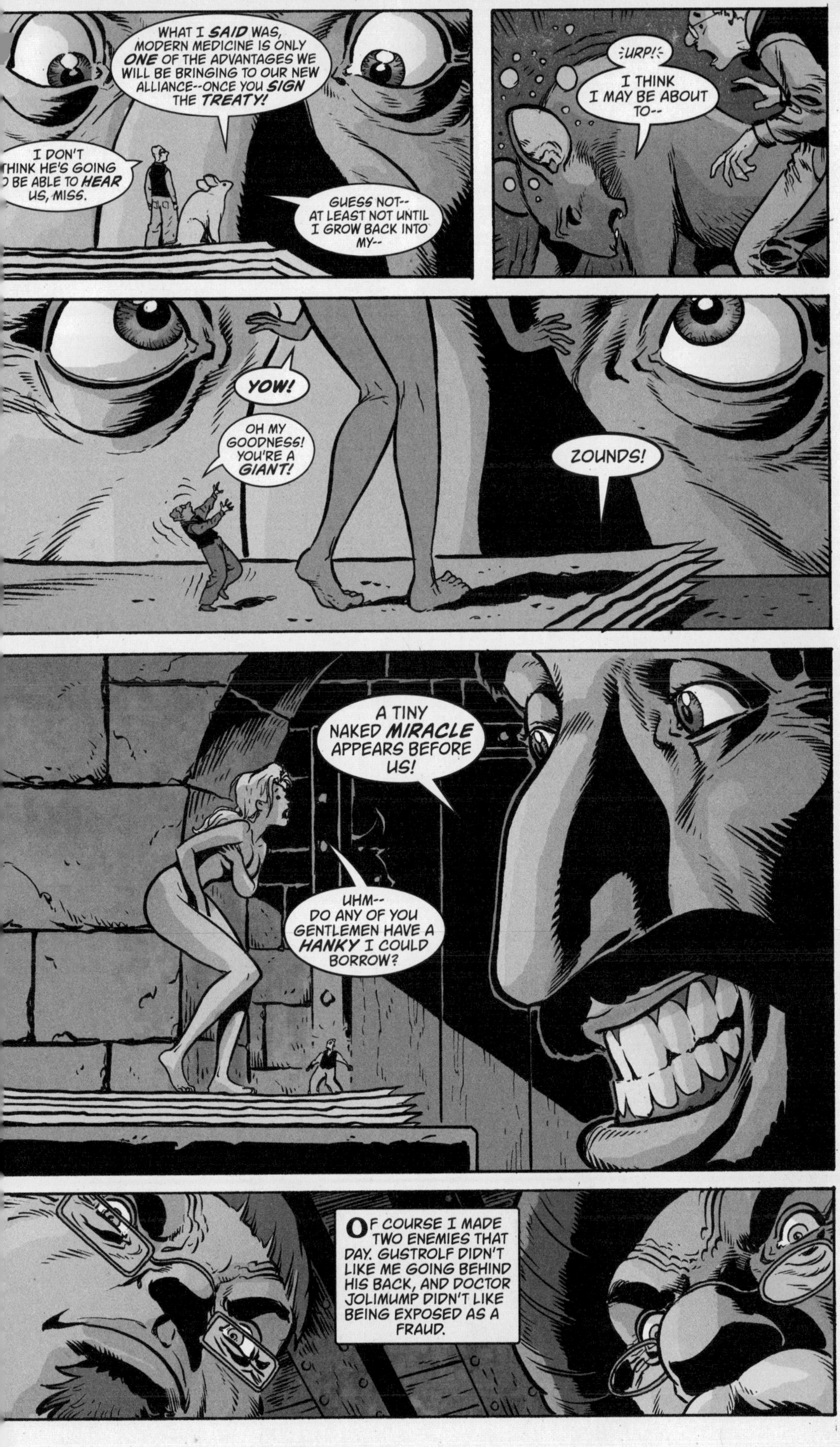
WHAT I SAID WAS, MODERN MEDICINE IS ONLY ONE OF THE ADVANTAGES WE WILL BE BRINGING TO OUR NEW ALLIANCE--ONCE YOU SIGN THE TREATY!
I DON'T THINK HE'S GOING TO BE ABLE TO HEAR US, MISS.
GUESS NOT-- AT LEAST NOT UNTIL I GROW BACK INTO MY--
URP!
I THINK I MAY BE ABOUT TO--
YOW!
OH MY GOODNESS! YOU'RE A GIANT!
ZOUNDS!
A TINY NAKED MIRACLE APPEARS BEFORE US!
UHM-- DO ANY OF YOU GENTLEMEN HAVE A HANKY I COULD BORROW?
OF COURSE I MADE TWO ENEMIES THAT DAY. GUSTROLF DIDN'T LIKE ME GOING BEHIND HIS BACK, AND DOCTOR JOLIMUMP DIDN'T LIKE BEING EXPOSED AS A FRAUD.

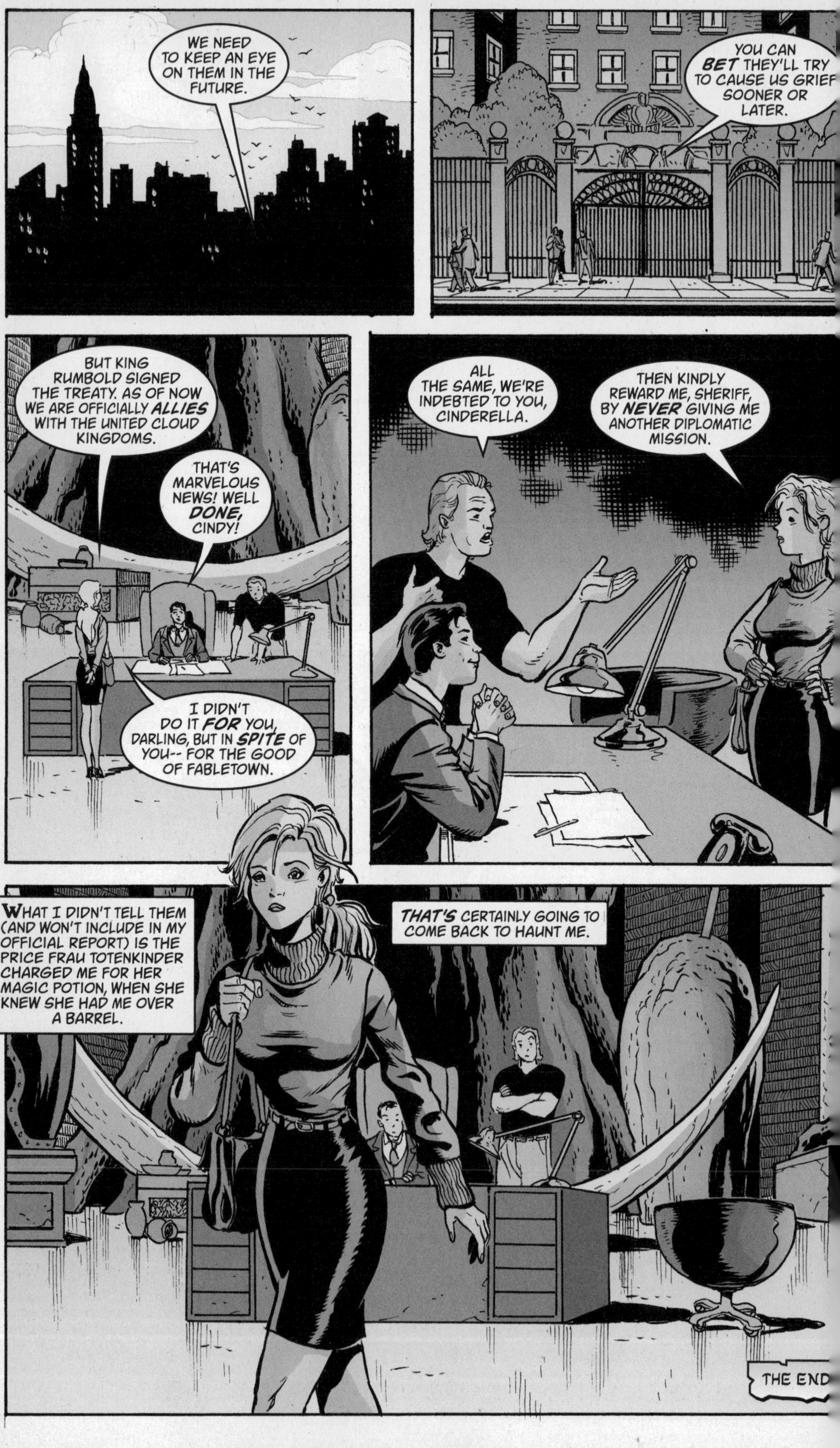
WE NEED TO KEEP AN EYE ON THEM IN THE FUTURE.
YOU CAN BET THEY'LL TRY TO CAUSE US GRIEF SOONER OR LATER.
BUT KING RUMBOLD SIGNED THE TREATY. AS OF NOW WE ARE OFFICIALLY ALLIES WITH THE UNITED CLOUD KINGDOMS.
THAT'S MARVELOUS NEWS! WELL DONE, CINDY!
I DIDN'T DO IT FOR YOU, DARLING, BUT IN SPITE OF YOU-- FOR THE GOOD OF FABLETOWN.
ALL THE SAME, WE'RE INDEBTED TO YOU, CINDERELLA.
THEN KINDLY REWARD ME, SHERIFF, BY NEVER GIVING ME ANOTHER DIPLOMATIC MISSION.
WHAT I DIDN'T TELL THEM (AND WON'T INCLUDE IN MY OFFICIAL REPORT) IS THE PRICE FRAU TOTENKINDER CHARGED ME FOR HER MAGIC POTION, WHEN SHE KNEW SHE HAD ME OVER A BARREL.
THAT'S CERTAINLY GOING TO COME BACK TO HAUNT ME.
THE END